SOLDIER

www.rbooks.co.uk

Acclaim for *Soldier*:

'Engagingly recounted with both intelligence and candour
. . . General Jackson is a man of high principles, who on
more than one occasion was prepared to lay his career on
the line to defend [his] beliefs. In this highly readable and
fascinating book, he speaks a great deal of good sense.
More importantly, he is able to publicly voice his concerns
for the future and defend the soldiers he clearly cares
about'
James Holland, *Sunday Telegraph*

'Utterly compelling . . . Jackson has provided a model of
the modern military commander, media friendly,
internationally minded and politically sensitive . . .
Indispensable reading'
Andro Linklater, *Spectator*

'Insightful and valuable . . . In his account of his career, he
has exposed the weaknesses and failures that led to the
challenges facing our troops in Iraq and Afghanistan
today'
Michael Evans, *The Times*

SOLDIER

The Autobiography of General Sir Mike Jackson

GENERAL SIR MIKE JACKSON

CORGI BOOKS

TRANSWORLD PUBLISHERS
61-63 Uxbridge Road, London W5 5SA
A Random House Group Company
www.rbooks.co.uk

SOLDIER
A CORGI BOOK: 9780552156028

First published in Great Britain
in 2007 by Bantam Press
a division of Transworld Publishers
Corgi edition published 2008

This book is a work of non-fiction based on the life, experiences and
recollections of the author. In some cases names of people, places, dates,
sequences or the detail of events have been changed solely to protect the
privacy of others. The author has stated to the publishers that, except in such
minor respects not affecting the substantial accuracy of the work, the contents
of this book are true.

A CIP catalogue record for this book
is available from the British Library.

Addresses for Random House Group Ltd companies outside the UK
can be found at: www.randomhouse.co.uk
The Random House Group Ltd Reg. No. 954009

The Random House Group Limited supports The Forest Stewardship
Council (FSC), the leading international forest certification organisation. All
our titles that are printed on Greenpeace approved FSC certified paper carry
the FSC logo.
Our paper procurement policy can be found at
www.rbooks.co.uk/environment

Typeset in 11/13pt Giovanni Book by
Falcon Oast Graphic Art Ltd.
Printed in the UK by CPI Cox & Wyman, Reading, RG1 8EX.

2 4 6 8 10 9 7 5 3 1

This book is dedicated to the British soldier
and his family, past, present and future.

Contents

List of Maps

Preface

What follows is an autobiography. It focuses more on my life in the Army than on my personal life. But my own experiences, reactions and observations provide the thread running through the book. If what I have written seems to some egocentric, this is the reason why.

I should like to stress that I make no claim to have written a history of the events I have lived through. I am aware that there is much else that could be included, were I writing a different sort of book. But to do so would be in a sense dishonest. I have tried to describe how these events seemed to me at the time, and to distinguish clearly the occasional afterthought reached with the benefit of hindsight.

There are many people with whom I've worked closely during my military career who are not mentioned by name in the pages that follow. To do so would be to burden the narrative with a weight of detail it could not support. These people know who they are, and I hope they know that I'll always be grateful to them for their advice, encouragement and support – particularly my various Chiefs of Staff, Military Assistants and ADCs. That they are not all named in this text does not mean that they are not remembered.

This book is therefore both a story and a statement. The story begins with youthful adventure and ends in rather less youthful high command. The statement is what that journey taught me. I also hope that this book might even inspire some of its younger readers to undertake a similar journey.

Acknowledgements

My heartfelt thanks go to all those people who have kindly helped and encouraged me along the way, and without whom I doubt the book would have been written. I would particularly like to thank all those who read and commented on the text, including: Edwin Glasgow QC, Major General David Howell (Director of Army Legal Services), Major General (Retd) Andrew Ritchie and William Shawcross; and of course various members of my family, but especially Mark, my elder son, who has been invaluable in scrupulously giving me the grass-roots view. Among those who shared their memories with me were Brigadier Mark Carleton-Smith, Lieutenant Colonel Ed Smyth-Osbourne, Major (Retd) Milos Stankovic and Lieutenant General Sir Freddie Viggers.

I am particularly grateful to Brigadier James Everard and Major General (Retd) Jonathan Bailey for lending me their Kosovo diaries, and to Brigadier (Retd) Nick Ridley for lending me his account of Warrenpoint. All three of these generously allowed me to make use of their material.

I should also like to thank Alex Bedford for stepping in at short notice to help with corrections, and Micola Neville for introducing her. James Cartwright kindly downloaded an early typescript in the Rift Valley in Kenya.

Derek Askew helped out by copying photographs from my scrap-books and other memorabilia.

Paul and Sarah Horsley generously lent us Ebbi, their beautiful villa in Tuscany, for a week at the beginning of the process, which allowed me to concentrate on the book free from other distractions.

I am most grateful to Adam Sisman for his professional and patient assistance with the text; to all the capable staff at Transworld, and particularly my editors Bill Scott-Kerr and Simon Thorogood, for their helpful comments on the typescript; to Gillian Somerscales for her excellent copy-editing; and to Sheila Lee for her part in the picture research.

Thanks are also very much due to Colonel Ben Bathurst and Nick Gurr of the MOD's Directorate General of Media and Communication for their rapid examination of the text for errors of security and fact.

For the avoidance of any doubt I want to make it clear that I have not always taken the advice I received, and I bear sole responsibility for the book's contents.

I particularly want to thank Annabel Merullo for encouraging me to write the book and helping me to place it; and my agent Christopher Little for delivering on what he promised.

Last, and greatest, of my debts is to Sarah, who has played a pivotal part at every stage of the preparation of the book, particularly in her professional role as a picture researcher – and, as a soldier's wife, in the past twenty-three years of my life.

List of Abbreviations

ACE	Allied Command Europe
ADC	aide-de-camp
AFOR	Albania Force
AFSOUTH	(NATO's) Allied Forces Southern Europe
AG	Adjutant General
ARRC	(NATO's) Allied Rapid Reaction Corps
CCF	Combined Cadet Force
CDS	Chief of the Defence Staff
CGS	Chief of the General Staff
CINCEUR	Commander in Chief US European Command
CinCLand	Commander in Chief Land Command (British Army)
CINCSOUTH	(NATO's) Commander in Chief Southern Europe
CJO	Chief of Joint Operations
CO	commanding officer
COMAFOR	Commander Albania Force
COMARRC	Commander Allied Rapid Reaction Corps
COMBRITFOR	Commander British Forces

COMKFOR	Commander Kosovo Force
CSCE	Conference on Security and Co-operation in Europe
DEFRA	Department of Environment, Food and Rural Affairs
DfID	Department for International Development
DIPTEL	diplomatic telegram
DPR (Army)	Director of Public Relations (Army)
DPR (Navy)	Director of Public Relations (Navy)
DS	directing staff
DSACEUR	(NATO's) Deputy Supreme Allied Commander Europe
DZ	dropping zone
EOD	explosive ordnance disposal
EP	entitled person
ETA	estimated time of arrival
FLOTUS	First Lady of the United States
FRU	Force Reconnaissance Unit
FRY	Federal Republic of Yugoslavia
FYROM	Former Yugoslav Republic of Macedonia
GOC	General Officer Commanding
ICRC	International Committee of the Red Cross
ICTY	International Criminal Tribunal for Yugoslavia
IEBL	(Bosnia) Inter-Entity Boundary Line
IED	improvised explosive device
IFOR	(Bosnia) Implementation Force
IRA	Irish Republican Army

ISAF	(Afghanistan) International Security Assistance Force
KFOR	Kosovo Force
KLA	Kosovo Liberation Army
KVM	Kosovo Verification Mission
JIC	(Kosovo) Joint Implementation Committee
JIC	(UK) Joint Intelligence Committee
MA	military assistant
MAFF	Ministry of Agriculture, Fisheries and Food
MOD	Ministry of Defence
MRF	Military Reaction Force
MTA	Military–Technical Agreement
MUP	Ministarstvo Unutrasnjih Poslova (Serb special police)
ODA	Overseas Development Agency
OTC	Officers' Training Corps
P Coy	Pegasus Company
Pifwic	person indicted for war crimes
PJHQ	Permanent Joint Headquarters
POTUS	President of the United States
PPS	pre-parachute selection course
PRT	Provincial Reconstruction Team
RUC	Royal Ulster Constabulary
RUF	(Sierra Leone) Revolutionary United Front
SACEUR	(NATO's) Supreme Allied Commander Europe
SFOR	(Bosnia) Stabilization Force
SHAPE	Supreme Headquarters Allied Powers Europe

SITREP	situation report
SRSG	Special Representative of the (UN) Secretary-General
TA	Territorial Army
Tac HQ	Tactical Headquarters
TAOR	tactical area of operational responsibility
UCK	Ushtria Clirimtare e Kosovës (Kosovo Liberation Army)
UDR	Ulster Defence Regiment
UNHCR	United Nations High Commission for Refugees
UNMIK	United Nations Interim Administration Mission in Kosovo
UNPROFOR	(Bosnia) United Nations Protection Force
UNSCR	UN Security Council Resolution
VJ	Vojska Jugoslavia (Yugoslav Armed Forces)
VTC	video conference
WMD	weapons of mass destruction
ZOS	Zone of Separation

1
Schoolboy

I am a soldier. I have held every rank in the British Army from officer cadet to four star general. I am now retired, but my almost forty-five years of service ensure that I remain a soldier at heart. My father was a soldier, my elder son has been a soldier and my younger son plans to become a soldier. My father in law, my brothers-in-law and my son-in-law have all been soldiers – so the Army is something of a family tradition. But my father didn't push me in that direction, and what I have said to my sons is that it is your life, and therefore your call, and you must decide what you want to do with it. I am pleased that both of them have decided to follow the path I took, but I would have been entirely content had they chosen otherwise.

My father George Jackson served in the Army for forty years, without ever rising beyond the modest rank of major. He suffered a serious heart attack in the early 1950s and that put the kibosh on any further promotion. The Army was pretty ruthless about such matters then. My father never showed any resentment at this setback. If it ever went through his mind that he might leave the Army, he never mentioned it to me. He was a great gentleman, very courteous, and scrupulously honest; a delightful man, who always had a wry smile on his lips, perhaps indicative of his humorous attitude to life. I liked him and I respected him; to me he was always 'Pop'. My mother too was very loving, and ours was a happy, secure home. My parents were not strict in the Victorian sense, but they did set rules, and I grew up with a definite sense of what was right and what was wrong.

Pop was a tall, lean, dark man with a long nose, all features which he handed on to me. He sported a neatly trimmed moustache, a practice I have not emulated! Pop was an active and practical man, who'd been a member of the Boys' Brigade and who was very fond of playing football. In adulthood he became a keen motorcyclist. Mother was dark too, slight but none the less forceful, a strong, bright-eyed Yorkshire woman, who had been quite a beauty in her youth. She loved walking, and in her teens had done a great deal of hiking in the Peak District.

My father joined the Army in 1935 as a private soldier, becoming a trooper in the Household Cavalry. I can remember his telling me about being a member of the Sovereign's Escort at the coronation of King George VI, which sounded very impressive to a young boy. He didn't make the big leap to commissioned rank until about halfway through the Second World War, when he became an officer in the Royal Army Service Corps. I suspect that my parents waited until my father was commissioned to get married.

George was the youngest of five children of Charles

Henry Jackson, the skipper of a deep-sea line-fishing vessel working out of Grimsby. My grandfather, whom I sadly never knew, had lost his father when he was only four and, having been sent to work on a Lincolnshire farm at the age of ten, had run away to sea in his late teens. The life of a long-line fisherman then was very hard, sailing small vessels up to Iceland and along the Greenland coast even in winter, often under brutal masters and in cruel conditions, defying icebergs and heavy seas in the search for cod and halibut up to 20 stone in weight. Such a harsh life left him unmarked, however, for Pop said that no family ever had a better father. My grandfather was patient, loving and fair; everyone who knew Charles Jackson respected him and his word, and looked upon him as a gentleman. In the First World War he served as a master of a minesweeper. In the Second World War, though by then well into his sixties, he again volunteered for service with the Royal Navy and was made master of a small vessel working out of Scapa Flow.

My parents must have met during the early part of the war when both were in their mid-twenties, though unfortunately I know almost nothing about the circumstances beyond the fact that Pop was then living in Bristol, and since my mother's death late in 2006 there is now no one left alive to tell me. My mother Ivy was from Sheffield, where her father, Tom Bower, had been an engineer in the steel industry who had lost his job in the Depression. She was a year older than my father, born five months before the outbreak of the First World War, and the only child of her parents, which was unusual for the period. (Her own mother had been one of eleven siblings.) An intelligent girl, she won a scholarship to

Sheffield Grammar School, and when she met my father she was working as a curator at the Sheffield Museum.

Along with so many British soldiers, my father spent the early part of the war kicking his heels. He and my mother married on 7 March 1942, soon after he received his commission. I was born two years later, at my mother's home in Sheffield, just ten weeks before my father finally went into action on D-Day, 6 June 1944. He was second-in-command of a squadron of amphibious vehicles (DUKWs) whose function was to ferry men and materiel ashore. His squadron commander was killed on the first run in to 'Gold' Beach, so my father had to take command from then on. For him, as for so many others, D-Day was a baptism of fire. For his actions then and subsequently he was awarded the Belgian *Croix de guerre* and was mentioned in dispatches. Like so many of his generation, he was reluctant to talk about his experiences and, judging that it would make him uncomfortable, I didn't seek to push him to do so.

I don't know much about what Pop did for the rest of the war except that he took part in the Allied advance through north-west Europe, finishing up on VE-Day in Germany. After the war he was posted to Palestine, in the Mandate days, before the creation of the State of Israel. British soldiers were trying to keep the peace between Arabs and Jews, and might be attacked by either; it was no place for wives and children. So my early years were spent in Sheffield with my mother's family, and then in Aldershot when Pop came back from Palestine. In 1948 he was posted to Libya, an Italian colony which had been occupied by the British during the war, and which would become an independent kingdom in late 1951.

My first memory is of sailing out by troop-ship with my mother to join him. I can dimly remember our cabin, and the fact that both of us were very seasick as the ship sailed through the Bay of Biscay. In Libya the sun seemed to shine every day. We lived in the capital, Tripoli, where I attended the British Forces primary school. I can remember the name of our street, the Via Generale Cantore. We had an Alsatian, Roly – too good-natured to be a proper guard dog – and a pre-war Lancia with running boards, no doubt a legacy of the Italian occupation. In 1949 my sister Lynne was born in the British Military Hospital in Tripoli.

My parents enjoyed their overseas postings and, unlike some British people of their generation, always embraced 'abroad'. But after two years in Libya we came back to England when my father was posted to a Territorial Army unit in London. We lived in Army quarters, a large flat in Putney. I attended the local primary school on the west side of Putney High Street. A few years later my father was posted to a staff job in Nottingham, and not long afterwards to Germany, but by this time I had already started boarding at Stamford School, a single-sex establishment situated as you might expect in the town of Stamford, in southern Lincolnshire. Many Service families send their children to boarding schools, to achieve continuity of education while their parents are posted from place to place. The Army makes a contribution to the fees in recognition of this.

I was still only a small boy of eight when I went away to school. We slept in big dormitories with the windows left wide open, even in winter. I can remember waking in the morning to find snow on the bed. St Peter's, the junior boarding house, was on the other side of town from the main school, so every morning and then again in the late afternoon we youngsters would set off in a long crocodile, escorted by one of the housemasters.

At breakfast, we all gathered in the dining hall where each form sat at a different long table, waiting for the arrival of the Headmaster and his wife before beginning to eat. The Head was known to us as 'Eee-Hee', because of his funny little laugh; boys home in on such things. Eee-Hee, whose real name was Basil Deed, always had a bowl of porridge for breakfast. He would read *The Times* for what seemed quite a long time, and then scoff his porridge in double-quick time before going back to his newspaper. We used to time him, and it became quite a thing to see how fast Eee-Hee would get his porridge down on any particular morning.

I don't remember being homesick, and in general I was quite happy at school. We were all in the same boat, after all. There was a fagging system in place which required small boys to 'fag' for their seniors, running errands and generally acting as drudges: perhaps a little archaic, but it taught you to obey orders unquestioningly. Like boys everywhere we fought, but I don't remember any bullying. Being taller than most, I was able to look after myself.

At the end of term I would travel back to my family, and once my father had been posted to Germany, this meant taking the boat from Harwich to the Hook of Holland and then boarding a special military train that wandered through the garrison towns of northern Germany. I can still remember the sense of adventure of one occasion when I went by plane, the first time I had ever flown. Like any first-time flyer, I found it all very exciting. A family friend had met me at King's Cross off the train from Peterborough and driven me to the West London Air Terminal, where I was handed over to the care of an air hostess. She and the steward fussed over me during the flight – the fate of an unaccompanied minor is not a bad one!

I suppose I was a typical 1950s schoolboy: a Boy Scout who read *Eagle* and *Hotspur*, made Airfix models and spent long hours playing with my model railway. Family holidays were spent camping throughout western Europe, travelling in Pop's old Mercedes, and after that in his lovely pale-green BMW, so big that Mother needed a sandbag under her foot to reach the pedals. At school I played rugby and tennis, a sport I still enjoy, and took part in middle-distance and cross-country running. I enjoyed swimming, too; the school opened a pool soon after I joined – unheated, of course! Perhaps I was a bit rowdy. When I was eleven my housemaster warned my parents that my behaviour 'must improve'; the following term he reported that I was 'noisy and impetuous', and the next term that I was 'wild and scatterbrained'. I was often walloped for 'ragging' by prefects, who were entitled to administer corporal punishment, using a cane. But by the time I was almost thirteen the housemaster informed my parents that I was 'sobering down and growing up'. Eventually I became a house prefect, which in retrospect was good preparation for my future life as an officer, in that it gave me some experience of maintaining discipline and taking responsibility for others.

In my early teens I joined the school cadets, the Combined Cadet Force (CCF), which encompasses all three Services. We didn't have a navy section, as Stamford was some way from the sea, but we certainly did have an air section. I remember a most improbable Heath Robinson glider, which boys would fly across the playing field only a few feet above the ground. I chose to go into the army section, probably because of my father. I used a .22 cadet rifle and practised on an indoor range, but to this day I have never managed to become more than a very run-of-the-mill shot. I enjoyed the CCF camps, which meant going away for ten days or so with boys from several other schools, sleeping in tents or huts and spending our days under the supervision of a handful of regular Army soldiers. I remember one in Scotland, at Cultybraggan, and another in Aldershot. This was my first taste of soldiering. We undertook tactical exercises under the direction of the regular soldiers – one group setting out to capture a hill, for example, while another group was tasked to defend it. 'Go left flanking!' the sergeant might bellow as we schoolboys advanced across the heather, taking advantage of any piece of natural cover, often flinging ourselves forward on to the wet ground. In those days there were no cadet rifles; we carried the heavy Lee Enfield No. 4s, bolt-action rifles loaded with blanks. When you fired there was a satisfying crack and a smell of cordite, but no recoil and, of course, no bullet.

It's fair to say that I wasn't an outstanding scholar at Stamford. If I excelled at anything, it was modern languages. I have always been interested in the structure of words and in etymology generally, and I found that I had a facility for languages. Perhaps I have a good ear. My mother was a talented musician, a pianist who might well have made music her career had she not met my father and got married, and she too was good at languages. She encouraged me to take up the violin, which I persisted with throughout my years at school, though I think that hearing me scratch away used to drive her crazy. I did a bit of choral singing as well, and I particularly remember the excitement of putting on a performance of Handel's *Messiah* with the girls of Stamford High School. We also put on a French play with Stamford High, Molière's *Le Malade Imaginaire*. Any contact with girls was of course very welcome!

French was compulsory, and I also took German, largely I suspect because my parents were living in Germany and I could practise my German in the holidays. More unusually, I also did Russian. Stamford was very go-ahead in offering Russian at O and A level in the late 1950s, when there was something almost exotic about it. From the late 1940s onwards the Russians had been the enemy, as they would be for forty years; the Soviet Union was a formidable opponent, very powerful and very menacing, and at the same time somewhat mysterious, hidden behind an 'Iron Curtain'. So there was a slight sense of forbidden fruit in studying Russian.

The sixth form at Stamford was grouped by study area, so that one had a modern language set, a science set, and so on. I decided to go with my strengths, studying French, German and Russian at A level, taking my exams in the summer of 1961, when I was seventeen.

It was about this time that I decided to join the Army. It's difficult to remember now what led to this decision. It was just one of those things that I seemed to have been thinking about for some time. Perhaps it had always been there in some way or other. I suppose that for me joining the Army meant a life of adventure, an escape from the humdrum alternative of working in an office. I was intrigued by the idea of putting myself on the line, of seeing how far I could push myself. And becoming a soldier offered the prospect of seeing something of the world. It's perhaps hard for young people now to realize how rare the opportunities for overseas travel were in those days if you weren't wealthy. My parents didn't push me into it, and I don't think that I had joined the CCF intending to join the Army in due course. But it was obvious to me that my father found his Army career satisfying, and I'm sure that my experiences in the CCF had a considerable influence in demonstrating the pleasures of soldiering.

Not many of the other boys at school were interested in a Service career, though there was one I recall, a bit younger than me: John Drewienkiewicz, known subsequently by his Army nickname, DZ, who would go on to have a successful military career, rising to become a major general. Our paths would cross again many years later when he was number two in the Kosovo Verification Mission.

My headmaster was a bit sniffy about my decision to join the Army. 'You know, Jackson,' he told me, 'you really should go to university.' There was a sense then, although it's completely changed now, that the Army was not the place for the brightest. I took it as quite a compliment that he thought I might be a candidate for university entrance, because in the early 1960s only a very small minority, perhaps about 5 per cent of all school pupils, had any form of tertiary education. But I had made up my mind and nothing he could say would alter it, though I did agree to go back to school for a term after taking my A levels as an insurance policy, in case the Army gave me the thumbs-down.

By this time my father had been posted to Malta, where I spent the 1961 summer holidays after my A levels. I remember sitting around the kitchen table with my parents and talking my career choice over with them, the application papers to join the Army as a regular commissioned officer spread out in front of us. I put in my papers, and in early November I was called before the Regular Commissions Board at Westbury, in Wiltshire. I would be away for three nights. I suppose I must have been quite nervous, aware that the stakes were high: I had been warned that around half of all candidates were failed by the Board. I took the train down to London and then another train out to Westbury, dressed in the suit that I would wear in the evenings. At Westbury station I was picked up by a minibus together with several other youngsters and driven to Leighton House, the home of the Regular Commissions Board (now known as the Army Officer Selection Board). The main building was a Georgian mansion, surrounded by lesser outbuildings, one of which provided the candidates' quarters.

There were about fifty of us on that three-day course, divided into three or four groups. We all wore colour-coded tabards with numbers on them – rather like the ones competitive runners wear – and throughout the course we would be addressed by number rather than by name. As well as standard intelligence tests, we were given a range of tasks, when there would be at least one member of the staff watching and listening to everything we did and said. One of the tasks was to give a 'lecturette' in front of the assembled company: five or ten minutes on the subject of your choice – which in my case was Malta.

Rather more taxing were tests of the kind widely used in

the military, and nowadays often also on management courses. The scenarios differ but the same principles apply. In the Army these are known as command tasks: for example, working as a team to get a burden – a heavy oil drum or something like that – over some notionally bottomless chasm. You're given some planks and ropes but nothing quite fits, and the goal is to work out what to do. For some of these tasks a leader is appointed, while others are so-called leaderless. In all cases the observers watch the dynamics of the group to see who emerges with the bright ideas, who is a team player or who isn't.

Back at school, the eagerly awaited envelope arrived a few days later. There was a place for me at the Royal Military Academy, Sandhurst, starting in January 1962.

I passed the good news on to my parents, but I can't remember how. Telephoning abroad back in those days was a nightmare. For one thing, you often had to wait hours until a line was available. If you were calling from a payphone, you had to insert exactly the right change, then press buttons A and B in the right sequence. If you pressed the wrong one, or pressed them in the wrong order, you risked losing all your money. I probably decided that it was easier to send them a telegram.

The rest of my last term at Stamford was fairly relaxed. The pressure was off, and this gave me the opportunity to study other subjects I hadn't been able to give a lot of time to before, like art. Unlike my son Mark I am no good at painting, but I enjoyed calligraphy. Our art master was quite a character, and oddly enough it was he who first suggested I read Clausewitz, the great philosopher of war. He said, 'You're going to be in the Army, boy, you must read Clausewitz's *Vom Kriege*, "On War"'. So I did. I confess that I found it intellectually challenging. This was my first introduction to the theoretical side of warfare. Like so many others before and since, I was particularly struck by Clausewitz's dictum that 'war is nothing but the continuation of politics with the admixture of other means'. It was a concept that would resonate throughout my career as a soldier.

Before going to Sandhurst I had to enlist as a soldier, because as an officer cadet you are a soldier, not an officer. I was summoned to the nearest recruiting office, in Leicester, where with one hand on a Bible and standing in front of a uniformed officer I swore an oath of allegiance to The Queen, Her heirs and successors. Then I signed my so-called 'attestation paper', and that was it: I was a soldier. I was given one day's pay and sent away on unpaid leave until the date I was due to report to Sandhurst.

2
Cadet

Very early, perhaps even on my first evening at Sandhurst, we were given a talk about what it means to be an officer. The Royal Military Academy's motto is germane: 'Serve to Lead'.

An officer is a leader of men. He has to exert the authority to ensure immediate obedience when necessary. To do so effectively it is essential for him to earn the respect of the men under his command. Of course, he has to show himself to be physically fit, able to do the things he asks his soldiers to do. Courage is another obvious requirement, moral as well as physical. If an officer loses the confidence of his soldiers then obviously he is in some trouble; so he's got to have a good brain in his head, he's got to show good judgement and he needs to be decisive, to show the men that he knows the job and is able to make up his mind about things, quickly if need be. But there's another side to this too. An officer has got to look after his soldiers, not in a patronizing sense, but to ensure their welfare, safety and, where possible, comfort. He is responsible for them in every aspect.

The training at Sandhurst is designed to produce officers who understand the range of qualities required of them and who are capable of exhibiting these in practice. To those who aren't used to it, the combination of military discipline, rigid adherence to standards of dress and behaviour, and hard physical training may seem strange – though less so if you've been educated at a British boarding school. A certain degree of humility is necessary; you have a lot to learn. Being shouted out by a sergeant reinforces this message. There's an Army tradition that at Christmas the officers and NCOs serve the men their lunch, a symbolic gesture of the principle enshrined in the Academy motto.

The big day arrived in January 1962 when I presented myself at Sandhurst, just north of Camberley, on the border between Berkshire and Surrey. I remember how imposing it seemed: large and handsome buildings set in several hundred acres of grounds, with parkland, woods and ornamental lakes. I was excited to be there, keen to make a good fist of it.

Back then there were two intakes to the Royal Military Academy every year, in January and September. Cadets took a two-year course, with three terms in each year, following the academic model. We worked a five-and-a-half-day week, with Saturday afternoons and Sundays free, though we were not allowed out for the first few weeks. In those days, more than half of the course was academic, with lectures, tutorials, essays and examinations, very much on university lines and taught by civilian academic staff. We studied science, mathematics, languages, international affairs and military history. In recent years the curriculum has changed, to reflect the fact that the great majority of the intake will be graduates, and the course has been shortened from two years to one, with a more condensed academic syllabus.

Some things were much like school. For example, there were three colleges, Old, New and Victory, much like school houses. Old College is a magnificent stucco-fronted Georgian building in the Palladian style, with a grand entrance of massive Doric columns supporting an ornate pediment. I was housed in New College, itself a large and imposing red-brick building dating from the Edwardian era. Slightly to my surprise, I found that I had my own room, which I quickly discovered had to be kept immaculate because, like everything else, it would get inspected. It was small, equipped with a single bed, a wardrobe, a hand-basin and a bookshelf, and heated by a heavy cast-iron radiator: all pretty basic, perhaps, but to me, accustomed to sleeping in large dormitories at boarding school, it seemed very comfortable. There were endless roll calls; I heard ours so often that I could soon recite the names of the cadets in my platoon by rote. On arrival, every cadet was assigned to one of four companies in each college, named after battle honours of the British Army – I was assigned to Ypres Company – and within the company to the junior platoon of about fifteen to twenty cadets (about half the size of a regular Army platoon). Each company consisted of four platoons at different stages in their training, and each platoon had an officer as the platoon commander and a platoon sergeant, both regular Army: ours were Captain David Martin, a jovial gunner, and Sergeant Ford, a Grenadier Guardsman, a small but fierce man with a bristling moustache.

A sizeable minority of cadets were from overseas; in my company there were cadets from Jamaica, Malaysia, New Zealand, Nigeria, Pakistan, Sierra Leone and Thailand – and two from Iraq; in my platoon, we had a Sikh from Malaysia, Sarjit Singh, a very good man, and Sam Mboma from Sierra Leone. Poor Sam chose the wrong side of an attempted coup and was executed only a few years after leaving Sandhurst. As for the British cadets, I'm always wary of making assertions when I don't have the hard evidence, but I would have thought that two-thirds or more of them were public schoolboys, whereas nowadays the proportion is more like one-third. Society was more hierarchical then than it is today, and this fact alone may have deterred many good candidates from state schools from applying to Sandhurst. I would maintain that the Army has always been open to talent, however. The First World War general Sir William Robertson may have dropped his aitches, but he rose from private soldier to become Chief of the Imperial General Staff. My own view has always been that I don't give a damn where somebody comes from; if he's good, he's good, and that's the end of the matter. I loathe snobbery in any form.

Unlike today, there were no women at Sandhurst at that time. The then Women's Royal Army Corps was completely separate, and female officer cadets had their own nearby but separate college.

To say that there was a lot to get used to would be an understatement. For one thing, everything seemed to have to be done at the double, and we were inspected all the time to make sure we'd done everything properly. Then there was the novelty of being addressed by grown men as

'Sir' (I was still only seventeen). All the warrant officers and senior NCOs would address you as 'Sir', even if they prefixed this with an unflattering description, such as: 'You horrible lazy idle officer cadet, Sir.'

I remember very early on being on parade and addressed by the great Academy Sergeant Major, the senior warrant officer for the entire British Army. 'Now that you are at Sandhurst,' he barked at us, 'I will call you Sir and you will call me Sir, because I am a warrant officer. But there's one difference: you will mean it and I most certainly won't.' This was the legendary Jackie Lord, the Academy Sergeant Major for most of my time at Sandhurst. A tall, lean man with a well-trained moustache and piercing eyes, he stood ramrod-straight. Lord had been a Grenadier Guardsman; having joined Airborne Forces on their formation, he had fought at Arnhem and had been captured. The story is told that, by the time his prisoner-of-war camp was liberated, Jackie Lord had rounded up the remaining Germans and put them in custody, and was ready at the front gate with an immaculate salute and a guard of honour when the Allied liberators arrived. He was a hell of a man, much admired and respected by all the cadets.

Right at the beginning we were issued with our kit. Sandhurst has its own uniform, given that none of the cadets at this stage is a member of any particular regiment. We were issued with a smart full dress uniform, known as 'Blues', khaki serge battledress (which despite its name wasn't worn in the field), combat kit (which was), a peaked cap for smart wear and a beret for field and non-smart wear, and several pairs of very stiff boots: best boots that had to be kept highly polished, and boots for the field. In those days they were hobnailed, believe it or not, and you had to put the studs in yourself to a set pattern. The boot had to be soaked first to make the leather supple enough, and then you banged in the studs with a hammer. Boots were inspected like everything else. The sergeant would bark, 'Mr Jackson, Sir, let me see your boots' – then, 'Those boots are fucking idle, Sir. Show again.'

We spent a lot of time cleaning our kit, and usually we'd sit doing this together, in and out of each other's rooms, or at tables in the corridor, chattering away with one another. The shared tedium of it all helped build a sense of comradeship.

Cadets were issued with their own weapon, the standard rifle of the day, which was known as the SLR, the self-loading rifle. 'This is yours, look after it very well, Sir,' I was instructed. We kept our rifles in our rooms when not in use, with the bolt extracted and locked in a small safe. Nowadays this would be an unacceptable arrangement; the complete weapon must be kept in a secure armoury.

The first term's training was all military, essentially the same as any recruit going into the Army gets: basic weapon handling, basic fieldcraft, basic infantry tactics, basic communications – and of course we began square-bashing. We learned all the drill: how to present arms, how to stand at ease, how to march in step and keep an exact distance from the next man while turning our heads to give the salute. The man on the inside of the row has to remain looking forward to ensure that the rest continue to march straight ahead. The slightest mistake and we had to do it all over again. There's plenty of hard physical exercise ('beasting' as it's known in the Army): cross-country runs, route marches, a lot of gym work, boxing, swimming and so on. Much of this is done on a competitive basis between the companies, encouraging an *esprit de corps*. Then there's the assault course. All assault courses are basically the same: there'll be a number of obstacles, such as rope swings and ditches. Some you can only really handle as a team. The high wall is one of those. You won't get over it on your own because it's too high for an individual to jump to the top, so you have to shove up one or two blokes, who, having got up there, lie on their bellies with their legs dangling on the other side and their arms reaching down, ready to catch people and hoick them up as they take a running jump at it. Plenty land face down in the mud. You're carrying your kit and being chivvied all the time, naturally.

It was soon borne in on us that to a large extent we would stand or fall by our ability to work as a team. In that respect the platoon is a microcosm of the Army as a whole. The sense that you're all in it together is very important. And of course that sense forms among a platoon of officer cadets as it forms in any other unit: you help each other through some of the difficult bits, and where somebody's a bit weak you'll offer to give them a hand.

Inevitably there were some cadets who dropped out, and a few who failed to come up to scratch, those who were told that there was no point in continuing. If you were struggling to keep up you might get 'back-termed', which meant you had to do the last term again and pick up the course with the next intake coming through. Fortunately this didn't happen to me.

In the battlefield exercises, some cadets would be given command appointments such as platoon or section commander for, say, the following twelve hours, and ordered to carry out some major tactical task. The permanent staff watch this sort of exercise particularly closely, because if there is any doubt about a cadet's suitability, this is where it shows. A cadet platoon commander might be charged with taking his platoon from point A to point B, and then ambushed on the way by the enemy (another platoon firing blanks). How do you handle that? Some guys freeze: Bloody hell, I've been ambushed, what do I do next?

Each December we travelled abroad for a big exercise. In my first year we went to Cyprus, which at that time of year has a climate much like England in early summer. In the second year we went to Libya, which was interesting for me personally because of course I remembered living there as a boy. We also did an exchange exercise with the French military academy, St Cyr: one year they came to us and then the next we went to them. I chatted with some of the French cadets, who impressed me as competent, professional and committed. This was a pleasant surprise, because in those days the prevailing wisdom was primarily to see the French as having been defeated by the Germans in 1940 and by the Viet Minh in the early 1950s.

Once the first term was over we were allowed out at weekends, after the Saturday morning parade on Old Building Square. The parade itself would usually take an hour or so, and afterwards we would be itching to get off. But sometimes, instead of the hoped-for 'Well, gentlemen, that's it, off you go for your weekend,' we would hear the Academy Sergeant Major utter the dreaded words: 'That was terrible. Go round again.' A groan would go out, as cadets realized that they would not be able to catch the planned train or make the arranged rendezvous.

By this time I had a car, a green 1937 Morris 8 Tourer known as 'Esmeralda' that I had bought for £20 – one of a collection of old bangers belonging to cadets, many of them pre-war, parked around the back of New College. I often had to crank-start the engine, but in general Esmeralda behaved herself. Those cars were so simple that even with minimal mechanical skills you could more or less maintain them.

Camberley was handily placed for heading up to London. There was a pub in South Kensington that we cadets frequented, The Bunch of Grapes, and often that would be the first – and last – port of call. We drank a lot of beer, and chased the girls in West London flat-land. Often we could go from party to party until very late on a Saturday night. We had a lot of fun in those days. Work hard, play hard: that was our formula.

It's been largely superseded, but there was then at Sandhurst a sort of prefect system: so-called 'cadet government'. Only in a minor way was this a disciplinary body, but cadets were ranked: cadet corporal, cadet sergeant, cadet colour sergeant, junior under-officer and senior under-officer. The senior intake provided a complete cadet command structure, which shadowed the real officers at Sandhurst: the senior under-officer shadowed the company commander, three junior under-officers shadowed the platoon commanders of the following three intakes, and so on. I made it to junior under-officer, one short of the highest rank.

*   *   *

A few days before the end of my time at Sandhurst the order of merit for our intake was published. A typed list was pinned up on the notice board, and everybody crowded around to examine it, inevitably with much leg-pulling. I was ranked fifth in the overall order of merit – 'jammy bastard', as one of my friends kindly put it. I sent my parents a telegram to let them know how I'd done. A day or two later came the prizegiving; I must have been a real inky swot in those days, because I won two prizes, for languages and military law.

On the morning of 19 December 1963, I was one of two hundred or so officer cadets in our 'Blues' who passed out on the Sovereign's Parade. General Sir Gerald Lathbury, the then Quartermaster General, took the salute on behalf of the Queen from the top of a dais. He had commanded the 1st Parachute Brigade at Arnhem, and was now Colonel Commandant of the Parachute Regiment, the tribal elder. We marched past in slow time and then in quick time, saluting as we passed the general. At last we marched up the wide stone steps of the grand entrance of the Old College, between the massive Doric columns and on through the open doors. In accordance with tradition, the Adjutant followed us up the steps mounted on his charger.

After the parade came a formal lunch. There was an end-of-term feeling, and when lunch was over we handed in our kit and then let off a bit of steam. It was a tradition for each platoon on commissioning day to pose for a photograph in the most ridiculous dress they could find; perhaps because we'd just got back from Libya, we chose a French North African theme, with guys dressed as legionnaires, matelots and other outlandish figures. In the evening we changed into our smart new regimental mess kit uniforms, ready for the Commissioning Ball that evening, attended by lots of pretty girls. For some reason I had two girls to escort that evening, one of whom I contrived to pass on to another cadet whose date had stood him up. Our rank as second lieutenants would be shown by a star, known as a pip, one on each epaulette. But we would not actually become commissioned until midnight, by which time most of the regular staff would be long gone – ever since the time when a newly commissioned young officer had tried to place his sergeant under arrest. And so the form was to cover each pip with a piece of tape. At midnight, to the popping of champagne corks, off came the tapes, and from that moment on we were all officers.

The one really big decision that any cadet has to make at Sandhurst is which part of the Army he's going to join. The regimental system is fundamental to the British Army (although something of a mystery to foreigners). The different components of the Army are known as the Arms and Services: broadly speaking, the Arms comprises the fighting elements – for example, the Royal Armoured Corps, the Infantry, the Royal Artillery, the Royal Engineers – and the Services the support and logistic elements, for example, the Royal Army Medical Corps and the Royal Logistic Corps. Furthermore, the Royal Armoured Corps and the Infantry in turn each comprise a number of regiments. British soldiers give their first loyalty to their own corps or regimental cap-badge, and only then to the Army as a whole. The British Army can therefore be seen as a federation of warrior tribes, each with its own history, hierarchy, customs, dress and so on. It is a peculiarly British structure, but one which self-evidently works well for the British Army.

I'd been attracted by the Parachute Regiment right from the start. The Paras had a reputation as a can-do organization, offering the young soldier the prospect of plenty of action. On enlisting in the Army you formally have to join one tribe or another, even if you are bound for Sandhurst. When I went to the recruiting office in Leicester after being accepted by the Regular Commissions Board I had chosen to enlist in the Parachute Regiment. Clearly it was in my mind even then that serving with the Paras would be an exciting challenge.

As my time at Sandhurst wore on, however, I came to the view that I could best use my languages in the Intelligence Corps. So when I filled out preference forms about halfway through my second year, that became my first choice, and in due course I was accepted and commissioned into the Corps.

After leaving Sandhurst, I was ordered to report to the Intelligence Corps training centre (then called a 'depot') at Maresfield, near Uckfield in Sussex, after completing twenty-five days' commissioning leave. To celebrate becoming an officer, I bought myself a used sports car, a green, soft-top Sunbeam Alpine, not very reliable but a lot more glamorous than my old Morris 8.

To be frank, Maresfield was a bit of an anti-climax after Sandhurst. I seemed to be treated as a sort of general dogs-body, doing the boring tasks nobody else wanted to do. This didn't last very long, however, because after three months I was sent on the fifteen-week infantry platoon commanders' course. The Intelligence Corps had, and still has, a commendable policy of ensuring its young officers get some combat-arm experience by spending a year or two as a platoon commander with an infantry battalion, and one had to do the course as preparation for that. The course takes the young subaltern beyond the very basic level of tactics he learned at Sandhurst and prepares him to join an infantry battalion as a platoon commander. So there were young officers on the course from every different infantry regiment, dressed in a startling variety of different uniforms and headgear.

The first part of the course was at the long-since closed Small Arms School at Hythe, on the Kent coast. This was primarily about weapons and was taught mainly by senior NCOs. The second part was all about infantry tactics, taught mainly by officers, and took place at what was then the School of Infantry at Warminster, on the edge of Salisbury Plain. It was an intensive course and we spent a lot of it in the field, some of the time carrying out practical tasks such as digging slit trenches – hard work in the chalk of the Plain. The exercises included 'all phases of war', i.e. advance, attack, defence, withdrawal. Sometimes these exercises were scripted very tightly, and at other times there was more scope for improvisation, what we call 'free play'. Umpires decided the casualties, handing out tags labelled 'gunshot wound' or whatever. We also learned how an infantry battalion works in the field, with its three manoeuvre companies, its support company equipped with anti-tank weapons and mortars, and its administrative company which runs the battalion's logistics.

Before I reached the end of the platoon commanders' course I was summoned to Birmingham University for an interview. While still at Sandhurst I had decided to apply to university to read Russian Studies, even though getting a place would mean postponing by another three or four years the day when I would begin real soldiering. Back then, as I have said, only a handful of the cadets at Sandhurst had degrees, but the Army took the view that a proportion of its officer corps ought to be graduates and therefore it funded a limited number of university places annually for newly commissioned young officers: about forty out of an annual intake of around four hundred, so around 10 per cent of the total.

My original A-level grade in Russian had been pretty poor, and as Sandhurst offered the opportunity to take A levels, I had decided to have another go. My Russian teacher was a splendid character, Count Constantinoff, a small and wizened old man who used to tell rather tall stories about sledges and wolves in the snow when he was in his cups. As a White Russian he had fought in the Civil War against the Reds, and only got out when it was clear that the Whites had lost.

I re-sat my Russian A level and obtained a better grade. Even with my improved Russian, however, my grades – a D and two Cs – were still not good enough for Oxford, which turned me down, rather to the disappointment of my parents. With hindsight, this was probably fortunate, because as a result I took a degree which interested me rather more and which I think has stood me in rather better stead. The Oxford degree focused on Russian literature, and while I had studied the Russian classics – Pushkin and Tolstoy, in particular – I felt that if there were something broader, that would be better for me. That's why I was attracted by a course in Russian Studies, whereby you studied the language as much as a means to read source material in Russian as for its own linguistic sake. At that time only two or three universities in Britain were offering such a course. In the first year, one would study straightforward politics, economics and sociology, and then in the second and third years one would move on to apply those disciplines to what was then the Soviet Union, and its history. I felt that it might be useful to 'know thine enemy'.

Birmingham accepted me, so a month or two after completing the platoon commanders' course, off I went to begin life as a student. The mid-1960s was an interesting time to be at university. A new Labour Government under the leadership of Harold Wilson had come in, after a long period of Tory rule. Change was in the air: there was the beginning of a youth counter-culture which rejected established values. Young men were starting to grow their hair long and dress in some pretty outlandish clothes. Students were in general left-inclined and pretty anti-war. Many of them were viscerally opposed to the use of force, whatever the circumstances. As a serving young Army officer I suppose I must have seemed an object of some curiosity to most of them, but I made no attempt to disguise who I was or what I thought.

My time at Birmingham coincided with an escalation of the Vietnam War. Professional interest led me to follow events as closely as I could. The strong opposition to the war felt by the majority of my fellow students was obvious. I wasn't opposed to the war in principle, and I did share the American belief that the march of Communism needed to be resisted. I can remember speaking at a formal debate in the Students' Union; the subject was a rather general pacifist proposition along

'King and Country' lines, but of course Vietnam was always in the background. Unsurprisingly, the vote went against us. Wilson made it clear early on that he was not going to deploy British troops to Vietnam to support our American allies. The British Army had mixed feelings about this. On the one hand, there was relief that British soldiers were not going to be sent into what was obviously a very difficult and dangerous situation. On the other hand, there was a sense of an opportunity missed.

I was two or three years older than most of my contemporaries at Birmingham, and perhaps a little more mature: certainly better off, thanks to my second lieutenant's pay. I used to go up to London quite a lot. Having a bit more money to spend as well as a sports car was no bad thing for my social life.

I lived in digs, in Edgbaston, just down the road from the university, as the only tenant of a middle-aged landlady, a widow as I remember. She would cook me breakfast, and then I would normally eat lunch and my evening meal in the university refectory. They were comfortable lodgings, though my landlady was very proper and there was no question of being able to bring girls back. To keep fit I used to swim and go pounding round the streets of Edgbaston in my Army boots. I kept my military hand in by doing the odd weekend exercise with the Officers' Training Corps (OTC), and I went on their camp on Dartmoor for a fortnight in the summer vacation. It was pretty tame stuff after what I was used to, but I enjoyed it all the same. I was relieved to be in the company of people who didn't disapprove of my choice of career. It must be admitted, too, that the OTC bar served some of the cheapest beer in Birmingham.

Russian Studies was not everybody's cup of tea, and only a handful of students took the course. We were taught in small groups or in one-to-one tutorials. It was a degree requirement to spend part of your second long summer vacation in Russia, to improve your spoken language as much as anything else. But the Ministry of Defence thought this was a bad idea and told me I couldn't go. I'm not sure what they thought might happen. Maybe they were worried that I might be seduced by some KGB beauty – not that I knew any secrets to betray. It was disappointing, because when you spend so much time studying a country, you want to go and see it for yourself. I didn't argue against the ruling, however. I had to get a special dispensation from the University Senate to relieve me of the obligation to fulfil that aspect of the course. In its place they sent me on a language immersion course at a summer school in Chester, a poor substitute. I was quite envious when my fellow undergraduates came back at the end of their stay and told me what I had missed. Ironically, ten years later I would be sent to the Soviet Union, courtesy of the MOD.

I got married in 1966, while still at university. It seemed very much the right thing to do at the time, but we were both rather young, even by the ways of the time. As the marriage regretfully broke down in the early 1980s, I will say no more, beyond that I became the father of two much-loved children, Amanda, who was born in 1971 when I was serving in Northern Ireland, and Mark, born in Scotland a couple of years later.

In 1967 I graduated with second-class honours. I didn't attend the actual graduation ceremony, because by the time it took place I was halfway across the world, with my wife and parents in Hong Kong, where my father had been posted not long before. We had flown out to join them under what is called an 'indulgence', a scheme that allowed you to take up an empty seat on any RAF aircraft for a nominal sum. I had applied for an indulgence and one came up, irritatingly the day before the graduation ceremony. Thankfully the university agreed to grant me my degree *in absentia*, so off we went to Hong Kong for a few weeks. I found it a vibrant, exciting place, though there was a sense of unease about the upheaval just across the border in Communist China. It was a treat to stay with my parents, who lived on the second floor of an apartment block with a big balcony overlooking Repulse Bay, one of the most beautiful beaches in Hong Kong. Then we flew back to England, and on 7 August 1967 I reported to the Parachute Regiment depot in Aldershot to begin my infantry attachment.

3

Subaltern

The Parachute Regiment considers itself to be special. It attracts a certain sort of soldier, with a lust for adventure and excitement, and terrier-like commitment and determination. The Regiment prides itself on its fighting qualities and its wholly professional approach. It is a young regiment, founded in the Second World War, and some see it as still having the brashness of youth. If that might have had some truth forty years ago, I believe it to be without foundation today. The Paras have come of age, matured by operational reality and experience. Officers of the Regiment – and never more so than now – have achieved high rank in the Army in competition with others of their peer group. The Paras provide over half of the regular Special Air Service – a statistic which vividly emphasizes their fighting qualities.

The Parachute Regiment, the infantry of the Army's Airborne Forces, has the unique ability to deploy directly to its objective over strategic distances, independent of any need for ports, airfields and other infrastructure in the theatre of operations. The airborne role is a dramatic one, not least because it carries with it inherent risk, but also because it provides the ability to surprise the enemy, to dislocate him. Helicopter-borne operations can produce a similar effect, but they can only be mounted at short, tactical ranges.

The Regimental motto is 'Utrinque Paratus', which means 'ready for anything' – a neat pun on 'Para'.

I had opted to join the Intelligence Corps, and at this stage I still had every intention of returning to them once I had completed my infantry attachment. But it was no coincidence that I opted to do my infantry training with the Parachute Regiment. I'd had the Paras in mind right back when, as a schoolboy, I went to Leicester to enlist – and in my second year at Sandhurst I had volunteered for the basic beginner's parachute course at RAF Abingdon, though this was more because I thought it would be fun than with any thought to the future. The course began with a fortnight's concentration on drills and landing techniques. As part of this you jumped from a platform about 10 yards high, wearing a harness attached through a pulley to an air fan, which slowed your descent so that you dropped to the ground as if wearing a parachute. Afterwards you did eight proper parachute jumps, the first two from a small cage dangling below a tethered balloon, in those days an old Second World War barrage balloon (this means of training went out of service years ago).

I wouldn't be honest if I didn't admit to being a little apprehensive the first time I jumped, but it was exciting too. The feeling of letting go when you step into space is so intoxicating that some people get hooked on it. And when you hit the ground you feel exhilarated. In some ways it's more daunting to jump from a balloon because the whole thing is that much more clinical, as deliberate as stepping off a cliff. In a military aircraft, on the other hand, it can feel somewhat claustrophobic. You're packed in like sardines, you've been sitting in an uncomfortable position for hours, it's hot and sweaty, and there's a hell of a lot of noise, especially once they open the door and the red light comes on. Low-level flying can be particularly unpleasant, with many people being airsick. It's a relief to get out into the fresh clean air. And as soon as you leave the plane you're in the propeller backwash – whereas if you step out of a balloon you fall vertically.

After a couple of jumps from the static barrage balloon, the other six training jumps were from aircraft. In those days we jumped from a Hastings or a Beverley, the four-engine transports of the day. There was a very clear drill on the ground beforehand, so we knew exactly what was coming. One of the drills to help you cope with the turbulence on leaving an aircraft involved using the so-called 'knacker-cracker', a cable running between two towers. You're harnessed to a slide, and after you jump off, you get bounced around as you slide – which can be quite painful in the nether regions if you haven't got the harness just so!

In the aircraft you're seated in a row with your back against the aircraft frame. Twenty minutes before jumping, you stand up and hook up your parachute to a static line above head height. About five minutes before you jump, one of the crew opens the door and after a short while the red light comes on. Then the light turns green and an RAF 'dispatcher' orders the first man in the line to jump – and so on, until it's your turn. You're on your feet, waiting in line. There's no time to hesitate: you just have to follow the man in front to the door and jump. The time interval between each man and the next is no more than a second.

Landing is not as difficult as one might imagine. Your vertical speed on hitting the ground is not that great; they say the impact is not much more than that of jumping off a kitchen table. That's in still air, of course; if you've got a brisk wind, that will give you lateral movement as well. But in still air you can sometimes remain on your feet when you land – the so-called 'stand-up' landing.

You did the first few jumps from an aircraft without your kit, but the training course was progressive, so after two or three jumps, you then started jumping with your equipment.

Jumping with all your kit is another matter altogether. It might weigh fifty or sixty pounds, more in some cases: a heavy pack filled with everything you will need on the ground, your weapon strapped alongside your pack in a canvas sleeve, and your webbing with your ammunition. Just carrying it makes you feel like a beast of burden. But this is what you've been training for – to be able to land in a potentially hostile environment and fend for yourself when you reach the ground. Of course, it would be dangerous to land carrying so much extra weight; so the pack is not on your back, but hooked on to your parachute harness in front, with a quick-release mechanism that you operate once the parachute opens, so that the pack falls on a length of rope perhaps 15 feet below you. There's a bit of a jerk when it reaches the end of the line, but then it dangles below you for the rest of the drop, and hits the ground first.

You finished by doing a night drop, which concentrates the mind because you can't see the ground unless the moon is very bright. As you drop you don't know how high you are, so it's important to keep a good landing position throughout. Just before you land you hear the thump of your pack hitting the ground, which gives you about a second's warning.

On successful completion of the Sandhurst parachute course, you were awarded a little parachute emblem – known as the 'light bulb' because that's what it looks like – which you wore on your lower sleeve. Afterwards we undertook a live jump as part of the Sandhurst exercise we carried out against St Cyr, the French military academy.

To qualify for Airborne Forces, you first have to pass the pre-parachute selection course (PPS) run by Pegasus Company (P Coy), so that was the next thing on my horizon in the late summer of 1967. It's a hard, physically demanding course: somewhat different from the SAS selection course, but none the less very tough. It is designed (a) to make sure each individual has a high level of fitness, and (b) to put him under stress and see how he copes with it. By no means everyone makes it through. For the duration of the course an officer is just a member of his squad, being shouted at by a sergeant along with all the others. As it turned out I was the only officer in my squad, which meant I came in for particular attention from our squad sergeant, a Geordie called Les Peacock. Sergeant Peacock was small, wiry, and extremely fit.

In those days, the course took place in Aldershot and in

South Wales, near Crickhowell, where the Black Mountains meet the Brecon Beacons. The location has since moved to Yorkshire, but the format remains the same. There are speed marches (known as 'tabbing') over the hills, when you've really got to move; log races between teams carrying big heavy logs; what's called 'milling' – individual boxing, without any Queensberry Rules; the assault course; and other similar delights. The last thing you do is the stretcher race. You're in a squad of eight; the stretcher is loaded to simulate the weight of a wounded man, and you take it in turns to carry this, four at a time. It's very hard work, but there's a wonderful feeling when you get to the end and know that you've finished.

Once I'd passed the PPS that September, the Great Men who decide these things told me that I had to go back to RAF Abingdon and do the same basic parachute course all over again. I felt that this was unnecessary, but they said there had been too long a gap since I had last parachuted while still at Sandhurst more than four years earlier. So I went through the whole course once more. At the end of it I emerged with my red beret and parachute wings, indicating that the wearer has qualified to become a member of Airborne Forces.

I was now a full lieutenant, and almost six years after enlisting had at last reached the stage when I was going to command real soldiers, in a real battalion in the field army. This is a moment every young Army officer looks forward to, with a mixture of anticipation and trepidation. I would be commanding a platoon of thirty-odd guys, some of them no doubt older than me and all serious soldiers, while I was a raw young man who wasn't even a proper Parachute Regiment officer.

The Regimental Headquarters of the Parachute Regiment posted me to the Second Battalion, 2 Para. On joining, I replaced the cap-badge of the Intelligence Corps with that of the Parachute Regiment – naturally a very proud moment. At the time, the whole Parachute Brigade – consisting of the three Parachute battalions and other airborne units from the Artillery, the Engineers, and so on – was in Germany on a very large exercise, so off I went to join them in the field. When I got there I was told, 'Right, you're going to B Company and you're going to command No. 4 Platoon.' Unusually, there would be no officer/officer handover, because the platoon sergeant had been in temporary command of this particular platoon. I was coming in over his head, which might have been a bit tricky.

The relationship between a new officer and the platoon sergeant is one that has been played out thousands of times over the centuries. The sergeant is almost inevitably older and vastly more experienced; typically he may have served ten years or more. In comes the young officer who has a lot to learn, but at the end of the day he is the one who has the authority. It is a very important part of the platoon sergeant's job, not only to be second-in-command of the platoon, but also to bring on his young officer, to show him the ropes.

No matter how much training you may have received, there's no template to show you how to work with your platoon sergeant. Everybody has to work it out for himself. So much of it is a matter of chemistry, of establishing the right relationship with this particular individual. Any young officer in those circumstances who starts to throw his weight around will become rather 'unloved'. You've got to walk a tightrope: you must show on the one hand that you are the boss, and on the other that you value your sergeant's opinion. There must be a bit of distance, even if it's only psychological. Physically you can be in a slit trench with the guy, you are sleeping next to him, you are crapping next to him: you can't be too standoffish in the field, but you mustn't be too matey either.

The sort of thing you might do is to have a quiet conversation with your platoon sergeant, maybe over a beer, certainly not in front of the soldiers, after you've been serving together three or four months or perhaps after a big exercise. 'How am I doing?' you might ask. If you give him the opening, you can have that conversation. But it's a delicate balance. Soldiers don't like being bullshitted. Some young officers make the error of trying to 'curry favour', and they soon learn that soldiers don't like that either.

In this case there was a further twist in the tale, in that the platoon sergeant I inherited soon moved on to other duties, to be replaced by . . . Sergeant Peacock! As it turned out this was a stroke of luck, because he knew me from the selection course, and if he hadn't thought then that I was OK, I wouldn't have passed. In fact we got on very well. He was a very dedicated and professional soldier, with a nice dry sense of humour, a remarkable man who finished up a lieutenant colonel. Many years later, I bumped into him on one of my last visits as Chief of the General Staff. I was at Bovington saying goodbye – and, lo and behold, there he was: Les Peacock. He was working as a retired officer down at the Royal Armoured Corps Centre. We had ten or fifteen minutes reminiscing together before I had to leave.

* * *

After the exercise in Germany was over I came back with the rest of the Battalion to Aldershot, where the Parachute Brigade was based at the time. Then early in 1968 2 Para headed out to the Far East for four months' jungle training. Malaysia seemed wonderfully warm after an English winter. We were based at a place called Kota Tinggi, about 20 miles north of the town of Johor Baharu, right at the southern tip of Malaysia, at the end of the causeway which links Singapore to the mainland. This was only my second time in the Far East – the first being my visit to Hong Kong to see my parents the year before – and the sights, the sounds and the smells all seemed very exotic. Malaysia and Singapore were then comparatively backward and undeveloped – very different from the way they are today.

Independent Malaysia was at this point just five years old. After the end of the Second World War, British and Commonwealth troops had fought a long counter-insurgency campaign in the Malay Peninsula against Communist guerrillas. The Malayan Emergency had lasted from 1948 until 1960, ending in the defeat of the Communists. The campaign had featured large in the Sandhurst military history syllabus. General (later Field Marshal) Sir Gerald Templar had been appointed High Commissioner, with extraordinary powers: one of his policies had been to move people out of the areas penetrated by guerrillas into protected areas, thus denying the insurgents a population to support their activities. In 1968, when we arrived in Malaysia to do our training, the US Army was already heavily engaged in what had begun as a counter-insurgency campaign in Vietnam. Interestingly enough, my company commander in

Malaysia was Sam Conn, an American officer with experience of Vietnam, serving with us under a long-standing exchange arrangement whereby there's always a Parachute Regiment officer with an airborne unit of the American Army and an American airborne officer with one of our parachute battalions. We were fascinated to hear of Sam's Vietnam experiences. At the time I questioned the American tactics, and wondered whether they were not too reliant on technology and firepower. Now I am not so sure that they could have done anything else, given the political constraints on them and the growing unpopularity of the war at home.

This was a period of dramatic developments in the Vietnam War. In January 1968 the North Vietnamese had launched what came to be known as the Tet (New Year) Offensive, a massive surprise attack involving half a million men. North Vietnamese troops reached the gates of the American Embassy in the South Vietnamese capital of Saigon before being repulsed. The Commander of US Land Forces, General William Westmoreland, requested a further two hundred thousand reinforcements. Faced with a storm of criticism at home, the American President, Lyndon Baines Johnson, announced at the end of March that he would not be seeking re-election, as well as directing a halt to the bombing of North Vietnam. There was no bigger scalp than that of an American President; the North Vietnamese had suffered a military defeat, but scored a political victory. For military strategists considering how best to respond to Communist insurgency, there was plenty to think about in the spring of 1968.

Before going out to Malaysia, we had practised jungle

tactics in thick woods back at home. There were soldiers in the Battalion who had operational experience of fighting in the jungle during the Borneo campaign in the early 1960s, when the British Army and its Commonwealth allies had successfully resisted Indonesia's attempt to take over the country. This had been largely infantry versus infantry fighting in the jungle – 'low intensity' operations, as opposed to high intensity, which involves tanks, artillery, air power: the full panoply.

Jungle warfare is the essence of infantry soldiering in many ways. You *can* use artillery, but it's not very effective because you can't tell where the rounds are landing. Usually you can't see very far, sometimes only three or four yards ahead. Then you have to decide: do you use tracks or do you not? If you follow a track, you're likely to make faster progress; but you may walk into an ambush, or step on a booby-trap. We tried to avoid unnecessary noise when moving through the jungle. Of course we carried machetes, and sometimes we were forced to use them, but only if there was no alternative. The area we were operating in was mostly secondary jungle, which is much thicker and harder to move around in than the original primary rainforest. It's hot and steamy, and you have to carry everything you need with you. In particular, you always have to think about your water requirements. Navigation in the jungle is very difficult. Before the days of GPS you had to navigate solely by dead reckoning, using a compass and a map and reading the contours. Two soldiers are nominated to count paces, and you have to check their counts one against the other: 'Right, how far have we come? Two hundred and fifty yards, OK, move off on a bearing of one-fifty.' If you get lost, well, Sir gets his leg pulled a bit. Serving in the jungle is a good way to get to know your soldiers because you're all living on top of each other.

One agreeable aspect of serving in the jungle is that you get eight hours' sleep every night. Sleep in the field is normally in short supply, because much operational activity takes place at night. But in the jungle the night is so dark that movement is almost impossible without using a torch.

Less agreeable were the leeches, thoroughly unpleasant creatures which would fasten on your legs and elsewhere. We took to wearing condoms after a young officer friend of mine found a leech disappearing up a precious part of his anatomy.

I was still commanding the same platoon I joined in Germany. The odd soldier came and went, but basically it was my gang, and I found the experience very satisfying. And we had a bit of fun, too. I remember nights out with other young officers in Singapore when we'd go on what the Navy calls 'a run ashore'. Though everyone knew I'd be leaving for the Intelligence Corps sooner or later, I was made to feel one of the tribe. Of course I used to get teased a bit – 'Where's the intelligence?', that sort of thing – but it was all very good-humoured.

While out in Malaysia we were warned that we would not be going home at the end of that tour. The Battalion was ordered to Hong Kong, then of course still a British colony, to reinforce the garrison. We flew there by RAF Hercules from Singapore. I remember that my parents came to meet me at Kai Tak airport.

On our arrival in Hong Kong, the tension was palpable. There had been unrest in the Colony the previous year, no doubt a spillover from events across the border. The Cultural Revolution in China was in full ferment. It was a bizarre period of upheaval in that vast country. China then was very different from the economic powerhouse of today. The Chinese leader Mao Zedong seemed semi-detached from the Government. His encouragement of ground-level revolutionary activism had unleashed violent forces, and the whole country seemed dangerously unstable. The Chinese were attempting to foment trouble – even revolution – in Hong Kong, and there were fears that fanatical Red Guards might pour across the border.

The Battalion was given the task of securing the border with mainland China. Of course, if the Chinese had really wanted to invade we could not have stopped them. They had a huge army millions strong, whereas the entire British garrison was then four or five battalions, just a few thousand men. We would have fought, but we would have been quickly overwhelmed.

B Company's focus was on a place called Mam Kam To, one of the few points where you could cross by road into mainland China. Here a river formed the border. A simple barrier controlled access over the bridge. We were on a small hillock overlooking the crossing, in a makeshift *Beau Geste*-style fort. On the far side was an area where the peasant farmers would bring their produce to sell to traders from Hong Kong, who would be up there with small trucks and carts to collect it and bring it back to the city. Every morning these Chinese farmers would have what we used to call the Red Book session. They would all line up and chant and wave their copies of Mao's *Little Red Book*. It was the most extraordinary business.

The People's Liberation Army sentries patrolling the

border took no part in these sessions. Not that we had any contact with them either. They were very disciplined, with precise orders how to react, depending on how close you came. So, for example, a sentry would be standing at ease with his weapon on the ground: when you approached within, say, thirty yards, he'd come to attention, and then within twenty yards he would hoist his weapon across his chest. You could tease them, just by approaching and retreating: very unkind really.

The barrier at Mam Kam To consisted simply of a red-and-white striped barber's pole, hinged at one end. I can still remember the first of the printed 'Orders for War' we were given, dating from many years earlier: '1. Close the barrier.'

In those days all you could see on the other side of the border were paddy fields stretching into the distance. Now there are skyscrapers everywhere you look.

As an American, Sam Conn had not been allowed by his superiors back home to accompany us to Hong Kong, and so for about a month, until his relief arrived, I took over command of B Company, about a hundred men, because I was the senior platoon commander. It was quite a privilege, given that I was still only a lieutenant of twenty-four.

And then I had another little stroke of luck. One of the tasks laid on the Battalion by the local Brigade Headquarters was to produce a young officer as a watch-keeper in the operations room back at Headquarters British Forces in Kowloon: POLMIL it was called, because it was run jointly with the police. Lieutenant Colonel Richard Dawnay, who was the Battalion commanding officer, asked me if I'd like to take it on and see a bit more of my parents. Of course, I said, I'd love to. So I spent a month actually living with my parents and commuting by duty vehicle to the Headquarters, where I did night duty manning the phones. After writing up the evening's report, you didn't have to stay awake: it was a sleeping duty, which meant that you'd only have to get up if the phone rang. So I got a reasonable amount of kip and then I had the days to myself.

The unrest was mainly confined to Kowloon, the urban area on the mainland; Hong Kong Island was more isolated from the trouble, both literally and metaphorically. But it was obvious to me that the vast majority of the population didn't want anything to do with Mao; on the contrary, what they wanted was to make money, and of course the Hong Kong Chinese are very good at that. It was pretty raw capitalism, with its downsides as well as its upsides. But I loved the energy, the colour, and the bustle; Hong Kong was an exciting place to be.

By the time 2 Para was withdrawn from Hong Kong, the crisis in China was coming to an end. Mao himself declared the Cultural Revolution over, and the Red Guards were disbanded. When the Battalion returned to Aldershot I was due to go back to the Intelligence Corps, but my return was delayed because 2 Para were again deployed early in 1969.

The British operation in Anguilla is an extraordinary tale, with many elements of comic opera; it would have made ideal material for Gilbert and Sullivan. Some people referred to it ironically as 'Harold Wilson's finest hour'. To those who wanted to see it that way, the story seemed to encapsulate the shrunken horizons of Britain in the late

1960s. While America was fighting a major war against Communist infiltration in South-East Asia, Britain was dealing with a little local difficulty on a tiny Caribbean island.

The origin of the problem was one of the many loose ends being tied up as Britain withdrew from Empire. At the time, there was a bit of a Whitehall fashion for putting federations together as a prelude to independence. The planners at the Foreign and Commonwealth Office tried it in Southern Africa, tying together Rhodesia and Nyasaland, and that didn't work terribly well. They tried to create a federation of all the British colonies in the Caribbean, which quickly fell apart. And following this collapse, they wanted to create a federation of three small islands in this particular bit of the Caribbean, St Kitts, Nevis and Anguilla – inevitably dominated by the first, as it was the biggest. The Anguillans, all six thousand of them, didn't like being lorded over by Kittitians, and they feared that with independence they would no longer be able to appeal to the British for protection. So, instead of demanding independence, the Anguillans insisted on remaining a colony. They made representations to London, which allowed matters to drift for a couple of years.

Then things began to get out of hand. There was talk of the Mafia establishing a foothold in this part of the Caribbean. A few dodgy characters appeared on Anguilla, including a fellow called Spector, Dr Spector, who – far from being an evil mastermind of the type faced by James Bond – was said to be a convicted abortionist from Cleveland, Ohio. A local politician made threatening noises, warning that he had caches of arms at his disposal to resist any attempt at imposing a solution on the island. Eventually a junior FCO minister was dispatched to Anguilla to persuade the inhabitants to accept the federation plan. On the very day of his arrival he sent a message back to London saying that he was under siege. It was alleged that shots were fired, though nobody was hit and no property seemed to have been damaged. The junior minister left the island shortly afterwards.

The British Government decided that it would have to act to restore law and order and to re-impose its authority by direct rule. So a force was speedily assembled to do this, based on 2 Para, because at that juncture we were the Spearhead Battalion – that is, the battalion nominated to be at very high readiness for any unexpected eventuality. It was 2 Para's good luck that they were on the Spearhead roster when the decision was made. We were all very keen to take part, however ludicrous the politics of it all, because soldiers always want to take part in operations. It is what we're trained for, after all.

It was clear that one company would be left behind. And of course there was great competition inside the Battalion to avoid drawing the short straw. Much to our chagrin, it was decided that B Company would be the one to suffer that terrible fate 'Left out of Battle', while the rest of the Battalion would form the invasion force, accompanied by a contingent of 120 policemen provided by the Metropolitan Police. We at Aldershot witnessed the strange sight of groups of senior police officers arriving to coordinate their planning.

At first the plan was to parachute into Anguilla. That was rejected as being overdramatic, and it was decided that the force should be flown out to Antigua and then taken to the island on board two frigates, HMS *Minerva* and HMS *Rothesay*. They steamed through the night, arriving offshore while it was still dark, only a week after the envoy had left so hurriedly. At dawn the force set out for the shore in small rubber boats. Richard Dawnay, the commanding officer, was up on the bridge of one of the two frigates, waiting anxiously for news. Flashes were seen on the beach, though there was no sound of gunfire. A moment later the radio burst into life, reporting contact: several journalists, no injuries. The flashes had come from the photographers' cameras.

As it turned out there was no opposition at all, and not a shot was fired during the whole operation. Most of the islanders were hugely pleased to see British soldiers, because most of them had never wanted to become independent. The world found the whole affair rather comical. Somewhat undignified photographs appeared in the press of large naked policemen disporting themselves in the tropical waters. A boatload of prostitutes arrived from the nearby island of St Martin and were promptly sent back again, despite their protests that they had come to offer their services to the islanders and not to the servicemen.

In due course it was decided that the force in Anguilla should be downsized, and at the same time that there should be a *roulement*, i.e. that the existing force deployed there would hand over to B Company, to spread the operational experience around the Battalion. Richard Dawnay came home and his second-in-command, Major Norrie Giles, went out to replace him, as a 'local' (i.e. temporary) lieutenant colonel, to give the Army that extra bit of clout. He needed a small staff, and since by that time I'd been a platoon commander for eighteen months or so, I was chosen to be the adjutant of the force in Anguilla, on promotion to acting captain. So that was good news, both for Norrie Giles and for me.

I'd never been to the Caribbean before. We staged through Antigua, where the logistic base was, and then flew on to Anguilla by RAF Hercules, landing on a dirt airstrip. It's a flat island, scrub-covered, with some glorious beaches. I paid a nostalgic visit to Anguilla early in 2007 to find it transformed into a high-end tourist destination; but then it was rather dilapidated, with just a couple of ramshackle beach hotels, and very little infrastructure. By the time B Company arrived, any tension there had been before had eased. A British Commissioner had been installed and things were starting to return to normal. The soldiers continued to patrol the island, to get to know the locals and to deal with any remaining unrest, but there were no incidents at all that I can remember. A squadron of Royal Engineers was already on the island repairing the roads, building a new school and constructing a deep-water jetty. The police, dressed in their British helmets but mercifully not in their serge tunics, did what police do normally. We played cricket with the locals and were thrashed every time. 'This has been most useful for the airborne soldier,' Lieutenant Colonel Giles was quoted as saying in an interview given to a reporter from the *Aldershot News* shortly before we left, in September 1969: 'It has taught him citizenship.'

As a postscript: St Kitts and Nevis became fully independent in 1983, while Anguilla remains a British Overseas Territory. The island is now stable and thriving. Comic opera it may well have been, but the operation served to stabilize the situation and to provide Anguilla with the foundation of a prosperous future.

After the Anguilla operation my time with 2 Para was over. This was very sad for me. As my infantry attachment continued, I had asked myself increasingly whether I'd made the right choice in opting for the Intelligence Corps. I was more and more drawn to the active life of an infantryman, and I loved serving with the Paras. I relished their commitment, their professionalism, their unpretentiousness and their energy. I'd made a lot of good friends, and there was a buzz about the Parachute Regiment which was heady stuff to me. So I made up my mind to ask for a formal transfer. Richard Dawnay was encouraging. The Army has a system of annual confidential reports on every serving officer, which are collected in a book, to be used by the selection boards when a candidate is being considered for promotion; he wrote in mine that 'by inclination, character, and physique' I was 'far more suited to an infantry environment than to his present Corps', i.e. the Intelligence Corps. The Parachute Regiment had obviously decided that I was OK: if I wanted to join them, they were happy to have me.

But the Intelligence Corps didn't like the idea at all. To them, this was poaching. And I wasn't the only one who'd decided to leave. Of course, it was the risk they took in having this commendable scheme whereby their young officers go on an infantry attachment. So there was a bit of irritation when I announced that I wanted to make the transfer. The upshot was that they insisted I went back to the Intelligence Corps and soldiered on, at least for a time: their argument was that I needed to gain more experience of intelligence work before I could make an informed decision. By this time their depot had moved from Maresfield in Sussex to Ashford in Kent, so that's where I went next. And the first thing I had to do was to go on an Intelligence Corps young officers' course, because even though at twenty-five I was by this time not quite so young, I had yet to receive any intelligence training.

I left 2 Para in July 1969 as an acting captain. My date for substantive promotion was December that year. Now, there are rules about this: you can only maintain acting rank if you are working in a post which is allocated to that rank, and of course being a student on a course is not a captain's post per se. The purists would say, 'Well, you lose your acting rank and you're a lieutenant again.' But it's a bit hard to go down, having gone up; so a deal was struck that I would be a 'local captain', i.e. unpaid, until my substantive promotion came through in December. Army logic, perhaps.

The following three months were spent learning how the Intelligence Corps operates. From what I can remember the course focused on operational intelligence: how do you find out about what the enemy's doing over the next hill? Some of it was interesting, some less so, though really I was just marking time. I hope I gave it a fair shot and wasn't resentful about being made to do it. But the longer I stayed, the clearer I was that I wanted to transfer back to the Paras.

The first job I was given, and the last as it turned out, had nothing to do with intelligence per se. I was posted to be second-in-command of the depot at Ashford, which was really about training recruits for the Intelligence Corps – important enough, but nothing special. If the

Corps had really wanted to keep me they might have given me something more exciting to do, so perhaps they'd given up on me by then. I had the sense that they didn't really approve of me; an earlier annual report had criticized my 'tendency to ebullience and flamboyant behaviour'. During my time with the Intelligence Corps I was sent on what was then called the 'Junior Division of the Staff Course', a three-month course intended to equip captains to become junior staff officers, and to initiate them into all-arms tactics – that is, tactics in operations involving all elements of the Army's various Arms and Services.

As time wore on I became more and more frustrated. Things had to be brought to a head. I asked for an interview with the Director of the Intelligence Corps. He must have guessed why I wanted to see him, because he gave me a less than encouraging look when I walked into his office and saluted.

'What's all this about, Mike?' he asked as I sat down.

I put the case that I had put forward the year before, when I'd been persuaded into staying on. 'Sir, I thought then that I'd made the wrong choice,' I explained, 'and now I'm convinced of it.'

He ran through the same old arguments for my remaining with the Corps.

'Look, Sir,' I said to him, 'I've given it a try, just as you asked me to. I've been back with the Corps for the best part of a year and I'm more convinced than ever that I made the wrong choice. I hope you will let me go, but you are probably going to lose me either way, because if I can't go back to the Parachute Regiment, I don't think I'll stay in the Army. I'll go and do something else.'

I fear this was bluff: I didn't have a Plan B. But I really wanted to move on. And I knew that, at the end of the day, he couldn't stop me. Every officer and soldier has the right to transfer between regiments if he wants to, though a great deal of pressure may be put on him to stay. With some reluctance, the Director of Intelligence agreed to let me go. On 9 November 1970 I received a posting order transferring me permanently to the Parachute Regiment. I reported back to the Regimental HQ, and they sent me off to join the 1st Battalion, which was already two months into an eighteen-month tour in Northern Ireland. This would be a residential tour, living with our families in Palace Barracks, Holywood, 10 miles east of Belfast. Like most people in Great Britain, I had not known much about Northern Ireland until the unrest had begun a couple of years before, but since then the Province had been in the media spotlight: as a result one was very conscious of the street violence and the fact that the Army had become heavily committed in trying to restore order. I was excited to be posted there. Northern Ireland was an operational theatre which offered an opportunity to see some action.

4

Troubles

The 'Troubles' in Northern Ireland seemed to go on so long that few people now recall how they started. Of course, there has been trouble between Protestant and Catholic in Ireland going back at least three centuries. But the modern 'Troubles' began in 1968, that year of upheaval – of *les événements* in Paris, of the 'Prague Spring', of the mass protests throughout America against the Vietnam War. Ironically, this was the only year since the Second World War in which no British soldier was killed on operations. Marches by the Catholic Civil Rights Association sparked Protestant reaction, and a spiral of violence began, with serious rioting in the main urban areas of Belfast and Londonderry. Houses were burned to the ground, families were driven from their homes, and civilians were killed in firefights between paramilitary groups set up on both sides of the religious divide. Rightly or wrongly, the Catholics felt that the police (the Royal Ulster Constabulary or RUC) sided with the majority

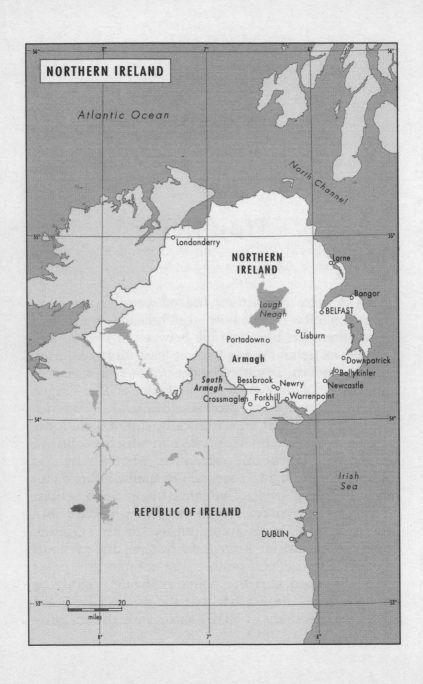

NORTHERN IRELAND

Atlantic Ocean

North Channel

Londonderry

NORTHERN
IRELAND

Larne

Bangor

Lough
Neagh

BELFAST

Portadown   Lisburn

Armagh

Downpatrick

South   Bessbrook   Newry   Ballykinler
Armagh   Newcastle
        Crossmaglen   Forkhill   Warrenpoint

Irish
Sea

REPUBLIC OF IRELAND

DUBLIN

0   20
   miles

Protestant or 'Loyalist' population and stood aside when Catholics needed defending. When the Army was first deployed on the streets of the Province late in 1969, at the urgent request of the Northern Ireland Government, the troops were welcomed and even cheered by many of the Catholic population, who saw them as protection from Protestant thugs. Looking back, I don't see that the British Government had any choice but to act as it did. However, the Irish Government, which had not then surrendered its constitutional claim to the Province, declared that the deployment of British troops on the streets of Ulster was unacceptable. British ministers described their intervention as a 'limited operation', with the idea that the soldiers should be withdrawn as soon as law and order was restored.

There was no reason for the soldiers to take one side or the other; so far as the Army was concerned, they had come to the Province simply to re-establish order, not for any political purpose. But it was impossible to avoid politics in Northern Ireland. So many things were sensitive, even the names of places. To call the Province itself by its ancient name, Ulster, could be an irritant to the Nationalists. The Royal Ulster Constabulary was therefore condemned by its very title. (It has recently been renamed, with a conscious effort at neutrality, the Police Service of Northern Ireland.) Whether you called the Province's second city Derry or Londonderry marked you out as Catholic or Protestant.

British soldiers entered a febrile situation. This was the first time that troops had been operationally deployed within the United Kingdom since the advent of a properly constituted police force. The Army was on a very steep learning curve in dealing with these intractable problems of civil disorder, not on some far-flung island but on domestic British territory, under the scrutiny of the ever-present press and television. To do so effectively required methods and skills that had not then been developed. There were new weapons, too: CS gas, then relatively untried, and baton rounds (generally known as rubber bullets), designed to disable without causing serious injury.

There is a story, perhaps apocryphal, perhaps not, from those early days when troops were first deployed to deal with rioters in Northern Ireland. It is said that the old colonial techniques of riot control were still being used, because they knew nothing else. I can remember watching a training film at Sandhurst in the early 1960s called *Keeping the Peace*, showing troops in box formation, the platoon commander surrounded by a square of soldiers. There was an escalatory procedure: first you addressed the crowd with a loudhailer, ordering them to disperse; next you unfurled the banner reading 'disperse or we fire'; and so on. The story has it that the first such banner unfurled in Northern Ireland was greeted with total incomprehension: apparently the phrase 'disperse or we fire' was written in Arabic, because the last time it had seen daylight had been in Aden.

By the time I arrived in Northern Ireland towards the end of 1970, the conflict had developed into a three-way struggle between Catholic paramilitaries, Protestant paramilitaries and the Security Forces. Soldiers were regularly taunted and stoned by young hooligans when they tried to impose order, in particular to prevent the traditional parades marching through areas where their presence was bound to provoke resentment. The Army had already largely lost the confidence of the Catholics, often described as 'Nationalists' because many of them were assumed to favour a united Ireland. Marches which had begun as a legitimate protest against social deprivation had become politicized. Soldiers were beginning to be shot at by snipers. The imposition of a curfew in the Falls Road area of Belfast in July 1970, and the subsequent violent reaction, had ended in several deaths and numerous injuries.

On 6 February 1971, Gunner Robert Curtis was shot dead in North Belfast by an Irish Republican Army (IRA) terrorist, the first British soldier to be killed in the Troubles. A line had been crossed: a British soldier had been killed on the streets of the United Kingdom, almost certainly by a fellow UK citizen. It was a shock, though we had all realized that this was bound to happen sooner or later. I was only a few hundred yards off at the time – close enough to hear the gunfire – taking part in the same operation, to contain rioting in the largely Catholic area of the Ardoyne.

The Northern Ireland Prime Minister went on television to announce that the Province was 'at war' with the IRA. But if this was a war, it was a war in which the Security Forces were at a disadvantage: they were, quite properly, required to operate within the law, while their opponents were literally outlaws. British soldiers serving in Northern Ireland were not immune from criminal prosecution for acts carried out on active service. They were given special powers to enter private property, stop vehicles, and so on – but in response to unlawful violence, they were permitted by law only to use 'reasonable force', a vague term that wasn't a great deal of help to the soldier on the ground. Nor could he rely on his commanding officer, because – particularly in this kind of situation – it was unusual for a soldier to be given an order to open fire; most commonly he had to make this decision for himself. As a result of the imprecision of the law, every soldier was issued with a set of rules of engagement, printed on a yellow card, to carry with him. Thus, for example, a soldier was entitled to return fire if he could see a weapon being used.

The violence got steadily worse. In March 1971, three off-duty soldiers in civilian clothes were lured to their deaths by women they had met in a pub. A soldier's Catholic girlfriend had her hair shaved by Republicans, and then was tarred and feathered and left tied to a lamp-post. Increasingly the IRA resorted to bombings rather than taking on the Army directly. A senior NCO in the Parachute Regiment, Sergeant Michael Willetts, sacrificed himself to save the lives of children by throwing himself on an IRA bomb at a Belfast police station. He was awarded a posthumous George Cross.

The increased risk to soldiers necessitated the introduction of further restrictions on off-duty activities, particularly within the most dangerous areas of the city itself. Outside these, however, life went on almost as normal. Only a dozen or so miles from the centre of Belfast, for example, was the largely Protestant seaside town of Bangor, where the boys used to go for a night out with no security concerns.

At this time 1 Para was the reserve battalion for 39 Brigade, one of three brigades stationed in the Province and responsible not only for the city of Belfast, but also for a considerable rural hinterland. Each of the ten or more battalions of 39 Brigade, minus 1 Para, was responsible for its own 'patch' within the Belfast area. As the reserve battalion, 1 Para was brought in wherever more troops were needed. At that stage we had four companies within the Battalion, and there was a cycle of readiness, so that the lead company was on, say, fifteen minutes' notice to move, the second company had thirty minutes, the third had an hour, and we would rotate through. My role for my first few months with 1 Para was as community relations officer/unit press officer. As such, I worked directly for the commanding officer, Lieutenant Colonel Mike Gray (later Lieutenant General), who had been my first company commander in 2 Para. My job didn't take me out on routine patrol, but I was out on the streets a great deal, because the press were everywhere, often crouching alongside soldiers to avoid being hit by bullets or stones. Some of the press were more sympathetic than others, but I didn't encounter any outright hostility. Everything we did was filmed by television cameras; the Army hadn't experienced anything like this before. A young corporal might give an interview in the street – 'I was here, I got shot at, I fired back' – and the public loved it: here was one of the boys, telling it as it was. This was my first real exposure to the media and, often flying by the seat of my pants, I found it very stimulating. I relished the challenge – not least because the job took me out on to the streets wherever there was trouble.

Like any other soldier serving in Northern Ireland, I got used to having bricks and petrol bombs thrown at me, and to abuse from passing civilians, particularly women, who would shout and spit. It was irksome, but best ignored. The first time I came under fire with live rounds was during the winter of 1970-1. I was with C Company, which had been given the job of protecting the Springfield Road police station, in the heart of West Belfast. We were lined up in anti-riot formation, wearing protective helmets with visors and carrying transparent shields to ward off missiles, while rioters pelted us with stones and petrol bombs. Even in this dangerous situation, there were press about. We were attempting to disperse the crowd with rubber bullets when I heard the sudden crack and thump of incoming rounds. The crowd vanished as we took cover. It was a strange sensation to be under fire. Of course there was an element of fear, and an adrenalin thrill as well; on the other hand, we had trained so much for this that it seemed oddly familiar. There is a sense of immunity – 'it's not going to happen to me' – so that when a soldier is hit by enemy fire, his first reaction is often surprise. It doesn't do to think too much about the possibility. I carried a pistol, but never used it except in training. The best people to return fire are not officers, who have other things to think about, but soldiers, whose job this is, and who are usually rather better at it.

In the spring of 1971 the IRA split into two wings, the old 'Official' IRA and the new, more militant and more radical 'Provisional' IRA, which soon emerged as the main enemy. Our role as regular soldiers was to deter the terrorists at a local level. The phrase used was 'framework operations', the aim being to create a situation within which, as much as possible, normal civilian life could continue. The boys on the ground would of course return fire if anyone opened fire on them, but there were other units who would take on the terrorists less openly. The Force Reconnaissance Unit (FRU), 14 Intelligence Company, the Military Reaction Force (MRF) – these were all cover names for covert armed units. Intelligence and the response to it were handled on a very tight, need-to-know basis. Even when I became a brigade commander, I would not necessarily be in the loop. There would be a directive that uniformed troops were to keep out of a particular area between this time and that time because it had to be 'sanitized' for a particular operation. I didn't always know what was going on, but I didn't always need to know.

The Commander of 39 Brigade was Brigadier (later General) Frank Kitson, a soldier with a very distinguished record of counter-insurgency operations in Kenya, Malaya, Oman and Cyprus. An incisive thinker and military theorist, he had just completed a year at University College, Oxford, on a Defence Fellowship, that is, a sabbatical period of study. Kitson was a small man with a piercing stare and a high, nasal voice, notorious for his dislike of small talk. The story is told of a dinner party at which some ambitious young wife sat next to him. Her opening gambit was to say with a smile, 'General, I've been bet I'll get at least half a dozen words out of you,' to which Frank replied, 'You've just lost,' and didn't say another word to her for the remainder of the evening. He had a reputation as cold and remote, but he commanded enormous respect among those who served under him, myself included. Kitson was not the most senior officer in the Province – as one of the three regional brigade commanders he reported to the General Officer Commanding, Northern Ireland (GOC, NI) – but within his area of responsibility he was the sun around which the planets revolved, and he very much set the tone for the operational style.

Kitson had used his year as an Oxford Fellow to write a book. *Low Intensity Operations*, published soon after I arrived in Northern Ireland, was to make him a hate figure for the far left, for in it Kitson detailed the pioneering techniques he had used to counter Communist insurgents and guerrillas in a colonial setting. His essential point was that counter-insurgency and intelligence-gathering needed to be integrated, and he advocated aggressive methods in the pursuit of these aims. Most controversially, he argued that internal subversion and civil disorder in the UK would loom large among the threats to be faced in the future. He envisaged that the unrest in Northern Ireland might spread to the mainland, requiring the rapid intervention of the Army to retrieve the situation. To some retired Army officers of a right-wing bent, such ideas would not seem so far-fetched in the 1970s, when strikes paralysed the economy and the sovereignty of the elected Government appeared to be threatened. But no serving officer I encountered took talk of such a scenario seriously.

The security situation in Northern Ireland deteriorated throughout 1971. There were almost seven thousand violent incidents that year, including 261 attacks on police stations and more than a thousand bombings. At Palace Barracks we developed an extraordinary operational routine. More often than not, trouble took place during the evening and the early hours. We would be relaxing in the officers' mess, watching television, reading the newspaper or having a drink, when we'd hear a bomb exploding in Belfast, even though this was a few miles off. Maybe the windows would shake. We'd look at our watches, reach a decision on the critical issue of whether we had time for dinner, and not long afterwards the phone would ring, requesting support, so off would go the lead company. Later the second company might be called out too. This became an almost nightly occurrence. Typically we might be out until the small hours of the morning.

The so-called 'Civil Rights' marches continued, as did the so-called 'Loyalist' marches, defying a ban introduced earlier in the year. These marches provoked further civil disorder. Riots were often used as a 'come-on' by the IRA to lure soldiers into an ambush. After a while, we learned that rioters apparently dispersing could be a signal that IRA gunmen were about to open fire.

The British Government was coming under intense pressure from the Northern Ireland Government to introduce internment without trial. Internment had been used in Northern Ireland before, during a previous, very short-lived IRA campaign in the mid-1950s, when both Dublin and Stormont had introduced it. I think that within the Northern Ireland Government there was a feeling based on a kind of collective memory: 'Well, it worked last time; it will work this time.' The difference this time around, however, was that there was no stomach for it south of the border. Terrorists would be able to find shelter in the Republic, safe from arrest. The round-up might catch a few of them, but most would escape the net. Meanwhile, many innocent people would be interned. The outrage at such injustice would undermine our attempts to isolate the men of violence. Internment was a blunt weapon which served to exacerbate rather than ameliorate the situation.

In midsummer the Northern Ireland Government had its way when London yielded, over-riding objections from the Security Forces. At dawn on 9 August 1971 a huge operation to round up suspected terrorists began. More than three hundred were taken away on that first morning. The reaction to internment by the Nationalist community was predictably violent: widespread rioting, shootings, bombings, and attempts to establish no-go areas with barricades constructed from burnt-out cars, rubble and anything else that came to hand. Northern Ireland seemed to be teetering on the brink. There were many firefights, and 39 Battalion was fully engaged. Frank Kitson would not accept no-go areas; as a consequence, 1 Para conducted a series of operations to remove barricades and re-establish some semblance of law and order. At first light each morning for a week or so, we would be in a different barricaded area. The job done and handed over to the local unit, we would return to Palace Barracks around lunchtime, sort ourselves out, get the briefings done for the next day and then get to bed before repeating the operation elsewhere the following morning. These intensive days were not without incident: when dealing with the barricaded Ballymurphy estate, for example, we found that the barricade across the Springfield Road had been booby-trapped, and in the course of the operation the Battalion fought a fierce three-hour gun battle with an estimated twenty gunmen. I was just around the corner, dealing with the press. Serving in Northern Ireland was sometimes surreal.

In the early summer I had taken over as the adjutant, a sought-after post for a young captain. The adjutant is the commanding officer's right-hand man, and so a pivotal figure in a battalion. This was my first staff job, albeit at unit level, meaning that I was assigned to a commander's staff rather than in command of a unit myself. The Army seeks to provide officers with broad experience, meaning that as they move up the career ladder officers switch back and forth between staff jobs and regimental commands. Much of the adjutant's job concerns personnel matters, including the administration of discipline: doing the paperwork, arranging the hearings and reading out the charges to an accused soldier. He has no disciplinary powers himself: those, of course, are the prerogative of the commanding officer and the company commanders. The adjutant does have the task of keeping rowdy young officers in order, but that's about the limit of it. In those days we had no operations officer, so I fulfilled this function too. But I kept the press job as well, because there was nobody else available. It was a particularly busy time in this respect, because we were very much in the spotlight. Nevertheless I was able to return to England briefly to undertake a specialist anti-terrorist training course under the auspices of MI6.

Because as unit press officer my name often appeared in the press I began to receive hate letters, saying for example that I'd been sentenced to die by a sniper's bullet – but they were very crude and I just laughed them off. I didn't show these to my wife.

Soon after I became adjutant a new battalion commander was appointed: Lieutenant Colonel Derek Wilford, who was not Parachute Regiment by origin, but an officer of the Royal Anglian Regiment. There is a system whereby both officers and soldiers can volunteer to do a tour with Airborne Forces (and if they are infantry, therefore with the Parachute Regiment), and this is what Derek Wilford did. I had known him previously when he had served as a company commander in 2 Para before taking command of the 1st Battalion. Wilford was a slim man, already greying in his late thirties, and a dynamic, positive, confident leader. He made it very clear that he would always support the men under his command, and as a result the soldiers adored 'the Colonel'. He struck me as intelligent and thoughtful. You'd sometimes come across him reading a volume of poetry.

During that winter, as the security situation steadily deteriorated, we received a succession of high-level visitors, including Lord Carrington, then Secretary of State for Defence, and General Carver, who had just taken over as Chief of the General Staff (CGS), the head of the Army. Christmas brought two visitors of a different kind, who had come to Northern Ireland to provide cheer to the troops: the comedian Frankie Howerd, and the reigning Miss World, Eva Reuber-Staier. As adjutant, I ensured that the onerous task of escorting Eva to the Combined Service Entertainment (CSE) show that year fell to me. Meanwhile we kept our parachute training going, making a weekly drop on Slemish Mountain in County Antrim, where St Patrick had lived and preached.

By the beginning of 1972 1 Para had been in Belfast for almost eighteen months, far longer than most of the other battalions, which were then on four-month tours. Our distinctive maroon berets made us immediately recognizable to the civilian population, and we had acquired a reputation for tough, uncompromising soldiering, going in hard and ready. We became particularly experienced at crowd dispersal: we developed the tactic of driving our squat armoured personnel carriers (nicknamed, for reasons obscure to me, 'pigs') into the middle of a rioting crowd before the soldiers debussed and set about the rioters, normally with batons. It was aggressive stuff, but it didn't always find favour with some other units. When they found themselves up against a problem without enough manpower to deal with it, we would arrive to support them, sort it out, get back in our vehicles and shove off back to Palace Barracks, leaving them to deal with the aftermath.

A front-page story in the *Guardian* in early January 1972 suggested that some other units had asked us to keep out of their areas, but this was strongly denied by HQ Northern Ireland. Another story in the following day's *Daily Telegraph* quoted 'Captain Mike Jackson' as describing attempts to stir up trouble between different units of the Army as 'contemptible'. I arranged for the *Daily Express* to run an interview with Derek Wilford headed 'My men are not thugs'.

All this came to a head in an incident towards the end of January, when C Company of 1 Para was deployed to assist soldiers from the Royal Green Jackets. I was not present myself, but I heard about it immediately afterwards from some of the officers involved. The Green Jackets were responsible for security at a place called Magilligan Point, an old army training centre at the end of a peninsula on the north coast, which had been converted into a temporary internment camp. On this particular day there had been a march from Londonderry to protest against internment, in defiance of the ban. A barbed-wire fence had been erected across the peninsula to keep out the demonstrators, but unfortunately this fence stopped at the high-water mark. It was low water when the marchers arrived at the fence, and some of the demonstrators strayed on to the beach in an attempt to go around the edge of the wire. There was real concern that they might try to release the internees. C Company responded with a spirited baton charge. The subsequent mêleé was captured on television, including a sequence in which it appeared that a soldier was kicking a marcher who was on the ground.

In the week that followed, bombs exploded within the compound housing our barracks at Holywood. Fortunately there were no casualties as a result, but this lapse in security caused a furore.

The following Sunday, 31 January 1972, would become notorious as 'Bloody Sunday'. What exactly happened on that day remains in dispute. There was an inquiry shortly afterwards presided over by Lord Chief Justice Widgery, but the findings were bitterly contested. Lord Saville's subsequent inquiry has yet to report. The controversy centres on the question of how British soldiers came to open fire on apparently unarmed civilians. It would be quite wrong of me to attempt to answer this question – indeed, as I write it is still *sub judice*, nearly ten years after the second inquiry was set up. I can only describe the events as I witnessed them, as fairly and as accurately as possible.

A 'Civil Rights' march had been organized for that Sunday afternoon, and it was anticipated that this would be much larger than usual, perhaps ten thousand people.

Of course it was illegal, but as usual that didn't seem to worry the marchers. Headquarters Northern Ireland decided to reinforce 8 Brigade with 1 Para for the operation to handle the march, probably because of our long experience in Belfast at handling public disorder on the streets.

Londonderry, Northern Ireland's second largest city, felt quite different from Belfast. While there was a significant Catholic minority in West Belfast, in Londonderry Catholics were in the majority. Londonderry lies very close to the border with the Republic, and the west side, on the far bank of the River Foyle and lying outside the city walls, was pretty well exclusively Catholic. This was known as the 'Bogside': here Nationalists had declared 'Free Derry', a barricaded 'no-go' area for the Security Forces, openly policed by armed and hooded IRA men. A community alert system was used to mobilize the IRA to repel incursions by the Security Forces. Women would sound the alarm by banging dustbin lids. The Irish flag flew over 'Free Derry', which to all intents and purposes was no longer part of the United Kingdom.

The point had been reached where the Army's street maps showed a big black dotted line, known as the 'containment line', beyond which the police and the Army hardly ventured. There was a bit of waste ground on this boundary known as 'Aggro Corner', where young hooligans considered it good sport to come in the early evening and 'brass up' the troops holding the containment line, hurling stones and petrol bombs, anything they could find. This became known as the 'five o'clock follies'. You would see it on television, night after night, soldiers wearing shin guards and carrying big shields, standing there and getting pelted. Some referred to these as matinee performances, because they seemed so obviously staged. As in Belfast, there were occasions on which snipers exploited such riots in order to fire at soldiers. On the very morning of Bloody Sunday, a young officer died of wounds received from such a sniper attack days before.

Londonderry lay within the area of responsibility of 8 Brigade, commanded by Brigadier Andrew McLelland. By comparison with 39 Brigade, it was 8 Brigade's practice to use CS gas in large quantities, while in Belfast we hardly used it at all. Although circumstances in Londonderry were quite different from those prevailing in Belfast, there was a sense in 39 Brigade that 8 Brigade hadn't been firm enough. We were very disapproving of the fact that a 'no-go' area had been allowed to come into being. The violence would never end unless the perpetrators were arrested.

The city centre, including the Guildhall and many other fine old buildings, was just outside the no-go area. This was the city's commercial heart. The Chamber of Commerce was very concerned about widespread destruction if lawless marchers were allowed to over-run the city centre. Once the mob was in, shops and offices would be in danger, and with them the livelihoods of owners and employees alike. As a result 8 Brigade had erected barricades along the containment line to keep demonstrators out of the city centre.

The basic plan was to hold the marchers on the containment line to protect the city centre; but it was also decided to take advantage of the opportunity to arrest the worst of the hooligans. This would be our task. It was a

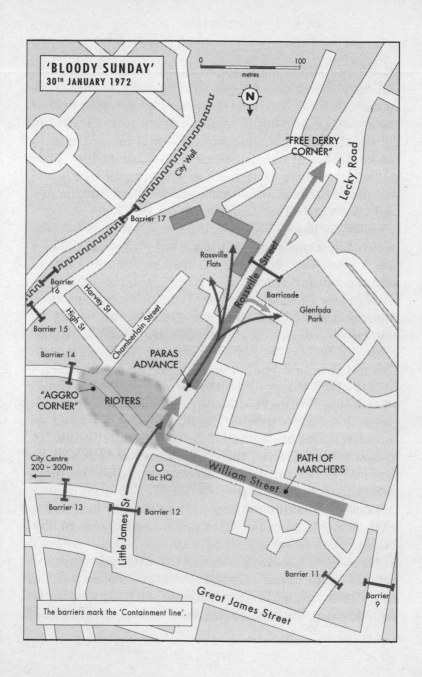

'BLOODY SUNDAY'
30TH JANUARY 1972

metres
0 — 100

N

City Wall

"FREE DERRY CORNER"

Lecky Road

Barrier 17

Rossville Flats

Rossville Street

Barrier 16

Barrier 15

Harvey St

High St

Chamberlain Street

Barricade

Glenfada Park

Barrier 14

PARAS ADVANCE

"AGGRO CORNER"

RIOTERS

City Centre 200 – 300m

Tac HQ

William Street

PATH OF MARCHERS

Little James St

Barrier 13

Barrier 12

Barrier 11

Barrier 9

Great James Street

The barriers mark the 'Containment line'.

snatch operation, of the type we did all the time. The main difficulty was to stop people running away: to put a cork in the bottle. We had evolved a tactic of going in behind the crowd or of coming in at the flank to cut them off. Clearly this was a large operation which would require a large number of troops. We envisaged using three companies, in a pincer movement, to surround the rioters and cut off their retreat, arrest them, bundle them into the pigs and take them off for handover to the RUC.

Derek Wilford gave us a briefing shortly before the march. His attitude was confident and professional. There was a sense that we might be heading for some sort of setpiece confrontation: it seemed unlikely that there wouldn't be at least some aggro. But it's worth stressing that the Battalion's mission was to capture rioters in the immediate vicinity of the barricades, which of course meant going over the containment line. The Colonel had thought long and hard about how to get in, how to get over the containment line into the area where the rioters would be. The main difficulty was vehicle access. Of course we anticipated that the IRA might react when we 'invaded their turf'. We had to be prepared to be attacked at any time. However, there was no sense in which we planned to use the arrest operation to 'teach the IRA a lesson'. That was not on the agenda.

I drove up to Londonderry early on Sunday morning in a vehicle we knew as the 'Gin Palace', a rather ancient box-bodied truck which served as a mobile HQ. It was fitted out inside with chairs, desks, map boards and communications equipment. Nowadays there is always an operations officer in the Battalion HQ, but then the adjutant usually fulfilled this role when the Battalion deployed, so more often than not I would be stuck in the Gin Palace during operations. However, on this occasion the Colonel asked me to accompany him, effectively to act as his 'gofer'. I remember being with him and the small group that formed his tactical HQ in a room on the first or second floor of a building looking south over the waste ground, towards the gable end of the dominating Rossville Flats, thought to be an IRA stronghold. We were in position by 14.30 hours, about an hour before the march was expected to pass. I recall going across to the window to get a better view. Derek snapped at me, 'Get back, you bloody fool, they could have snipers in those flats!'

A little later, there was a shot which holed a drainpipe close to the building in which we were standing. I cannot now be certain whether I actually heard the shot or whether I heard about it subsequently on the radio. But from this point we had every reason to believe that at least one individual out there had a weapon and that therefore we might come under fire again. About 15.55 hours we heard over the radio that Support Company had identified and shot a man attempting to detonate a nail bomb.

We heard reports over the radio of the marchers coming downhill. Then they came into view and we saw them pass by. There was a lot of shouting and chanting. The vast majority of them did not linger by the barricades, but moved on beyond the Rossville Flats to 'Free Derry Corner', a well-known gathering place, where they were addressed by various speakers. But the hooligans hung back by the barricades so they could take on the soldiers. This is what we had anticipated. The thugs and the marchers were now separated, so we could get behind the thugs and isolate them. I remember groans from those present when soldiers at the barricades began to use CS gas, because this made it likely that we would have to use our respirators, at least initially. They were uncomfortable and smelly, and worse still, they restricted your vision, which made you feel more vulnerable to snipers. In fact the gas had cleared by the time the snatch operation took place.

Our main force was further back with the pigs, poised to go forward into the waste ground and scoop up the hooligans. We were kept waiting for what seemed a long time for the order to go – Brigade Headquarters was concerned that there should be adequate separation between the violent and non-violent elements of the marchers. The Colonel became impatient. There were various communications over the radio, in which he expressed his desire to get a move on. He said something to the effect of 'They are all where we want them now.' Eventually, at 16.10 hours, we were given the order to go.

Through the window I saw our Support Company's vehicles moving towards the Rossville Flats, about two hundred yards off. The barricades had been pulled to one side to allow vehicle access. Now they were debussing in the shadow of the flats. Some soldiers were carrying batons ready to make arrests, their rifles slung across their backs, but some had their weapons ready to cover the others. There was nothing unusual about this; on the contrary, it was standard drill for some soldiers to cover those making arrests. Almost immediately it became apparent that they thought they had come under fire.

They began zig-zagging from side to side and looking for cover.

Derek Wilford was a commander who liked to be forward among his soldiers, to see what was happening for himself. After a few minutes, he decided to do just that. We tore down the stairs together, round the corner and out into the street, and then sprinted across the waste ground. There was a lot of noise. I saw soldiers hunched up, trying to make their bodies as small as possible. As I dashed forward with my head down I had the definite impression that someone was firing at us from a vantage point somewhere ahead. When you are used to the sound of gunfire you can estimate the range and the direction it is coming from. You first hear a crack, which is the sound of displaced air as the bullet passes close to you; then a thump, the delayed noise of the rifle being fired. The thump gives you an indication of the direction, the time gap between the crack and the thump gives you a sense of range.

It took us about thirty seconds to reach the gable end of the Rossville Flats, where Support Company Headquarters had taken cover. I remember the surge of relief when I reached them. The mood among the soldiers was tense. Major Ted Loden, the company commander, was one of them, and I remember his making it very clear that he and his company had been under fire. It seemed that most of the shooting stopped soon after we reached the Rossville Flats.

My view of what was happening was constricted. I didn't see any soldiers firing their weapons, nor did I draw my own pistol. Nor did I see any gunmen firing at us. It was a confused situation. People were running here and there. The ground was scattered with debris left behind by the demonstrators. I noticed a low barricade across the road. I can recall 'losing' Derek Wilford, and I think he ran across the road, but after a while he was back. Everything seemed to calm down and go quiet. The Colonel was working out what to do. I heard him say something into the radio to the effect of 'What do you want me to do now?' After a few minutes the order was given by HQ 8 Brigade to pull back behind the containment line. This was about twenty or thirty minutes after we had gone in. But I do have a clear memory of seeing a pig with bodies lying in the back. These were three civilians who had been shot near the gable end of the flats.

My next clear memory of that day is of being back in a factory building in Drumahoe, just outside the city, which we had been allocated as a holding area. It was early evening, and it was becoming clear that there had been a large number of fatalities. In fact, thirteen civilians had been shot dead, and a fourteenth died later. I was deeply shocked, because although the British Army had shot a number of persons in the past, there had never been deaths on this scale. To this day it remains the most tragic such episode in the whole sad history of the Troubles.

I was left with some very mixed and worrying feelings. I imagine that others in the Battalion felt the same. I hated the thought, as some commentators would state straight away, that our soldiers might have lost control. It would be very unprofessional to have done that, and in the Army one is very proud of professionalism. I knew these men, and I knew their quality. So far as I was concerned the Paras were tough, but they were disciplined. I found it

Aged nineteen, in full dress uniform ('Blues') on Sandhurst commissioning day, 19 December 1963.

My father and mother in Bristol 1941, the year before they married, and before my father had obtained his commission.

Sitting with my mother on the running board of our pre-war Lancia near our home in Tripoli, late 1940s. Our dog Roly poses on the pavement.

Candidates on the officer selection course at the Regular Commissions Board, November 1961. I am in the middle of the back row, no. 35.

Ypres Company cleaning parade, Sandhurst, 1962. Sarjit Singh polishes a boot in the foreground; Sam Mboma is seated in the middle of the picture, and I am standing in the corridor behind him.

With my father, a keen motorcyclist, in Tripoli, 1949.

As a young officer, behind the wheel of the green Sunbeam Alpine that I bought second-hand in the mid-1960s.

Shortly after being commissioned, with my mother and sister Lynne in Germany.

Preparing to jump on the basic parachute training course, RAF Abingdon, September 1967. I am seated fourth along the row.

Left: *One of my duties during my first tour of Northern Ireland in the early 1970s was to act as unit press officer. Here I am talking to the press after an arms find in March 1972.*

Above: *Seated in the car talking into a radio is Brigadier Frank Kitson, a controversial figure who took a robust approach to counter-insurgency operations. Almost two decades later I would step into his shoes as Commander of 39 Infantry Brigade. Standing beside the car is my battalion commander, Lieutenant Colonel Mike Gray. The so-called 'Gin Palace', our mobile TAC HQ, can be seen in the background. The figure who appears to be standing on the running board may be me.*

9 August 1971, the day internment without trial was introduced in Northern Ireland.

Left: *Security operations in Belfast, 1971. I am standing at the right of the picture; my commanding officer, Lieutenant Colonel Derek Wilford, is standing just to the left of the lamp-post.*

Above: *A young woman who has lost both legs in a huge IRA explosion is comforted by Lance Corporal Wayne Evans, central Belfast, 20 March 1972.*

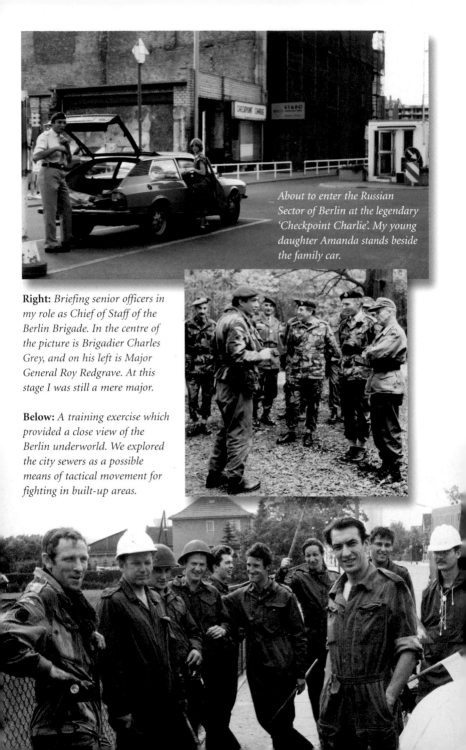

About to enter the Russian Sector of Berlin at the legendary 'Checkpoint Charlie'. My young daughter Amanda stands beside the family car.

Right: *Briefing senior officers in my role as Chief of Staff of the Berlin Brigade. In the centre of the picture is Brigadier Charles Grey, and on his left is Major General Roy Redgrave. At this stage I was still a mere major.*

Below: *A training exercise which provided a close view of the Berlin underworld. We explored the city sewers as a possible means of tactical movement for fighting in built-up areas.*

Moscow, October 1976, as part of a Staff College visit to the Soviet Union during the Cold War.

Johnny Frost, the hero of Arnhem, took a keen interest in the Parachute Regiment. As commander of B Company of 2 Para during my second tour of duty in Northern Ireland, I had the privilege of showing him around the 'bandit country' of South Armagh. Also in the picture is Lieutenant Colonel Colin Thompson.

Warrenpoint, August Bank Holiday 1979, when two coordinated bombs were detonated by the IRA, inflicting the highest number of casualties suffered by the British Army in a single incident since the Second World War.

Above: *The vehicle destroyed by the full force of the first explosion.*

Right: *My notes on hearing the first report of the incident.*

Below: *The scene of the carnage. On the left is the tidal estuary of the Newry River, which forms the border with the Irish Republic; in the foreground is the crater formed by the first explosion; and on the right of the dual carriageway is the ruined gate-lodge where the second bomb detonated. I set up my HQ in the stone tower opposite.*

1st explosion
w' pk docks   blessed → cas
2nd   200 yds
all ca
still some dead
contact   2 hits claimed
one body in view

difficult to accept that there could have been any mass breach of discipline. Other people would suggest that there had been some sort of conspiracy, a hypothesis which the facts do not sustain. Though the two theories were mutually inconsistent, some tried to argue both at once: that there had been some sort of conspiracy and that the soldiers had run amok. But however incredible the accusations, it was a terrible thought that we might have killed innocent people, whatever the stress of the moment, and whatever the provocation. There was no doubt in my own mind that we had come under fire, and in those circumstances it was legitimate to return fire at properly identified targets. The question remains whether the response of some of our soldiers was proportionate or not, considering the nature of the threat.

In the factory that evening, the standard 'after action' drills were cutting in. There were a lot of military police-men around. It was an absolute rule in Northern Ireland that military police took statements from any soldiers who had fired live rounds. Every soldier was allocated a certain number of live rounds, and had to account for them to his platoon sergeant. The rounds have batch numbers so that they can be identified after firing. As adjutant, I helped in the administration of the statement-taking exercise, making a list of those who needed to be interviewed. There was absolutely no question of briefing the soldiers about what they should say.

I remember speaking to a staff officer at HQ 8 Brigade over the telephone. Such was the scale of the casualties, he said, that there could well be a special inquiry. The Brigade HQ required statements from Derek Wilford and each of the company commanders. My job was to act as a scribe, interviewing each of them, writing out a statement and then getting him to read it through before signing it. The work took most of the night. In the process it became clear that the only soldiers from 1 Para who had fired their weapons came from Support Company, and that quite a large number of rounds had been fired.

The announcement of an inquiry presided over by the Lord Chief Justice was made very quickly afterwards. Lord Widgery decided to hold his inquiry in the Province at Coleraine on the north coast, so that he would have ready access to witnesses. I was not called upon to give evidence myself, but back at Palace Barracks I was involved in some of the administration, dealing with witness requests from the inquiry and arranging helicopter flights to Coleraine. Part of the preparation for Widgery was that each soldier who had fired his weapon had to indicate where he was when he fired and where his target was. I remember large charts spread out on the floor, with soldiers marking their positions and their targets in blue and red.

Widgery reported his findings within a couple of months or so of Bloody Sunday. His inquiry pretty much exonerated the Army, and concluded that there had been no general breakdown in discipline, though it also concluded that some of the firing 'bordered on the reckless'. As soon as it was published, the Widgery Report was criticized as a whitewash. It failed to assuage the anger of the relatives of those shot on the day, or to quell the speculation, which continued to poison attempts to reach a peaceful settlement in the Province.

In 1998, the recently elected Labour Prime Minister Tony Blair announced the setting up of a new inquiry under the Law Lord, Lord Saville. At the time of writing this inquiry has yet to publish its findings, though the cost to the British taxpayer is said to be approaching an astonishing £400 million. I myself testified before the inquiry on two occasions in 2003, and until Lord Saville has concluded his contemplations on the matter I am constrained in how much I can say. The fact that the Saville Inquiry has taken so long to report and consumed so much public money is perhaps in itself evidence of the difficulty in establishing the truth of the events on that tragic day.

I found the charge that the Paras had 'run amok' on 'Bloody Sunday' difficult to accept. A decade later the self-discipline and the humanity of the Parachute Regiment soldier would be tested on the far side of the world. One of the closing battles of the Falklands War, the Battle of Wireless Ridge, was fought by 2 Para. This was a completely different environment from Northern Ireland, where we were always operating among civilians: the Falklands was straight force on force; the Army's job was to kill the enemy and win the war. Come daylight, 2 Para had pushed the Argentines off the ridge, the final piece of high ground they occupied. To the west was Tumbledown Mountain, which the Scots Guards had taken the same night, at some cost. After fierce fighting on Tumbledown, the Argentine soldiers broke and ran. My friend David Chaundler, who was in command of 2 Para, described the scene to me afterwards. From the ridge looking south-east, you could see Port Stanley about three miles off. To the south-west, the eastern slopes of Tumbledown Mountain were covered in Argentine soldiers fleeing towards the town. And of course, the gunner forward observation officers were firing artillery at them as they fled. It was a 'turkey shoot', though legitimate within the laws of international conflict. David Chaundler ordered the guns to cease firing. It was a big decision, because no formal surrender had been taken at that point, and theoretically the soldiers he spared might have regrouped to fight us again; but he chose to stop the killing, in the interests of common humanity. And the guns of the British Army fell silent.

5
Behind the Curtain

Though Frank Kitson was a brusque man, he knew his soldiering. He would have understood that Derek Wilford was feeling bruised and battered and worried about what had happened that Sunday in Londonderry. Shortly after we got back to Belfast, Kitson came to see the Colonel. To reach the office of the commanding officer one had to pass through that of the adjutant, so I greeted the brigadier and ushered him in, before leaving the two of them alone together. Kitson has a very distinct nasal voice, so it would have been difficult not to overhear what he was saying even if I had been trying not to. 'Well, Derek,' Kitson began, 'you'd better tell me what happened.' So I heard the Colonel describe the snatch operation across the containment line into 'Free Derry'. Kitson was generally supportive, but when Wilford had finished, he offered a trenchant comment. 'What I don't understand is why, having got that far in, you didn't go on and sort the whole bloody mess out.'

Kitson expressed himself pretty brutally, but he had a

point. There was no doubt that we could have gone on to retake the 'no-go' area, though this would almost certainly have resulted in more deaths.

In the aftermath of Bloody Sunday, a crowd in Dublin burned down the British Embassy while the Gardai stood by and watched. In February the IRA took their bombing campaign to mainland Britain, exploding a bomb at the officers' mess of the Parachute Brigade HQ in Aldershot, killing six civilians and a Catholic padre. The following month the Provisional IRA detonated a huge bomb in the centre of Belfast that killed six people and injured a hundred and fifty more, many of them horrifically. A young lance corporal from 1 Para was photographed cradling in his arms a young woman who had just lost both her legs in the explosion. The Official IRA attempted to assassinate John Taylor, Northern Ireland's Minister for Home Affairs; despite being shot six times, he survived. On the streets, thousands of Protestant paramilitaries paraded in uniform, and let it be known to sympathetic journalists that they had built up a large stockpile of weapons. In Belfast, 1 Para intervened to break up a running battle between Protestant and Catholic gunmen which left eight people dead. The Province appeared to be heading for civil war. Less than two months after Bloody Sunday, the British Government decided that enough was enough, suspending the Stormont Parliament and imposing direct rule. A temporary truce was agreed while senior British politicians held secret talks with represent-atives of the IRA – but no agreement was reached, and in the summer the bombing campaign resumed with a vengeance when twenty-six IRA bombs exploded in

Belfast, killing eleven people. With grim symmetry this day, 21 July 1972, became known as 'Bloody Friday'.

By this time 1 Para had reached the end of its eighteen-month tour and we had returned to the mainland; but we had barely settled back in Aldershot before we were recalled to Northern Ireland for a mammoth operation to remove the no-go areas, mainly in Londonderry, as Frank Kitson thought should have been done long before. Heavy Royal Engineer armoured vehicles were brought over from Germany by landing craft to clear the barricades. In all, twenty-one thousand troops took part in Operation Motorman, the greatest number of British soldiers committed to any one operation since 1945. As there was a shortage of available barracks, we were garrisoned initially on HMS *Maidstone*, a Royal Navy ship in Belfast dock that had previously served as an internment centre. I spent much of my time aboard ship running the operations room. Fearing a bloodbath, the authorities had made no secret of the imminent operation. The IRA decided not to stand and defend 'Free Derry', melting away before we arrived. In the event there were few civilian casualties, and no soldiers were injured. The most violent response occurred at Claudy, a small village not far from Londonderry and the border with the Republic, where nine people died after three terrorist car bombs exploded in succession. At first companies of 1 Para were farmed out to other battalions, but after a while we were given our own 'patch' in northern Belfast, straddling the two communities. We remained in the Province for a few more months and finally went home in November. It had been a long haul.

*   *   *

The Battalion's next deployment was to be a six-month UN tour in Cyprus, but I was told that I wouldn't be going with them. Instead I was off to Scotland to join 15 Para, one of the then three Territorial Army battalions in the Parachute Regiment that supplemented the three regular battalions. It was quite a wrench to leave 1 Para after the shared experience of dramatic events, and disappointing to miss the operational tour in Cyprus – but the TA was an important part of the Army of which I knew little, and the job carried with it welcome promotion to acting major. The Army's career structure is designed to give officers a broad range of experience as they move up the ladder. In any event, I've always taken the view that whatever I'm asked to do, I'll give it a good try.

A TA unit has a small number of regular Army staff who are the oil in the engine. The commanding officer can be either regular or TA, but the so-called training major, who writes all the training programmes and plans all the exercises, is always a regular officer – and that was me. My new battalion was widely spread: Battalion Headquarters, A and Support Companies in Glasgow, B Company in Aberdeen, C Company in Edinburgh.

Part-timers TA soldiers may be, but they too are professional, and 15 Para trained hard. A demanding weekend's programme would begin with a parade in the TA Centre on Friday evening after work, following which the troops would move to a local airport, where several RAF Hercules aircraft would be waiting: then fit parachutes, emplane, take off at 23.00 hours, fly south and jump on to Salisbury Plain at 01.00 hours the next morning, going straight into a 36-hour exercise. The exercise would finish at 13.00 or 14.00 on Sunday afternoon, and after a quick clear-up we would be driven to RAF Lyneham to fit parachutes, emplane and jump back into Scotland around 17.00 or 18.00 hours on the Sunday evening. Then home to bed, and back to work on Monday morning. That's real commitment. Yes, they got paid for it, but not a huge amount of money.

There is an ill-informed view that the Territorial Army is only playing at soldiers. For myself, I've always been a great admirer of the TA. They bring a lot of colour to the Army, because they have a foot in both the civilian and military camps. There is a slogan, 'One Army' – i.e. not a regular army and a territorial army but a single army – and in my view that says it all. There is a tendency nowadays to refer to the TA as reservists, perhaps founded on the idea that, as a title, 'Territorial Army' may be old hat. But plenty of people continue to think the name an honourable one.

In those days the TA essentially had one job, which was to fill out the order of battle – to do or die against the Warsaw Pact in north-west Europe. For the forty years up to 1989, the core strategic requirement for the British Army was to play its part in NATO's defence of western Europe, and most of the fighting Army was dedicated to this task. That role would be overtaken by events when the Cold War came to an end. Now the TA plays an important part in helping the regular Army to sustain current operations. It's not always easy, of course. Although the Reserve Forces Act 1996 gives the Army the legal power to mobilize TA soldiers, compulsory mobilization is kept to a minimum in peacetime. Much depends on an individual TA soldier's circumstances. If he works for himself, he can come to his own decision. The real rub comes if you get a TA soldier who is a key player in a small family firm, when it's obviously very difficult for him to go off for a six-month tour. Some of the big firms are extremely generous with their employees' time, and actually see the TA as a benefit, not a detriment. I remember a conversation with a senior executive of a large manufacturing company. 'Thank you very much,' I said to him, 'for letting your chap go to Iraq for six months.' His reply was quite unexpected. 'I'm the one who should thank you. I sent out a shop-floor worker, and I got back a foreman.'

Many TA soldiers join a part of the Army which has no relation to their civilian life, just to have the change. But we also try to make use of an individual's skills where appropriate. For example, there are many people in the TA Royal Signals who work for BT. And we have a wonderful group of railway repairers, maintainers and train crews within the Royal Logistic Corps who have been used in at least two operations that I can recall, Kosovo and Iraq. Almost by definition they are professional railwaymen in civil life; they can repair railways, they can run railways and they can drive trains, all of which can be extremely useful at times. But we only need them on an occasional basis. It would be a very expensive capability to maintain within the regular Army, and therefore it makes sense to keep that expertise within the TA and draw on it when you need to.

The regular defence medical services were severely reduced in the cuts that followed the ending of the Cold War. Now the Army relies very heavily on TA medics – which means in effect the National Health Service, because that's where most of them work normally. The MOD has chosen not to employ many of the top specialist surgeons needed operationally in full-time service; so TA medical personnel can mean the difference between life and death for a wounded soldier.

I became a strong advocate for the TA, though I suspect that while with 15 Para I may have ruffled a few feathers. 'If he has a fault,' read a comment in my generally favourable annual report for 1973, 'it is that because of his extrovert nature and that he is so capable, he occasionally gives some of those less endowed the impression that he is arrogant.'

There was one tragic incident during my two and a half years with the TA which still casts a shadow over my memory of this period.

Exercise 'Bold Guard' in September 1974 was a very big NATO manoeuvre, involving American, British, Danish and German forces. We were rehearsing one of the Battalion's possible war contingencies: what we would do in a time of tension, or indeed if the Warsaw Pact actually attacked. The specific purpose here was to put an airborne force into Germany in a reinforcement role – and, on the assumption that runways had been knocked out, to deploy as quickly as possible: by parachute. We in 15 Para were due to make the second of two battalion parachute drops with 'heavy drop platforms' carrying our vehicles, following a drop the previous day by 2 Para. We were flying from RAF Lyneham, a journey of two or three hours in a large stream of C130 Hercules aircraft. Once the Battalion reached Lyneham, my job as training major was done. I took on the role of umpire, observing what went on and adjudicating on tactical engagements. We were all loaded with heavy packs, carrying weapons, ammunition and supplies sufficient for an eight-day exercise: approximately eighty pounds in weight per man. The dropping zone (DZ) chosen was in northern Germany near the border with Denmark, immediately south of the Kiel Canal, which links the North Sea to the Baltic. During the Anglo-German naval race before the First World War, the canal had been dug wide and deep, deep enough to take battleships. It might seem strange to choose a DZ so close to such an obvious hazard, but it was always hard to find the amount of space necessary for a drop; this DZ met the required safety criteria, and precautions had been taken in the event of anyone dropping into the water. In the event, these precautions proved tragically inadequate.

The drop was to have taken place in the morning, but because of local fog over the canal it was postponed to 21.00 hours, not long after last light, the same day. The run-in was north–south, i.e. the stream of thirty-six RAF Hercules aircraft flew at right angles over the canal before the drop. As always, flares in the shape of an 'A' (the 'Alpha') had been positioned to show where the first parachutist should land, about 350 yards south of the canal bank. If all goes as intended, the first man out lands on or very close to the Alpha. The first one out of the aircraft is not normally the commanding officer; where he drops varies, but often it's in the middle of the 'stick', depending how one wants to rendezvous on the ground. The lighting in the aircraft is subdued to promote night vision. As you approach the DZ, the dispatcher gets the line of parachutists to their feet. The doors on both sides open, and there's a rush of air into the aircraft. When the green light is illuminated, it's time to go.

In the event we jumped from rather higher than we

need have done, from a thousand feet, and the speed of the light southerly wind had been underestimated because of undetected wind shear. This meant that both the personnel and vehicle drops began a few seconds early.

I was one of the first few out of my aircraft. I could see the Alpha clearly, and I could tell straight away that I was going to drop short. I could see the canal, too, because there was a large ship going past, all lit up like a Christmas tree. At that point I knew with a horrible sense of foreboding that something had gone very wrong, because the canal was supposed to have been closed to shipping before the drop. I pulled down very hard on the rigging lines to try to steer the parachute away from the water. In the event, I splashed down in the shallows, and was able to wade ashore easily.

I was lucky. Fourteen paratroopers landed further out into the canal, along with three heavy equipment platforms. They would have felt the shock of the cold water, followed immediately by the pull of their heavy packs dragging them down. We had trained for this contingency, of course. If you find yourself dropping towards water, the drill is to get rid of your equipment by emergency release, and then to get out of your parachute just before you hit the surface: you bang the quick release box to undo the harness. You keep hold of the straps until the last moment, and then release them as you splash down, so that you won't get dragged under by a waterlogged parachute. But at night it's difficult to judge how high you are, and obviously you don't want to let go of your parachute too early.

Some of those who landed in the water managed to

make it to the shore, or were rescued by the German safety boats which had been standing by as a precaution, but six men drowned. It was particularly upsetting for me, because these were men I knew. When the bodies were recovered it was found that not all of them had been able to jettison their packs. Like the rest of us they were all wearing lifejackets, but none of them had been inflated in time. One man's parachute was wrapped around the propeller of the ship that I had seen from the air.

In a further tragedy, the German engineer colonel whose job it had been to provide the safety boats and to liaise with the authorities to close the canal hanged himself the day afterwards.

The Battalion quite rightly got on with the exercise. Intense activity is a powerful antidote to shock and grief. But instead of acting as umpire, I stayed behind for the next few days to liaise with the German police, the British military police, and an RAF board of inquiry which arrived the following day. I camped by the canal, living on my field rations, while I watched German frogmen make a systematic search of the canal bottom. My abiding memory of that time is of bodies lined up on the bank. I had the unpleasant task of identifying the corpses: to do so I had to reach down, unzip the combat jackets, extract the dog tags and verify the name and number stamped on each with a young military police officer standing beside me.

Earlier in the year I had sat the staff promotion examination. This was a crucial stage in any officer's career. The Staff College was the intellectual powerhouse of the Army, taking 120 of the 400 or 500 or so officers in each age group and grooming them for senior ranks in the future. If you were accepted by the Staff College, you had a chance of making general; if not, the odds were against you.

In those days everybody had to take the basic exam to be promoted to the rank of major, and those applying to the Staff College had to take additional papers. Candidates were also assessed by the so-called 'book' of their confidential reports, a system which continues to the present day. Each year a report is written on every officer and NCO in the Army by his or her superior in the chain of command, with comments from at least one other officer further up the chain. These reports assess both performance over the past year and potential for promotion, and are collected with past reports in the 'book'.

The Army is a meritocracy. Officers benefit from careful career planning. Career progression is very tightly structured – quite properly, in my view. At each stage some move forward, while others fall by the wayside. Officers are assessed for promotion by annual selection boards, a system that continues all the way up to the top of the Army: No. 5 Board looks at candidates for promotion to major, No. 4 at candidates for lieutenant colonel, and so on up to No. 1 Board, which looks at candidates for promotion to general. The Army is rightly proud of this rigorous system, designed to be as objective as possible, avoiding any possibility of nepotism or favouritism. Each member of the board works alone to score each candidate on the basis of his 'book'; if there's a wide discrepancy between any two scores, the relevant board members are asked to mark again, and to continue to do so until the discrepancy is reduced to the acceptable level. Then the scores are aggregated to produce an order of merit, and those with the highest aggregate scores are the ones selected for promotion. The boards are also responsible for appointments. The Military Secretary, who is the officer responsible for career matters, circulates a list of posts coming up as their holders are promoted or move on in some other way, you indicate your interest, and the boards decide who goes where.

Promotion lists are distributed under embargo down the chain of command. Each list is printed on differently coloured paper: the list of promotions to major is beige, to lieutenant colonel pink, to colonel blue and to brigadier green. There isn't an annual list for generals because there are so few such appointments; these are made as and when required. For obvious reasons the lists are known as the 'beige list', the 'pink list', and so on.

Typically, an officer will hear news of his promotion or future appointment from his commanding officer, at whatever level, an announcement often accompanied by a congratulatory drink. Those promoted to major general and above will receive a personal telephone call from the CGS. It does occasionally happen that an officer at this level will decline to take up a posting, but the system is so refined that such an occurrence is rare.

In April 1974 I received a letter from the Ministry of Defence confirming that I had qualified both for promotion to the rank of major and for entry into the Staff College when I finished my tour with the TA. In the autumn of the following year I began a three-month course at the Royal Military College of Science, at Shrivenham near Swindon, as a precursor to my Staff College year. This was a crash course on military technology: armoured vehicles, explosives, that sort of thing. Science was never my strongest suit, and I scraped through with a C grade. 'Major Jackson had some difficulty keeping pace with the technical aspects of the course,' my report read afterwards. Not my finest hour.

At the beginning of 1976 I became a student at the Staff College. This was based at Camberley in Surrey, another large mid-Victorian building built in a style somewhat reminiscent of Haussmann's Paris, with dormer windows projecting from the roofline.

Years later, when I was myself on the Directing Staff (DS) at Camberley, I used to say to my students at the beginning of the year, 'I hope you've enjoyed everything you've done in the Army before this moment, but frankly it counts for little enough in terms of your future, because you start again here. What happens to you in the future will be almost exclusively determined by how well you do on this course.'

The Staff College syllabus was broad: basic staff duties; conventional tactics; counter-revolutionary warfare, as it was then called; 'out-of-area operations', meaning operations outside what was then considered as the main theatre in north-west Europe; joint operations, i.e. with the Navy and the Air Force; how the MOD works and other non-Army matters. The syllabus reflected the Army's core roles as they were then defined. The emphasis was understandably on how the Army should play its part in the defence of north-west Europe, but the course also took account of possible unexpected challenges in the future – such as we would face when Argentina invaded the Falkland Islands.

Students are taught in groups of ten, known as

'syndicates', by a member of the DS; these are all lieutenant colonels, supposedly picked from the most promising in that rank within the Army. There's a lot of writing involved: students learn how to write operation orders, and to prepare what is called a brief, i.e. a paper a staff officer would give to his boss as an aide-memoire or decision-making tool. For example: 'The divisional commander will be coming to see you next week; we know he wants to talk about these subjects and here are some notes on them; these issues may arise; etc.'

Your written work is very carefully marked, and a report is written on your performance at the end of each term. What the DS are looking for all the time is the power of analysis, i.e. the ability to digest complex material rapidly, to identify what's really important, and then to express your thoughts – whether verbally or in writing – in succinct and lucid English. It was a great wartime leader, Major General 'Windy' Gale, commanding the 6th Airborne Division, who stated very succinctly and lucidly that the one purpose of communication is to take a thought from one human being's brain and to transmit it to the brain of others with the minimum possibility of misunderstanding, confusion or ambiguity. You also take part in map exercises, where there are no troops involved, and by which you practise the intellectual process of handling quite large formations. There are visiting speakers as well, of all sorts. In my time as a student at the Staff College they ranged from General Sir John Hackett, a brigade commander at Arnhem, to the left-wing union leader Hugh Scanlon. Ken Livingstone has also visited several times over the years, always ensuring good cut-and-thrust at question time.

We learned more about battle procedure: the sequence of warning orders, operations orders and confirmatory orders. It's a top-down process, and the procedure is the same at every level, from corps right down to platoon. For example, a battalion commander might receive from his brigade commander a warning order, telling him to get ready to do something. There will be a task – e.g. 'capture hill 123' – probably some timings – 'by first light on Wednesday' – and any other relevant information available at that point. When a battalion commander receives such a warning order – whether in writing or verbally – he will immediately then think, 'Right, what does this mean, what are my options?' The ensuing mental exercise of analysing the mission, evaluating the various factors involved (the ground, the enemy, time and space, etc.) and developing possible solutions was then known as 'the appreciation of the situation' (the Army has subsequently adopted the American term 'the estimate'), and putting it down on paper was one of the skills taught in the written work. The point is to lay out clearly each stage in your thinking so that it can be examined critically, and any flaws detected and eliminated. If at all possible, the commanding officer should make a reconnaissance. The outcome of the process is a series of possible courses of action, along with a list of the advantages and disadvantages of each. The commander must now make his decision. What will then emerge will be a battalion scheme of manoeuvre: e.g. 'A and B Companies, you are to attack the objective from the right flank; C Company, you are in reserve but be prepared to exploit tactical success.' The timings are very important: everything revolves around H-Hour, the moment when the action commences. Hours are expressed as H+3 or H−3. The same applies to dates: a campaign or an operation commences on D-Day, and dates are expressed as D−1, D+2, and so on.

As soon as he's worked out his preliminary thoughts, the commander will issue his own warning order to the companies in the battalion – 'Be prepared for so-and-so' – with timings and probably some logistic information at that point. So everybody is starting to think about the task that they've been given, and as the orders come down through the ranks, right down to section level, they become more and more specific and more and more limited.

It's always the preferred option for the commander to give his orders personally, because he can then discuss face-to-face any questions his subordinates may have. Almost certainly, at the level of brigade and upwards, these oral orders will be supplemented by a written operation order, which will provide all the supporting detail. As you go further down, the requirement for written orders diminishes. There is also a mechanism for feedback up the chain of command, known as the 'back-brief'.

The final part of this sequence is the confirmatory order, which is not always given, depending on the circumstances. So the commander at any level has the authority to proceed without receiving a confirmatory order, unless he's been told to wait for one.

All these principles and procedures are set out in the commander's field manual, a type of aide-memoire, which provides a useful checklist of details, particularly if you're tired and under pressure.

One of the teaching methods used at the Staff College and elsewhere is the TEWT, the tactical exercise without troops. You are set a tactical problem and given all the necessary information (perhaps on your own, perhaps as a small group of two or three). You go out and walk the ground and form a plan, which you subsequently present to the other students, and they are invited to comment. It isn't a question of getting it right or wrong; this is a means of getting students to think about operational planning and execution, at whatever level. The TEWTs are jocularly contrasted with NEWDs (night exercises without darkness) and JEWTs (jungle exercises without trees).

All students at the Staff College were roughly the same age, in their early thirties, and at the same level, senior captains or newly promoted majors. In addition, there were a handful of officers from the RAF, the Royal Navy and the Royal Marines, plus fifty-odd students from overseas. This can lead to some strange encounters afterwards. During the Falklands War, an Argentine graduate from Camberley would surrender to a fellow Staff College graduate.

There is a system whereby each overseas student has a British student as a sponsor. I looked after one of the Germans, an officer called Rudiger Drews who became a good friend of mine. Many years later, when I was head of KFOR in Macedonia, he visited my HQ in Skopje in his capacity as the three-star general commanding the German land forces. Another of the foreigners I got to know pretty well was Itzik Mordechai, a veteran of the 1973 Yom Kippur War who became a major general and later the Israeli Minister of Defence. So there is a bit of a Staff College old boy network.

It was professionally stimulating to be at the Staff College, of course, but one abiding memory of that year at

Camberley is that hardly any of us seemed to have any money. Here we were, 120 of the allegedly most promising officers in the Army, all – except the odd one with family means – flat broke. The economy in 1976 was in a terrible state; annual inflation soared to over 20 per cent. We seemed to be always worrying about how we were going to manage. I can remember being delighted to get my posting overseas, both because of the job, of course, but also because I would qualify for Local Overseas Allowance, which I think saved my financial bacon. By this time I had two young children, and we were living in married quarters within the college grounds, boxy 1960s houses nicknamed 'Legoland'. My parents were just up the road, literally ten minutes away, close enough to see their grandchildren regularly. They had come back from Hong Kong in 1970, when my father retired from the Army. He then took what's known as a retired officer's job at a local Army training centre.

There comes a memorable day two-thirds of the way through the year at Staff College when the syndicate DS doles out brown paper envelopes to the students, each of which contains a posting order. This is the moment you find out what you're going to be doing for the next two years. It's known as black bag day, for reasons that are lost in the mists of time. Someone described it as 'the annual pit-head disaster, complete with wailing wives' – because of course the students' wives may have their own views about the postings, not always positive.

The jobs on offer are very varied. Some students open their brown paper envelopes and groan. Others, confronted by an indecipherable alphabet soup, mutter, 'What the hell's that? I don't even understand what the job is.' I was delighted because I had been appointed Chief of Staff of the Berlin Brigade: a plum job in a fascinating place. Perhaps not the ripest plum; a purist would have said that I'd have been better off with a brigade in West Germany, because that was where the real centre of gravity of the British Army was to be found. But I certainly wasn't complaining; I was very pleased and excited to be heading for Berlin, and so were all the family.

At Christmas 1976, right at the end of the course and following longstanding tradition, we staged a pantomime, produced, directed and put on by the students. Ours was loosely based on the Cinderella story; I remember that I had a small part in the second row of the male chorus. In the time-honoured tradition of the genre, the script was extremely irreverent, with plenty of leg-pulling of the Commandant and his DS, and Ugly Sisters who needed a shave. The overseas students watched in bemused amazement. So this is the conclusion of the great British Army staff course? Some kind of comic opera?

The mid-1970s saw various moves to try to reduce the tension between East and West. The buzz word of the time was détente, meaning an easing or relaxing. As part of the so-called Helsinki Accords of 1975, it was agreed that there should be bilateral UK–Soviet military exchange visits, staff college to staff college, starting in 1976. There was considerable excitement in Camberley at this prospect. I saw this as a great opportunity. I had missed out once on a visit to the Soviet Union; I wasn't going to miss out again. I decided to corner the Commandant, Major General John Stanier, whenever I had a chance. There are moments in your life when you have to blow your own trumpet, because no one else will blow it for you. This was one of them. The opportunity arose at some social occasion, the kind of environment in which it is easiest for a young major to talk informally to a major general – particularly a somewhat august and patrician general like John Stanier.

'General,' I said, taking the plunge: 'We hear there's a trip to Russia coming up.'

'Yes,' he replied, 'looks like that.'

'Well,' I persisted, 'you do know, don't you, that I'm the only student who speaks Russian?' I wasn't entirely sure of that, but since only two places had been allocated for students, all the rest having been grabbed by the Ministry of Defence and DS, I said it anyway. It seemed to work, because I was chosen to be one of the two student members of the party, the other being John le Quesne from the Royal Electrical and Mechanical Engineers.

Nowadays, when Russia is largely seen as just another foreign country much like any other, this visit might seem unexceptional. But in 1976, with the Cold War still icy, it was unusual for anyone to go there, let alone a British Army officer. The Soviet Union was a totalitarian state, secretive and forbidding. Its citizens were rigidly and sometimes brutally controlled, and constantly monitored. Just to converse with a Russian was quite something.

Everything was to be done strictly according to the published programme. In mid-October we flew by Aeroflot to Moscow. We were picked up from the airport in a fleet of long black Zil cars and driven to a pretty basic Ministry of Defence hotel on the Lenin Hills, quite near Moscow University. After a gruesome evening meal, the senior escorting officer announced that we would now go and tour Moscow by night, as the programme indicated. We were in uniform, and assumed we would change into civilian clothes for our tour of the capital, as we would have done had we been in London. When this was put to our senior minder, there was considerable surprise. 'We are military,' he replied, making it clear that we were expected to wear uniform throughout. Strap-hanging on the Moscow underground and strolling across Red Square in British Army uniform was an interesting experience – though I can't pretend that we noticed any particular reaction from the Muscovites. Perhaps they thought we were officers from the army of some more obscure member of the Warsaw Pact.

The next morning John le Quesne and I laid a wreath at the Tomb of the Unknown Soldier at the Kremlin Wall. We would do quite a lot of wreath-laying on that trip. After an appointment with Colonel General Makarov, the Chief of the Main Directorate of Military-Educational Establishments, we were driven to the Frunze, the Moscow staff college, which turned out to be a very imposing neo-classical building in the centre of the city. You entered a very large vestibule, and on the left as you went in there were racks and racks of coat hooks, though we never saw a single student in the whole place. Maybe they were away on an exercise, but more likely they were being kept out of our way. Inevitably, the British military attaché in Moscow was a member of our party, and of course it was part of his job to find out as much as he could about the Soviet armed forces. I noticed his eyes roving across the coat racks and his lips moving, and I realized that he was surreptitiously counting the coat hooks. One of the Russians spotted what he was doing at the same moment.

'My dear Brigadier,' he interrupted with a smile, 'five hundred and sixty-four.' Everyone laughed hard at that point. The ice was thawing.

We were given lunch at the Frunze, with many vodkas and much toasting. The Commandant was an ancient old boy, and we got the impression that he wasn't very well; but he came in for lunch and reminisced about the old days, becoming very maudlin, almost to the point of tears, telling a long story about his horse being shot from beneath him (the Red Army still having cavalry in the Second World War). That evening there was a lively cocktail party in the residence of the military attaché, and the next day we were given a tour of the Kremlin. One obligatory engagement, of course, was a trip to see the embalmed body of Lenin in his mausoleum. We arrived there to be confronted with a huge queue, and we imagined that we were in for a long wait in the October cold. But we needn't have worried, because we were marched directly to the head of the queue. Before we entered, one of the escorting officers indicated that he had something to say. We all gathered round expectantly. 'I am required by law to ask if any of you have any explosives about your persons,' he said very solemnly, 'because if you have you must surrender them before you go in.'

I was very struck by the Soviet Armed Forces Museum, which was organized by rooms depicting different stages of the Second World War. We British could hardly fail to notice that of these thirty or forty rooms only one was given to the Anglo-American Allies – just one, dealing with the Normandy invasion. This was how Russians perceived what they know as the Great Patriotic War: they believed that what the Western Allies did was peripheral, that the war had been fought and won largely by Soviet forces. I wondered how my father would have responded to that.

After an evening performance of *Nutcracker* at the Bolshoi, we caught the overnight train for Leningrad, the Red Arrow express. John le Quesne and I shared a compartment. Before we had left England the security authorities had given us a fairly stern wigging to beware of being subverted; to beware especially of Olga, the beautiful spy. John and I were teasing each other about this very subject when the compartment door opened and a woman's head appeared – but it belonged to a babushka, a grandmother with her samovar, enquiring whether we would like any tea.

The next morning we arrived in Leningrad, now once again known by its pre-revolutionary name of St Petersburg, and were taken to visit a Sandhurst equivalent, the wonderfully named Leningrad Higher All Arms Twice Red Bannered School. This time the cadets paraded for us, and General John Stanier, a polished public speaker, addressed them. I can't now remember exactly what he said, but no doubt it was something anodyne about building bridges, and I expect that he referred to the great wartime alliance against the Nazi menace.

After the obligatory tour around the sights of Leningrad – and the glorious Summer Palace just outside the city – we were taken that evening to the opera, something very modern and not to my taste. But I was interested by the theme: the life and achievements of Peter the Great. It was clear that he was still a great hero in Soviet Russia, even though he had been a tsar.

By the time the opera ended it was already late, and we

were due to return to Moscow by the night train, which left at 23.55. It must have been the first night, because the applause went on and on, with ovation after ovation. Our Russian hosts began looking at their watches, caught in an awful dilemma: we couldn't miss the train, that would be a terrible loss of face; but nor could we walk out while the audience was still applauding this great work of Soviet art. Eventually we were hustled out into another convoy of big black cars, and driven hell-for-leather across the city. As the lowliest members of our party, John le Quesne and I were in the last of these. Suddenly a taxi shot out of a side street and drove into the side of us. Our driver, who had been silent until now, became very voluble. We had visions of being left behind in Leningrad while the rest of the party took the train to Moscow. Fortunately, neither car was seriously damaged. As ours drove away, John and I looked back to see the poor old taxi driver up against the wall, being given a hard time by members of our police escort. We made the train by the skin of our teeth. Arriving in Moscow the following morning, we were met by one of the senior Russians, whom by this time we had got to know quite well. After the usual greetings I mentioned the crash and expressed the hope that the taxi driver was OK. I received a stony-faced denial: 'There was no crash.'

I found this response an insight into the real Soviet Union. The accident was certainly unprogrammed, and obviously embarrassing – so it didn't happen. For me it had been fascinating to be in Russia, to get a sense of the Soviet Union from the inside, to snatch a peep behind the curtain. Back in 1939 Churchill had described the Soviet Union as 'a riddle wrapped in a mystery inside an enigma' – and almost forty years later its citizens were still just as difficult to fathom. I was always trying to understand the Russian paradox. Did they think of themselves principally as Russians or as Soviet citizens? As Marxists or patriots? Europeans or Asiatics? They were such a cultivated people, yet their government was so brutal. In so many ways they were like us – yet in as many others they were not like us at all.

6

City on the Edge

The fall of the Berlin Wall is already receding into history. For young people, it must be hard to imagine Europe as it was for almost half a century after the end of the Second World War: divided down the middle, from the Arctic to the Black Sea. The border was sealed; the peoples of the eastern side were imprisoned, and those who tried to escape were frequently shot in the attempt.

This absolute divide between East and West was most apparent in Berlin, then a city like none other. Right up until 1989 Berlin remained an anomaly, still under military occupation as it had been since 1945. As all of Germany had once been, so Berlin remained, carved by the victorious Allies into Zones of Occupation as prescribed by the Yalta Conference of early 1945. There was a British Sector, an American Sector, a French Sector – and, on the eastern side of the city, a Russian Sector, by far the largest of the four. These arrangements had been frozen in the Cold War that had begun almost immediately after the

Germans were defeated. It had been intended that Berlin should be a unified city administered jointly by the four Allied powers, but very soon after the end of the war the Russians had walked out of the quadripartite institutions, in particular the Kommandatura, the military government. The Kommandatura continued to meet monthly, year after year, with an empty place at the table left for the Russians should they ever decide to return – which they never did.

West Berlin was an island, isolated more than a hundred miles within Russian-occupied territory, accessible only along restricted road and rail links, and by three narrow air corridors. In 1948 the Russians had sealed the land links and tried to starve West Berlin into submission, but a continuous airlift had kept the city supplied until, over a year later, the Russians relented and lifted the blockade. Germany divided into two separate states, the Federal Republic in the West and the 'Democratic' Republic in the East, with formidable armies stationed in each, under the umbrella organizations of NATO and the Warsaw Pact respectively. But Berlin continued to be administered in the same way, because any changes would have upset the delicate balance prevailing in the city. For example, the Western forces in Berlin were not under the NATO chain of command, because their status had been defined under the Potsdam Agreement between the Allied Powers in the summer of 1945, predating NATO which did not come into being until 1949. The Western Allies refused to recognize East Germany, so all road traffic up 'The Corridor', as it was known, was regulated by the Russians.

Within Berlin, civilians could move fairly freely

between the sectors until 1961, when mass emigration of skilled workers to the West prompted the building of a wall between the Russian Sector and the others, preventing any further passage across the city. This infamous wall became a dramatic symbol of Communist oppression. Along the west bank of the River Spree, which in the vicinity of the Reichstag formed the boundary between the Soviet and the Western sectors, was a row of crosses, in memory of people who had been shot dead by guards while trying to reach the West. In 1963 President Kennedy flew into Berlin and famously declared his solidarity with the people of the city: 'Ich bin ein Berliner.'

So Berlin continued from decade to decade, and so it was when I was posted there in January 1977. The house which I was going to take over from my predecessor being not yet available, I drove out alone, the rest of the family following by air two weeks later. In any event, I thought it would be fun to drive across Europe in my recently acquired Rover 2000. This was the first new car I'd ever owned; as I was going abroad I was able to buy it tax-free, and the garage did me a good exchange deal on the old car. I took the overnight boat from Harwich to the Hook of Holland, arriving at six o'clock in the morning, and then drove east the whole day. Of course, to reach West Berlin you had to drive through East Germany. Afterwards I'd drive that route between the West German border and Berlin so many times that I would come to think nothing of it, but that first time was memorable.

Crossing the Inner German Border was an elaborate ritual. The form was to report first to the Royal Military Police post at Helmstedt, with all your documents: your ID card, your passport and your posting order. The military police would fill out transit documents and give them to you, along with very detailed maps. You'd be warned not to stray from the prescribed route, and not to drive too fast, because it would be very embarrassing if you were arrested for speeding by the East German police (the 'Vopos'), given that we did not recognize their status. After that you were on your own. Having left the military police post, you would negotiate various chicanes and other obstacles until you reached the Soviet checkpoint. There you had to park your car, get out and walk across towards a little office building. The sentry would salute you, and you would salute him back, even if you were in plain clothes. On the outer wall of the building was just a little counter with a hole in the wall through which you shoved your papers. A hand would take them away. You waited, hoping everything would be in order, and after a while the papers would re-appear at this hole, duly stamped. Then you could set off.

It was late on a wet January afternoon and getting dark when I set out along the East German autobahn to Berlin for the first time. There seemed to be no traffic at all. It was uncanny to drive through dripping forests as the light was going, with no headlights behind me and none coming towards me. Bloody hell, I thought: into the heart of darkness go I.

After driving for two hours I arrived at the Berlin Russian checkpoint (known as Bravo), where I had to go through the same rigmarole as at the inner German border, and then on through the Allied checkpoint, and eventually there I was, in West Berlin. I drove straight to the officers' mess of the Berlin Brigade Headquarters for what I felt was a very well-earned whisky.

* * *

My appointment as Chief of Staff of the Berlin Brigade was what the Army calls an 'all-arms' staff job, i.e. where one's tribal identity is of no consequence to the job itself, and where one serves alongside officers and soldiers from many other tribes. My brigade commander, Charles Grey, was a Sapper, for example. The Brigade Headquarters was in the administrative building of the 1936 Olympic stadium, an imposing edifice in the Nazi neoclassical style, designed by Hitler's architect Albert Speer. There were amazing facilities, including two huge swimming pools, one outdoor, one indoor: all free, of course, because under international law we were still the occupying power, though we did not use that term to avoid any possibility of offending the Germans. The Brigade consisted of three infantry battalions, two of them based in Spandau, which is almost a satellite town but still within the perimeter of West Berlin, and the other right up against the East German border on the other side of the Havel, the long thin lake which runs north–south through the city. In support we had engineers, a logistics base, communications, a military hospital – in fact, all the infrastructure one could want, including schools, one of which my two children attended.

The four-thousand-strong Berlin Infantry Brigade was the sole British force in Berlin, and one of three Allied brigades, one per Western ally. In a unique arrangement the three brigade commanders reported to three major generals, the commandants of the Allied Sectors. Our commandant was Roy Redgrave, a cousin of the left-wing actors Vanessa and Corin. The strategic role of the Allied Forces in Berlin, and thereby the British Brigade, was to play their part in deterring and, if need be, resisting a Warsaw Pact attack. Of course, if it came to resistance we probably wouldn't last very long, because we were completely outnumbered. But our presence was symbolic, a powerful signal of the West's determination to remain in Berlin.

Operating as we were in such a confined area, organizing military exercises was not easy. For some exercises – armoured manoeuvres or parachuting, for example – we would have to decamp to the Federal Republic. But we were able to conduct set-piece exercises in the great forest, the Grünewald, and put much effort into maintaining our ability to ferry across the Havel, because that would be important if the bridges were destroyed. The West Berliners were very tolerant of any disruption resulting from our activities, because they were well aware that their continuing freedom depended on our presence. Our exercises led to some comic incidents. In summer young Germans like to prance around naked in the sunshine, and Berliners were no exception. On more than one of our exercises we burst out of the wood into a large clearing at the centre of the Grünewald to find bare Berliners disporting themselves. British soldiers concealed in camouflaged gear encountered German girls playing volleyball with everything on view – very good for morale!

We also had what were known as 'crash-outs': no-notice exercises, designed to test the speed of our reactions. As the Chief of Staff I would plan these, keeping the details on an absolute close hold, so that only about four or five people knew when the hooters would sound. Typically, this would be at about 01.00 or 02.00 hours, so of course on such occasions I wasn't the most popular man in Berlin. The boys were expected to be out of barracks within an hour, and they always were; for them, it was almost a point of honour which battalion was first out. I remember one occasion when we were given the opportunity to exercise in a derelict area of the city that was about to be demolished. This would provide a rare opportunity to practise house-to-house fighting, what is known in the Army as FIBUA ('fighting in built-up areas'). I planned the exercise to simulate a counter-attack on an enemy-held urban position, negotiating very discreetly with the *Stadt* authorities to avoid giving any warning of the crash-out.

If war came, our job was to hold West Berlin until we were relieved. Short of general war, had the autobahn corridor been cut, there was a plan for an Allied armoured division to fight its way up the corridor towards us. Of course, being surrounded by enemy territory made us vulnerable to attack from all sides. When I arrived in Berlin, each Western Ally had its own plan to defend its own bit of the city, but there was no fully coordinated defence plan. I found my brigade commander a difficult boss, but he clearly saw the need for an integrated defence concept; he pushed this hard, and it was eventually accepted. I did a great deal of work on this new plan, and in the process learned a lot about multinational operations which would come in useful later in my career, not least the friction that can result when national interests do not entirely coincide.

The main obstacle to any integrated plan was establishing an integrated chain of command, and this was particularly difficult for the French. They were always slightly prickly about their position in Berlin anyway –

perhaps a legacy of their difficult experience in the war. France had been a founding member of NATO in 1949, but traditionally disliked the idea of American pre-dominance. In 1966, de Gaulle had withdrawn French forces from the integrated NATO military structure, though they remained political members of the Alliance. The NATO political headquarters, which had been in Fontainebleau, moved to Brussels; the military HQ, Supreme Headquarters Allied Powers Europe (SHAPE), moved to Mons, also in Belgium. A French corps remained stationed in Germany, based in the Black Forest as it had been since 1945, but throughout the Cold War period we in the British Army (and no doubt the other NATO members) could never be sure what the French would do if it came to the crunch. They would say, 'Of course we will be there' – but there was always this un-certainty, because they weren't part of the integrated forces and therefore they weren't part of integrated planning.

So the development of an integrated plan for the defence of West Berlin was a very delicate business. Obviously the US Commandant in Berlin would have to be *primus inter pares*, but the French found that difficult. And there was a further complication: the Allied forces in Berlin were not part of NATO, and so the plan needed to be coordinated with the NATO chain of command in West Germany. The Allied armoured division forcing its way down the autobahn to relieve West Berlin would be under NATO control. So getting our Gallic Allies on board required considerable diplomacy, and my A-level French was often tested – but we had just about cracked it by the time I moved on.

I remember the drama when a British Army convoy,

heading back to West Germany, took the wrong turning on the autobahn. They had seen a sign saying Frankfurt, and thought, 'That's fine, we know Frankfurt'; but it turned out that they had taken the turning not for the familiar Frankfurt am Main, which is in the Rhineland, but for Frankfurt an der Oder, which is on the Polish border. So there was a British Army convoy driving east through Warsaw Pact territory: the kind of thing that in those days made people very nervous indeed. The convoy had actually reached Frankfurt an der Oder, clearly about to invade Poland, before somebody twigged. Sector Headquarters were going spare: 'What the hell's going on? Can't these people map-read?'

One enjoyable way to get into and out of Berlin was by rail. Each of the three Western Allies had a train service to the West: the American train went to Frankfurt, the French to Strasbourg and the British to Brunswick. We could ride on each other's without payment. Trains ran every day, no matter how few passengers there were, because the train service was, like so much else about Berlin, of symbolic importance. Each train was guarded by six soldiers, with an officer commanding, a duty that was handed out in turn to units throughout the Brigade. This was the only duty I ever volunteered for: not for altruistic reasons, but because I enjoyed it and found it interesting. You would leave Charlottenburg station early in the morning, and very quickly the train would reach the East German border. As the officer in charge, you had to have 'move-ment orders' ready for every passenger on the train, together with either passports (for families and civilians) or military ID cards (for servicemen). With all of these documents in your possession you would disembark, walk down the platform, and present them to a Russian officer – Russian, not East German – who sometimes would take a long time and peer at each and every one and sometimes would just say 'Fine'. Some would even offer a glass of vodka, and maybe there would be some idle chat. There was a civilian interpreter in tow – but being a Russian-speaker I could to some extent dispense with his services, which would immediately establish more of a rapport: people are always appreciative if you can speak their language, however haltingly. Some few hours later, around midday, after passing through a further set of Russian and then Allied controls on the border between the two Germanies, the train would reach Brunswick, where passengers would disembark, perhaps to catch a connecting train. There were two or three hours of free time in Brunswick to have a wander round and do whatever you wanted – perhaps shop a little, take a stroll by the river, visit an art gallery, or just sit in a café – before the train left on its return journey at around four o'clock in the afternoon. Meals on board were provided free of charge, in a restaurant car run for some historical reason by a group of elderly Polish displaced persons. As officer commanding the train you were made a bit of a fuss of: you'd be served with a full English breakfast soon after you left, then (having had lunch in Brunswick) afternoon tea just as the train set out on the way back, and some hours later dinner. Wine didn't cost very much, and so you arrived back at Charlottenburg in the early evening feeling absolutely no pain at all, after a very good day out.

*   *   *

135

Living in Berlin was exciting. Every morning you got up with a spring in your step. Of course, it helped that I was a reasonably competent German-speaker. I remember talking to a good friend of mine, a German, and saying to him, 'What a wonderful city this is, what an amazing place. Despite all its problems,' I said, 'life here is like nowhere else.' And he replied, *'Jawohl, heute leben, besonders heute abend – morgen, wer weisst, vielleicht die Russen'* ('Live today, especially tonight – tomorrow who knows, perhaps the Russians'). That was very much the Berlin philosophy.

And life was good. We were quartered in Charlottenburg, very close to the Olympic stadium, in a comfortable house on the south side of the long straight road which heads west out of Berlin. It was very pleasant, set in well-tended gardens surrounded by mature trees. I had to wait until I was made a general before I would be allocated quarters as good as that again. One was extremely fortunate.

Under the terms of the Potsdam Agreement, the Western Allies had absolute right of access to East Berlin, as the Russians did to West Berlin, because Berlin was considered as a single city. All ranks were encouraged to exercise this right, and of course it was a fascinating thing to do. The old classical heart of Berlin, all the museums, the beautiful old opera house – all this was in the East. The only condition was that you had to go in uniform. My first venture into the Soviet Sector was on one of the bus tours organized by the British authorities every Saturday morning. We passed through the only access point for Allied personnel, the infamous Checkpoint Charlie, the funnel for all our traffic between East and West. This was the front line of the Cold War, a place immortalized in thousands of books and films and magazine articles. Passing through the checkpoint was a potential problem, because we did not recognize the authority of the East German guards. For those wearing it, the uniform itself was sufficient proof of identity, but other members of the family would make a slight concession by holding their passports open against the car window. Once through the checkpoint, we were taken to see the sights: the Brandenburg Gate, Hitler's bunker and so on. That first trip into East Berlin was just to get my bearings really, but I liked it and afterwards I would go often, usually with the family. Everything seemed very cheap there. While West Berlin used the Deutschmark – then one of the strongest currencies in the world – East Berlin had the Ostmark, the East Mark, which was another matter altogether. The official exchange rate was around four to one, but you could go into any bank in West Berlin and get fifteen or sixteen Ostmarks for your Deutschmark – so your Western currency went a long way in East Berlin. Unfortunately, there wasn't much worth buying, except cheap LPs, Meissen porcelain if you could find any, cameras, binoculars and children's clothes.

Often at the weekend we'd wander around Alexanderplatz, which was the big central area, do a bit of shopping, and then find somewhere to have a half-decent lunch. In the evenings you could go to the opera for next to nothing, and there were two or three places we knew where one could have dinner afterwards, dressed in full mess kit, bow tie, medals, the whole shebang. One favourite restaurant was called the Ganymede; its interior was like a relic of the 1930s, with potted palms and a little string orchestra. Once, as we came in after the opera with four or five other British couples, the string orchestra struck up 'God Save the Queen'! The East Berlin restaurants would pretend to serve lurid cocktails and offer an elaborate menu when in reality there would only be Wiener schnitzel or whatever, accompanied by some vinegary East European red wine. It would be difficult to over-estimate the vivid contrast between West and East Berlin: the change as one drove back through Checkpoint Charlie from the darkness and the gloom of the East to the bright lights and *joie de vivre* of the West was abrupt and extraordinary.

Occasionally you would see Russians in West Berlin doing what we did, exercising their right of access and no doubt spending such money as they had on Western goodies. Sadly, we had very little contact with Russians, except on a very formal basis. One exception to this was the summer party given by the British Military Liaison Mission (known as Brixmis).

At the end of the Second World War, all four Allies had agreed that they should have military liaison missions, one commander in chief to another, with right of access throughout occupied Germany. Thus the British mission had right of access throughout East Germany, as did the French and American missions; and likewise, the Soviet mission had right of access throughout West Germany. Once the Cold War started these liaison missions became essentially intelligence-gathering operations, but they retained a semblance of their old liaison function. The British Mission's HQ was an elegant *fin de siècle* house in Potsdam, only half an hour from the British Sector in West Berlin, but in East Germany. Members of the

Mission lived with their families in the West, but this Headquarters was kept in Communist-controlled territory as a symbolic gesture. And every summer a reception would be held in the garden there. Many Russians would be invited, and some of the other Allied Grands Fromages as well. I was invited *ex officio*, and very intrigued to be attending. Apart from anything else, we got there not by going through Checkpoint Bravo, which was the one on the main autobahn from West Germany, but by going across Glienicke Bridge, the spy exchange bridge. So there we were, on a warm summer's evening, all in uniform of course, with the Pimm's flowing, and I was enjoying the rare opportunity to use my rusty Russian. Towards the end of the party, when I was probably not entirely sober, I found myself talking to some Russian officer. I hadn't taken on board who he was until I suddenly noticed his five-pointed star on a ribbon: the emblem of a marshal of the Soviet Union. I had been banging on to the Soviet Commander in Chief in Germany. I stopped in mid-sentence, aghast. He looked at me with a rather quizzical expression for a moment, and then said, 'How very interesting, Major,' before turning on his heel and walking off.

The only other place where I would have 'face time' with Russians was at Spandau Prison, a grim fortress built of dark red bricks with turrets and watchtowers. This was another of those bizarre Berlin anomalies, a prison with only one prisoner: Rudolf Hess, 'the loneliest man in the world'. Only once or twice did I ever catch sight of him, a stooping, gaunt, frail figure strolling in the garden alone. Hess had been Hitler's deputy; now he was the last surviving Nazi leader, and as such was deemed to be potentially a focus around whom neo-Nazi groups attempting to revive the glories of the Third Reich could rally. For the Russians in particular, his continued incarceration was a matter of the utmost importance.

Hess was guarded by a platoon of thirty soldiers from each of the four Allied powers in turn. Each platoon would be on duty for a month, before handing over to the next. It was a dreary duty, and the soldiers used to hate it. But on handover day there would be a lunch, for the incoming and outgoing platoon commanders, plus other representatives of all four Allies. As the Brigade Chief of Staff, I used to work out the rota, so I would be invited, as would my opposite numbers: American, French and Russian. There would be between a dozen and twenty young officers, four or five from each country, and all at roughly the same level. It was an opportunity to mix informally, and of course it helped that I could speak some Russian. I recall idly remarking to one Russian officer, 'What a dreadfully boring duty this is!' and the Russian getting quite cross with me. 'No,' he said, 'this is a very honourable duty. You should not forget what Hess represents, and all those who died in order to remove people like him.'

From time to time Hess, who was already in his mid-eighties and who had been in prison almost half his life, would need medical treatment. Again, I was responsible for making the arrangements, since the prison was in the British Sector. He would be treated in the British military hospital, about three miles up the road towards the city centre. He would be taken there by convoy, with a military escort and representatives from all three other Allies in attendance, watching everything that we did – particularly the Russians. Like so many other aspects of Berlin, Spandau Prison was surreal.

* * *

Ceremonial was an important part of life in Berlin. There was the annual Allied Forces Day Parade, when contingents of the three Western garrisons would march through the centre of West Berlin, close to the Wall itself. The British also celebrated the Queen's Birthday with a larger parade every summer in the grounds of the Olympic stadium complex. The Great and the Good of Berlin would be invited to watch. One year, despite several rehearsals, Charles Grey got his word of command wrong; the result was a bugger's muddle on the parade ground and huge embarrassment all round. Against my strong advice, he instigated one of those early-morning crash-out exercises only thirty-six hours afterwards. We all can and do make mistakes, but this lost him any sympathy he might originally have enjoyed.

My appointment as Chief of Staff of the Berlin Brigade had been for two years, concluding at the end of 1978. The next step along the usual Army career path was to go back to the Regiment as a company commander, and at the beginning of 1979 I was posted to the 2nd Battalion, 2 Para – which coincidentally was coming towards the end of a tour in Berlin, so the Jackson family was able to stay on there another six months. I was given B Company to command, the company I had joined when first posted to the Regiment as a young lieutenant. Among the hundred-odd men now under my command were some from my original platoon, including 'Banzai' Burton, who had succeeded Sergeant Peacock as my platoon sergeant while I was still a platoon commander, and who now was to be B Company Sergeant Major.

We were conducting one of our field exercises, in a rural

area which was outside the city but still part of the British Sector, when the Prince of Wales visited the Battalion in his capacity as Colonel in Chief of the Parachute Regiment. It was the beginning of a long relationship with the heir to the throne, culminating in the six years I served as Colonel Commandant of the Regiment. Soon afterwards I learned with much pleasure that I had been awarded the MBE, for my 'exceptional contribution' to the new integrated Allied plan for the defence of West Berlin.

Bizarrely, most of my last six months in Berlin was taken up with special training for Northern Ireland, which is where 2 Para were headed again. Civilians might ask themselves whether this was a welcome posting. The fact is that, as a soldier, you take what you're given. Some of this preparation was carried out at 'Tin City', a mocked-up urban environment the size of an English village constructed predominantly of corrugated iron in Sennelager, West Germany. We undertook various kinds of minor tactical training: patrolling, anti-ambush drills, anti-bomb drills – and what we called 'judgemental shooting': training in when we were authorized to open fire according to the rules of engagement stipulated on the 'yellow card'.

We left Berlin in June and, after summer leave, reassembled at the Army camp at Ballykinler, a small village at the southern end of County Down, right on the coast. This would be another two-year residential tour, with the families housed within the barracks' perimeter for their own security. Ballykinler was a pretty place, in sight of the Mourne Mountains and with a glorious sandy beach, but isolated: Downpatrick, the nearest town, was 7 miles away, and it was 25 miles to Lisburn, the main military base.

The primary role of 2 Para on this posting was to act as reserve battalion to 3 Infantry Brigade, headquartered in Dungannon, whose tactical area of operational responsibility (TAOR) took in the south-east of the Province, including South Armagh. Our particular role was to support the South Armagh *roulement* battalion – headquartered at Bessbrook, about twenty minutes' flying time from Ballykinler – which when we arrived in Ballykinler was the 1st Battalion, the Queen's Own Highlanders. At any one time 2 Para provided at least one company to serve under their command, on a monthly rotation. For most of 2 Para's tour, the South Armagh company was based at the tiny village of Forkhill, in the old police station, which had been expanded with Portakabins and other temporary buildings and was protected by a high fence.

For me this tour would prove totally different from my tour with 1 Para seven years before. Our patrols then had been almost entirely in built-up areas. Now we would be operating in the fields and villages of South Armagh, the region that had become notorious as 'bandit country'.

7

Bandit Country

The landscape of South Armagh is exceptionally beautiful. Rough moorland studded with glacial moraines covers the hills, which look down over a patchwork of green fields. Armagh is the smallest of the six counties of Ulster, and very rural, noted for its orchards. There are no big towns or busy roads here. Modest villages huddle in the valleys; tracks end abruptly at small farmsteads. Only a small painted cross on the road surface informs the traveller that he has reached the border with the Republic.

This seems like a peaceful place, quiet and tranquil. So it is again, perhaps. But until recently, these lanes and hedgerows were laced with menace. The lush green countryside had been a battleground between the Security Forces and the IRA since the Troubles began, with innumerable bombings, shootings and mortar attacks. Lack of vigilance here could prove fatal.

The people of South Armagh never accepted partition. The locals were always staunchly Republican, resenting

144

the border that legally if not culturally had divided them from the rest of Ireland since 1920. Smuggling in and out of the Republic was so commonplace as to be mainstream, encouraged by the absurd agricultural subsidies in both countries. I well remember stopping a large truck somewhere on a lane in South Armagh to search the vehicle. The driver had a load of pigs on board which he had brought in from the Republic.

'Right, so where are they going?' I asked him.

He told me that he was taking them to Warrenpoint, the small port just south of Newry. Was he hoping to sell them there?

'Not exactly,' he answered. 'I'll just be taking them there and bringing them back again.'

Puzzled, I asked why.

'Because when we cross this way I get a subsidy from the British Government for doing it, and then when I cross back I can get a subsidy from the Irish. Then I take the pigs back to the fella I've rented them from.'

'Give me that again,' I said. 'You're joking, aren't you?' But he wasn't.

An unhealthy contempt for the forces of the British state prevailed throughout this close-knit community. South Armagh was a stronghold of the IRA, which enjoyed the sympathy if not the active support of local people. Even priests could be part of the conspiracy, and it was rumoured that a local doctor had laughed as he walked past a badly wounded British soldier. In this part of the Province terrorists could be sure of shelter and assistance, and if threatened with capture it was easy for them to slip across the border into the Republic. IRA gunmen carried out a series of atrocities here, some in response to killings by Loyalist death squads. In 1976, for example, a minibus carrying men home from work had been stopped at a bogus vehicle checkpoint near Bessbrook. The Catholic driver was allowed to go, but the passengers, all Protestants, were massacred with automatic weapons. Ten men died at the scene; one survived, despite being shot eighteen times.

South Armagh was particularly dangerous for the Security Forces. Almost half of all the British soldiers murdered by the IRA in the first decade of the Troubles had been killed in this sparsely populated rural backwater, only about a hundred miles square. Scores of policemen and Ulster Defence Regiment (UDR) part-timers had died here too. This was enemy territory, with a sullen and hostile population; behind every pair of eyes lurked a potential spy. What we were involved in here was counter-insurgency, of the type the Army had conducted in Malaya and elsewhere, but fought in what should have been a sleepy corner of the British Isles.

The South Armagh IRA specialized in ambushes, exploding roadside bombs as Security Force vehicles were passing. Many of these were detonated by a signal carried along dug-in wires, but they had also developed bombs that could be detonated by radio, which were harder to deal with and involved much less risk for the bomber. There were also frequent gun attacks on British foot patrols, using long-range sniper fire. The IRA had recruited a large number of 'scouts' whose job it was to watch the Security Forces and record their habits, with the aim of identifying potential targets. They placed their bombs in locations where they knew soldiers were likely to pass. Travelling overland in South Armagh became so dangerous that the Army had to use helicopters to move troops and supply its bases, just as the Americans had done in Vietnam. The landing site in the village of Bessbrook became the busiest heliport in Europe, more so than those supplying the North Sea oil rigs. Everything was transported by helicopter – even the rubbish. Army helicopters would take off and land every few minutes, flying at rooftop level to reduce the risk of missile or small-arms attack.

Our job was to put boots on the ground, to support the beleaguered police and to show that the rule of law still held in South Armagh. We almost always patrolled on foot; paradoxically, it was safer that way. Vehicles on the whole have to use roads or tracks, and it was simplicity itself for the IRA to put an explosive device in a culvert under the road or dig it into the verge and leave it there, sometimes for months, until an Army vehicle happened to come past. On foot, you could choose your own route. You never went through a gateway because that was an obvious place for an improvised explosive device (IED). Instead, you always went from one field to another by forcing your way through the blackthorn hedges, despite the inevitable scratches and discomfort. The IRA used both command wire and radio signals to detonate IEDs; neither was simple to defeat, whether by tactical or technical means.

Another reason for patrolling on foot was that the soldiers were spaced out, so if a bomb was detonated it was unlikely that many of them would be within range. In a vehicle, on the other hand, you're packed in, and the likelihood is that if a bomb explodes several of you will be killed at once.

Every patrol would be carefully planned in advance, with possible firing points identified and covered. Sometimes we'd carry out a 'route clearance', searching a road for bombs in advance of a convoy, checking every culvert for IEDs. The Belfast–Dublin railway was a favourite target for the IRA. For them it was a propaganda coup to be able to close this line, so they tried to sabotage it whenever possible. One especially vulnerable place was the infamous Kilnasaggart Bridge, where the railway crossed over a road only three or four hundred yards from the border. We tried to protect this by maintaining a presence on the ground, but of course this made the soldiers a target.

As well as bombs, the South Armagh IRA would use home-made mortars, but their range was only two to three hundred yards and they were not very accurate, so they would only use them to attack static targets like exposed bases – and there were not many of these in South Armagh.

In many ways this was a cat-and-mouse game, particularly where IEDs were concerned. Those of us operating overtly – the so-called 'Green Army' – were not there primarily to flush out the IRA, but if they attacked us, it was game on. There were some fierce gun battles, some lasting an hour or more. But most often it would be frustrating: if you didn't hit one of your attackers in your opening burst of fire, you probably wouldn't hit them at all, because the terrorists had their escape route planned in advance. A car would be waiting, and they'd race off towards the border, which would be only a few minutes' drive away. Even if we did hit someone we wouldn't necessarily know it, because the wounded would be whisked away for treatment in the South. Sometimes they would open fire on us from across the border, and in those circumstances we were permitted to return fire into the Republic; but of course then you'd have even less chance of knowing whether you'd hit one of them.

We had no formal contact with the Irish Army. If we were doing an operation right up against the border, a request would be put in for a Security Forces presence on the other side to deter IRA activity. This would always be done through the RUC, who would talk to the Garda, who in turn might call on the Irish Army for support. By and large the Irish Security Forces were cooperative at a local level. Officially they were not supposed to fraternize with us, but sometimes I might have a brief chat with an Irish Army officer at the border.

The IRA in South Armagh were not to be underestimated. They knew the lie of the land extremely well and they were pretty cunning. Operations in the area were a real battle of wits. It was said that if you stopped thinking, you'd start dying. Our job, operating alongside the police, consisted of 'framework operations', routine patrols, searches, manning vehicle checkpoints and so on, just to show that we had the presence, the boots on the ground. In many ways the real war of attrition against the IRA was carried out by covert forces of one sort or another, working 'on very close hold', meaning on a strict need-to-know basis. Some of the time we didn't even know when they were around. To avoid the risk of mistaken identity and a blue-on-blue ('friendly fire') contact, the standard procedure was to impose a so-called 'out-of-bounds area'. For example, we might be told that an area of two or three square kilometres was out of bounds to us, and mark this on our maps. Sometimes a quick reaction force would be put on standby, in case things went wrong and the covert operation needed backup. Occasionally when we'd stop a covert vehicle at a checkpoint, the driver would produce ID showing that he was a member of the Security Forces.

The four companies of 2 Para rotated on roughly a monthly basis between Forkhill, guard duty at Ballykinler, and specific operations such as reinforcing Newry and protecting the railway line. Rural patrols from the company base would be out for several days at a time. Living in an improvised base like Forkhill was cramped, unpleasant and uncomfortable; for one thing, there never seemed to be enough hot water. The boys had to sleep in dormitories, with beds crammed in close to each other and very little storage space for clothes and other personal possessions. But at least the food was consistently good, thanks to the excellent Army chefs. Occasionally we would join a 'surge' operation in a different part of the South Armagh TAOR, when troops would flood an area in the hope of making arms finds and deterring terrorist attacks. After a month or so on deployment, it would be a relief to get back to barracks in Ballykinler. We would always hold a company party the night we got in – an opportunity for the boys to let off steam. As the evening wore on, we would belt out what had become the company song: 'You'll Never Walk Alone'.

In between all of this there was some time for leave. This kind of *roulement* was essential to morale, but of course it made us more vulnerable to attack every time a company moved into or out of a deployment. Even helicopters were not entirely invulnerable to IRA attack; and there were insufficient helicopter hours to avoid road moves outside South Armagh. It was a road move between Ballykinler and Newry – not in South Armagh proper – which provided the IRA with the opportunity for their single most devastating attack in their long campaign against the British Army.

The August Bank Holiday Monday of 1979 was hot and sunny, coming at the end of a month of fine weather. B Company had been conducting operations along the railway line for several days, and we had come into the HQ of the Queen's Own Highlanders at Bessbrook to sort ourselves out and grab some rest. The plan was to stay there a night or two before going back to the railway line. We set up an ops room, while anyone not on duty wandered off in various directions: to the Naafi to get something to eat, to find a bunk for a kip or a shower for a wash. Bessbrook was a huge building; originally a Victorian textile mill, it had been heavily reinforced and reconstructed to house up to a thousand men. Its windowless corridors were lined with pipework, and the constant throbbing of generators gave one the feeling of being in a ship below the waterline.

Meanwhile 2 Para's Support Company in Newry was due to be relieved by A Company later that day. My opposite number Major Peter Fursman, commanding A Company, was already in Newry in the process of taking over from Major Barry Rogan, commanding Support Company. We were all company commanders together, and good friends. The main body of A Company would be coming in by road, which was always a concern; the operations room back in Ballykinler had identified a number of different routes, and would pick one of them at random to try to vary any pattern we might have been setting. This time, the random choice was to result in mayhem.

The convoy of a Land Rover and two four-ton lorries carrying a platoon of about twenty-six soldiers from A Company was sent south along the coast and then up the eastern shore of the estuary of the Newry River. For several miles above the port of Warrenpoint, the river estuary funnels into a tidal lough several miles long and about two hundred yards wide known as Narrow Water, which marks the border with the Republic. A dual-carriageway road ran along the eastern (Northern Irish) shore, while thick woods came down to the water's edge on the Republic side. It was an ideal place for an ambush. The woods provided cover for the terrorists, who had a clear view of traffic passing along the road on the other side of the estuary. There were no obstacles to interfere with a radio signal detonating a bomb on the eastern shore. Being already in the Republic, the terrorists had a good chance of escaping after making their attack.

The Army had long recognized the vulnerability of this stretch of road and frequently put it out of bounds. However, there were only a few routes into Newry from Ballykinler, and if we were to avoid establishing a predictable pattern which would be vulnerable to ambush elsewhere, we had to use this one from time to time. The IRA had in all probability targeted the Royal Marines, who often used this route after conducting their regular checks on the container port at Warrenpoint docks.

In studying the Army's procedures following a bomb attack, IRA analysts had noticed that we would invariably set up an incident control point near the scene of an explosion, from which we would evacuate casualties and collect forensic evidence. They had decided to exploit this procedure by placing two bombs close to each other, the second located where they thought the incident control point was likely to be. The first bomb was hidden beneath straw bales in a trailer which had been parked the previous night in a lay-by. The second bomb was hidden about two hundred yards further along the road towards Newry, in the gate-lodge to a large country house situated higher up the slopes of the Narrow Water valley. Opposite the gate-lodge, on a small promontory that projected almost halfway across the lough, was one of a series of stone towers built in Elizabethan times to defend the east coast of Ulster. It was a noted local beauty spot.

We in B Company were relaxing back at Bessbrook when the dreadful news of Lord Mountbatten's murder came through at about midday. He and members of his family had been heading out to sea on a fishing-trip from Mullaghmore, the village in County Sligo, on the west coast of the Republic, where the Mountbattens had spent every summer for the previous thirty years. Apparently a radio-controlled device had been hidden in his boat and then triggered by somebody on the shore. As well as the Earl, three others had been killed: his fourteen-year-old grandson Nicholas Knatchbull; the boy's grandmother, Lady Brabourne; and Paul Maxwell, a fifteen-year-old local boy who had been acting as boatman. Several further members of the family, including Mountbatten's daughter, were in hospital being treated for their injuries.

Service in Northern Ireland hardens one to atrocities, but even so everybody was deeply shocked by the cruel murder of such a distinguished figure, and the wanton killing of his companions. The news subdued us all, eliminating the normal exuberance you usually feel after completing an operation in the field. But if this was bad, it was about to get much worse.

Later in the afternoon, shortly before five o'clock, I was having a cup of tea in the officers' mess downstairs at Bessbrook when the intercom buzzed. It was my colour sergeant. 'I think you'd better come upstairs,' he said. 'Now.' I raced up to the ops room, two steps at a time. He looked up at me with a sombre expression. It was not a clear picture, he informed me – it never is in these early stages – but he had heard a report on the Battalion radio net from Royal Marines in the area that there had been some sort of explosion on the main road from Warrenpoint to Newry. I had a sinking feeling in the pit of my stomach as I realized that 2 Para was involved.

The bomb in the lay-by had been detonated at 16.40 hours as the rear lorry of the convoy was passing. It took the full force of the explosion and was hurled on to its side. The other lorry driver put his foot down and drove on before parking under the cover of some trees, while the Land Rover swerved across the central reservation and turned around to face the direction from which it had come, towards the smoking debris of the trailer and the wrecked rear lorry. Here the platoon commander set up an incident control point, while he tried frantically to raise Bessbrook on the radio, without success. Radio communications between Bessbrook and the company at Newry had broken down, and the resulting inability to talk to the troops on the ground greatly complicated the Battalion HQ's ability to control the incident and provide support. The crew of a Wessex helicopter on a routine mission intercepted the soldiers' distressed and increasingly desperate transmissions, and contacted Bessbrook. The helicopter was ordered to return to the Battalion HQ, collect a medical team and the four-man Battalion quick reaction force, and take them to Warrenpoint.

Bodies of the soldiers who had been riding inside the lorry were scattered across the road, many of them in flames. All this time the air was filled with the crackle of ammunition and blasts of explosive detonating in the ruined lorry, mixed with the screams of the wounded lying across the road. The surviving soldiers were very jittery. Convinced that they were being shot at from the other side of the water, they returned fire, killing an innocent tourist and wounding another. One soldier became aware of movement behind a roadside wall; pointing his gun, he shouted an order to come out with hands held high. Several shocked children appeared; they had been picnicking with their mother.

Lieutenant Colonel David Blair, commanding officer of the Queen's Own Highlanders at Bessbrook, was himself airborne in a small Gazelle helicopter when he heard the news. He quickly decided that his presence was needed on the ground. Meanwhile, in Newry, Barry Rogan dispatched his own eight-man quick reaction force to the scene in two Land Rovers, and a few moments later he and Peter Fursman followed in two further Land Rovers. On arrival they made the fateful decision to set up the incident control point at the gate-lodge, parking their vehicles beside the building and positioning two Land Rovers on either side of the incident, to prevent civilians entering the area. The Wessex helicopter landed on the central reservation of the dual carriageway, between the wrecked vehicle and the gate-lodge. The medical team alighted immediately, followed by the quick reaction force from Bessbrook. A few moments later a soldier returned to the helicopter to tell the crew to expect only two casualties, as the other six men who had been travelling in the lorry were all dead. About five minutes later the first stretcher was on board, and the other was alongside the Wessex, which was ready for take-off.

It was now almost 17.00 hours. Colonel Blair's Gazelle helicopter had dropped him and his signaller in the grounds of the country house before leaving. These two ran down the drive to join Peter Fursman and his mobile HQ at the gate-lodge. At this moment the watching terrorists detonated the second bomb. The building disintegrated in a huge explosion, disappearing in a cloud of dust and smoke. Lumps of granite were hurled through the air. The Wessex shifted slightly in the shock wave, which blew out one of its Perspex windows. It was then bombarded with fragments of stone. One boulder as big as a football came down through the rotor blades, bouncing off the nose of the aircraft. Though severely damaged, the helicopter managed to take off and fly low over the trees towards Bessbrook.

By this time I was in the Battalion ops room trying to follow what was happening on the Queen's Own Highlanders battalion net. I realized with a sense of mounting dread that there had been many casualties. I still have the scrap of paper on which I scribbled some notes. They read: '1st explosion W[arren]p[oin]t docks, Wessex [bringing] cas[ualties], 2nd 200 yds, all cas[ualties], still some dead, contact 2 hits claimed, one body in the river.' There was still much confusion about what had happened: the Royal Marines' initial contact report had implied an explosion at Warrenpoint docks. Details became clearer over the next few minutes. It was feared that both Peter Fursman and David Blair were dead. Barry Rogan had been bowled over by the second bomb, but miraculously had escaped serious injury.

Brigadier David Thorne, Commander of 3 Brigade, arrived at Bessbrook from his HQ in Dungannon and took control of the situation, issuing orders very rapidly. The Queen's Own Highlanders urgently needed a new battalion commander, and as bad luck would have it Colonel Blair's second-in-command, Major Jeremy Mackenzie, was in Hong Kong reconnoitring their next deployment. The senior company commander, Major Nick Ridley, was in Crossmaglen, 15 miles to the south-west. Thorne made ready to fly to Crossmaglen, where he would promote Ridley to local lieutenant colonel on the spot, ordering him to fly immediately to Bessbrook to take command of the Battalion. Then he noticed me.

'Hello, Mike,' he said. 'What are you doing here?'

I explained that we were untasked, having just come off an operation.

'Right,' he said. 'You're the people to do this, because it's a company from your battalion that's been attacked. Get down to Warrenpoint and sort it out.' Within minutes I was flying to the scene with my immediate command team, followed in fairly short order by the rest of the company. Our job was to relieve the soldiers on the ground and contain the scene until the clear-up operation was completed. I was anxious that there might be further bombs. I remember saying to 'Banzai' Burton, 'We want to be bloody careful that there isn't a third one around here somewhere.'

I arrived at the incident within half an hour of the second bomb explosion. As we circled before landing I could see two craters and large scorch-marks on the road marking where the bombs had been. The gate-lodge had been completely destroyed, with large lumps of granite scattered as far as a hundred yards off. The police and the ambulance service were already on the scene. We landed on the road about three hundred yards south-east of the first bomb-crater (see sketch-map), reckoning that this was a spot with nothing distinct about it that might have caused the IRA to identify it as a potential target. Other helicopters were evacuating the wounded. We relieved the Queen's Own Highlanders' quick reaction force and the survivors of the two bomb blasts. I found Barry Rogan, now the senior officer on site, his forehead covered by a field dressing; after a quick briefing, he handed over the situation to me and returned to his company HQ in Newry.

I knew what I had to do as incident commander under those circumstances: deter further attack, put a cordon around the whole area, preserve the scene of the crime, help the investigative agencies to do their job, and keep all other people out. I set up my HQ in the stone tower opposite the wrecked gate-lodge, after having had it thoroughly checked out for any further IEDs. Only then could I take stock. It was a horrifying scene. There was human debris everywhere, in the trees, on the grass verge and in the

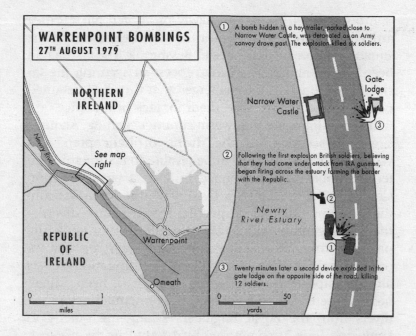

WARRENPOINT BOMBINGS
27TH AUGUST 1979

NORTHERN
IRELAND

Newry River

See map
right

REPUBLIC
OF
IRELAND

Warrenpoint

Omeath

0 ———— 1
miles

① A bomb hidden in a hay trailer, parked close to Narrow Water Castle, was detonated as an Army convoy drove past. The explosion killed six soldiers.

Narrow Water
Castle

Gate-
lodge

③

② Following the first explosion British soldiers, believing that they had come under attack from IRA gunmen, began firing across the estuary forming the border with the Republic.

Newry
River Estuary

②

①

③ Twenty minutes later a second device exploded in the gate lodge on the opposite side of the road, killing 12 soldiers.

0 ———— 50
yards

water: mostly unidentifiable lumps of red flesh, but among them torsos, limbs, heads, hands and ears. I had seen the effect of bombs before, of course, but never carnage on this scale. When a bomb goes off, the air inside the body is compressed, and often forces its way out through the joints. There were some very gruesome sights. All that was left of the driver of the rear lorry was his pelvis, which had been welded to the seat by the intense heat. In these circumstances your emotions shut down and the training takes over. Soldiers try to remain as professional as possible. If anyone felt sickened by what he saw, he would go into the bushes so as not to be seen vomiting by his mates.

Around 18.00 hours the newly promoted Nick Ridley arrived, and we spent some time together assessing the situation before he flew back to Bessbrook. The Garda had been alerted and were in the process of securing the far side of the lough. It later emerged that they had detained two men, but had released them for lack of evidence.

It stayed light late that warm summer evening. An eerie silence descended, as the drone of helicopters and vehicles faded. It seemed unbelievable that something so terrible could have happened in such a beautiful spot. Gradually the specialists arrived: CID, the forensic team, the weapons intelligence people, search teams, divers – the whole gamut. At this stage we still did not know the precise number of casualties, and we were trying to work out who was missing by a process of elimination. It was almost impossible to identify who had been killed, because there were so few remains. I remember one of the divers from the Royal Engineers asking me quietly to come and look at something he'd found in the water. It was a human face that had been blown clear of the man's skull. The line of a moustache was still visible. The diver asked me if I recognized the man. I felt a shiver of horror. 'Of course I do,' I said in a shaky voice. 'He's a good friend of mine.' It was Peter Fursman; that was all we ever found of him. David Blair was identified only by the crown and the star on his epaulette.

I was told that back at Ballykinler it was like the Village of the Damned, while the wives and families waited to hear who had been killed. Apparently there was a rumour that I was one of the dead.

The final body count was eighteen soldiers killed, sixteen Paras and two from the Queen's Own Highlanders.

Six more Paras were seriously wounded. This was the highest number of soldiers killed in any single incident during the whole bloody history of the Troubles. Lieutenant Colonel David Blair was one of the most senior officers killed. The loss to the Paras in a single contact was the worst since Arnhem in 1944. The death toll might have been even higher but for some miraculous escapes. One soldier survived uninjured despite being blown 30 feet through the air; another remained unscathed even though he was taking cover behind a bush beside the lodge-gates when the second bomb exploded.

We maintained the cordon for five days while the emergency services carried out their grisly work, painstakingly clearing the human remains, gathering forensic evidence and removing the debris. Astonishingly, they found the window of the Wessex helicopter intact; I eventually sent it back up to RAF Aldergrove, where I think it's still on display.

The clear-up was very hard for the soldiers, because these were their mates. All the time we were down there by the water's edge I was anxious about the danger of further sniper attacks from the far side. I charted the possible enemy positions for a shoot and placed my cordon accordingly, though of course we could not fully protect those involved in the clear-up.

I still have ugly pictures in my head from that terrible day. Once you've seen such appalling sights, you can't close your mind to them. But I don't have nightmares; fortunately my temperament isn't like that. My attitude is: move on, put that away, because if you get bogged down in thinking too much about it, you might start losing your own courage – and that wouldn't do at all.

Peter Fursman's widow, Christine, said she wanted to see where her husband had died. Lieutenant Colonel Colin Thomson, 2 Para's commanding officer, was very unsure about this, but Christine was insistent. I took it upon myself to escort her around the site of the bombing; it seemed to me that I owed it to them both. For me this was the hardest moment of the whole incident. Christine's fortitude was tremendously affecting; I felt close to tears myself as I watched her holding back her own. I was very anxious that there might still be body parts lying around, but if she did catch sight of anything of that kind, she didn't react. Peter and I were the same age and the same rank. We'd been friends for years, and spent a lot of time together. It occurred to me later that if the cards had come off the pack in a different order it could have been B Company rather than A Company travelling along the road that day, and then it might have been Peter who would have pulled my face out of the water.

Humphrey Atkins, the Secretary of State for Northern Ireland, visited us at the scene the next day, and on the Wednesday Mrs Thatcher, only three months into her tenure as Prime Minister, flew to the Province. She first visited the wounded in hospital, and then spent some hours in Belfast before flying on to South Armagh. Nick Ridley and I briefed her on what had happened in the presence of the Secretary of State, the GOC, Lieutenant General Sir Timothy Creasey, Brigadier David Thorne and Barry Rogan. I was impressed by the way she listened carefully and asked pertinent questions. At the end she instructed the Secretary of State that increased effort should be put into developing new technology to counter the threat of bombs detonated by remote control, and directed him to establish a much closer relationship with the Garda. Both these initiatives were to prove valuable in countering the IRA threat over the two decades that followed.

A month after the Warrenpoint killings, a memorial service was held at the garrison church in Aldershot, attended by the Prince of Wales in his capacity as Colonel in Chief of the Regiment. I was among many 2 Para personnel who flew back to England for the ceremony. The church was packed with wives, girlfriends, parents and other family members. The Prince of Wales read the lesson, and then the names of the dead were read out, before the Last Post sounded. We resolutely sang 'Onward Christian Soldiers', followed by the National Anthem. Finally the Regimental Colours were carried from the church, followed by Prince Charles and the families of the fallen.

I received a letter from Jeremy Mackenzie, who had taken over command of the Queen's Own Highlanders on his return from Hong Kong. He commended the men of B Company for their fortitude and resilience in the most harrowing circumstances. It later emerged that Catholics across the Province feared a massacre in reprisal for the terrible deaths of so many soldiers at Warrenpoint. It was a tribute to the discipline and restraint of the Paras that no such reprisals occurred.

The most direct result of the massacre at Warrenpoint was the cessation of road movement between Ballykinler and South Armagh. More helicopter hours were made available, so that from then almost all troop movements were by air, though we sometimes used covert, unmarked vans. Even movements by air were not risk-free, however: on a number of occasions helicopters came under fire from small arms or even medium machine guns. A Wessex operating out of Crossmaglen came under fire from a heavy machine gun mounted on the back of a truck with armour plating. Unfortunately there was not enough room inside the compound at Forkhill for a helipad, so it was located outside the fence. This meant that helicopters on the ground were vulnerable to attack, but luckily the IRA never scored a hit on one.

During our tour the base at Forkhill was completely rebuilt with mortar-proof buildings, improved facilities and fortified defences. To protect the convoys bringing the building materials, we took part in large set-piece operations at battalion level. It required approximately a thousand soldiers to picket the whole route from Bessbrook to Forkhill, both close-in to the road itself and, crucially, on the high ground overlooking the road. The aim was to deny the IRA any point from which they could fire or plant or detonate a bomb. The pickets were maintained for three or four days while large convoys brought in building materials and then came out with the waste.

A complex of permanently manned observation towers on stilts was erected to provide surveillance over South Armagh. They were known in the Army as 'sangars', an Arabic word taken into British use. We put up one of the first, on high ground above Forkhill. These towers gave excellent surveillance over the TAOR, being equipped with, among other things, optics which could read a number plate a mile or so off. The IRA didn't like these at all, and attacked them from time to time, but without a lot of success. By definition they were not overlooked, and they were well defended with lots of barbed wire and security lights. The soldiers manning the towers were changed over at quiet times such as the small hours of the morning, always varying our procedures to avoid becoming predictable. The South Armagh towers have now been dismantled as part of the peace process.

Over the months that followed, 2 Para suffered further casualties. One of our soldiers was killed by a bomb blast while checking a culvert. On New Year's Eve 1979 there was a dreadful 'blue on blue', after one of our platoons had set up a speculative ambush on a border crossing. The platoon commander broke one of the golden rules: once the ambush is set and everybody's in position, you don't move until the ambush is formally lifted. For whatever reason, perhaps because he saw something suspicious and decided to take a look, he left the ambush, taking his signaller with him. On his return he walked straight into the trap that he himself had laid. As the lieutenant and his signaller approached the soldiers opened fire, killing both men. Then one of our sergeants died when he took a short cut through a gate where a bomb had been laid. With these deaths 2 Para gained the unenviable record for the most casualties sustained by any unit during a Northern Ireland tour.

Johnny Frost had commanded 2 Para at Arnhem; he was the figure immortalized by Anthony Hopkins in the film *A Bridge Too Far*. Of course, Frost was a living legend to us for what he'd done at Arnhem, holding the bridge for much longer than anyone had thought possible. The plan for Operation 'Market-Garden' had been for

Ist Airborne Division to secure the bridge over the Rhine until relieved by heavy armour coming up the road from Eindhoven, but this failed to break through to Arnhem, and Frost's lightly armed force had fought a desperate battle against SS Panzer troops with much heavier firepower. Frost still took huge interest in the Battalion, and I'd met him several times. On Arnhem Day 1980 he came out to see us at Forkhill. Though almost seventy by this time, he was still spry, and of course he was intensely interested in all aspects of soldiering. I took him up to a bit of high ground above the railway line, a very good vantage point from which you could see much of the company area and across the border. This was rugged, Dartmoor-like country, and on the high ground we were quite secure. It was a privilege to spend some time in his company.

The end of 1980 marked the end of my two years with the Battalion. The military situation in Northern Ireland had reached stalemate, with each side developing tactics and counter-measures. There had been little political progress, but the very fact that terrorism had not prevailed was itself some kind of victory.

I left 2 Para at Christmas, even though they had another four or five months of their tour remaining. I was headed for the National Defence College at Latimer, near Aylesbury in Buckinghamshire, where I would undertake a six-month course with officers – all British – of similar age and rank from all three Services. The aim of the course was to provide selected officers with a broader and deeper understanding of defence on a joint-Service basis. This was a welcome change after eighteen months of full-on field soldiering.

But there would be a footnote to my second tour in Northern Ireland. On 4 July 1981 some 2,500 people attended the annual Airborne Forces Day Parade at Aldershot. There were marches, fly-pasts, and a parachute display by the Red Devils. The Colonel Commandant of the Regiment, General Sir Anthony Farrar-Hockley, presented awards. For my service as a company commander in Northern Ireland I was awarded the oak leaf symbol of a mention in dispatches 'in recognition of gallant and distinguished service'. It was a proud moment.

8
Commanding Officer

In June 1981, while still at the National Defence College, I was promoted to lieutenant colonel. I felt very gratified to have reached this rank at only thirty-seven, the earliest age at which you can do so.

The Army career structure dictates that officers from the rank of major upwards will alternate every two years or so between command and staff jobs. The concept is that you're getting a rounded person coming through at each level. Accordingly, my next posting was back to the Staff College as a member of the Directing Staff – a really plum job for a young lieutenant colonel. The DS consisted of, dare I say it, some of the sharpest of the younger officers of this rank, while the students were the cream of the generation of Army officers about five years younger, senior captains and young majors in their early thirties. It was stimulating to teach these bright young people in an invigorating environment. Having said that, I have to admit that I was frustrated to be in a staff job when the Falklands crisis blew up, early in 1982.

The events leading up to the Falklands War were in their own way as bizarre as those leading to the invasion of Anguilla. There is an atavistic Argentine belief that the Falkland Islands – which they call the 'Malvinas' – are theirs. The islanders, on the other hand, had for as long as anyone could remember been overwhelmingly in favour of remaining British. The Argentinian military junta headed up by General Galtieri had been making threatening noises towards the 'Malvinas' for some years, but it was not at all clear that this was any more than bluster. The Chiefs of Staff had anyway concluded some years before that the Islands were indefensible. The crisis began absurdly enough, with an Argentinian scrap-metal dealer landing illegally on the island of South Georgia just before Christmas, and escalated from then until the Argentinian invasion of the Falklands early in April. The Foreign Office and even the MOD were inclined to regard the whole thing as a *fait accompli* even before it happened, but the First Sea Lord, Admiral Sir Henry Leach, was made of sterner stuff. As soon as news of the invasion came through he went to the House of Commons to beard the Secretary of State for Defence, John Nott. It turned out that Nott was in a meeting with the Prime Minister at the time. When Mrs Thatcher learned that the First Sea Lord was waiting, she summoned him in to join them, whereupon he brushed aside the defeatist advice she'd been given by the Foreign Office and MOD bureaucrats. 'Prime Minister, we can do this,' he told her. Then and there she gave him the authority to start forming a Task Force to sail to the South Atlantic. Word has it that Nott went as white as a sheet on hearing her words. A few days later she announced in the

House of Commons the British Government's determination to retake the Islands.

At the Staff College we were all totally absorbed by the developing situation. Of course everyone was behind the Government's decision 100 per cent. But the stakes were very high. I remember one of my more far-sighted colleagues saying to me, 'One government will fall, whatever happens. If Britain wins, Galtieri cannot survive. And if we lose, Thatcher will be out. Maybe both governments will fall.'

Then the question arose: who's going to go? We hadn't had a real war for more than a generation, and everyone wanted a taste of the action. Here was an opportunity to do what we'd all spent our lives training for. Within the Army, there was some rapid force generation, as everyone scrambled for a place aboard one of the many troop-ships, including the liners *Canberra* and *Queen Elizabeth II*. A force of approximately ten thousand soldiers was assembled very swiftly from a standing start, incorporating 3 Commando Brigade Royal Marines, with its three battalion equivalents, and two battalions of the Parachute Regiment, 2 and 3 Para. My previous battalion was now under the command of Lieutenant Colonel Herbert 'H' Jones, who had succeeded Colin Thomson after the latter's premature death from cancer the year before. Like Derek Wilford, 'H' had come in to command a parachute battalion from another regiment, in his case the Devon and Dorsets. Ian McLeod, the lieutenant colonel commanding 1 Para, flew from Belfast to London in order to lobby for his Battalion to form part of the Task Force – unsuccessfully, as it turned out – and his soldiers bombarded Downing Street with letters demanding the same.

It soon became clear that the military staff within the MOD would need extra bodies. Lieutenant General James 'Jimmy' Glover, Deputy Chief of Defence Staff (Intelligence), wanted a second military assistant (MA). He already had one MA, but the work was expanding at such a rate that he needed another, to concentrate solely on the Falklands campaign. So they cast around for someone suitable and alighted on me, probably thinking, 'The Staff College can spare him.' I'd known Jimmy Glover from my second tour in Northern Ireland, when he'd been Commander Land Forces there, deputy to the GOC. I knew him to be a demanding boss who didn't suffer fools gladly, but also to be highly intelligent with a good sense of humour. All in all, he was a good man to work for. Perhaps my Intelligence Corps background counted in my favour, plus the fact that I had learned something of the other two Services during my time at the National Defence College. I received a phone call out of the blue one day, telling me to get up to London as quickly as I could be released from the Staff College, to report to General Glover at the huge MOD main building on Whitehall. If I wasn't going to be part of the Task Force itself, at least I could be part of the planning. Within a day or two I was there.

An MA works directly for a general, of two-star rank or higher. He is usually a lieutenant colonel, though he can be a major. It's one of the sought-after jobs for an officer in his mid- to late thirties – usually, though not always, followed by the command of a battalion. The job of the MA is to process the work that goes through his general's office. A general will also have an ADC (aide-de-camp), who will handle all of the mundane but necessary tasks such as organizing his diary, his daily programme and his social activities, fixing transport, and so on; and he may well have a PA as well, who will be a staff sergeant or warrant officer. But it will be the MA who handles major policy issues: he will draft letters and papers after discussion with his general. It's a very personal relationship, and the chemistry has to be right for it to work. You are the general's right-hand man, and you share his confidences. It's a position of great influence, of course. The MA is always on the telephone: people will use him as a sounding board. 'How's the old bugger going to react to this?' they might ask, and he might say in response, 'I think this is the way the general sees it.' This sort of thing goes on all the time, and much of it doesn't reach the ears of the general, but occasionally the MA will come and tell him that so-and-so over at such-and-such is trying to find out what he's thinking about this or that. Or he might tell the general that he's had a worrying phone call, and that he suspects that all is not well for some reason or other. It's a very privileged position, and you learn a great deal, so it requires somebody who knows the importance of discretion.

The role of Defence Intelligence is to know as much as possible about the enemy, to understand what he is doing and what his intentions are. In the Falklands context, the job was to analyse the resources Argentina had at its disposal: what capabilities the enemy had on the Islands; what were his naval and air capabilities; and what was his ability to resupply. Of course, up until this point Defence Intelligence had been focused on the perceived threat from the Soviet Union and the Warsaw Pact; now we had been attacked from a completely unexpected direction. It's fair to say that we didn't know very much about the Argentinians' military resources at the start of the campaign. Fortunately, however, we were familiar with the capabilities of their most potent weapon, the air-launched Exocet missile, because the Royal Navy was equipped with the ship-launched version. Their Super Etendard fighter-bombers, which carried the Exocet, were French-manufactured, so we knew quite a bit about them as well.

My routine revolved around the daily meeting of the Chiefs of Staff at 09.00 or 09.30 hours, before which a great deal of work went on to ensure that they were in possession of all the latest information. I would be in for 05.00 every morning, as part of a small assessment group within the Defence Intelligence staff. We would see what had come in overnight, and pull together a briefing for General Glover at 08.00. Such long working hours, seven days a week, meant that commuting back to Camberley was not an option. Instead I cadged a bed off David Reece, an old friend of mine from my days in the Intelligence Corps, who was also working in the MOD as a lieutenant colonel and who lived in Clapham.

This daily Chiefs of Staff meeting was attended by the heads of the three Services – the First Sea Lord, the Chief of the General Staff and the Chief of the Air Staff. It was chaired by the Chief of the Defence Staff (CDS). The Vice-Chief was also present. The Secretary of State would often be there as well, together with other senior MOD staff, including of course Jimmy Glover. Jimmy was very keen on visual aids, and he always had several prepared for each Chiefs of Staff meeting. Nowadays everybody uses PowerPoint, but back in those days you used 'vufoils' –

sheets of clear plastic on a light tray, which would be projected on to a large screen. In the Chiefs of Staff's conference room, this projection was done from a cubby-hole on the other side of the screen. Maddeningly for the operator, this meant that the vufoils had to go on to the light machine upside down and back to front. Sometimes things called flips were used: overlays hinged to one edge of the cardboard frame of the vufoil, which could be flipped over the original image to build up the detail. Obviously the two images needed to match up; you kept the flips in position by taping them to the cardboard. All a bit of a fiddle.

It was my job to put the vufoils on to illustrate Jimmy Glover's briefing. Every morning I would be in the cubby-hole, waiting for the moment when Jimmy would give me the cue for a new display: 'Now, can we please have the map of East Falkland,' that sort of thing. I couldn't see him and he couldn't see or hear me, but I could hear what was being said through a pair of headphones. And of course, in order to respond when Jimmy wanted a new display, I had to listen in to all their discussions. This was a remarkable learning experience for a young lieutenant colonel, to be able to listen to the Chiefs as they discussed the progress of the war. What struck me most forcefully was the political dimension to any big military decision. In 1982 the political pressure to get a move on was intense, not least because the American Secretary of State Alexander Haig was still shuttling backwards and forwards between London and Buenos Aires, trying to broker a diplomatic deal.

It was the role of the Chiefs to define the strategic parameters; the actual operation was commanded from

Fleet Headquarters at Northwood, in north-west London, and that's where the details were worked out. At least in theory, British military doctrine gives operational and tactical freedom of action to the in-theatre commanders. I say 'in theory', because the temptation to interfere from on high – to apply the so-called 'long-screwdriver' – can be difficult to resist, particularly for politicians. The Americans are much more 'top down', but we prefer to let the man on the spot get on with it.

However, the Chiefs of Staff were closely involved in the fate of the *General Belgrano*, the Argentinian cruiser that was eventually sunk by one of our torpedoes. This episode was especially fascinating to me, because the *Belgrano* was being tracked by HMS *Conqueror*, one of our nuclear-powered hunter-killer submarines, captained by Commander Christopher Wreford-Brown, whom I happened to know very well because we'd been students together at the National Defence College. The intelligence was that the only Argentinian aircraft carrier, the *Veinticinco de Mayo*, had sailed from its base halfway up Argentina, therefore north of the Falklands, and the *Belgrano* group of warships had set sail from the south. The obvious conclusion was that they were moving out in a pincer movement to attack the Task Force as it approached the Islands. The *Belgrano* was an old Second World War cruiser which the Argentinians had bought from the Americans, pretty outdated in many ways but nevertheless equipped with impressive firepower, capable of outgunning anything we had, while the *Veinticinco de Mayo* was assumed to be carrying Super Etendards armed with Exocet missiles. Merely by putting to sea, it considerably extended the range of the Argentinian aircraft on the mainland. This was a real issue, because the Falklands were at the limit of their range from their shore base, and as things turned out some aircraft had to ditch in the sea on the home run when they ran out of fuel.

After stalking the *Belgrano* for several days, Wreford-Brown received permission to attack. The effect of the *Belgrano*'s sinking was to bottle up the remainder of the Argentinian navy behind their 12-mile territorial waters line for the rest of the war for fear of being torpedoed, thus effectively removing the threat posed by the Argentinian surface navy. Later, some suggested that it had been wrong to send so many Argentinian sailors to their deaths when the *Belgrano* was sailing away from the Task Force. I've never understood this argument. If she had not been sunk at that point, and had re-emerged a week later to attack one of our aircraft carriers, that would have been an appalling outcome. The loss of life was very sad, but the *Belgrano* was an enemy warship, at sea, a perfectly legitimate military target. At the moment she was sunk she might well have been heading away from the Task Force, but a few minutes later she could have been heading back towards us: the question of her heading at the time of the attack was irrelevant.

Given the Royal Navy's command of the sea, the only practical means the Argentinians had of resupplying their garrison on the Falklands was by air. It was decided to deny the Argentinians this supply route by a bombing raid on the airfield at Port Stanley. One result of this was a very embarrassing moment for me.

The raid itself was an extraordinary feat of airmanship, given the huge distance between Port Stanley and the nearest available airfield at Ascension Island – over four thousand miles of featureless ocean. The operation involved two Vulcan bombers – one of which became unserviceable and had to return to Ascension – and fifteen Victor tankers, with seventeen air-to-air refuellings: the margin of error was minuscule. The point was not only to make holes in the runway, important though that was, but to demonstrate strategic reach: if we could hit Port Stanley, we could hit air bases on the Argentinian main-land, which would give the enemy something to think about. In those days, before the so-called 'smart bombs' which have GPS on the bomb itself, it wasn't easy to render a runway unusable by bombing; but the RAF pulled it off. The following morning the Chief of the Air Staff, who hadn't had a lot to say up until this point and who had been feeling a bit left out, was elated.

'Right,' said Jimmy Glover at his early morning briefing, 'I think we have some satellite photographs showing the damaged runway.'

My RAF colleague offered to produce the necessary visual aids in time for the 09.30 Chiefs' meeting.

At 09.29 all the Chiefs had assembled, but I still hadn't got the vufoil for the Port Stanley airport attack. I stood at the door of the projection room, somewhat concerned. I could hear Jimmy's forthcoming words in my head: 'If we can have the first vufoil now, please, Mike . . .'

Down the corridor came a sprinting wing commander. I saw with a sinking heart that there were several flips on the vufoil. As he handed it to me, all the flips fell off. I cursed, scooped them off the floor, dashed inside and put on the earphones just in time to hear Jimmy's dulcet tones: 'Now, Mike, if you could put on the base map, we'll build the picture up from there.'

I managed that all right, but then came the difficult part.

'Now, on the next flip you will see the bombing run and the distribution of the craters.'

Well, of course, this had to be upside down and back to front. I tried to get it right, but each time I did so it seemed to get worse and worse. I could hear the Chief of the Air Staff becoming irritable. 'No, no, it wasn't like that at all.' Everybody started to chip in with suggestions – 'Up a bit, no, down a bit' – while the Chief of Air Staff became crosser and crosser, because I'd ruined his big moment.

I apologized to Jimmy Glover afterwards. He gave a wry smile.

'Hmmm . . . Better not happen again, Mike, otherwise it's back to Camberley for you, my friend.'

He didn't mean it. At least, I don't think he did.

Goose Green was the most remarkable battle. I've now walked that bit of ground twice: the terrain is gently undulating grassland, with very little cover of any kind. Moreover, the sea on both sides of the isthmus restricts your room for manoeuvre. For infantry assaulting an enemy already dug in, this is about as difficult as it could possibly get. Nevertheless, 2 Para commenced their attack on prepared Argentinian positions shortly after 02.00 hours local time, and after more than a day's very hard fighting defeated, against the odds, a much larger number of defending Argentinians. As a Parachute Regiment officer and, moreover, as an officer who had not so long ago commanded a company in 2 Para, I was very proud of what they had achieved.

It was during the battle of Goose Green that my friend Lieutenant Colonel 'H' Jones, the commanding officer, was tragically killed at a critical moment. As in life, as in death: he was mortally wounded whilst leading from the front. The forensic analysis as to whether he should or should not have been so far forward is of course professionally absorbing; but it is entirely academic because H's total and passionate commitment to leading his soldiers made it impossible for him to be anywhere else. He was posthumously awarded the Victoria Cross. His second-in-command Major Chris Keeble took over and brought the battle to its stunningly successful conclusion. In the process he had there and then become a 'local' lieutenant colonel, just as Nick Ridley had done after David Blair was killed at Warrenpoint. This presented the Army with a dilemma. It was clear that 2 Para needed a new commanding officer. Chris Keeble had done everything that could be expected of a second-in-command under those desperate circumstances. But he had not yet been selected for command of a parachute battalion at the previous Command Board. The decision the Army had to take was whether to confirm Keeble as the new commanding officer, ignoring the fact that he had not yet been selected by the Command Board, or, hard though it might be for him, to put in someone else who had. This was discussed until late into the night by the then CGS and the Military Secretary. The Colonel Commandant of the Parachute Regiment also had his tribal say in the matter. These three Great Men had concluded that Chris Keeble should not be confirmed, and that an officer already selected for command should be sent out to relieve him. There were only two possible candidates: my close friend David Chaundler and myself.

Early the next morning David and I breakfasted together in the MOD's greasy-spoon café. We were pulling each other's legs, each making out that he would be the one to take over command of 2 Para. In fact there was never really any doubt about who would go. We'd already been given the nod that when the time came I'd be going to command 1 Para, and David would be going to 2 Para. He was H's designated successor: the only difference was that he would now be taking over much earlier than planned. As luck would have it, David had also been heavily involved in technical intelligence regarding the Argentinian Exocets.

David flew out to the Falklands three or four days later. The quickest way for him to get there was to parachute into the South Atlantic, as near as possible to one of the Task Force ships. They picked him up out of the water, and he assumed command shortly thereafter. Later, 2 Para fought their second major set-piece battle at Wireless Ridge (2 Para was the only battalion to fight two such battles). It wasn't easy to take over command of a battalion halfway through a campaign, and it was particularly difficult to have to say to Chris Keeble, 'Well done, Chris, but I'm in command now.'

Under the command of another good friend of mine, Lieutenant Colonel Hew Pike, 3 Para fought and won their fierce battle for Mount Longdon, one of the crucial final objectives leading to the capital, Port Stanley. Sergeant Ian McKay posthumously won the second VC of the campaign for his gallantry during this battle, and Hew was awarded the Distinguished Service Order for his leadership.

For me, missing out on the Falklands was frustrating, but I knew in my heart of hearts that there had been absolutely no reason to change what had already been decided.

*   *   *

I remember going out to RAF Brize Norton to meet the two Parachute Battalions when they came back from the war, a month or so after the Argentinian surrender on 15 June. It was a warm summer's day, and lots of people were there to greet them: the families, of course, but plenty of well-wishers too, including HRH the Prince of Wales in his capacity as Colonel in Chief. The two Battalions had taken a serious number of casualties, and the atmosphere was mixed: great pride in their military success, set against the sorrow for the forty soldiers who had not come home, and sympathy for their families.

Both 2 and 3 Para had come by sea from the Falklands to Ascension Island, and then flown on from Ascension by VC10. The aircraft landed and taxied to a halt in front of us. Steps were wheeled up. Then the doors opened, and the two commanding officers, David Chaundler and Hew Pike, appeared, pausing at the top of the steps. The crowd cheered their hearts out, with the Regimental Band playing 'Congratulations' as soldier after soldier came through the doors and down the steps. It had been only eighteen months since I'd left 2 Para, so of course it was a very poignant moment for me. I felt privileged to be able to congratulate Johnny Crosland, a superb fighting soldier who had been my successor as commander of B Company, and who would be awarded the Military Cross for his leadership in the Falklands. I was able to shake the hands of many of the soldiers with whom I had served.

The Falklands conflict had been proof of the competence, determination and resourcefulness of all three Services. The message was not lost on more formidable opponents than the Argentinians. At home, the effect of the war was to prevent cuts that were already in the pipeline. The Secretary of State, John Nott, was forced to backtrack.

This was the end of my secondment to the MOD. I said goodbye to Jimmy Glover and returned to the Staff College in the high summer of 1982. In his personal report on me Jimmy Glover commented that 'provided that he can temper his ambition and retain a sense of humility and humanity, he should go far, both in command and on the staff'. According to him I still had both, but I needed to ensure that I didn't lose either in the future. Perhaps I was a bit pushy; you have to be, if you're going to get on.

My father died later that year, at the comparatively young age of sixty-seven. It was a cruel blow to us all, but of course particularly to my mother and my sister, Lynne. There was a void in all our lives. Though I was frustrated to have missed out on the Falklands, my presence in England did mean that I was able to be on hand during the long illness leading up to his death. It was fortunate indeed that I was at the Staff College at the time, so close to where my parents lived. At his funeral, with his coffin covered by the Union flag, I gave the tribute to his memory.

I still had another eighteen months at the Staff College, but as time went on I became increasingly impatient to move on to what is to a large extent the pinnacle of any officer's ambition – so much so, that some officers choose to leave the Army once they've done it: to command a battalion.

The commanding officer is lord of all he surveys. 'The Colonel' is like the captain of a ship. Like a ship, the battalion is a discrete entity, and like the captain, the colonel is solely responsible for its performance and personnel. Within the battalion he has almost unlimited responsibility. By the same token, if anything goes wrong, it's the CO's fault.

I had known for some time that I was destined for 1 Para. At that time the Battalion had a unique role. In 1983 it became the British component of the Allied Command Europe Mobile Force (Land): NATO's 'fire brigade', a lightly armed multinational force intended to deploy in times of tension to the flanks of Europe as a demonstration of Allied resolve. In particular, NATO planners envisaged attacks through Scandinavia in the far north and towards Turkey in the south-east. Norway was particularly vulnerable, both because of its common border with Russia, and because it was a large country but sparsely populated. The Norwegians were therefore especially reliant on NATO reinforcement, part of which would be supplied by 1 Para. An attack might take place at any time of the year, so we had to be prepared whatever the weather conditions; we had to be ready to live and fight in a Norwegian winter. The conditions can be very harsh indeed. One morning while we were conducting an exercise the temperature suddenly dropped from a mild −10 degrees Celsius to −30. One moment we were operating under a clear blue sky, the next we were enveloped by a howling blizzard. This happened within just a few minutes, forcing us to abandon the exercise: peacetime safety conditions dictate that you stop training when the temperature reaches this low level. In such conditions the margin of survival gets very tight, as one's mental and physical reactions slow right down.

The Battalion spent the months before I was due to take command in March 1984 on specialist Arctic training in the area inland from Bergen, around the Hardanger Icecap, in preparation for a big NATO exercise. I was due to take over command immediately afterwards. As the time drew nearer I began to feel uneasy about the fact that they would have done this training and I would not. It seemed to me that this wasn't an ideal position for a new commanding officer to be in. So I left the Staff College three months early and engineered a deal to do five weeks' basic Arctic warfare training near Lillehammer with the Royal Marines, who also had a reinforcement role to Norway. I was the most senior person on the course by quite a long way, but since we were all students, rank was immaterial. I was starting at the bottom again.

The aim of this basic Arctic training was to teach you how to survive in such extreme conditions: how to move on cross-country skis and snow shoes, pulling sledges (known in Norwegian as 'pulks'); how to live in the Arctic in the open, with all your kit on your back, if need be. I learned how to dig a snow hole, which will keep you comparatively warm whatever it's doing outside. Another of the training exercises is designed to prepare you for the shock of falling through ice into the freezing water below. You cut a hole in the ice on a frozen lake and then jump in with your kit on. You must climb out of the water and then strip off your wet clothes as quickly as possible, even if you're out in the open, because if you don't, your wet clothes dramatically increase the risk of fatal heat loss. It was therefore vital to keep a change of dry clothes in your rucksack.

It's actually safer and more pleasant in the Arctic if the

temperature is below freezing. A thaw can be miserable, because everything starts to melt and you get wet – and then if the temperature drops again it can be dangerous, because your wet clothes will freeze.

Another risk comes when moving across deep powder snow: if you fall carrying a heavy pack, you will create a hole in the snow, and it is often very difficult to climb out again. You will probably lose one or both of your skis in the process, which makes it all the more difficult.

Map-reading in the Arctic is a problem, because the snow covers any recognizable features, altering their shape; you have to rely on reading the contours. Any flat bit of snow-covered ground is likely to be a lake. The Norwegians use an augur – a giant corkscrew – to check the thickness before venturing out on to the ice in vehicles.

Of course I came in for a bit of ribbing from my Army colleagues for training with the Navy – all par for the course. Though the Marines might refer to me as a 'bloody pongo',* the Navy nickname for a soldier, in fact they were very welcoming and hospitable, and they taught me the basic Arctic warfare skills. After I had finished the course I still had a little time left before joining 1 Para, so I volunteered to be an umpire on the big NATO exercise inside the Arctic Circle, learning all the time. The purpose of the exercise was to practise how NATO would defend north Norway; our defence plan envisaged a Warsaw Pact attack either through Sweden, or, if the Russians were minded to

---

* 'Anyone from the Army', according to the Royal Marines' website. The derivation of this term is apparently from the quip: 'Where the Army goes, the pong goes.'

observe Swedish neutrality, through the north Norwegian plateau of Finmark. Among those taking part in the exercise were a Canadian battalion, an Italian Alpini battalion and elements of the US Marine Corps, which also had a re-inforcement role in the Arctic. It was interesting to be in a position to observe such a multinational exercise at close hand. While serving in Berlin I had become aware of how different armies can be: each has its own style and its own culture, reflecting its national culture. The exercise also pro-vided a chance to learn more about operating in these Arctic conditions. In such extreme cold a lot of equipment needs particular care: helicopters, for example, need very rigorous de-icing drills, because ice on the rotor blades means loss of lift. By the end of my first winter I felt that I probably understood how to operate in this environment as well as any of the soldiers I was about to command. I was up to speed.

Naturally the Battalion was taking part in the exercise, and in fact my predecessor, Ian McLeod, handed over to me while we were still out there in Norway. It was an important moment, but there was nothing formal about it: just a handshake. We flew back to England a couple of days later.

The Battalion was based at Bulford, on the edge of Salisbury Plain. From Easter 1984 I lived in a large, com-fortable 1930s house set aside for the CO called Stephen's Mount. Though by this time I was divorced, there was no question of my living in the officers' mess like the other single officers. Whether the CO is married or single, he will almost invariably occupy the house designated for the purpose, because his subordinates would find it awkward to have him around in the mess all the time. That said, the officers' mess was for me, as for all the officers, a form of social club, a place to wind down and to mix informally.

And so it is for the sergeants' mess. It is often said that a good sergeants' mess makes a good unit; it is as important as a good officers' mess, and many would argue even more important. Warrant officers and senior NCOs have their own parallel hierarchy, presided over by the regimental sergeant major just as the colonel presides over the commissioned officers. The RSM is always a formidable figure, one who commands enormous respect from everybody, soldiers and officers alike. It is not unknown for junior officers to receive a bollocking from the regimental sergeant major, and it would be foolhardy indeed to answer back. No officer would dream of calling on the sergeants' mess without prior invitation. From time to time I would be invited to the sergeants' mess on some kind of occasion, usually for dinner. At Christmas each mess entertains the other to drinks, and the two messes compete with each other on the playing field. Cliché it may be, but without doubt the sergeants' mess is the backbone of the British Army.

It was while CO of 1 Para that I somehow acquired the nickname 'the Prince of Darkness', though why I have little idea. That said, I am fond of the odd glass of whisky and a cigar in the evening, while putting the world to rights. Only occasionally did people find it a strain to keep up.

I first met Sarah at a dinner party in the summer of 1984. She had been working for some years as a picture researcher for a publisher in London. I thought that she was a breath of fresh air, sparky and fun, and we fell for each other immediately, though it took a while for her to agree to marry me. As the daughter of a career soldier, an officer in the Royal Engineers, she perhaps had an inkling of what she might be taking on. We married the following May, in the little Saxon church across the road from Bulford Manor, the house which would become our home fifteen years later. David Chaundler was my best man, and my son Mark – then aged twelve and about to start at Wellington College – his deputy; my daughter Amanda was the only bridesmaid. Sarah has been a wonderful wife to me, and a true friend and loving stepmother to the children. By their early teens, both Amanda and Mark were at boarding school, but we saw as much of them as we possibly could.

I took the Battalion to Norway for ten weeks' training in each of the following two winters. We would rent youth hostels and camp sites, and then go out into the country for exercises lasting about a week. It was challenging and demanding and sometimes very tough, but it was also very enjoyable and I have great memories of that time. There's something very satisfying about pushing yourself hard. As well as the Battalion itself, we had very good back-up: support and recce helicopters, artillery, engineers, communications, logistics – my own train set, you might say. Everything is slower in the snow, with vehicles skidding around, and you need special oils for your machinery to function properly. The Norwegians used the German Leopard tank, with an electric heater in the sump to get the oil warm enough to start the engine; in the Second World War, fires were lit under the sump to achieve the same effect. We also used over-snow vehicles: small trucks with rubber tracks to make them grip on snow- or ice-covered ground. In fact, one of the quickest ways to get about in the Arctic is on skis: we could travel between 15 and 20 miles overnight. As light infantry we would practise digging in, using blocks of compacted snow as cover. If you pack it hard enough it becomes as solid as concrete. To combat an armoured attack we carried anti-tank weapons and practised laying minefields.

One special memory that lingers in my mind is of a night move on skis. The conditions were perfect: dry, with not a breath of wind. The temperature was just at that point when you hear a squeak as you dig the point of the ski pole into the snow, about −6 degrees Celsius. There was a bright moon, and not a cloud in the sky. The snow reflected the moonlight, so that you could see for miles. And then the Northern Lights commenced, lighting up the sky with flashes of colour, an unforgettable and ethereal display. 'And they're paying me for this,' I thought happily.

The Allied Mobile Force (Land) was also responsible for defending NATO's southern flank, and we carried out a couple of exercises in Turkey, in midsummer, which provided a good contrast to our Arctic training. We exercised in Turkish Thrace, west of Istanbul, on a defensive line near the Bulgarian border, the idea being to simulate defence against a possible Warsaw Pact attack from the north. The countryside around there is rolling grassland, quite similar to Salisbury Plain, except of course that it was much hotter. South-east Turkey, down towards the Syrian border, was another deployment option for the Force.

In 1985 a new General Secretary of the Communist Party, Mikhail Gorbachev, had taken power in the Soviet Union, and had immediately initiated a reform process, epitomized by his concepts of *glasnost* ('openness') and *perestroika* ('restructuring'). I watched these developments with great interest, and indeed they were much discussed within NATO. While they seemed positive, the feeling was that we should not let our guard down.

One curious deployment was guard duty outside what was then the massive US Air Force base at Greenham Common, near Newbury in Berkshire. Since 1981 there had been a rather messy 'peace camp' of protestors living outside the base in a jumble of tents, tarpaulins and plastic sheeting, as part of a much wider campaign against the stationing of so-called 'intermediate' nuclear missiles in Europe. There was widespread unease that these new weapons – 'cruise' missiles and Pershing II ballistic missiles – meant an end to the policy of 'Mutually Assured Destruction' which had restrained both sides since the 1950s; strategic thinkers began to discuss the possibility that the superpowers might fight a 'limited' nuclear war in Europe. There were large demonstrations against the introduction of these new missiles in many European capitals. The peace camp had been set up as part of this campaign, and had attracted special attention as it consisted exclusively of women. The protestors would regularly cut the perimeter wire and trespass on the base. The implied message was that women were resisting the male madness of war.

The Secretary of State for Defence, Michael Heseltine, was determined to face down the protests and to press ahead with the introduction of these missiles. For a while battalions were tasked in six-week rotation to go and guard the base against the threat posed by these ladies, and in due course 1 Para was given this onerous duty. There was something ludicrous about the deployment, giving rise to inevitable undignified stories, including the rumour that a soldier and one of the protestors had engaged in congress through the chain-link fence. I cannot comment on the veracity of this rumour.

In the summer of 1986 my two-and-a-half-year term as CO of 1 Para came to an end. 'Right, Colonel, that's it,' said my second-in-command: 'Time's up.' It's very much a matter of 'The King is dead; long live the King' when the moment comes. I was handing over to Lieutenant Colonel John Reith, whose career and mine would be increasingly intertwined as we moved up the Army ladder. As always when the CO leaves, there was a bit of light-hearted theatre to mark my departure: I was mounted on an armchair tied to the top of an over-snow vehicle, which was driven out of the barracks while the Battalion lined the route applauding. It was a poignant occasion for me, because this was the last time I would directly command troops on the ground, and my last experience of serving in the Regiment itself. From this time on I would continue to wear the red beret, but I would swap the regimental cap-badge for that of the General Staff. But it was time to leave the Battalion and move on.

On promotion to full colonel, I joined the Joint Services Defence College as the senior Army member of the Directing Staff. The new college was in effect Latimer Mark II. The MOD had closed Latimer in the mid-1980s as part of a cost-cutting exercise, but they wanted to keep the course going, as it was felt to be valuable to bring together mid-career officers from all three Services with a handful of civil servants. So they found some spare space at the Royal Naval College in Greenwich and established the Joint Services Defence College there as successor to the

National Defence College. More recently, the Joint Services Defence College and the three single-Service staff colleges have all been merged into the Joint Service Command and Staff College, housed in a new building at Shrivenham, outside Swindon; combined with the old Military College of Science, it became the Defence Academy of the United Kingdom.

As my time with the Battalion had drawn towards its end I had looked at the list of available appointments and seen that this post was coming up. It looked attractive, so I had applied and the Board had decided to appoint me. I was pleased to get this job because I like teaching, and I enjoyed the cut and thrust of vigorous debate that went with it. I was succeeding my friend David Chaundler, who had been able to give me the inside story beforehand.

My boss for the first part of my time at Greenwich was Air Vice-Marshal Barry Newton, a strong believer in the joint Service approach and in the College itself. He was followed by Rear-Admiral Guy Liardet, an erudite man with an irreverent sense of humour and great fun to work for. In one of my personal reports from this time he said of me: 'quite a character, tall, dark, dashing, with a lived-in face and a touch of flamboyance. I would expect to see a ruffianly component in the field.' What he meant by that I cannot imagine.

The old Royal Naval College building, once the home of naval pensioners and now the University of Greenwich, is magnificent. In particular, I had lunch most days and some splendid formal dinners in the Painted Hall, renowned as one of the finest dining halls in Europe. The ceiling, by Thornhill, depicts a series of allegorical and maritime themes. It was, of course, where Nelson had lain

Our wedding day, 4 May 1985: Sarah has her arm around my daughter Amanda, while my son Mark stands in front of me.

Jacko senior and Jacko junior. **Left**: *Mark's first parachute jump, with the Red Devils, summer 1989.* **Right**: *Mark's Sandhurst commissioning day, April 1995.*

Left: *As Commander of the 3rd Division, I had responsibility for organizing the British dimension of the events commemorating the fiftieth anniversary of D-Day. Towards the end of the day veterans paraded before HM The Queen on 'Gold' beach, where my father had led his squadron ashore half a century earlier. Unfortunately the programme ran late, and some of the veterans had difficulty with the incoming tide.*

Arctic training as commanding officer of 1 Para, mid-1980s. In this watercolour sketch for an oil painting by Peter Archer, I am the figure speaking on the radio, binoculars around my neck.

The 3rd Division contributed troops to the ill-fated
United Nations Protection Force (UNPROFOR) trying
to keep the peace in Bosnia. As their Divisional
Commander I visited them in Goradze, wearing a UN
beret. During this visit I encountered the Bosnian Serb
General Ratko Mladic, later indicted for war crimes.

Things did not settle down
immediately after Dayton. Here
I visit the scene of a firefight on
the 'confrontation line' between
two of the rival factions soon
after Dayton 'D-Day'. At the
centre of the picture are the two
Discoverys of my mobile HQ.

Left and main picture: *NATO's Implementation Force (IFOR) replaced the comparatively ineffective UNPROFOR after the Dayton Agreement. I commanded one of IFOR's three divisions in Bosnia. We had a lot of firepower at our disposal, as we demonstrated in this display to the local faction commanders.*

Bottom: *After a meeting of the Joint Implementation Committee (JIC), with the faction commanders in our sector. Some of these men had until very recently been fighting each other. On the left is Richard Dannatt, then commander of the 4th Armoured Brigade, who would eventually succeed me as Chief of the General Staff.*

Above: *Demonstration by relatives of Serb POWs at our Banja Luka HQ. Some of the placards are addressed to me personally.*

Right: *Al fresco lunch with General Dudakovic, one of the faction commanders, Bihac, spring 1996. Dudakovic is sitting opposite me, second from the right.*

NATO Secretary-General Javier Solana and Supreme Allied Commander, Europe, General George Joulwan visit our Banja Luka HQ. On the left is my Chief of Staff, Colonel Andrew Ritchie, and on the right is our artillery commander, Brigadier Freddie Viggers.

With my ADC, Captain Rory Gilbert, in a Lynx helicopter.

Left: *Major General Jackson lends a hand.*

Right: *In August 1996 I handed over command of the 3rd Division, and as usual there was a light-hearted ceremony to mark my departure. Here the Headquarters staff tow me in a knackered old car to a farewell lunch.*

With Prime Minister John Major in Banja Luka, early summer 1996. My son Tom (then aged six) commemorated the occasion in this picture.

Tuesday June 12th

This is my daddy in B

Bosnia with the prime

minister.

Tom had been looked after by Aida, a Bosnian au pair, whose parents Munir and Minka Pijailovic (right) were living in Sarajevo, then under siege by Bosnian Serb forces. We sent them food parcels, and in February 1995 I was able to meet them for the first time, during my visit to British forces serving with UNPROFOR. It was a moving occasion.

in state prior to his funeral. Each year the Hall saw a splendid Trafalgar Dinner, with all present singing sea shanties. Thornhill's painted ceiling includes many naked or semi-clad ladies on view. Apparently there are 293 boobs up there – though I never counted them myself.

We weren't at all averse to living in London. Sarah had lived and worked there for years before we married. For the first six months we lived in an apartment in the College, over the residence occupied by Admiral Sir John Fieldhouse, Commander in Chief of the Fleet during the Falklands War, and now First Sea Lord. We then bought a house in Clapham, and for two years I commuted every day to Greenwich. It was a very happy time. But all the time I was thinking: what next? The next potential step was brigade command, but the competition was very fierce. There were then fourteen manoeuvre brigades – i.e. all-arms deployable brigades – and three Northern Ireland brigades in the British Army. About half of them changed hands each year, but there were five or six officers eligible for each available brigade command. By the promotion rules, my opportunity would come in 1988, my second full year at Greenwich – but it didn't happen. It was a blow.

Maybe I wasn't doing as well as I had thought. By this time I was forty-four. I knew perfectly well that if you don't get promoted to brigadier by your late forties, further progression is unlikely. Brigadier rank is the first rung on the ladder to the 'stars', a major general having two stars, a lieutenant general three and a full general four. Up to this point everything had gone reasonably smoothly for me. Perhaps I'd got as far up as I was going to go. Either I was going to have to settle for rather less than I'd hoped – or maybe this was the signal to move on.

I started looking around, trying to make up my mind whether to stay within the Army or to try something else. I went to see a few headhunters and careers advisory people, without identifying anything in particular that seemed right for me. It was at this point that Colonel Johnny Hall telephoned and suggested we meet for a chat. Though I've come to know him well since, I didn't really know him then, and I was intrigued to know what he had in mind. Johnny was serving under the Military Secretary, the two-star general responsible for appointments and promotions. As such he was in the best possible position to evaluate my prospects within the Army. I told him of my disappointment and that I was thinking about leaving.

Johnny didn't seem surprised. Perhaps he'd already had word that I was looking around. 'Mike,' he said, after a pause, 'I've had a good look at your book and I've done some thinking.' He was referring to the book of confidential reports, written on every officer by his superiors at the end of each year. Johnny reminded me that it was unusual – though not unheard-of – to be selected for brigade command at forty-five years of age. He had my complete attention.

'My strong advice to you,' he continued, 'is to give it one more year.'

9

Onward and Upward

When Johnny Hall had recommended that I should give it another year, he had also hinted that I had a good chance of being selected for the following year's Higher Command and Staff Course. This was a new three-month course at the Staff College for a dozen or so high-flying officers, mostly colonels, but with a few sailors and airmen as well. Although it had been held for the first time only the previous year, in 1988, it was already clear that selection for this course could put you in the fast lane.

The rationale of the course was to bring fresh thinking to the whole question of 'operational art', i.e. the level between tactics – how to attack that hill and take it – and strategy, which draws in political and other considerations. Operational art is the business of how to fight a campaign within a given theatre, how to sequence events and battles, in order to further the overall strategy.

The new course was the brainchild of Nigel Bagnall, CGS in the late 1980s and known to everybody as 'Ginge' because of his shock of red hair. General Bagnall, who had commanded 1st British Corps in Germany and afterwards had been Commander in Chief of the British Army of the Rhine, had thought long and hard about how to fight the battle against the Warsaw Pact, if it ever came to that, and he had come to the conclusion that our planning was unimaginative. Our assumptions were attritional, expecting both sides to sit there and slug it out. Bagnall had studied the German Army's campaign on the Russian Front during the Second World War, and he had been enormously impressed by their extraordinary ability to manoeuvre and regroup very quickly. Bagnall wanted the British Army at theatre level to think more in terms of manoeuvre, striking paralysing blows by removing the enemy's freedom of action, creating doubt in the enemy's mind, rather as the Israeli General Sharon had done so effectively during the 1973 Yom Kippur War. More generally, Bagnall hoped to get the Army's younger commanders thinking out of the box.

Johnny Hall was no false prophet. Not long after our discussion, I found my name on the list for the next Higher Command and Staff Course, starting in January 1989. It was at least a partial recovery. On the course with me in that second year were thirteen other colonels, one Royal Navy captain, one RAF group captain, plus one American, one Australian, one German and one Frenchman. It was three months of concentrated intellectual study and hard work, but enormously stimulating and rewarding. Everyone had to write a thesis: I chose the topic of 'out-of-area operations' – i.e. out of the NATO area – and argued that these might become more relevant in the future. The course involved lectures, syndicate discussions, private study, map exercises and the so-called 'staff ride', a sequence of battlefield tours that took us to sites in Normandy, Verdun and the Ardennes, among others. We were fortunate that our tour was conducted by Professor Richard Holmes. There was a lot one could learn from studying these past campaigns on the ground. Though of course the tactics and technology were completely different, many of the principles remained the same.

As it happened, the Assistant Commandant of the Staff College then was Jeremy Mackenzie, now a brigadier, who had been second-in-command of the Queen's Own Highlanders at the time of Warrenpoint, and whom I had come to know quite well as a result. As you get nearer the top of the Army, the same names tend to crop up again and again. From being a huge, seemingly anonymous organization when you join, it becomes quite intimate as you reach the senior levels.

Having missed out in 1988, I was hoping to be selected for brigade command in 1989; of course, this was by no means certain, but I felt encouraged by that conversation with Johnny Hall. If I were to be selected, I would not take up the appointment until the end of the year, leaving a gap of almost nine months. So I decided to make the most of this opportunity. I applied for a Services Fellowship, under a similar arrangement to the one taken up by Frank Kitson almost twenty years before. This would give me the chance to undertake a study of a chosen area of defence in an academic environment.

Towards the end of the 1980s there was the sense that the old superpower stalemate that had governed strategic thinking since the Second World War might be opening up. Gorbachev had initiated a reform process inside the Soviet Union which was gathering its own momentum. An arms reduction process was taking place, with both sides scaling down their arsenals in a series of negotiated agreements. Meanwhile, the prospect of the Strategic Defense Initiative or SDI, Reagan's idea of a satellite-based defence system, was threatening the strategic balance. Suddenly, many of the assumptions that had governed our thinking for so long were in the melting-pot.

In the autumn of 1988 I had a number of discussions about what I might find interesting to study if I undertook one of these fellowships. Many of those I talked to argued that change was coming, and that the Army would have to adapt accordingly. I decided to look at the future of the British Army, in terms of size, organization and structure, should the Cold War become less cold. This topic would, incidentally, bring in my longstanding interest in the Soviet Union, with an opportunity to examine Gorbachev's changes. I submitted an outline for a thesis along these lines, and the powers that be gave it the thumbs-up.

Having decided to study the future of the British Army, the only question remaining was: where? Dr Gwyn Prins, a don at Emmanuel College, Cambridge, had been a frequent visiting lecturer at Greenwich, and I had come to know him quite well. He said he'd be delighted to act as my supervisor. As the idea of a few months at Cambridge also found favour with Mrs Jackson, I went up there to see if I could find a suitable college to take me on. Gwyn gave me lunch at Emmanuel, an obvious possibility. The experience was enough to make me realize that I might feel out of place among the undergraduates, who were much the same age as my own children. 'Gwyn,' I said, 'would you be very cross if I looked elsewhere?' The upshot was that I settled on Wolfson, the postgraduate college. There was a very varied collection of people studying there, not only from Britain but from abroad: members of the judiciary, senior policemen, journalists on scholarships, all sorts – company in which I would find kindred spirits.

I could have commuted to Cambridge from London, but both of us thought that this would be a wasted opportunity. Instead we rented a charming little two-up, two-down cottage in Eden Street, just off Parker's Piece, owned by a young don who was doing an exchange year at Berkeley, California. It was in a lovely part of Cambridge and very central. For us it was aptly named, a little paradise. We were beholden to nobody and it seemed like a golden interlude, time out of normal life. Sarah carried on with her freelance picture research, just as she had done before, taking the train to London when she needed to. Meanwhile we tried to make the most of our time in Cambridge. I set out to try to dine in every college: I didn't quite manage that, but I did dine in most of them.

It was a very happy time, an idyllic summer of bow ties, bicycles and boats . . . and a baby. Though we'd been married for four years, nothing had happened, so we'd investigated and established that there was a problem. By a happy coincidence it turned out that one of the pioneering fertility treatment clinics – Bourn Hall – was only just outside Cambridge. We thought, well, why not? And as luck would have it, it worked, first time. So that was another piece of serendipity. If I hadn't missed brigade command in 1988 I'd have missed both the

Higher Command and Staff Course and the Services Fellowship, but, far more important, Sarah might never have become pregnant.

Earlier in the summer I had received the news I'd been hoping for: I had been selected for brigade command, starting in November. And it was to be Northern Ireland once again: 39 Brigade, based in Belfast, the same brigade that Frank Kitson had commanded during my first tour.

I had to choose my moment to tell Sarah that we would be going there, as I knew that her heart would sink at the news.

We were sitting on the river bank when I broke it to her. I had punted us up the Cam, and eventually we stopped for one of our many picnics. I moored up and we spread out a blanket in the grass to sit on. It was then that I told her. She was pleased for me, but I could tell straight away that it had given her much to think about. We would be living behind the wire, and that concerned her rather more than security issues. She worried that it would be too much like living in a goldfish bowl. I remember urging her to keep an open mind.

We went over to Northern Ireland to have a look around, staying with the chap I'd be taking over from, Brigadier Bryan Dutton, in the house that we'd be living in. Sarah also had an opportunity to talk to Bryan's wife Angela and some of the other Army wives, as well as some civilian friends of Angela's. She realized that you could make a life outside the wire if you chose to do so. For such a free spirit – and a pregnant one, at that – being independent and having her own life was important. She's that sort of person.

* * *

The idea was that I should finish my thesis before we left Cambridge. I had done all the necessary research, but we were having such a good time that I am afraid I neglected my writing, leaving it until the last moment like a typical student; so October 1989 was spent with my head down, writing furiously. I finished just before we left Cambridge and went back to London to pack up the house. It had been a close-run thing.

In the end I think it helped my thesis that I came from the Parachute Regiment, and as a result my career hadn't been focused on what was then seen as the main theatre in central Europe. At various points in the past, people had recommended that I should spend some time with 1st British Corps in north-west Germany, deemed to be the centre of gravity of the Army, where the crucial conflict would take place, if it ever came to that. In fact, of course, the British Army of the Rhine was about to lose its strategic significance, once the Cold War came to an end. So my being on the periphery, so to speak, actually proved an advantage.

I used the Staff College facilities to print and bind about fifty copies of my thesis. A lot of people knew of the work I'd been doing and asked me to send them a copy. Then it started being passed around. A second edition had to be printed. I occasionally go back to it and it still holds up reasonably well in principle. I concluded that a shift in UK defence policy and planning was required to take account of the increasing likelihood of conflict outside the NATO area, with the Army being restructured to provide a more balanced and flexible force capable of undertaking such operations. I highlighted the need to 'expect the unexpected', which now seems rather prescient. However, I must confess to a howler. One of a set of assumptions which I listed in the thesis was that change to the status of Berlin was 'unlikely in the time-frame of the next ten years'. In fact the ink was barely dry on the page before the Berlin Wall came down. Within the year, the city was once again capital of a reunified Germany.

The television pictures of the Wall being demolished by jubilant protestors made electrifying viewing. Gorbachev had made it clear that the Soviet Union would not interfere. The inevitable conclusion was that the Cold War was over. This was a seismic shift, which would require NATO to rethink the strategic assumptions on which planning had been predicated. Within a few years the threat which had dominated our thinking since the end of the Second World War had virtually evaporated. Germany would cease to be the front line, becoming instead a parking lot for forces to be used elsewhere.

It was time for the move to Northern Ireland. We sold the house in Clapham, actually managing to complete the sale on the very day we were due to leave London. We stopped in the Lake District and had two nights' stay in the much-feted Sharrow Bay Hotel before continuing up to Stranraer. There we caught the ferry across the Irish Sea to Larne, where we were met for the first time by our close protection team – a reminder, for Sarah in particular, that for the next two years or so security issues were going to be ever present. And so my new life as a brigade commander began.

This was a challenging assignment. The Brigade which I was coming in to run was big: varying in size, it usually consisted of about ten battalions, including two resident battalions and a number of Ulster Defence Regiment (UDR) battalions, so well over five thousand soldiers overall. It was based at Thiepval Barracks in Lisburn, about 10 miles south of Belfast, a very big Army base which was also the home of Headquarters Northern Ireland. As Commander of 39 Infantry Brigade, I was one of three brigadiers reporting to Lieutenant General Sir John Waters, GOC in the Province. The other two brigades were based in Portadown and just outside Derry. As well as the Belfast area itself, I was responsible for the east of the Province, down to and including South Armagh. Halfway through the tour the Brigade shed quite a lot of this area in a complete boundary reorganization, done in order to harmonize the Army's areas of responsibility with those of the police. Ideally the two should work hand-in-hand at each level of command, but this had not been possible while there had been this mismatch, so the boundary change made complete sense.

In some ways not much had changed since my last tour in Northern Ireland. There was less mass rioting on the streets than there had been at the beginning of the Troubles, but the violence between the Protestant Loyalist and Catholic Republican communities was continuing, with appalling atrocities committed on both sides. There were also vicious feuds between factions within the terrorist groups, as the killers killed each other. The IRA had become technically much more proficient. They continued to target the Security Forces, within the Province and on the mainland, and also abroad, particularly British bases in Germany. A month before I left England they had killed eight members of a Royal Marine band in an explosion at a barracks in Kent. I had been in the Province only a few days when another terrorist incident provided a stark reminder of the risks. Mark and Amanda had flown out to join us for our first weekend in Lisburn – not least to choose their bedrooms and sort out their things. We were still unpacking when the phone rang: four soldiers from the Parachute Regiment had been killed by a road-side bomb, which had detonated as their Land Rover was driving past. This had happened by the racecourse outside Downpatrick in the southern part of County Down. 'I'm sorry,' I said to the family, 'but I've got to go.' Welcome back, Brigadier.

One reason why the IRA had taken its campaign to the mainland was that Security Force casualties in Northern Ireland had become routine: the death of another soldier, or of another policeman, no longer resonated with the British public as once it might have done. As if playing some kind of deadly poker game, they kept increasing the stakes in an attempt to force the Government to concede. Five years earlier they had bombed the Brighton hotel where many leading British politicians were staying during the Conservative Party Conference, almost killing Margaret Thatcher, the Prime Minister. In 1991, while I was still in Northern Ireland, they would launch a mortar attack on Downing Street, which, had it been more accurate, could have wiped out John Major's entire Cabinet.

The function of the 'Green Army' was the same as it had always been: so far as possible, to provide security, and maintain law and order in support of the police. Our aim was to stabilize the security situation and to contain the violence. One of the biggest challenges came during the Loyalists' summer marching season. These big set-piece marches were seen by the Nationalists as provocative triumphalism, and often sparked violent incidents. We did what we could to prevent the latter, essentially by flooding the areas with soldiers and policemen. We attempted to restrict the IRA's control of the Catholic areas by providing regular patrols, but it was next to impossible to prevent the intimidation that took place, enforced, for example, by the cruel practice of 'knee-capping' with electric drills. In a community too frightened to report such crimes to the legitimate authorities, the Army could only do so much to prevent hideous deeds taking place in the dark.

My job as Commander 39 Brigade did not involve me in manoeuvring troops on a day-to-day or hour-to-hour basis: that was for the battalion and company commanders. In Northern Ireland, as in any counter-insurgency campaign, each battalion has its own area, and within the battalion each company has its own patch. My job was to task, to coordinate, to encourage and to support the soldiers: to ensure that everybody knew what they were supposed to be doing, and that they had the resources they needed, including reinforcements if necessary. Each Friday morning at ten-thirty I held a meeting with my battalion commanders at Thiepval Barracks. The Brigade intelligence and operations staff would give a briefing, laying out the overall situation and the tactical picture; then each battalion commander would take a few minutes to summarize what had happened in the previous week. We would discuss future operations and logistical considerations. Sometimes there would be set-piece operations, for example during the marching season. Each

Wednesday morning at ten I would gather with the other brigade commanders for a similar meeting at HQ Northern Ireland. I was glad that the selection board had given me a Northern Ireland brigade: it suited me perfectly, not least as I was able to draw on a good deal of experience, both urban and rural, in the range of areas for which 39 Brigade was responsible. I was a round peg in a round hole.

One of my responsibilities was to liaise with the other Security Forces and the wider community. I held a weekly meeting at the Knock Police HQ in East Belfast with my RUC opposite number, the Assistant Chief Constable for Belfast. In the first few years of the Troubles, when the RUC had been in such a bad way after the events of autumn 1969, the Army had taken the lead; but by 1989 we were long into the era of so-called 'police primacy'. Major decisions about how to prosecute counter-terrorism operations lay with the RUC; the Army played a supporting role. Nearly all our patrols – at least in the urban areas – were accompanied by a policeman. The police handled the Protestant paramilitaries, so we were not routinely required to patrol the strongly Loyalist Shankhill Road. I also used to hold meetings with local church leaders, who acted as spokesmen for their communities. I saw quite a bit of the Secretary of State, Peter Brooke, a patrician but wise and kind figure who lived in great style in Hillsborough Castle, a fine country house which in the old days had been the home of the Governor General. On 9 November 1990 Brooke made a speech in which he stated that Britain had no 'selfish strategic or economic interest' in Northern Ireland and would accept Irish unification if that was the wish of the people of the Province. Many regard this speech as paving the way for political progress after decades of stalemate.

Intelligence was handled by the intelligence branch at Headquarters Northern Ireland, and I had my own intelligence section in the Brigade. We were both consumers and collectors of intelligence: we received general intelligence about the IRA's thinking and tactics, with the occasional nugget of information that had a specific operational usefulness, and we fed back intelligence gathered on the ground to HQ Northern Ireland. A soldier on patrol with a sharp pair of eyes may spot something, or he may have a chance conversation on the street which might be important. The drill is that after every patrol the soldiers have a very thorough debriefing with their local intelligence section at company level. But the Brigade was not directly involved in the covert war against the IRA. Special Branch had the lead in this area, and details of their activities were restricted on the 'need to know' principle. Suffice it to say that detailed, specific intelligence would almost certainly be exploited by non-Green Army forces.

Though the IRA had taken their campaign to the mainland in an attempt to force a political settlement, there continued to be a succession of shootings and bombings in the Province, with my soldiers taking casualties. For the man on the ground it was a constant strain, testing his judgement and his patience to the limit: one wrong move and he could be dead. Equally, the consequence of a split-second decision could be desperate. If you put soldiers into a very tense and difficult situation in which they are under constant threat from the civilians around them, tragic mistakes are bound to happen. Rules of engagement are carefully drafted to ensure soldiers act lawfully, and in the end soldiers' actions will be judged under the law. However well soldiers are trained in the rules of engagement, they always face the risk of allegations that they have overstepped the mark and committed an offence. It's essential that the process of law continues, even if the judgments are very hard. Soldiers must be subject to the law like every other citizen: once you begin to depart from that principle, you are lost. My time as CGS was to see a number of such incidents stemming from the Iraq campaign.

Sarah's concerns about living in a goldfish bowl were quickly allayed. People were extraordinarily welcoming, and very soon we found ourselves part of a lively and generous circle of military and local friends. Though we lived behind the wire, we certainly weren't confined there. On the contrary, Sarah became involved in a charity called Women Caring for the Children of Northern Ireland, through Judy Lindsay, who had already become a firm friend; the purpose of the charity was to bring together families from both sides of the sectarian divide. This enabled Sarah to visit some of the hard-line areas in Belfast, such as the Ardoyne and the Divis Flats, to assess new projects. It was an opportunity for her to see what sectarianism meant for women and children at grass-roots level. We would often go out in the evening, though as a brigade commander I had to have close protection all the time. There was a team of four Royal Military Police and they would work in pairs, so there would always be two minders wherever we went. Off duty, we would use our own car and they would follow in a car equipped with security devices. I remember one evening attending a packed concert, marking the bicentenary of Mozart's death, at St Ann's Cathedral, not far from one of our regular haunts, the pretty little opera house which had already been bombed two or three times by the IRA. The concert was about to resume after the interval – the conductor had his baton raised ready to start – when a loud explosion rocked the cathedral. Few, if any, of the audience batted an eyelid. Only car-alarms triggered by the bomb interrupted an exceptional evening's performance.

I left immediately and went to find that the IRA had bombed the opera house again. The façade had been damaged, with rubble spilling on to the street. Police and soldiers were already on site. Once the concert had ended, Sarah joined me there. We were both saddened to see the damage to this lovely building where we had passed many enjoyable evenings. I am glad to say that it was once again rebuilt to its former splendour.

Commanders at brigade level and above benefit from having an NCO appointed to their personal staff to help with military administration in the house, which is used not only for official entertaining but also as an alternative office and, indeed, conference centre from time to time. It is in this role that Corporal Pete Mawby of the Parachute Regiment entered our lives. He had just rejoined the Army after finding life outside not to his liking. Pete is a stocky figure, and, like me, he is follicly challenged. Always cheerful, ever staunch, he would remain with us for most of the next eighteen years or so, until he retired from the Army as Colour Sergeant Mawby MBE.

Sarah was well into her pregnancy when we arrived in

Northern Ireland. Though rather younger than me, she was comparatively senior to be having her first child. Medical advice was that she should have a series of tests at a precise time in her pregnancy – our first week in Northern Ireland – which could only be carried out at the Royal Victoria Hospital in West Belfast, a strongly Nationalist area. So Sarah became the subject of a major security operation: three armoured personnel carriers and an escort of sixteen policemen and soldiers escorted the new brigade commander's wife from Grosvenor Road police station to the hospital. I thought she would be horrified, but she was quite amused by the whole thing.

In due course our son Tom was born in the City Hospital, on the south side of the city. The obstetrician arranged, on security grounds, for Sarah to occupy an isolation ward, two nice big rooms all to herself. A day or two after Tom's birth, I found Sarah surrounded by girl-friends. It was a very obvious sign of how quickly she had found friends. Sarah has observed that it was a help to her for Tom to have been born so soon after we arrived in Northern Ireland, because people responded so immediately and warmly. They could see that she was looking for support, and they provided it.

On Friday 16 November 1990 I spent an hour or two with the Prime Minister. She'd flown over to Northern Ireland for the day, and spent the morning with the Secretary of State and other leading political figures. But in the afternoon, before leaving, she had decided to spend some time with the soldiers. That was typical of Mrs Thatcher. She liked soldiers and they liked her: she knew how to relate to them, and she liked to be photographed with them.

Maggie was a popular figure with the Army. The boys liked her no-nonsense style and they admired her courage. And of course after the Falklands her reputation in military circles was sky-high.

I escorted her about that cold, wet November afternoon. We had met before, when she had come to South Armagh after the Warrenpoint massacre. But she wasn't there to see me; she had come to talk to the soldiers. She knew instinctively how to convey to them that sense of, 'Yes, I'm with you, I'm supporting you, whatever you're doing.' And they greatly appreciated it.

I was a little surprised that she hadn't cancelled her visit, because she was in the middle of a political crisis. In a sense this had been precipitated by the IRA, who had murdered her old confidant Ian Gow back in the summer, triggering a by-election in which the Conservative Party had suffered a crushing defeat. But that result was an expression of a deeper discontent with her Government, which by now had been in power for more than a decade. Sir Geoffrey Howe, her former deputy and the last survivor in Government of the close associates who had been with her throughout, had resigned a fortnight earlier. Three days before she came to Belfast he had made a damaging speech in the House of Commons, and the next day Michael Heseltine announced his intention of standing against her for the leadership of the Party. The election would be decided by the ballots of the Parliamentary Party, which were scheduled to continue until one candidate achieved a clear majority. The first of these ballots was due to take place on the following Tuesday, while Mrs Thatcher was attending a meeting of the Conference on Security and Co-operation in Europe (CSCE) in Paris.

There had been indications that the vote would be very close, and it was by no means certain that she could hold off the challenge.

As it turned out, she did not. Two days later she would announce that she would not contest a second ballot, and a week later she resigned. But there were only two votes in it; had she gained those two votes she'd have won on the first ballot and been free to continue, to 'go on and on' as she had once put it. Many people believe that had she not gone to Paris but instead had remained in London to canvass more support, working the tea-rooms as the cry has it, she would have gained those extra two votes. Who knows what might then have happened? At the very least, she would have had more freedom to choose the time of her departure.

It seemed typical of her that despite all this pressure she carried on regardless, fulfilling her engagements with us and in Paris, scorning those who were trying to bring her down.

All this was in my mind as I accompanied Mrs Thatcher that November afternoon. We must have made an incongruous combination: I tall and lean, she much smaller, but indisputably the boss. It was getting dark at Thiepval Barracks when I walked with her along the concrete path towards the helipad. She was about to board a helicopter to fly to Aldergrove, the main Belfast airport, where she would take an RAF jet back to London, staying there only a day before flying on to Paris. It was wet and windy, and she was wearing a mackintosh and headscarf, carrying her trademark handbag.

As we walked together I passed on the pleasantries appropriate to the end of such a visit. 'Well, Prime

Minister, thank you very much, your visit has been much appreciated by the soldiers.'

We reached the pad where the helicopter was waiting, its rotors turning in the rain. I said goodbye, raising my voice to make myself heard. Then an impulse induced me to give voice to my thoughts:

'Prime Minister, are you sure you should be going to Paris at this time?'

She looked at me fiercely. 'Brigadier,' she said, in a tone that made it clear there should be no further discussion on the topic: 'You attend to your soldiering and I will attend to my politics.'

One of Mrs Thatcher's last acts as Prime Minister was to put pressure on the Americans to use force to expel the Iraqis from Kuwait, which they had invaded in August 1990. President George Bush Senior had been somewhat hesitant, but she had told him firmly that this was 'no time to go wobbly!' Early in 1991 the American-led Coalition launched Operation 'Desert Storm', which very quickly succeeded in driving the Iraqi Army out of Kuwait. I had been watching developments with a keen interest, of course. It was clear from the start that as a brigade commander in Northern Ireland I would not be involved. But though this was frustrating, I was very happy to be doing what I was doing. And although it must have been exciting to be there, and the Coalition troops won an over-whelming victory, it was all over very quickly – the one-hundred-hour war, as it has been described. No Parachute Regiment battalions were sent to the Gulf, though my old friend Rupert Smith served there, as the major general in command of the 1st (UK) Armoured

Division. He had been a Para, and so had his Chief of Staff, Colonel John Reith, to whom I had handed command of 1 Para five years before.

In November 1990, during the planning for 'Desert Storm', the Assistant Chief of the General Staff circulated a selection of comments made by MOD civil servants in the previous year, questioning the need for a significant 'out-of-area' (i.e. outside Europe) capability. Events had already shown these comments to be short-sighted. 'It is hard to conceive any set of circumstances where the UK would engage another country OOA . . . equipped with armour,' read one. 'It is difficult to see UK participation in a "larger Allied Force" in a conventional OOA conflict,' read another. A third was particularly scornful. 'Can one seriously imagine a British Prime Minister seeking the approval of the House of Commons for a military adventure . . . to embroil the UK in a Middle East war?' It would have been nice to think that those who had penned these comments felt embarrassed by them when only a few months later the UK went to war in the Middle East as a part of a coalition – but somehow I doubted it.

A few months after Operation 'Desert Storm' I was back in England, having a drink with my son Mark. He was still at Wellington, and I'd taken him out for the evening. We were chatting through his plans, because he was due to leave school that summer. Some years earlier, when he was only fourteen or fifteen, Mark had decided that he wanted to go into the Army, and had secured a place at Sandhurst with an Army scholarship. At first he thought of joining a cavalry regiment, but a 48-hour visit to Aldershot had convinced him he should opt for the Paras. He certainly wasn't influenced by me: if anything, the opposite was true, because Mark was something of a long-haired rebel in those days. Subsequently he had applied for and obtained an Army bursary to fund him through university. Before that he planned to take a gap year, travelling with Amanda. They had it all worked out. They were going to St Moritz in December, where he would act as one of the 'tower boys' on the Cresta Run, while Amanda was going to be in charge of the Club shop. Then in February they would go travelling in Africa. What he hadn't fixed is what he'd be doing between leaving school and December.

'Look, Mark,' I said, 'here's a thought.' I'd done a bit of homework. I explained how he could join what was then the Ulster Defence Regiment on a wonderfully Irish basis of 'full-time, part-time'. That is, one could join the part-timers and work full-time, the advantage being that one had to give only twenty-eight days' notice to leave. 'The thing is, Mark,' I said, 'it means that you can come out to Northern Ireland as soon as you leave school, and you can serve as long as you like, gain some experience, save some money and then go off travelling.'

Mark's eyes lit up. 'Absolutely bloody marvellous, Dad,' he said. 'Great idea.'

As soon as he left school a few months later Mark came out to join us in Northern Ireland. He had passed his driving test, so I bought him an ancient pale blue Mini from a farmer just down the road from the barracks, and he had an extended teenage party travelling around with some of his Northern Irish friends. Then he joined the UDR, and at the end of his basic training I was very proud to be able to present him with an award as 'Champion Recruit' for his intake. From the late summer until about

November, he served as a private soldier in the UDR. Mark was living with us at home in Lisburn, so it made sense for him to join the Lisburn-based UDR battalion. This was part of 39 Brigade, so theoretically he came under my command, though of course there were quite a few people in between.

The day came for his first early morning patrol, when he was due to report for duty at 05.00 hours. His UDR Centre was only a five-minute walk from our home. The night before I had tried to get him ready: 'Right, Mark, are you organized, have you got your kit ready, have you set your alarm clock?'

'Yes, Dad, all fixed, sorted.'

Knowing what teenagers are like about getting up, I set my own alarm for 04.30.

When I awoke the next morning I could hear some horrible music blaring from along the corridor. I found Mark still fast asleep. He had slept through his radio alarm – though how he could sleep with that racket blaring was a mystery. 'Come on,' I said, kicking him: 'You're going to be late.' Just then I heard the doorbell. I was wearing nothing but a towel around my waist, but of course I had to answer the door. It was a member of Mark's section, Lance Corporal Hagan, with two grinning soldiers in the background. 'Good morning, Sir,' he said, putting up a slightly exaggerated salute: 'Is that son of yours coming out to play?' It was bit cheeky, perhaps, but I was in no position to pull rank because my wretched son was late on parade – on his very first day!

Of course I was concerned about Mark, as any other father would be in the circumstances, but perhaps being in the firm myself made me a little less so, because I had a greater knowledge of the risks involved. The Army loses far more people to road traffic accidents, disease, heart attacks, and the kind of afflictions which might just as easily strike a civilian than it does to enemy action. It's a matter of perspective. Even in Northern Ireland, we weren't taking a lot of casualties at that point. We'd lost some people, and we'd had people wounded, but not in shocking numbers. So yes, of course, there was a fatherly concern, but I was also rather proud of him: proud that the boy had the bottle to do it. And the fact that Mark spent some time as a private soldier before he became an officer stood him in very good stead later. In my view that was a real feather in his cap.

I took a week's leave that winter, and we went out to St Moritz to join Mark and Amanda. Mark had been riding the Cresta Run. 'Come on, Dad,' he said. 'You've got to get down this; come on, if I can do it, you can do it.' He didn't leave me much choice! You lie flat on your chest on a special toboggan, with your face only six inches or so above the ice, and you must steer the toboggan precisely or you will come out of the run. Towards the finish, experts can reach a speed of 80 miles per hour. The main risk comes as you negotiate the 180-degree bend called 'Shuttlecock', round which the centrifugal forces are particularly powerful. If you do lose control and go over the edge, there's plenty of soft snow and straw to break your landing. The important thing is to hurl the toboggan away from you as you fly through the air, because otherwise you can be badly cut up by its razor-sharp runners. Coming out does qualify you to wear the Shuttlecock tie – and that very much includes me!

It's an addictive experience and I've been doing it off

and on ever since. One year Mark and I entered the Cresta 'Fathers and Sons' event as a team. Sadly, this was a little too ambitious on my part, and we took the wooden spoon. For my last five years in the Army I was President of Army Winter Sports, which had the incidental bonus of a week in the Alps every year.

By this time I'd fulfilled my allotted two years as commander of 39 Brigade, but I stayed on another few months because my designated successor, Alistair Irwin, had been selected for the Higher Command and Staff Course. I was very happy to do so because I enjoyed the job so much. Around Easter 1992 we finally said farewell to Northern Ireland. We left with some sadness, because we had come to feel so much part of the place and made such good friends there. I was awarded the CBE, then customarily conferred on Northern Ireland brigade commanders.

We didn't know it then, but in fact an end to the Troubles in Northern Ireland was in sight. On the ground the security situation remained much as it was, but politically things were on the move. In December 1993, a 'Joint Declaration on Peace' (more commonly known as the Downing Street Declaration) was issued by the British and Irish governments. The following summer the IRA announced a ceasefire. In 1998, encouraged by President Clinton, the two governments and the political parties in Northern Ireland reached what became known as the 'Good Friday Agreement', renouncing violence and setting out a programme for political progress in the Province. The agreement was subsequently accepted by large majorities in referenda of the population on both sides of the border. I remember the cruel but accurate comment:

'The Prods have won but they're too stupid to understand it.'

For a long time the IRA had derived succour from the Irish political constituency within the United States. But the terrorist attacks on 11 September 2001 transformed American attitudes and meant that the IRA was no longer welcome in Washington. The IRA began decommissioning its weapons, a process said to have been concluded in 2005. In that same year the British and Irish governments issued another joint declaration. This contained a security annex laying out an end-state for the British Armed Forces within the Province. And in due course, at midnight on 31 July 2007, the Armed Forces did indeed go non-operational. This provided considerable relief to our resources; for much of the previous forty years, there had been up to twenty thousand soldiers stationed in Northern Ireland, one-fifth of our total manpower. There were two important caveats to this decision: the police could call on military assistance to help contain widespread public disorder; and the Army would continue to provide technical assistance, in particular with EOD (explosive ordnance disposal). Going non-operational required a major planning effort. We were particularly concerned to retain the specialist capabilities, skills and equipment accumulated during the long struggle against the terrorist threat to the Province.

While still in Northern Ireland I was, of course, wondering what I should do next. In the normal course of events I would have been expected to do a staff job as a brigadier before being considered for promotion. As the end of my tour in Northern Ireland drew nearer I scanned what's known as the 'dream sheet', the list of upcoming jobs circulated by the personnel people at the MOD. One job caught my eye: Director of Public Relations (Army). I thought this looked particularly interesting. It would mean managing the interface between the Army and the media, spending a lot of time talking to the hacks, particularly of course the defence correspondents, largely off the record – 'Let me explain the thinking behind this' – and also negotiating with ministers as to when senior officers in prominent positions like the CGS or GOC Northern Ireland should give interviews.

Nowadays every senior officer undertakes media training. During any big exercise the commanders will be interviewed by professional journalists, and these interviews will be filmed and evaluated later. They will also be played back to the interviewees, the evaluators pointing out when they seemed evasive or shifty, drawing attention to body language and all those other unintended signals. Nevertheless, some officers remain uneasy with the media, and some even resent the press, concerned that they're going to get shafted. While I don't share these concerns, I accept that the media can be irritating. But they are an essential part of modern life, and soldiers need to adapt to this like everybody else. It is very important that senior military leaders understand how to work with the media, not least because they represent a significant additional dimension in any operational theatre.

So the job as DPR (Army) was right up my street. It was London-based, and both Sarah and I liked the idea of coming back to London for a while. I put in for the job, and was appointed. But then something rather unusual happened. I can only surmise, knowing what I do of the system, that somebody dropped out, or decided to leave the Army unexpectedly, so that the dominoes started falling. A two-star appointment in the MOD, Director General of Organization and Territorial Army, suddenly became vacant. It appeared that the Army couldn't find an existing major general to do the job, so they said: Right, some lucky brigadier is going to get promoted. And that lucky brigadier was me.

It was a bitter-sweet feeling: I didn't get the job I would have relished, but I did get promotion after only one job at one-star level, which was very unusual in peacetime.

Almost as soon as this had been settled, everything changed again. There was yet another reorganization in the MOD, and the post to which I had been appointed disappeared. So then the Army offered me another two-star job within the Ministry, as Director General Personal Services. It was a job that covered an eclectic mixture of personnel functions in the Army: discipline and legal matters, welfare, pay and allowances, conditions of service and ceremonial, including Army bands. I reported to the Adjutant General, the Army Board member responsible for personnel matters. The Army Board, which has five members, is the Cabinet of the Army, chaired by the CGS.

We set ourselves up in London, renting a light and airy house in Putney belonging to an artist and his wife. Sarah resumed her freelance career, hiring an au pair to help look after Tom, who was now walking and causing mayhem in the way that active toddlers do. Working regular hours and wearing civilian clothes, I commuted every day to an MOD outpost called Empress State Building, a stone's throw from Earls Court tube station. I did feel a bit of a military bureaucrat, but I told myself that these functions have to be fulfilled: somebody needs to set disciplinary policy; somebody needs to engage the Armed Forces Pay Review Body over pay and allowances. These functions are necessary to make the Army work well. And the directorate mattered to people. The welfare side was particularly important, including welfare arrangements for veterans, liaison with the various Armed Forces charitable bodies, and so on. It was a broad portfolio and an interesting one. The job also made me consider much more deeply social issues that I hadn't really focused on before, and in that sense it widened my horizons. And in the process one learned rather more about the byzantine workings of the Ministry of Defence.

At this time there were big changes happening in defence as a result of the end of the Cold War. The Government was anxious to cash in its so-called 'peace dividend'. There was much debate about the future shape and size of the Armed Forces – not a debate in which I was directly involved, but one I watched very carefully. A series of policy documents followed one after another: especially significant were *Options for Change* (1990) and *Front Line First* (1994). There were three particular economies in the personnel area which the MOD wanted to impose on us, and which I remember discussing with my boss, the then AG, David Ramsbotham (lately HM Inspector of Prisons), a man I admire a great deal. I remember a group of us sitting around David's table and saying, 'AG, we can't sign up to these.' They wanted to get rid of high-street recruiting offices, which have since had to be reinstituted. Then they wanted to abolish the junior entry, the scheme that allowed youngsters to join the Army at sixteen under somewhat different and more liberal terms of service. That had always been very successful. We pleaded with them not to jettison the scheme, but they went ahead and did it anyway, and to some extent we've had to reintroduce it subsequently. The third decision was to downsize the medical services very significantly, doing away with military hospitals, and so depending much more heavily on the National Health Service to treat military patients. This was truly a dreadful decision, and one that we have not been able to get rescinded, because the investment required is too great. But there remains a great deal of concern about the way wounded soldiers are cared for when they come back from the field. While I applaud the quality of clinical care, not all NHS staff really understand the psychology of the soldier. The psychological benefit of wounded soldiers being together in the same ward and being treated by military medical staff has been woefully underestimated.

I chaired the Board which considered written appeals on behalf of those who had been turned down for the Long Service and Good Conduct Medal. This was a 'soldier-only' award (on the Victorian basis that officers are assumed to be of good conduct), given for fifteen years' service and an unblemished conduct sheet. Many of the candidates were very great men indeed – regimental and company sergeant majors, for example. Our job was to hear appeals from those who had been turned down for the award on account of some unfortunate entry in their record. The morning of the Appeals Board was always one to look forward to in an otherwise humdrum routine. A typical charge would be for 'conduct to the prejudice of good order and military discipline contrary to Section 69 of the Army Act, in that he discharged a fire extinguisher at the guard commander' – or whatever. The appeals tended to follow familiar lines and often elicited wry smiles: 'I was a young soldier. I fell into bad company. This conduct was totally out of character . . .'

One policy in which I was deeply involved was the introduction of compulsory drug testing, to which everybody in the Army is now subject on a random basis, just as many are in sports and other professions. This measure was introduced in response to the growing drugs problem in society as a whole. We felt that we had to draw a line in the sand on this issue. Of course it's particularly important that soldiers should be drug-free because, for example, you don't want somebody on a 'high' when he's carrying a weapon. There were practical concerns: the cost of running the programme, and the fact that inevitably we would lose soldiers because some would be discharged after failing drug tests. But we felt it was something that we had to do. Random testing applies right throughout the Army, at every level. I have peed into a bottle several times myself. I call this 'leading from the front'.

There were a number of policy issues that arose as a result of the presence of women in the Army, especially of course the vexed issue of whether women should serve in the front line. The essential question is not one of ability or discrimination, but whether the presence of women in close-quarter battle is detrimental to operational effectiveness. The evidence suggests that it is. The issue came to a head in Geoff Hoon's time as Secretary of State for Defence; like so many others, I was much relieved when he accepted the unequivocal advice of the Chiefs of Staff that women should not serve in tanks, in the infantry, in submarines or in the RAF Regiment, the Air Force's own infantry force. There are also issues that arise when men and women are serving alongside each other, of privacy for example. Sexual relations can cause serious problems if the two people involved both live within the same tight little community, particularly if one or both are married. Human beings being what they are, and human nature being what it is, soldiers do have extra-marital affairs, but they can have very corrosive effects – particularly if you get an officer sleeping with a soldier's wife, or vice versa. (It is just as damaging when a woman in the Army sleeps with another female soldier's husband.) The problem is not one of morality per se, but rather of the effect of such conduct on the operational effectiveness of the unit.

The Armed Services were still intolerant of homo-sexuality in the early 1990s, and there was genuine concern about the effects of taking a more liberal approach. But change here did happen – and that concern proved groundless. Exactly the same rules now apply to homosexual behaviour as to heterosexual: sexual behaviour, whatever it may be, must not impinge on operational effectiveness, for example by undermining the chain of command.

Bullying was a concern throughout my time, but in the 1990s it did not seem to be the serious problem it became later. The subsequent deaths at the Deepcut recruit train-ing centre have led some commentators to question whether there is a culture of bullying within the Army. I do not believe this to be true. While the death of any young person is a tragedy, such incidents must be con-sidered in the context of the tens of thousands of young soldiers who have passed through recruit training, and the fact that, sadly, in any cross-section of the population there is bound to be a proportion of suicides. The Army does not tolerate bullying at any time, and if it is detected, the perpetrators can expect to be prosecuted.

The job as DG Personal Services involved quite a lot of travelling, visiting Army bases to address gatherings of officers and soldiers. My opening gambit would be to say, 'You probably don't know what I do, but let me explain. After bullets, bombs and bangs in Belfast, now it's everything else beginning with "b" – bands, belts, berets, badges, buttons, banners, bars (medals), bars (booze), burglary, bullying, barbiturates, bosoms, babies, bonking and buggery.'

That was always good for a cheap laugh, just to warm up the audience.

Some time during the summer of 1993 I had another of those father–son conversations with Mark. After the winter of 1991–2 in St Moritz, he and Amanda had spent the next six months or so in Africa together. I remember going to meet them at Heathrow off a flight from Nairobi the following summer. Two scruffy urchins came through the gate, still dusty from the African bush and bursting with stories of their adventures. That autumn Mark went off to Southampton University to read archaeology and anthropology, while Amanda found herself a job in an advertising agency in London and moved into a flat. A year later, Mark and I met for a drink.

'Dad, this studying is not me,' he said. 'I want to get soldiering.'

I understood how he felt, though I was a bit disappointed that he wasn't going to see his university course through to the end.

'Look, Mark,' I said to him, 'whatever you end up doing – whether you stay in the Army or leave in due course – it'll be useful to have a degree.' But Mark was adamant that he'd had enough of university. I sensed that he'd made his decision, and I didn't argue any further. The upshot was that he took up early the place at Sandhurst which would otherwise have been his after he had completed his university course. I remember meeting him there at the back of Old College on his first day, when he rolled up with his sister Amanda in his old soft-top Land Rover. It is almost a tradition that every cadet brings his own ironing-board. My great friend Hew Pike had insisted on carrying his son William's ironing-board two years before, so I did the same – despite the hideous floral cover.

As my two years in the MOD went by, I was thinking, as ever, about what might come next. What I really wanted was to command one of the so-called 'manoeuvre divisions', which is the job that any major general would give his eye teeth for. But there were only two possibilities, the 3rd Division in Britain or the 1st Division in Germany. One day I picked up the telephone to find the CGS on the line.

'I want you to go and command the 3rd Division,' he said. 'Is that OK with you?' It most certainly was.

It was a great thrill to be chosen to go and command the great 3rd Division, which has a long and distinguished history. Formed early in the nineteenth century by one of my great heroes, the Duke of Wellington, it had fought in the Peninsula and at Waterloo. During the bitter fighting of the First World War it had earned the nickname the 'Iron Division'. At the outset of the Second World War it had been commanded by Montgomery, and he had chosen the sign of three black triangles surrounding an inverted red triangle to represent the Division, composed as it was of three infantry brigades, each of three battalions. After being evacuated at Dunkirk, the Division had been the first British formation to return to France, landing at 'Sword' beach on D-Day. The divisional motto is 'Drive On', though typically the soldiers have adapted this to FIDO, short for 'Fuck It, Drive On'.

I left the MOD early in 1994, after saying my goodbyes to all the various aspects of the Army for which I'd been responsible. Brigadier Charles Bond and his staff at the Kneller Hall School of Army Music came up with this adaptation of Gilbert and Sullivan which is now framed and displayed on the wall of the loo at home (along with much other bog-ography, as Sarah calls it).

He's been the ve-ry mod-el of a mod-ern Maj-or Ge-ne-ral,
He came from bangs and bul-lets in the bogs sur-round-ing
    Cross-ma-glen,
To con-cen-trate on bonk-ing, bands and bull-ies armed
    with just his pen,
He's coped with drugs, a-llowing-an-ces and certain matters
    mu-si-cal,
He's chaired the odd com-mit-tee on tend-en-cies
    be-hav-iou-ral,
He's nailed some jell-ies to the wall but not been too
    pon-tif-i-cal,
With style and guile he's done it all but now be-comes
    di-vis-ion-al,
Thank God – he's been the mo-del of a mod-ern Ma-jor
    Gen-er-al.

I had managed to engineer a bit of extra leave before taking up my new command, and as this fell in the dreary winter months of February and March and I was about to turn fifty, Sarah and I decided to celebrate by taking a holiday in Zimbabwe. We took Tom, now almost four, and Amanda and Mark joined us for a fortnight. It was the most wonderful six weeks, and we fell in love with the country and its people. The recovery from the civil war that had ended only a dozen years before seemed miraculous. It was a happy, vibrant place – a far cry from the tragedy of Mugabe's Zimbabwe today.

While in Zimbabwe I was especially keen to see the marshalling yards of Bulawayo. There's a bit of me that will always be a small boy when it comes to trains. I have a deal with my eldest grandson Casper that when he gets his own model railway, grandpa may give him a hand. Like many of my generation I feel nostalgic for the age of steam, which ended in Britain while I was still young.

Anyone who knows anything at all about trains knows that the railways of Africa were the most extraordinary engineering achievements. I had done some reading in advance of flying out there, and I knew that if the golden age of the railways had in any sense entered your soul, you had to see these marshalling yards of Bulawayo. So we went there one morning – and there they were, these huge black machines, hissing and puffing and emitting steam from every orifice. We stood about twenty yards from one particular pair of vast back-to-back engines, with eight wheels either side, front and back. I took photographs while young Tom clutched Sarah's hand, a little overwhelmed by the heat and the noise. Suddenly the engine-driver, a middle-aged black man wearing overalls and a red and white polka-dot neckerchief, leaned out from the footplate and gave me a friendly wave. I waved back – and then he beckoned to me. I wasn't sure what he meant, and the din of the engine precluded conversation, so I pointed at my chest in a gesture of enquiry. He beckoned harder, so I walked across until I was standing beside the engine and we could talk without shouting. Tom stayed behind with Sarah. I said hello to the driver, whose name was Moses. I suppose we were about the same vintage. We started chatting.

'What are you doing here?' he asked.

'I've come to see these machines,' I said. 'I think they're just amazing.'

'Humph. Well, they're very old-fashioned,' Moses replied loftily; 'I would prefer a diesel.'

And then he asked: 'Do you want to come up?'

'Do I want to do *what*?' I said, not quite believing my ears.

So up I climbed on to the footplate, and Moses and his fireman Aloysius showed me around his cab. Both were glistening with sweat: the heat of the boiler hit me as I climbed in.

'Maybe you would like to drive it?' Moses asked, sipping his tea out of a chipped enamel mug.

'You're not serious?' I said, but he nodded.

'Yes, I am. Steam's up, and we're ready to go.' He told me what to do: pull this, watch that, shove the other – and the mighty engine began to lumber forward, slowly at first. Aloysius shovelled coal into the boiler. I held up five fingers to indicate to Sarah that I would be back in as many minutes, and she nodded. Tom looked a little apprehensive as we moved off, but I smiled at him reassuringly from the footplate.

We steamed three or four miles down the track and then back again. It was pretty gentle stuff, never travelling at more than about twenty miles an hour at most, but I felt a sense of the massive strength of this great beast. At the end I thanked Moses and we shook hands, before I climbed down from the footplate and walked back to Sarah and a relieved Tom, still not quite believing what had happened.

10

A Modern Major General

I came back to England after that relaxing holiday in Africa full of enthusiasm for the job that lay ahead. We packed up the house in Putney, which was a bit of a wrench, and drove down the A303 to begin our new life on Salisbury Plain. Our home for the next few years would be Clive House in Tidworth, a substantial pre-war villa in a leafy setting set aside for the divisional commander. My headquarters were nearby at Picton Barracks in Bulford, where 1 Para had been stationed, and where I had been living when I met Sarah, so the area had good memories for us both.

I took over the 3rd Division in April 1994 from my long-standing Parachute Regiment friend Hew Pike, one of Tom's godfathers. The Division was then about twenty thousand strong, consisting of three brigades: the 1st Mechanized Brigade, stationed in and around Salisbury Plain, mainly at Tidworth; the Airborne Brigade, 5 Airborne Brigade as it was then, in Aldershot, less than an hour's drive east; and the 19th Mechanized Brigade, then based at Colchester, on the far side of London. With me in my Bulford HQ were my staff and the Division's signal regiment.

Very soon after I arrived, the Divisional HQ had the task of running the British dimension of the fiftieth anniversary of the D-Day landings in Normandy. With heads of state and other political leaders in attendance, there was no room for error. Nevertheless the stars of the show were the veterans, many of them by then in their seventies or even eighties. I had the privilege of meeting some of these old boys and spending some time in their company. This was a very moving occasion; there was a strong sense that this was the final such commemoration for many of them. I often thought of my father during that emotional day, wishing that he had lived long enough to share it with me. I felt proud that he had been one of these brave men.

The scheduled climax of the British celebrations was to be a parade on 'Gold' beach at Arromanches, to be reviewed by Her Majesty The Queen. Thousands of veterans were lined up on the beach waiting for her, the concrete hulks of the Mulberry harbour still protruding above the waves behind them. Several landing craft lay beached with their ramps down as they had been half a century earlier. The Queen's review of the veterans was programmed as the last event of the day, at 17.00 hours. Unfortunately the timing was very tight against the incoming tide, and earlier delays to the programme meant that The Queen arrived a few minutes late. I fear that the veterans on the far side of the hollow square got a bit damp – as no doubt many of them had fifty years before. After The Queen had reviewed the parade, the veterans

FORMER YUGOSLAVIA - Showing the Republics and the autonomous district of Kosovo and the autonomous province of Vojvodina.

AUSTRIA

HUNGARY

LJUBLJANA
SLOVENIA
o ZAGREB
CROATIA

ROMANIA

Vojvodina
o Novi Sad

45°

BOSNIA
AND
HERZEGOVINA
SARAJEVO °

BELGRADE

SERBIA

45°

A d r i a t i c   S e a

MONTENEGRO
Podgorica °

Pristina o
Kosovo

BULGARIA

o SKOPJE

ITALY

TIRANA o

MACEDONIA

ALBANIA

Thessaloniki
o

40°

GREECE

40°

I o n i a n
S e a

ATHENS
o

International border
Republic border
Autonomous district/province border
Former Yugoslavia

0   100
miles

15°

20°

15°

20°

marched past, singing wartime songs. On the beach, there was hardly a dry eye – and plenty of wet feet.

One of the veterans dropped stone-dead just after The Queen had passed him. After attempts to resuscitate him failed, he was stretchered off – to the applause of his old comrades. Later, one said to me, 'What a way to go: just been reviewed by The Queen, among your mates, straight to Valhalla.'

As the months passed my attention was increasingly focused on the deteriorating situation in Bosnia. Serbs, Croats and Bosnian Muslims (known as 'Bosniacs') had been fighting each other since 1992, when the former Yugoslav republics of Bosnia and Macedonia had declared their independence from Yugoslavia, following the successful secession of Slovenia and Croatia. Armies of these three ethnic factions – the first two aided by their 'parent' countries, Serbia and Croatia – were involved in a bloody struggle for control of territory. The Bosnian Serb army had occupied parts of Croatia: the Krajina (frontier) region in the west, and the area around Vukovar in the east, bordering Serbia itself. The consequent civilian suffering was causing increasing concern throughout Europe and in the wider world, particularly in America.

Yugoslavia had been created in 1918, as a union of south Slavs in territories formerly part of either the Austrian or the Ottoman empire. Though designated as a union of Serbs, Croats and Slovenians, Yugoslavia incorporated other national groups, including Bosnian and Kosovar Muslims, in an ethnic patchwork across the territories of the former empires. Initially a kingdom, it had become a Communist state after the Second World

BOSNIA AND HERZEGOVINA 1996 (Post-Dayton)

CROATIA

Vojvodina

Prijedor

Bihac

Banja Luka

Republika Srpska

Tuzla

SERBIA

'The Anvil'

BOSNIA
AND
HERZEGOVINA

Srebrenica

Gornji Vakuf

SARAJEVO

Pale

Gorazde

Split

Mostar

Republika
Srpska

Adriatic Sea

MONTENEGRO

- - - - - Inter-Entity Boundary line

0   50
miles

War, under the leadership of Josip Broz Tito, who had led the resistance to the Nazi occupation. Tito created what was in many ways an ideal multinational state, made up of semi-autonomous republics. Though Communist, Tito's Yugoslavia refused to join the Warsaw Pact, and maintained a neutral position during the Cold War. But after Tito's death in 1980 ethnic tensions increased, whipped up by nationalist politicians. The rise to power of Serbian President Slobodan Milosevic precipitated the break-up of Yugoslavia.

The disintegration of the Yugoslav state presented a challenge to national governments and international institutions. The Clinton Administration in the United States was extremely reluctant to become embroiled in the Balkans; and without American involvement, neither NATO nor the UN seemed capable of effective action. At the outset of the crisis the President of the Council of the European Union, Jacques Poos, then Foreign Minister of Luxembourg, had declared that 'the hour of Europe has dawned' – but in reality, the response of the European nations had been divided and ineffectual.

Bosnia and Herzegovina (to give it its full name) is a small country, approximately the same size as the Republic of Ireland, with a similar-sized population but a very different geography – varying from a high mountainous interior, which can be very cold indeed in winter, to a flat plain in the north and a very small length of coastline on the Adriatic Sea, where the climate remains temperate throughout the year. Its pepperpot ethnic distribution meant that there were isolated ethnic enclaves in many parts of the country.

Units of the 3rd Division were already deployed in

Bosnia, serving with UNPROFOR, the United Nations Protection Force. Sadly, UNPROFOR had a very limited mandate, so although it was able to provide a certain amount of humanitarian aid, it was unable to provide real security for the civilian population. UNPROFOR was asked to police so-called 'safe areas', but this often led to the troops themselves being threatened. Sarajevo, the capital of Bosnia, was under siege from Bosnian Serbs, who regularly attacked anyone trying to negotiate the only route into the city, the road across Mount Igman, which became known as 'the most dangerous road in Europe'. The people of Sarajevo suffered severe shortages of food and other essential supplies, while being subject to regular sniper fire, as well as occasional shelling and mortar attack.

As a family we felt a personal connection with Bosnia, because for the past year or so a Bosnian Muslim girl had been living with us in London as an au pair, looking after young Tom. Aida's elderly parents lived in an apartment in the medieval part of Sarajevo, and she was naturally very anxious about their welfare. Day after day the television was showing images from Sarajevo of sniper victims, ruined buildings and hungry people trying to eke out a miserable existence. Sarah and I wanted to help Aida if possible, and we found a way to do this. I got in touch with an officer I knew fairly well, Andrew Cumming, a brigadier serving with UNPROFOR, and asked if it would be possible for him to convey a 'Red Cross parcel' to Aida's family. He agreed, and we assembled a large collection of basics, with a few goodies – birdseed for the budgerigar, lipstick for Aida's mother, chocolate, and some dollars, the universal currency of the black market. Aida was often exhausted with worry, and so she was relieved that something was being done to help her parents in this desperate situation. Andrew gave the parcel to a chap called Milos Stankovic, Yugoslav by birth but brought up in Scotland, and now a major in the Parachute Regiment serving with UNPROFOR in Sarajevo. As a fluent speaker of Serbo-Croat he was much in demand as a translator, and so he tended to go wherever the commanders went. He managed to get the parcel to Aida's parents; a month later I sent him another parcel, and so we went on. 'This is your own personal humanitarian mission,' I wrote to him.

We had been sending these parcels for almost two years before I took one to Bosnia myself. In February 1995 I flew out to Bosnia, partly to visit 3rd Division units serving with UNPROFOR, but also to see the place for myself. There already seemed a strong possibility that the Division might have to become more involved as the situation worsened. Milos gave me a whistle-stop tour of Sarajevo before taking me to see Aida's parents, Munir and Minka Pijailovic. It was a very emotional meeting, with tears and embraces all around. Their gratitude was almost overwhelming – without our help, they maintained, they would not have survived this long. The old lady put her arm around Milos: 'He is like a son to us,' she told me. There was something particularly poignant about this scene: in the midst of this ghastly war, while Serbs and Croats and Muslims were killing each other without compunction, here was an elderly Muslim lady embracing a young man of Serb origin. I handed over the parcel and some letters from Aida. I had also brought some photographs of Aida with young Tom, and we sat and looked through them together, with many sighs and exclamations from the elderly couple.

Milos and I returned to the Residency in Sarajevo, the headquarters of my old friend Rupert Smith, now a lieutenant general, who only weeks earlier had succeeded General Sir Michael Rose as Commander, UNPROFOR. Like Mike Rose, Rupert was frustrated to be operating with such a limited mandate. I was due to visit one of our battalions in Gorazde, a Muslim enclave deep in hilly Serb territory to the east of Sarajevo. The Serbs controlled all traffic in and out, by road or by air, and it seemed that they were refusing to give clearance for my helicopter flight into Gorazde. Milos, who acted as UNPROFOR's liaison officer with the Bosnian Serbs, telephoned their headquarters in Pale, a little skiing village on the east side of Sarajevo. He managed to obtain their agreement to my flight the following morning, the only stipulation being that the commander of the Bosnian Serb Army, General Ratko Mladic, wanted to meet me for lunch afterwards.

Mladic had not yet been indicted for war crimes, but he had already earned an ugly reputation as a brutal, boastful and manipulative thug – somebody to be very wary of. In August 1994 the American three-star general Wesley Clark, who had flown in for a quick fact-finding visit, had allowed himself to be manoeuvred into a PR disaster: he was photographed smiling alongside Mladic, having swapped hats in an apparent gesture of bonhomie. The photograph was widely published and caused Clark great embarrassment back at home, where two congressmen called for his dismissal. 'It's like clowning with Hermann Goering,' one of them reportedly commented. I was a little apprehensive about our forthcoming encounter, though of course I knew that Mladic was a key player in the region and I was intrigued by the prospect of meeting him face-to-face.

The next morning snow was falling. We took off from Sarajevo Airport and after only ten minutes or so in the air landed again on the school football field at a mountain village called Sokolac. The Serbs insisted that, having crossed the line into Serb-held territory, you then had to land and be checked on your way in and then again on your way out. They would stop the UNPROFOR resupply convoys and search them from top to bottom. It reminded me of going in and out of Berlin. They wanted to ensure that we were not carrying any personnel who were not UN, or taking in weapons, ammunition or indeed rations to give to the Bosnian fighters. Everything UNPROFOR did had to be sanctioned by whichever faction controlled the ground. It was a humiliating sign of how weak the UN Force was.

I flew on to Gorazde, accompanied by Brigadier Robert Gordon, then commanding UN Sector South-West. It was useful to see the place for myself, and I hoped that the soldiers were encouraged by the fact that the Divisional Commander had made the effort to get to Gorazde and thank them. They were operating in very difficult circumstances, and it was important for them to receive some kind of acknowledgement. There was a lot of concern back home about what might happen to them if the UN effort collapsed. Though the terrain would have made it extremely difficult, there was none the less an extraction plan to go in, under NATO auspices if possible, create corridors to the isolated UN detachments and get them out – abandoning Bosnia to its fate.

On the way back we landed again at Sokolac to meet Mladic. Serb minders took us from the landing zone to an anonymous concrete building dating probably from the 1960s. This turned out to be a modest hotel, and there in the lobby, surrounded by his immediate staff and accompanied by a civilian interpreter, was Mladic – a squat, thick-set man in combat dress, with a ready grin and cold grey eyes. As he waved his hands in the air I noticed a gold ring on one finger, set with a large black stone. He greeted us effusively and led the party through into a dining room, where a dozen of us were seated around a simple wooden table. This was my first of many long and large Balkan lunches, often washed down with local wine and slivovic, a brandy made usually of plums and sometimes with pears. In this case, however, there was no alcohol: a plain meal of beans and a burger was served, which Mladic laughingly described as Serbian rations. Beaming and expansive, he presented himself as a simple soldier. He affected to be impressed that I had taken the trouble to come out here to see how my soldiers were doing.

I knew that Mladic was a cunning operator, and that I would have to keep my guard up in dealing with him, choosing my words with care. Robert Gordon did most of the talking. He had thoroughly briefed me beforehand on the issues that Mladic was likely to raise and how to handle them. The conversation centred on the logistic maintenance of the British battalion in Gorazde: what Mladic would be prepared to allow through and not allow through, and along which routes. Mladic's demeanour ranged from oiliness to bombast. His contempt for UNPROFOR was obvious. From his point of view, UNPROFOR was just an irritation, without the strength or the authority to impose itself in any meaningful way.

I was not sorry when the time came to leave. As a major general in the British Army, I found it irksome to have to come to a wretched place like this and to be harangued by such a despicable character as Ratko Mladic. But, as I was to experience time and again in the Balkans, it was essential to appear unemotional and to remain – at least outwardly – entirely objective.

I went back to Bosnia a month or two later and again visited the Pijailovic family in Sarajevo. The situation remained desperate, but the international community still seemed unwilling to risk more decisive action. In July 1995, however, an especially shocking massacre at Srebrenica outraged opinion all around the world, and proved to be the tipping point that at last drew in the United States. Until now NATO involvement had been limited to the sporadic enforcement of 'no-fly' zones – and without the commitment of NATO's lead nation the threat from NATO forces remained an empty one.

Srebrenica was another of those Muslim enclaves deep in Serb territory, very near the Serbian border. It too was a so-called 'safe area', protected by a Dutch battalion forming part of UNPROFOR. In the summer of 1995 Mladic's army, emboldened by the supine attitude of the Western powers, closed in on Srebrenica, determined to eradicate this Muslim enclave. The Dutch battalion, vastly outnumbered, let them pass after firing vainly into the air. The Dutch Government refused to allow NATO air strikes until all their troops were safely out of the area. The Serbs occupied the city, rounded up the Muslim men and massacred them, in the worst example of genocide in

Europe since the Second World War. Reliable authorities estimate that at least seven thousand Muslim males were systematically murdered by the Serb forces. Many of those who fled Srebrenica on foot had a very long and difficult journey through the forests to the city of Tuzla, constantly harassed by Serb forces as they tried to escape. Of the ten to fifteen thousand who fled Srebrenica in a column of men, women and children, only three to four thousand are said to have reached their destination.

The massacre at Srebrenica concentrated Western minds. President Chirac of France was particularly active in calling for action. The Clinton Administration was at last stirred into activity. The British Prime Minister, John Major, called an international crisis meeting in London at short notice, at which Rupert Smith presented a very important paper entitled 'The Fork in the Road'. He laid out the alternatives in stark terms. One option was to get out. If you cannot, or will not do more than you are prepared to do now, he said, you will achieve nothing, and the sensible thing is to leave. If, on the other hand, you want to secure an outcome that will last, then you must up the ante. This meant securing a stronger mandate for UNPROFOR at the very least. Thankfully, the London Conference took the view that it would be ignominious for the great powers of the Western world to withdraw from this small European country, with relatively small numbers of antagonists.

It was agreed at the London Conference that NATO would draw 'a line in the sand' around Gorazde, and that the decision whether to use air power to protect the enclave would be made within NATO, not by UNPROFOR or any UN body. These terms of engagement were later

broadened to include Sarajevo. Rupert Smith also concentrated such artillery as UNPROFOR possessed on
Mount Igman, to assist NATO air power in enforcing the
decisions of the Conference – and, not least, to deter
further shelling by the Bosnian Serbs.

Meanwhile President Clinton's special representative in
the Balkans, Richard Holbrooke, was working hard to
broker a diplomatic deal leading to peace. He knew that it
was not enough to engage the parties on the ground; any
lasting deal would need the consent of their paymasters in
Belgrade and Zagreb, the rulers of Serbia and Croatia,
Presidents Milosevic and Tudjman. General Wesley Clark
was appointed to Holbrooke's team as military adviser.
With the get-tough policy that had emerged from the
London Conference beginning to bite, and a new
Croat–Bosniac military alliance winning ground from the
Bosnian Serb army, it began to look as if the warring
parties would agree to some form of compromise. If this
happened, the plan was to deploy a NATO Force to
replace UNPROFOR. NATO's Allied Rapid Reaction Corps
(ARRC), commanded by British Lieutenant General Mike
Walker, would form the ground force headquarters under
NATO's Allied Forces Southern Europe HQ in Naples,
with three so-called 'framework nations' heading up
multinational divisions in different parts of the country:
France, the United States and the UK. Should this scenario
come about, the 3rd Division very much wanted to be
part of the action. This was nothing to do with me
personally. The British Army is by nature operationally
hungry – particularly when there's a new challenge.

One evening in late June, Sarah and I were guests for
dinner at Bulford Manor, the splendid old home of the

Commander in Chief, Land Command, the second most senior officer in the Army and the one responsible for so-called 'force generation'. At one point during the meal our host, General John Wilsey, who had been GOC Northern Ireland for the latter half of my time commanding 39 Brigade, was called away from the table to take a telephone call. Afterwards he took me aside. 'Things are moving, Mike,' he said. 'You may have to go out to Bosnia very soon.' My first thought was of my daughter Amanda's wedding in a week's time. I was of course due to give her away. No sooner had I been presented with this dilemma than all the lights went out. It was only a fuse, but in my situation it seemed somehow appropriate. Fortunately, the apparent urgency went as quickly as it came.

Rupert Smith's appointment as Commander UNPROFOR was only for one year, due to finish at the end of 1995, when he would become GOC Northern Ireland. In the late summer I received a telephone call informing me that I had been selected as his successor. My reaction was somewhat mixed. On the one hand, this new appointment meant promotion to lieutenant general; on the other, it would mean inheriting a position that both my predecessors had found immensely frustrating. I can remember thinking long and hard before deciding to accept. The new post would mean handing over the 3rd Division to my already nominated successor earlier than planned, and I began to make the necessary arrangements. On a practical level, I would have to find somewhere else for Sarah and Tom to live, because Clive House was tied to the post of GOC 3rd Division.

As Holbrooke's team engaged the factions in a whirlwind round of diplomacy, my own future was on hold. If an agreement was reached and the UK became one of the framework nations for the peacekeeping operation, this would mean putting a Corps Headquarters in the field, something we hadn't done since Suez. If, on the other hand, the parties failed to reach an agreement, my task as Commander, UNPROFOR might well be to oversee the Force's withdrawal from the region, which was bound to be messy and difficult.

All this was in the melting-pot when we took a late holiday in Singapore and Malaysia, tied in to an exercise being run by the Five Power Defence Agreement (FPDA) – UK, Singapore, Malaysia, Australia and New Zealand – the successor to the defunct South East Asia Treaty Organization (SEATO). Sarah, Tom and I stayed in an unpretentious but delightful beach guest-house on the east coast of Malaysia. It was a very simple place, with no landline telephones, and we were the only people there. On our second evening, the owner took a message from the British High Commission that Colonel Andrew Ritchie, my Chief of Staff at 3rd Division, needed to speak to me urgently. Our host kindly lent me his mobile telephone, warning me that reception was poor. To get a better signal, I walked on to the beach. 'Bosnia's looking more and more likely,' Andrew told me, 'but I think the Commander in Chief has his eye on 1 Div to do this. You might want to intercede now.'

The timing was not good. Here was I, sitting under a palm tree as a warm breeze blew in off the South China Sea, on the other side of the world from where the decisions were being taken. It was about nine in the evening local time, and I was dressed simply in a sarong. As I strolled up and down the sand in the moonlight, I managed to get hold of John Wilsey, and reminded him of all the planning for various Bosnian options we had done. 'Frankly, General, this makes 3 Div self-selecting,' I argued. I must have convinced him, because we heard no more after that about the possible involvement of the 1st Division.

Richard Holbrooke pressured all the parties involved in the Bosnian conflict to attend a conference at Dayton, Ohio – a US Air Force base chosen for its remoteness, which it was hoped would encourage the participants to hammer out an agreement. This was in mid-November, by which time I was once more in Bosnia. I had flown to Sarajevo via Zagreb, where I had met Kofi Annan, then Special Representative of the Secretary General (SRSG) for the Balkans. I stayed the night in Zagreb, in the rather upmarket hotel used by UN staff – contrasting sharply with the conditions in which UN soldiers were living in Bosnia. I found the ranks of smart white UN 4×4 vehicles in the hotel car park an uncomfortable sight; they seemed to be used only to commute between the hotel and the UN HQ by the airport.

When I reached Rupert Smith's HQ in Sarajevo the following day, I found he was away in Bihac for the night, which meant that I could borrow his bed – a good thing, because spare accommodation within UNPROFOR HQ was not easy to find. There were a lot of press hanging around, and much speculation about what was happening at Dayton. By midnight the general impression was that the Conference had failed. I went to bed in the early hours thinking: This is going to be where I sleep for the next year or so. It's a blue beret for Jackson, and three stars.

Rupert Smith returned the next day and we agreed a handover date in mid-December. Then I flew up to the UN Sector HQ at a small town called Gornji Vakuf, which had been on the front line between the Croats and the Bosniacs before they formed a federation to combat the Serbs. This Sector Headquarters was provided by the British 4th Armoured Brigade, commanded by Richard Dannatt – who, eleven years later, was to take over from me as CGS. In the late afternoon, just as it was getting dark, we were driving back from a visit to a British battalion when the radio in the vehicle burst into life, announcing that they'd settled at Dayton. I thought: Right – reference Plan A, cancel; insert Plan B. Back at Gornji Vakuf I watched the initialling ceremony on satellite television up in Richard's office.

So I finally knew where I was. I would not be the three-star commander of UNPROFOR, headquartered in Sarajevo; I would be the two-star commander of the new Multinational Division South-West – one of the three divisional commanders in the new NATO Force, known as IFOR (Implementation Force), remaining a major general and in command of the 3rd Division. I would deploy to Bosnia within a matter of weeks. HQ Multinational Division South West would be in Gornji Vakuf. Sarah and Tom could stay at Clive House. And this very room in which I was sitting would become my new office.

It had been a rollercoaster ride, not knowing what I was going to be doing right up until the last moment. But in the scheme of things my career was insignificant; the key thing was that, for the first time in five years, the outlook for Bosnia was hopeful.

*   *   *

I went out to Bosnia before Christmas, a few days before D-Day, 20 December 1995, the date when UNPROFOR handed over to IFOR. A couple of evenings earlier Sarah and I had thrown a party for the Headquarters staff, an event that became known as the Duchess of Richmond's Ball – although the comparison with Waterloo was more than a little far-fetched. In a short speech I urged the wives not to worry about their men: a forlorn hope, I suspect. In a symbolic gesture, the British soldiers who had formed part of UNPROFOR and were now coming under NATO command paraded formally to take off their light blue UN berets and put on their own British Army headgear. This was my first experience of commanding a multinational force: though more than half of the soldiers under my command were British, the Division also included Canadians, Czechs, Dutch and Malaysians. Of course, it would be unfair to expect the same capability from all national contingents. The Malaysians, for example, were hard pressed since they found – unsurprisingly – the Bosnian winters to be very harsh. And it is a curse of multinational operations that governments impose con-straints on their national contingents, usually for domestic political reasons. Some may do this or that, some may not: the outcome is a complicated matrix of permitted actions for each nationality – and this is the bane of a multinational commander's life. Each national commander carries a so-called 'red card', allowing him to opt out of a specific operation if his national government finds it unpalatable.

Nevertheless, IFOR was a pretty formidable force of some sixty thousand soldiers. Though many of these, at least at the outset, were erstwhile members of UNPROFOR, they were now serving under NATO command with much tougher rules of engagement – and, moreover, with plenty of fire-power at our disposal, including of course the threat of air strikes. UNPROFOR had possessed no heavy armour, and little enough artillery. We now shipped in tanks and self-propelled guns, which were brought up to our area on transporters in impressive convoys. My artillery commander, then Brigadier Freddie Viggers, moved quickly to open a live-firing range, and then organized a series of highly impressive live-firing displays for the faction leaders, as a clear demon-stration of what they would face if they were unintelligent enough to take on IFOR. It was another way of getting over the message, 'We're serious, don't mess around.' They had nothing to compare with our firepower, of course.

During the Bosnian war the territory controlled by each of the warring factions had expanded and contracted depending on the success of their forces. Much of the fighting had concentrated around various 'pockets', where a population from one ethnic group – usually Bosnian – found itself isolated. At Dayton there had been a lot of horse-trading, with deals being done about control of this piece of territory or that. A so-called 'Clark Corridor' had been created to the Gorazde pocket, for example. Both the Serbs and the Croats had wanted to hive off as much territory as possible and join their parent states, leaving the poor Bosniacs in the middle with a tiny amount. But Dayton maintained the principle of a single Bosnian state, divided into two so-called 'entities' in a loose federal structure. One entity was the Croat–Bosniac Federation; the other, semi-autonomous entity became known as Republika Srpska, forming an extraordinary horseshoe shape around the east and north sides of the old Bosnian republic. Dayton laid down a boundary between the two entities, known as the 'Inter-Entity Boundary Line' (IEBL), which in many areas did not tally with the ceasefire lines on the ground. The Bosnian Serbs would try to treat the IEBL as an international boundary, though Dayton had insisted on the territorial integrity of Bosnia and the right of free movement within it.

Though the Force which I commanded was named the Multinational Division South-West (a hangover from the UN Sector South-West), we were in fact responsible for north-western Bosnia bordering Croatia, which curled round the country from the north right round to the south-west, cutting it off from the Adriatic Sea. In the early part of the war the Bosnian Serbs had dominated this part of Bosnia, though they had never eliminated the so-called 'Bihac pocket' in the north-west. Latterly a combined assault by Croats and Bosniacs had pushed the Bosnian Serbs back, nearly driving them out of the mountains on to the northern plain around their capital, Banja Luka.

In the freezing midwinter there were some heart-rending scenes: lines of old vehicles, horses and carts, donkeys – anything to carry people who did not want to remain living in a place where in many cases their families had been for generations, once they could no longer rely on the protection of their own ethnic forces.

The boundaries agreed at Dayton were to be enshrined in detailed maps, but we hadn't received them by D+1, when I travelled up to Sarajevo for a meeting with Mike Walker and the other divisional commanders. In the airport car park I chanced upon an American full colonel with his driver and sidekick, who were asking the way to IFOR HQ. 'We have some urgent deliveries for them,' he explained.

'What have you got?' I asked.

It turned out that they had the newly printed Dayton maps.

'Aha,' I said, introducing myself. 'Perhaps I could have my slice now?' We transferred the maps directly from his vehicle into ours, and so – hallelujah! – we had our maps before anybody else.

The Dayton Agreement had been well thought through, with enough detail to make it all work, a tribute to the work of Richard Holbrooke and his team. Dayton laid out an end-state to which all the parties had agreed, with a clear mechanism for getting from start to finish. This clarity would prove invaluable in the weeks and months to follow. Dayton also stipulated strict timelines: what had to be done by D+30, D+60, D+90. For us, the Dayton Agreement became a kind of 'bible' to which I would refer whenever any kind of dispute arose. I carried a copy of Dayton with me everywhere. If there was any friction or altercation with any of the factions I just produced the document and pointed to the relevant clauses: 'This is what it says, this is what your leaders have signed up to.' That shut them up.

The military provisions of Dayton imposed three major obligations on the parties: a durable cessation of hostilities; support for IFOR; and security and arms control measures to promote a permanent reconciliation between the factions. These formal stipulations were amplified by a very detailed statement of procedures to be followed. The obligations thereby laid on the factions enabled IFOR to demand rigorous implementation of this or that provision – in the early days almost on a day-to-day basis.

Among many requirements, Dayton stipulated that the IEBL be marked on the ground, that no combatants from the opposing entity remain on the wrong side, and that weapons be centralized so that we could count them. Forces were not allowed to train without our permission. Those areas which were to be transferred from one entity to the other had to be vacated by D+45, and they would remain our responsibility until the forces of the other entity were permitted to enter at D+90, forty-five days later. In particular, there was a region shaped like an upturned anvil that had been occupied by the Croat–Bosniac alliance that was due to be handed back to the Serbs. This was a substantial area, as large as a medium-sized English county such as Leicestershire or Warwickshire. For the interim period between D+45 and D+90, we would be responsible for all the functions of government in the 'Anvil' – and in other areas where the IEBL did not tally with the ceasefire line – including security, policing, justice, civil administration and reconstruction. Many of the bridges had been destroyed, and the Royal Engineers enjoyed themselves putting in new ones. There is only one thing that engineers love more than building bridges, and that's blowing them up.

I had the Dayton Agreement and the accompanying IFOR statement of procedures translated into a set of orders which I gave to each of the factions, saying: Here, this is what you have to do and when. By D+30 forces would have to have withdrawn outside of what was called the 'Zone of Separation' (ZOS), 2 kilometres either side of the agreed ceasefire line. In the first few days, there were some exchanges of small-arms fire as each side took a last shot at the other, or – very occasionally – some bunch decided to have a go at us. But by and large the whole thing went more smoothly than we had dared hope. During these early days we were obliged to open fire on a number of occasions, but apart from one or two firefights on the cease-fire line, it was never very serious. Usually the trouble was sorted out at company commander level. But there were other risks. About a month after D-Day, a mine left over from the war detonated under one of our armoured vehicles, resulting in the deaths of a young officer and two of his soldiers.

The military annex to Dayton provided for a mechanism known as the Joint Military Commission, or Commissions: meetings between the faction commanders – both at national level, in Sarajevo, and locally, in each of the three areas. I called my first commission meeting on the morning of D+3, when I met for the first time the local big cheeses, so-called 'corps commanders' as they styled themselves, who were going to be part of my life for the next six months. There was no blueprint for these meetings, and to a large extent we were forced to make up the rules as we went along. The atmosphere was bound to be extremely tense, considering that these characters had only very recently been fighting each other.

The first meeting was held at a tented site astride the ceasefire line in the Vrbas valley, about halfway between Gornji Vakuf and Banja Luka and close to a big hydro-electric dam which by some miracle had kept functioning throughout the conflict. We assembled in a gloomily lit tent around four trestle tables arranged in a square. It was a cold day, with a bitter wind that kept the tent flapping throughout. With me were my Chief of Staff Andrew Ritchie and two or three others, including of course our interpreter. The Bosnian Serb side was led by General Momir Talic, commander of the 1st Krajina Corps: a short man with a deceptively easy-going, almost avuncular manner, who would later be indicted for war crimes by the International Criminal Tribunal for Yugoslavia (ICTY). His Croat opposite number was the bullet-headed Brigadier General Zeljko Glasnovic, who spoke disarmingly perfect English and who, I later learned, had served as an NCO in the Canadian Army. The commander of the Bosniac forces in the Bihac pocket was another large man, General Atif Dudakovic, who regarded himself as a Balkan Rommel. Accompanying him was General Mehmed Aligic, a crude, sexist and bombastic individual. Aligic later attempted to bribe me over lunch, at which point I got up and walked out.

I was determined to stamp our authority on these individuals from the start, to show them that the days of the soggy UNPROFOR mandate were over. We were not going to permit them to intimidate us or to dictate the agenda. I decided that this first meeting should be on a strictly formal basis. Status was everything to such people. Instead of going out to greet them as they arrived in their convoys, I waited for them inside the tent. The faction commanders were compelled to surrender their weapons to British military police before entering. As each party arrived there were rather a lot of hard stares, but they all sat around the same square of tables. We had arranged that once all three parties were settled in the tent, armoured vehicles would drive past and then come back again several times over, to give the impression that we had far more of these than we in fact possessed. It was all part of the attempt to impress on them that we were in charge. The device worked almost too well, in that it was difficult to hear what was being said above the rumble of the passing vehicles.

I opened the meeting, speaking slowly and emphasizing my words. 'I'm not interested in the past,' I told them, 'and this is not a discussion forum. I'm here to tell you what your political leaders have agreed at Dayton and how we're going to implement this.'

I emphasized that this was a NATO operation, and whatever might have happened in the past, NATO did 'joined-up soldiering'. They weren't going to be able to play on differences between the different nationalities as they had done with UNPROFOR.

The reactions were difficult to discern, but I carried on, eyeballing each man in turn. 'Orders are orders, gentlemen,' I said in conclusion.

The Joint Military Commission went into formal session as often as necessary. In those early days it was once every ten days or so, but as things settled the intervals became longer. But of course I met each of the individual commanders regularly on a one-to-one basis, over many, many long, large and liquid Balkan lunches – all part of confidence-building, listening to their complaints, assessing whether these were legitimate and if so what we might do to help, trying to diminish their fears of being caught unawares by a resumption of hostilities.

While we had no hard evidence that any of these individuals had been involved in dark deeds, we inevitably had concerns. However, we had to do business with these people to make Dayton work.

In the latter days of the war, while soldiers from Croatia itself were heading up the Vrbas valley, Dudakovic had fought a critical battle at Sanski Most, only 25 miles or so west of Banja Luka. The planned pincer movement had been curtailed by Dayton. But pretty soon afterwards the erstwhile allies had fallen out. The Bosnian Croat forces were due to have withdrawn from Kulan Vakuf, a small village about 20 miles south of Bihac. In the days immediately before the deadline they seemed very reluctant to fulfil their obligation. The stocky Dudakovic responded in the typical Balkan way: thumping the table and shouting, 'This means war.' His forces began to move south towards the Croats, and we deployed to block them. We also put together a formal operation to evict the Croats if it came to that, and we manoeuvred in a very obvious way to show that we were serious. We were concerned, but I was confident that we could handle the situation, however the parties behaved. Dudakovic's tablethumping was best understood as typical Balkan bombast, theatre rather than a real declaration of intent. The incident continued over several days, running up to the deadline. The Croats withdrew with only a few hours to spare.

I was lucky enough to have an excellent and highly intelligent interpreter, Elizabeth Soldo. The relationship with an interpreter is a very close one, because you spend a lot of time together, and it's crucial that it works well, because nuance is often everything when negotiating. Though a Bosnian Croat, Elizabeth accompanied me everywhere, even into Bosnian Serb territory, which obviously involved an extra element of risk for her personally. Not being able to communicate directly with those with whom one was dealing had some advantages, in that it gave one extra 'thinking time' in situations which often required careful consideration and in which a careless remark might easily have proved inflammatory. I was delighted when she was awarded an MBE at the end of 2007.

Our final timeline would be D+120, when all forces were due to return to barracks and all heavy weapons had to be assembled in what were known as 'cantonment' areas, an expression straight out of British India. Once corralled, the weapons would be subject to IFOR inspection, to ensure that they remained so.

By D+30 the factions were required to release their prisoners of war, each to the other, and predictably they were all very worried that they might release the prisoners they held without getting their own people back from the other side. One large exchange was due to take place right on the confrontation line, on the main road between Banja Luka and Gornji Vakuf, in the valley of the River Vrbas. This was really an International Red Cross (ICRC) function, but we were providing security and for obvious reasons we tried to help. The prisoners were brought up to either side of the confrontation line in buses. Families were waiting there for them to be released: women in headscarves, elderly mothers, children, fathers and brothers. But then the officials from each side started to argue about how many prisoners were there, comparing the numbers on the buses with their lists of those missing. The ICRC did their absolute best to broker the deal, but in vain. Neither side could bring itself to trust the other. So the buses turned around and drove away again, the prisoners pressing their faces against the windows in the hope of glimpsing their loved ones, the families completely distraught.

I had an early warning of what we were up against on the morning of D-Day itself, 20 December 1995. That day 4 Brigade set up a deliberate operation to move into Serb-held territory. The main road north led down the valley of the River Vrbas through a spectacular gorge, before emerging on to the plain around Banja Luka, the biggest and most significant town in Republika Srpska. In the last days of the war, Croatian forces had launched a major offensive in this direction, pushing the Serbs back and threatening to advance down the Vrbas valley towards Banja Luka itself. As our soldiers were getting ready to move down the valley, I noticed three bodies lying in a field quite close to the road ahead. There was something strange about them. Looking through the binoculars I could see that they were soldiers: all three were face down, their trousers around their ankles. I asked one of the local interpreters what this meant. He explained that these were Serb soldiers who had been buggered before, during or after the moment of death – almost certainly by withdrawing Croat forces.

Liberal-minded people from civilized Western countries struggled to comprehend the savagery unleashed in the Balkans when Yugoslavia began to fissure. Such passionate loathing between different ethnic groups is outside the experience of most of us. In our largely secular Western world, religious fanaticism is anachronistic. These ethnic antagonisms seemed a throwback to earlier, more primitive periods in the distant past. In the Balkans, though, the past is the present – yet not, I fervently hope, the future. I learned not to be surprised when Bosnian Serbs referred to Muslims as 'Turks', for example, or when locals cited battles from past centuries as if they had occurred the day before. There is a sad parallel with the attitudes I had encountered in Northern Ireland, where the Protestants could provoke the Catholics to violence by celebrating battles that had taken place three hundred years earlier.

As time passed, we uncovered further grisly evidence of war crimes. The ICTY sent representatives to the area, to take forensic evidence and carry out exhumations. It was our job to protect them, because inevitably there were people around who did not want this evidence to come to light. I remember going up to Prijedor, a mining town about 25 miles north-west of Banja Luka, in the centre of the region where many of the worst atrocities had taken place. It was a very unpleasant feeling to be in an area where such terrible crimes had so recently been committed. The Chief of Police was himself a pretty distasteful character, very rude, very loud and bombastic – so much so, indeed, that he was told to quieten down by some of his own town worthies. This man was later indicted by the ICTY, thus becoming a 'Pifwic' (person indicted for war crimes). He and another man were the targets of the first Pifwic arrest operation, after I'd left Bosnia. He attempted to pull a gun and was killed by British Special Forces.

The two most notorious Pifwics were of course Ratko Mladic and the Bosnian Serb 'President', Radovan Karadzic. Later IFOR would be heavily criticized for not having arrested them in the early days of its mandate. Both men had gone into hiding after the indictments had been served, though we would receive the occasional report that one or other of them had been seen. But in the early months of IFOR's deployment the political situation remained delicate, with the NATO chain of command reluctant to do anything that might jeopardize the fragile peace that had so recently come into being. Both Mladic and Karadzic were believed to be hiding in the American-controlled area, and the Americans were very nervous about mounting operations that might put their soldiers at risk. IFOR originally stipulated that soldiers might arrest Pifwics 'in the normal course of their duties', but that no special operation would be mounted to arrest them for the time being. Given that these two indicted war criminals are still at large, I believe that IFOR should have been bolder when it had the greatest authority, immediately after the handover from the UN to NATO.

Two or three days after D-Day, I received an invitation via our Special Forces people from Rajko Kasagic, the so-called 'Prime Minister' of Republika Srpska, to go and meet him in Banja Luka, the following morning if possible. This seemed to me a remarkable opportunity. There was a tendency for the Bosnian Serbs to be regarded as denizens of the outer darkness. But we had already recognized that there was real political rivalry between the more moderate Bosnian Serb faction in Banja Luka and Karadzic's more extreme faction in Pale. It was clear which side should be encouraged. So I decided to go. I checked with the helicopter crew beforehand whether they were happy to take me, given that Serb territory was potentially hostile. They had no hesitation. We flew up the Vrbas valley and out on to the snow-covered plain, heading towards the city. The best place to land seemed to be the football stadium. Special Forces personnel met us there and drove us to their 'safe house' in the town. After a short briefing we then walked the short distance to Banja Luka town hall, an impressive early twentieth-century building in the local style, to be met by a crowd of local journalists.

And that's where I met the Bosnian Serb Prime Minister, a man in his fifties who seemed a decent fellow with moderate views. We held a civilized private meeting, away from the press, accompanied by just a few aides and translators. It was the first bit of direct liaison with the Serb civil authorities that I had been able to achieve, and it was encouraging.

Before we'd even deployed to Bosnia, we'd done some careful thinking about where to site our HQ. The existing regional UNPROFOR Headquarters was sited in Gornji Vakuf, a small town with no airstrip. The result was that we had to slog by helicopter over the mountains from Gornji Vakuf to get to an airport capable of taking fixed-wing aircraft at Sarajevo or Split. Flying to and fro by helicopter was often difficult and sometimes, if the weather closed in, impossible. I frequently had to continue a journey by mountain road when the helicopter carrying me could not continue, and even then it was not always straightforward. I vividly remember flying back from Sarajevo on one occasion when the weather closed in. It was getting dark, and snow began to fall so heavily that visibility was reduced to zero. The helicopter pilot did his best, but it wasn't safe to continue. He put us down at Vitez, a British base, where we borrowed a couple of Land Rovers and continued on the unmetalled road over the mountains. It wasn't long before we were bogged down. Major General Jackson could be found outside in the cold and dark in the middle of nowhere, pushing with all his might to get the vehicle out of a snow drift.

As a rule we used a pair of Land Rover Discoverys, perhaps the ideal vehicle for the purpose. My capable driver

Sergeant Jim Heron was an example of that modern phenomenon, the soldier married to the soldier: as circumstances extraordinarily had it, his wife was also deployed to Bosnia and was working in a base only a mile or two from our HQ in Gornji Vakuf. Not wanting to embarrass the Herons, I asked another soldier whether they were able to see each other from time to time. 'Indeed they are, Sir,' came the reply, 'and, before you ask, the romantic rendezvous is the back of your Discovery!'

The other two Divisional Headquarters were both in sizeable towns with airfields big enough to take fixed-wing aircraft, the French in Mostar and the Americans in Tuzla, but neither of these two, nor – once the IEBL was in place – the Force Headquarters in Sarajevo, was on the Serb side. The obvious place for us to site our HQ was therefore in Banja Luka. It was a political as well as a practical move that we were contemplating. Of course it was sensitive to site a NATO HQ on Serb-controlled territory, because NATO had bombed and shelled Serb forces; but if we could pull it off, this would inevitably diminish the influence of the hard-line Mladic/Karadzic faction in Pale. If Dayton was to work properly, the centre of gravity within Republika Srpska had to shift towards Banja Luka. Kasagic knew this, and was therefore very keen for us to come to his 'capital'. I handled the negotiations personally, because of their sensitivity. Eventually, after much looking, we found the Banja Luka Metal Factory, about 5 miles north of the city centre, which seemed ideal for our needs. It had an office block, a big industrial canteen, a huge hangar-like building where we could store equipment under cover, space outside to build

a helipad, and a security fence. Under the Dayton
Agreement IFOR had the right to requisition property
without payment, but we felt that this was not the best
way to win friends and influence people, so I negotiated a
price. Something like half a million Deutschmarks (then
about £150,000) was required to secure the deal. Then I
spoke by satellite radio to the man with the money: my
Civil Secretary, Simon Wren. Simon paid our bills, ran our
locally employed workforce and answered the plethora of
MPs' Questions forwarded by the MOD, managing it all
with great aplomb. 'Simon,' I said, 'we've got the Metal
Factory, can you get up here today with some cash?' From
that moment on we were in business, with a headquarters
in Republika Srpska.

We decided to mark our arrival in Banja Luka by giving
a reception, done in the best British Army style: Pimm's,
canapés, a military band and a free-fall parachute display
by the Red Devils. The British Ambassador came, the local
politicians came, the military came: it certainly put us on
the map in our new location.

Another tick in the box for the Metal Factory was that it
was only twenty minutes' drive from Banja Luka airport.
This had been closed for some years as a result of the war,
but we hoped that it could be re-opened. I drove up to
take a look at the place late one January afternoon, just as
it was starting to get dark. The airport manager was
amazed to see us, and even turned on the runway lights
for our inspection. The airstrip was big enough to take
RAF Hercules aircraft, and the RAF liaison officer inside
my own headquarters, Squadron Leader Steve Smith, was
tasked to get it up and running. A few weeks later there
was another great extravaganza: the formal re-opening of

Banja Luka Airport, known to us as Banja Luka International.

A succession of VIPs arrived in an almost daily flow. I remember in particular the then Prime Minister, John Major, changing out of his suit into casual clothes in one of the offices at the Metal Factory before coming out to see the soldiers.

I learned much from my experiences in Bosnia that was to prove invaluable later on in Kosovo. In particular, the experience of administering the 'Anvil' and other such areas, where for a limited period there would be no machinery of government or security, stood me in very good stead.

I use the analogy of a rope to describe peace support operations in a post-conflict situation. The provision of security is only one strand; the other strands are political progress, humanitarian aid, demobilization of the factions' armies, reconstruction and economic progress. Once the strands are woven together, the rope is stronger than the sum of its parts. It's essential to demonstrate that, for the vast majority of people, the future is going to be better than the past.

I spent a lot of time with the local media, giving interviews and doing phone-ins, spreading the message that IFOR was here to ensure that war didn't restart, and to help people rebuild their lives.

In fostering political progress we were lucky to have the assistance and support of Carl Bildt, who had succeeded Kofi Annan as SRSG. Carl is a Swede, a thoughtful, bespectacled character, a very experienced and impressive man and a great internationalist. Before coming to the

Balkans as SRSG he had been Prime Minister of Sweden. I got to know him early on when he arrived unannounced at our Gornji Vakuf HQ after bad weather had curtailed his helicopter flight. We were in the middle of a farewell lunch for some of our staff officers and invited him to join us. A good discussion over lunch and a glass or two of wine followed, after which Sergeant Jim Heron drove him to Sarajevo. It was a good start to our working relationship, and we went on happily from there. Unlike us, Carl had virtually to beg, steal and borrow what he needed to do his job. He also had to contend with an attitude in IFOR's senior leadership which very largely shunned any civil dimension – which again I found difficult to understand. It was clear that not all shared my analogy of the strands of the rope. There was a lesson here which would prove invaluable in Kosovo a few years later.

For the Brits at least, the dual-track approach of military and civil measures was a given. There is a deep understanding in the British Army of how to run a post-conflict situation – or, to use an expression which, at least latterly, has been anathema to the Americans: how to nation-build. This understanding was shared by the Overseas Development Agency (ODA), then a sub-set of the Foreign Office, which had a positive, can-do approach and welcomed partnership with the military. Sadly, the ODA is no more. It has been replaced by the Department for International Development (DfID), which has a rather different culture – although to be fair the Department is constrained by the Act under which it was formed to 'the relief of poverty'.

We were lucky that the ODA sent out a consultant called Gilbert Greenall to handle the civil reconstruction dimension. Gilbert is a man of many parts: doctor, pilot, landowner and a reconstructor of vast experience who has made a special study of post-conflict situations. He was probably worth a battalion or more in terms of the effect he achieved. His key point is that you've got to get a move on: the first hundred days is when you'll get it right or fail. If you can show the local population the prospect of a better future in that crucial early period, you have your best chance of winning them over.

We had a modest amount of money from the ODA for local development and rehabilitation projects: putting a roof back on the local school, for example, or reconnecting the water supply to a village. Gilbert Greenall instituted a very simple system, requiring the minimum of paperwork. The local commanding officer would identify a project and Gilbert would authorize it. Whenever possible we would get local workmen to do the work, so that we spent the money in a way that would benefit the local economy.

The 3rd Division's tour with IFOR finished at the end of June 1996, seven months after the Dayton Agreement. Afterwards I received many gratifying letters of congratulation on what we had achieved in Bosnia. Among those who wrote in such terms were the Prime Minister, John Major, and the Secretary of State, Michael Portillo. He was kind enough to mention my 'outstanding contribution to the civil effort'. According to him, we had shown 'a remarkable degree of sensitivity and even-handedness' and had 'established excellent relations with all three communities'. I also received several such letters from senior figures in the Army. I replied to one of these, a letter from the then CDS, Lord Inge, reflecting on the uncertainty in the months before my deployment, and telling him that I was pleased to have commanded a multinational force rather than UNPROFOR. 'I did not relish the prospect of keeping UNPROFOR on the road when just about every ploy had been tried,' I wrote. 'It may have cost me a bob or two, but far better to have commanded Multinational Division South-West under IFOR with its thoroughly positive objective.'

I was honoured to be appointed a Commander of the Most Honourable Order of the Bath in recognition of my services in Bosnia. Three years later I would receive a knighthood, the Knight Commander of the Bath – the so-called 'Deep End of the Bath'.

Already things were beginning to return to normal in Bosnia, and in the intervening eleven and a half years there has been no renewed outbreak of serious conflict. There is still an international force in Bosnia, now under EU rather than NATO auspices; Britain's contribution has been scaled right back to a handful of staff officers. Bosnia, which threatened to expose the impotence of Western governments, has so far proved a notable success.

And so the day came – D+189 – to hand over to HQ 1 (UK) Armoured Division under the command of Major General John Kiszeley. A little research showed that it was the first occasion on which one British Divisional HQ had relieved another in the field since the closing stages of the Second World War. John and I shook hands. I wished him luck and drove to the airport.

We had managed to arrange for a very smart BAe-146, a thirty-seater jet used mainly by the Royal Family and Government ministers, to take the command group home, flying from Banja Luka International directly to Boscombe Down. I thought we deserved it, since most of us had hardly seen our families for six months or more, other than a few days' break mid-tour. I did a round of farewells beforehand, when bottles of slivovic were pressed upon me at every turn. Many of these were consumed on the flight home, to the slight discomfiture of the cabin staff. It was a happy return.

11

Back to the Balkans

'I hope duties on Salisbury Plain do not seem too tame after Bosnia,' Carl Bildt wrote after I had left. In fact, my time with the 3rd Division was up: my original two-year appointment had already been extended by four months or so because of the Bosnia deployment. In August 1996, little more than a month after arriving back from the Balkans, I handed over to my successor, Major General Cedric Delves. As usual, there was a light-hearted ceremony to mark my departure. There is a picture of me in the 3rd Division's in-house magazine standing on the passenger seat of a camouflaged car, my upper half projecting through a hole in its roof, a glass of wine in my hand, watched by the amused staff. 'While Major General Jackson familiarises himself with the cupola of his new staff car,' the caption reads, 'his ADC, Captain Rory Gilbert, realises that the car has no brakes.' Afterwards volunteers towed the knackered vehicle to a farewell lunch.

I took a few weeks' leave after handing over, and we

flew with Tom, then six years old, to Namibia for a holiday. Sarah and I both felt the need to get away from it all, and re-engage with each other after almost seven months' separation. All Service families know from experience that it is not always easy to settle back into family life after an operational tour – and that it's not going to happen overnight.

Then in September I began my next appointment, as Director General, Development and Doctrine, head of the Army's think tank at Upavon, on the north side of Salisbury Plain. We were busy revising our concept for peace support operations in the light of the NATO Bosnian experience, work which would prove useful to me later on in Kosovo. But I didn't have too long to think, because quite soon after taking up this post I received the welcome news that I would be succeeding Mike Walker as Commander of NATO's Allied Rapid Reaction Corps (ARRC), headquartered at Rheindahlen, near Düsseldorf. This entailed promotion to lieutenant general, the rank I would have assumed fourteen months earlier had I taken command of UNPROFOR towards the end of 1995.

And so we moved to Germany early in 1997. This was our seventh move in twelve years of marriage (by the time I left the Army in late 2006, the score was ten moves in twenty-one years, a rather better average).

One of the travel guides to Germany describes Rheindahlen as 'Little England', which says it all. Within this British Army base – the largest in Germany – there is in many ways a self-contained community, with all the facilities families need inside the wire. Foster House was one of the two generals' 'residences' set in woodland in the grounds of Wegburg Hospital, formerly one of the main military hospitals for British Forces Germany. A psychiatric unit remained, and we would occasionally see men in white coats walking patients in the hospital gardens. We were a short distance from the headquarters complex in Rheindahlen, and Tom would more often than not bike with Sarah through the woods to one of the three excellent British Forces primary schools on the main camp.

The ARRC had left Bosnia in November 1996, IFOR's role in Bosnia being taken over by a new NATO-led Force, SFOR, the Stabilization Force. A number of non-NATO countries contributed units to both IFOR and SFOR – including Russia. Thus Russian soldiers were serving under NATO command, only a few years after the ending of the Cold War. We had certainly come a long way in a short time. The Russians had a longstanding interest in Serbia, going back at least a century, and it was Russian support for Serbia that had started the dominoes falling in the summer of 1914. Since the West was trying to persuade Serbia to act responsibly as part of the international community, it seemed right to involve the Russians, with whom the Serbs had such well-established historical ties.

For the NATO nations, the gruesome civil war in the Balkans had been a searing experience, cruelly dashing the hopes raised by the ending of the Cold War. In 1992 a young American academic, Francis Fukuyama, had earnestly pronounced 'The End of History', prophesying the inexorable spread of Western liberal democracy throughout the world. Even those who judged this theory naïve had not predicted the eruption of primitive ethnic struggle within Europe itself. It rapidly became clear that the Cold War had contained ancient tensions, not destroyed them. Well might one Balkan specialist entitle his book *The Re-Birth of History*. Places that had seemed docile backwaters for almost a century were revealed as seething with ethnic hatred. For those trying to make sense of the post-Cold War world, it was back to the future.

The ARRC had emerged from the re-appraisals that followed the end of the Cold War. It was clear that NATO's structures had to change as a result to reflect the transformed situation. Much of the Alliance's organizational structure had been designed to fight the Warsaw Pact on the German plains, as part of the general defence plan for northern Europe. After this threat evaporated, there was a realization that NATO was going to need a more expeditionary capability, able to operate over long distances, and to this end the Rapid Reaction Corps had been created, devoid of any responsibility for territorial defence in Germany. It is in essence a Corps Headquarters of around four hundred permanent staff, a head to which a number of bodies can be attached. The ARRC Commander (COMARRC) does not command a substantial force on a permanent basis. But when the need arises, the contributing NATO nations will generate forces to come under his direct command, for the purposes of that specific deployment – as happened in Bosnia.

A parallel process of adjustment took place within the British Army, reflecting the shift in its focus from fighting a land war on the grand scale to mounting operations right across the spectrum of conflict, of greater or lesser intensity, from large-scale conventional warfare to modest humanitarian missions. Peace support operations seemed likely to form a priority for the future – an area in which the British Army was especially well qualified, for it had been pursuing what was fundamentally a peace support operation in Northern Ireland for the past quarter of a century. At the same time it was thought to be essential to maintain our full war-fighting skills at a high level. As with NATO as a whole, there was a shift of emphasis towards a more expeditionary capability, which implied a greater emphasis on joint operations with the other Services. These changes of role necessitated changes in attitudes, affecting every soldier from private to general. British soldiers were going to have to be yet more flexible and yet more resourceful in dealing with the more varied challenges of the future.

In peacetime, individual nations assign divisions to the ARRC for command and control training, but though we devised command post exercises to train their head-quarters, we didn't get involved in field training, since they remained under their national commands. And so we had a constituency, with which we formed a close training relationship. My first year with the ARRC was spent working hard on getting our war-fighting skills back up to speed, following the Bosnia peace support operation. If and when the ARRC deployed on another operation, it would be up to each individual nation to decide under the particular circumstances what force contribution it would make, if any. Under Article 5 of the original North Atlantic Treaty, an attack on one member state is considered an attack upon all. This is the superglue of the Alliance. But since the end of the Cold War we've been in non-Article 5 territory, intervening outside the NATO area, and an individual nation can decide not to take part in one of these operations if it chooses – even if that nation's permanent representative (in effect, its ambassador to NATO) on the North Atlantic Council has agreed that NATO should take on this task.

When the ARRC HQ was formed in the mid-1990s, the UK volunteered to become the so-called 'framework nation', providing much of the funding and many of the staff, including the Commander. The first COMARRC had been Lieutenant General Jeremy Mackenzie, second-in-command of the Queen's Own Highlanders at the time of Warrenpoint and Deputy Commandant of the Staff College when I was on the Higher Command and Staff Course. He had been succeeded by Mike Walker, and I was the third COMARRC. The success of the ARRC concept has led to several other such HQs being formed within NATO; but in the late 1990s we were the only one of our kind.

HQ ARRC is supported by a small permanent force of specialist soldiers from the UK as framework nation: a signal brigade of two communications regiments, and one support battalion to handle all the admin and logistics, including tentage, vehicles, food, rations, fuel and so on. But on deployment the HQ is designed to command a very large force of corps dimensions (approximately fifty thousand soldiers). The ARRC insignia is a spearhead, signifying that the Corps' role is to be the leading element, the sharp point of the weapon. Its motto is 'Audentis Fortuna Iuvat', meaning 'Fortune Favours the Brave'.

The ARRC HQ is under operational command of the Supreme Allied Commander, Europe (SACEUR), and as COMARRC I therefore reported directly to him. The post of SACEUR is always filled by an American four-star general, reflecting the preponderance of American military might within NATO. He is so-called 'double-hatted', because he also holds the national post of Commander in Chief, US European Command (CINCEUR). When I took up my appointment these two jobs were held by General George Joulwan, whom I had come to know quite well while in Bosnia. He was a large, outgoing man, a soldier's soldier, and I found it easy to get on with him. Quite soon afterwards, in the summer of 1997, he came to the end of his term and was replaced by General Wesley 'Wes' Clark.

Wes Clark was something of a loner, a driven, intensely ambitious man with a piercing stare. Often described as 'tightly wound', he seemed to bring a disturbing zeal to his work. He had a reputation as a very political sort of general, antagonizing his military superiors by going over their heads when they did not give him what he wanted. He was not popular among many of his colleagues in the US Army, who knew him as the 'Perfumed Prince'. Like Bill Clinton he had adopted his stepfather's name, and like Bill Clinton he came from Little Rock, Arkansas. A Vietnam veteran, Wes Clark was a highly educated man – and, again like Bill Clinton, a former Rhodes Scholar. Shorter than average, wiry and youthful-looking in his mid-fifties, he was not a man who relaxed easily.

On Clark's first visit to the ARRC HQ at Rheindahlen, we briefed him on the lessons learned from the Bosnia deployment. When we put up a slide emphasizing the importance of impartiality and even-handedness, Clark reacted sharply. 'You cannot be impartial where the Serbs are concerned,' he declared. I was taken aback, because all our thinking was contrary to what he was saying. I had plenty of reasons to mistrust Serb leaders like Mladic, but I had also encountered Serbs who had behaved reasonably in very difficult circumstances. I had found that if you dealt in a straight manner with men like Kasagic, they reciprocated. Nor did I think the other sides without blemish: on the contrary, all my experience in the Balkans led me to believe that there was not much to choose between them. But even then, Clark seemed to see the Balkans in very black-and-white terms.

Clark remained deeply involved with developments in Bosnia, so much so that, as I learned afterwards, Jeremy Mackenzie – by now Deputy SACEUR (DSACEUR) – had felt the need to counsel him against interfering so closely and so often with the commanders on the ground. 'The boys are grumbling a bit,' Jeremy warned him. 'You really ought to leave them to it.'

In May 1998, we NATO commanders gathered at SHAPE for SACEUR's annual conference. During the conference Clark called a lunchtime meeting for his key subordinates. 'Things are beginning to hot up in Kosovo,' he told us. 'NATO may have to intervene.'

For years, informed observers had been warning of a potential bloodbath in Kosovo. This was where the break-up of Yugoslavia would reach its climax.

Kosovo is felt by Serbs to be the homeland of their nation. Many of their beautiful medieval Orthodox monasteries are located there. 'Wipe away Kosovo from the Serb mind and soul,' wrote the Yugoslav writer, politician and theorist Milovan Djilas, 'and we are no more.' In 1389 the Serbs had fought the Ottomans at the battle of Kosovo Polje, also known as the Field of the Blackbirds, suffering a heroic defeat that looms large in the national mythology: Serbs see themselves as Christians in the front line of the millennium-long struggle with Islam. Kosovo became, and for more than five hundred years remained, part of the Ottoman Empire, before being reconquered by Serbia in the early twentieth century. At the end of the First World War, Kosovo became part of the new kingdom of Yugoslavia. Under Tito's postwar Communist rule, it then became a province of Serbia, one of the new republics within the federal system. Nevertheless Kosovo enjoyed a degree of autonomy, and ethnic tensions were kept in check.

Kosovo is small, less than half the area of Northern Ireland, though with a similar-sized population. It is strategically important, being a landlocked plain, almost surrounded by mountain ranges. High mountains ring Kosovo on its northern border with Montenegro, on its western border with Albania and on its southern border with Macedonia.* It is only on the eastern side, the Serbian side, that the ground is relatively open.

Like the Serbs, the Albanians also consider Kosovo important as the cradle of their own national movement. The proportion of the indigenous Kosovar population that is ethnically Albanian had been increasing steadily for many decades, and by the late 1990s had reached almost 90 per cent. Yet despite the demographic predominance of the Albanian Kosovars, most of the official positions were taken by Serbs, who dominated the security forces in particular. Kosovo was ruled as if it were

* The Former Yugoslav Republic of Macedonia, officially known by its initials FYROM, because of Greek objections to the use of the name Macedonia, which is also the name of the northern province of Greece. Pace Athens, Macedonia is used in this text out of convenience.

KOSOVO 1999

SERBIA

Montenegro

Podujevo

Kosovska Mitrovica

Pec

PRISTINA

Kosovo

Gracanica

Presevo Valley

Dakovica

Gnjilane

Prizren

Kacanik

Kacanik Defile

Kumanovo

ALBANIA

SKOPJE

0   20
        miles

FORMER YUGOSLAV REPUBLIC
OF MACEDONIA

a Serb colony. Ethnic Albanians in Kosovo speak a different language from the Serbs, a form of Albanian; and their religion is Islam, in contrast to the Christian Serbs.

After the death of Tito in 1980, Serb concern about the 'Albanianization' of Kosovo fuelled the rise of Serbian nationalism within Yugoslavia, and was skilfully exploited by Slobodan Milosevic in his rise to power. It was Serb nationalism that provided the pretext for the republics to start breaking away from federal Yugoslavia in the early 1990s. Thus it was said that 'the break-up of Yugoslavia began in Kosovo, and would end in Kosovo'. When he became President in 1989, Milosevic began the process of stripping Kosovo of the autonomy the province had enjoyed under the Yugoslav federal system. The result was to stimulate a movement for Kosovan independence. For some years in the 1990s, the Albanian Kosovars maintained their own parallel administrative structures under the benign leadership of Ibrahim Rugova, who advocated non-violent resistance to Serb rule. But not all were content with this approach, and in the mid-1990s the Kosovo Liberation Army (KLA, known also by its Albanian acronym, UCK) was formed and began a guerrilla campaign against the Serb security forces.

The KLA received support from Albania itself and from ethnic Albanians abroad, particularly in the United States, and by the summer of 1998 claimed to have 30,000 men under arms. Clashes between the KLA and the Serb security forces intensified. A pattern began of KLA attacks and heavy-handed Serb reprisals, often involving civilian casualties. Ethnic Albanians fled the Serb security forces; by the autumn there were estimated to be several hundred thousand internal refugees living in the woods, and the prospect of a humanitarian disaster loomed. Richard Holbrooke warned Milosevic against repression in Kosovo and allowed himself to be photographed alongside KLA fighters, indicating US support for the KLA. On 23 September the UN adopted Security Council Resolution 1199 calling for a ceasefire and dialogue between the warring parties. It also called for a withdrawal of Serb security forces used for repression, particularly the Serb Army, still then known as the Vojska Jugoslavia (VJ), and the Serb special police (MUP).

Back in Rheindahlen, we tracked all these developments very closely. As the summer of 1998 turned to autumn, the odds began to shorten on an ARRC deployment to Kosovo. We carried out a series of increasingly complex planning exercises, from which emerged a clear concept of the ideal composition and structure of a peace implementation force. At one stage in the autumn there was an absurd proposal for HQ ARRC alone to deploy to Kosovo, which would have left us exposed as potential hostages, just as UNPROFOR had been. Mercifully, this idea came and went almost overnight. We decided that, prior to entry into Kosovo, our in-theatre HQ should be sited near the Macedonian capital Skopje, only about 10 miles from the Kosovo border. Our line of communication would be from the Greek port of Thessaloniki, about 150 miles to the south, connected by a good, motorway-style road and a railway line. There were political difficulties, in that there was tension between Greece and Macedonia – not least over the name 'Macedonia' – but this seemed the only sensible supply route. The alternative through Albania, although shorter, was much less attractive, given that country's rudimentary infrastructure, inadequate ports and poor road network. There was also reason to think that the Albanian bridges could not support the weight of tanks and other armoured vehicles.

In October Holbrooke visited Milosevic, and came back with a deal. Faced with the threat of NATO air strikes, Milosevic offered concessions, and agreed to allow into Kosovo a two-thousand-strong force of unarmed observers, known as the Kosovo Verification Mission (KVM). Within NATO there was little faith that this deal would outlast the winter. We sent in a recce party, disguised as members of the KVM, who provided us with intelligence reports, both political and military.

In fact there was never a complete ceasefire, and towards the end of the year the fighting intensified. NATO deployed eighteen hundred troops to Kumanovo in northern Macedonia, ready to extract the KVM from Kosovo at short notice if they seemed threatened. There was already an American battalion in Macedonia, 'Task Force Able Sentry', stationed there some years before with a mission to deter Serbian aggression and, very unusually for US troops, serving under UN auspices.

In mid-January 1999, reports of a massacre of some 45 ethnic Albanians by the Serb security forces in the southern Kosovan village of Racak evoked memories of Srebrenica and prompted calls for NATO intervention. Talks between Serbs and Kosovar Albanians, organized by the so-called 'Contact Group' of France, Germany, Italy, Russia, the UK and the United States, took place at Rambouillet, near Paris. The proposed agreement provided for an independent military implementation force under NATO auspices to compel compliance. Four countries –

Britain, Germany, France and Italy – decided to deploy battalion-sized forces to Macedonia on a nation-by-nation basis, in anticipation of a successful agreement which might then have to be implemented in very short order.

By then I had visited Macedonia several times. The plan was for the ARRC to integrate the various scattered forces there under a single unified NATO command known as KFOR (Kosovo Force). KFOR's outline mission at this stage would be to provide stability in Kosovo following a political settlement, to prevent any further outbreak of fighting, and to ensure the return of all refugees once the Serbs had withdrawn.

By early February we had narrowed down our choice of a headquarters site in the Skopje area to two: the Intercontinental Hotel, which would have been comfortable but was expensive and rather small for our requirements, and might have given out the wrong message; and the 1970s-style Gazela Shoe Factory on the outskirts of the city. This was largely disused, though a little shoe-making was still carried on at one end, even after we had taken over most of the building. Like the Metal Factory at Banja Luka, it had much of what we needed: an office block, a works canteen good for feeding large numbers, warehousing for storage under cover, hard standing outside for parking vehicles, an area where we could site a helipad, and a perimeter fence for security. I had no hesitation in opting for the Shoe Factory, though it meant that we would be living in what had been offices, working and sleeping on camp beds in the same rooms. My team occupied a suite of offices on the upper floor, which included a slightly shabby conference room big enough to accommodate a meeting of thirty people or more. It was all fairly spartan, but none the worse for that. I must admit that I did begin to wonder about my decision later on, when my Chief of Staff, Major General Andrew Ridgway, entered his office to find himself confronted by a large rat. But by then we were committed, and after all it wasn't the first rat we'd encountered on operations, some of whom had only two legs. By early March our Rear Headquarters was already in place, handling the logistics, liaising with the Macedonian Government and attempting to corral the various national forces, although no formal command authority had been granted.

One thing still worrying me was the question of my new military assistant. In the middle of 1998, Miles Wade, the MA I had inherited from Mike Walker, had reached the end of his tour. I was given a list of three young lieutenant colonels from which to choose his replacement. None of them had what I was really looking for. I remember telephoning the Military Secretary and asking, 'Is there nobody else?' and his reply: 'I'm afraid not.' So I chose the best of them, as I thought, but with some misgivings.

Some months later, I realized that, for whatever reason, it wasn't working – and eventually, only about ten days before we were due to deploy to Macedonia, and with so much at stake, I told him so. I then telephoned the Military Secretary and said that I wanted the best man on his books by the next Monday morning. Faxes flew back and forth, and pretty soon I had a list with five names on it. Two of them I didn't know and there wasn't time to get to know them, but of the three I did know, one candidate stood out above the rest: James Everard, a scruffy cavalryman (for some, a contradiction in terms) who'd been

Richard Dannatt's Brigade Chief of Staff in Bosnia. I'd got to know him very well out there, and I thought him an outstanding young officer: highly intelligent and well read, a lateral thinker, and great fun. So I rang him up. He had just finished a tour in Germany and started a new desk job back in the MOD.

We chatted inconsequentially for a bit, and then there was a pause.

'Very nice to hear from you, General Mike,' he said cheerfully, 'but why on earth are you ringing me up?'

'I'm in a pickle,' I explained. 'I've just had to part company with my previous MA. I'd like to offer you the job. If you're on, it would be great to have you. I think we're off to the Balkans imminently, maybe as soon as a week from now. I cannot promise you a great adventure, but it should be interesting. What do you think?'

'Great idea, General,' he replied. 'But there are one or two difficulties. We've just packed up the house in Germany. All our kit's on the road now, I've put down a thousand quid for young Archie's nursery school in London, and the dog's been in quarantine for four months.'

'OK, James, I get the picture.'

'No,' he said, 'you haven't got the whole picture. Caroline's having twins in August.'

'OK, James. Great to speak to you. Good luck with the new job.'

'Hang on a minute,' he interrupted. 'I'm not saying no, I'm just laying it out for you. Give me half an hour to square it with Caroline and I'll ring you back.'

He called back well within the half-hour. 'OK, General, you're on,' he said. 'But there are one or two things you could do for me.'

'Anything,' I replied, still not quite believing that he had said yes.

'First, get us a decent house in Rheindahlen.'

'Done.'

'Next, can you find Mr Pickford's van and stop it?' And we did: we actually found it on the autobahn and said, do not go to Calais, turn left, drive to Rheindahlen. We got James his money back for the quarantine fees as well.

'Oh,' he added, 'one more thing.' What now? I thought. 'Can I be home for the twins' birth?'

'Of course,' I said, and that was that. A couple of days later he was at my side in Rheindahlen, and a week after that we were both in Skopje.

By mid-March 1999 the ARRC was established at the Gazela Shoe Factory, and was in the process of coordinating the various national contingents already deployed in Macedonia. At this stage there was still a hope that last-ditch efforts might salvage a diplomatic solution, even though the Serb negotiators at Rambouillet had refused to sign the agreement. Meanwhile, the Serbs in Kosovo began to step up the activity of their security forces. Richard Holbrooke flew to Belgrade in yet another unsuccessful attempt to persuade Milosevic to comply with the demands of the international community. He threatened that if Serbia did not comply, NATO would take military action. The crisis was seen as a test of Europe's ability to deal with problems 'in its own backyard'. For NATO, searching for a new role in its fiftieth anniversary year, this was both a challenge and an opportunity. For almost ten years commentators had been asking whether NATO's unity and resolve would persist after the ending of the Cold War. Here was an issue that could either show the way forward, or expose the weakness of the Alliance now that its original *raison d'être* was no more.

This was a test which threatened the stability of several west European governments, whose ruling parties were deeply divided on the issue. For all of them, the decision to take military action against Serbia was a tough one, but the unacceptable actions of Milosevic's security forces left them with no alternative. Grim stories of ethnic cleansing emerged from Kosovo in a steady stream. American politicians began to use the term 'genocide' to describe what was happening there.

Three former Warsaw Pact nations, the Czech Republic, Hungary and Poland, were in the process of joining NATO, and there was to be a ceremony at Rheindahlen on 19 March to mark their accession. Wes Clark had wanted me to remain 'on the scene' in Macedonia, but I felt that my presence was not absolutely essential at that moment and I wanted to get back home, not just for this important ceremony, but to brief the ARRC families at Rheindahlen on what was happening in the Balkans. It was very important on this occasion for them to hear what was going on from the Commander personally. There had been much uncertainty, much 'on the bus, off the bus', and it was right that they got as realistic a picture as possible from the horse's mouth. People who marry soldiers take on a lot, and the soldiers themselves are far happier when deployed if they know that their loved ones are being properly looked after and kept informed. Despite heavy snow, we managed to reach the community centre in Rheindahlen just in time for the briefing. This was the first of what became a regular monthly event, which our families much appreciated, and which helped to dispel misinformation from whatever source. It was an anxious time for the families, especially for the non-British wives – for many of whom this was their husbands' first operational deployment. I wasn't usually able to attend, of course; the briefings were given by whichever senior officer was available at the time.

The families' briefing was followed by a simple but symbolic ceremony at HQ to mark the accession of the three new NATO nations. But during the day we got the news that the KVM had been directed to withdraw from Kosovo the following day because of the deteriorating security situation. I had to get back to Skopje as soon as possible, in case the KVM withdrawal went wrong.

Captain Ed Sandry, my rock-solid ADC, moved heaven and earth to get us an aircraft, and managed to wangle us a 'pocket rocket', an RAF HS-125 six-seater executive jet, which had us back in Skopje before midnight. I spent the following morning up at the border crossing-point greeting the withdrawing KVM observers, who arrived in a long stream of orange vehicles; they included some of our own recce party and some familiar Special Forces faces. The number two in the KVM was my old schoolmate 'DZ', now Major General John Drewienkiewicz. It was great to see him, and of course we were relieved that everyone in the mission had got out safely. That night they had a celebration dinner in what was known as the 'Ally Pally', the Alexandra Palace Hotel in Skopje. Much red wine was drunk, and in the small hours of the morning I returned to the Shoe Factory feeling ready for whatever the next few days and weeks might bring.

The following day, 21 March, was my fifty-fifth birthday. Because of the sudden ending of the Rambouillet talks two days earlier and the need to get back to meet the KVM observers, we had not had time to collect much of our personal kit, so I decided to fly back to Rheindahlen again for one quick pit stop. By this time it was obvious that we would be going on to a war footing; NATO air strikes were due to commence imminently. We arrived back in Rheindahlen in the evening, and stayed for fourteen hours. I told Sarah that I was unlikely to be back for a while. She knew what that meant: she is a soldier's daughter. Ever practical, she asked me to remind her where all the family documents were kept, 'just to be on the safe side'. When the doorbell rang the next morning, I knew it would be Ed Sandry. I opened the door and told him I'd be with him in a minute. Sarah and I said our goodbyes. I picked up my beret, shouldered my rucksack, walked out to the car and slung it into the boot. Sarah had followed me out, and I gave her one last hug standing by the car. Then I climbed in and we drove away.

Two days later, on the evening of 24 March, NATO began air strikes. The bombing campaign dragged on for seventy-eight days, and during this period we in the ARRC were very much in the supporting role, almost spectators. In fact we were concerned about our vulnerability, being so close to the border. A quick attack towards Skopje by Serb units, particularly from Serbia proper down the Presevo valley, would have been a real problem. We were also within range of Serb artillery fire. As time passed and we were reinforced by air into Skopje and by regular convoys by road and rail from Thessaloniki, our fighting strength increased steadily, but at first we had only a few thousand troops to call on, scattered in different locations across northern Macedonia. SHAPE at last agreed to give HQ ARRC a degree of formal command over the various national troop contingents, now developing into five multinational brigades led respectively by France, Germany, Italy, the UK and the United States. As COMK-FOR, my immediate superior officer was US Navy Admiral Jim Ellis, NATO's Commander in Chief for Southern Europe (CINCSOUTH), who in turn reported directly to SACEUR. In practice, Wes Clark often bypassed Jim Ellis and dealt directly with me; this was very frustrating for both Jim and me. I got on very well with Jim, a sympathetic and understanding man who was always supportive. His staff and mine worked easily together – which wasn't always the case with the SHAPE staff.

There was also a concern about assassination attempts. On the day after the bombing commenced, Brigadier General Marcel Valentin, the French Brigade commander, was attacked with a Molotov cocktail. He escaped un-injured, though two British soldiers were not so lucky: they were hospitalized when their vehicles were stoned. I had a close protection team of two SAS soldiers, one very tall and one very short – unkindly nicknamed Pinky and Perky – who accompanied me everywhere I went for the next seven months or so. For getting about, we had two dedicated Lynx helicopters.

That same evening a mob attacked both the American Embassy and the Intercontinental Hotel in Skopje, where the KVM was staying. I learned that SACEUR in his national US role had ordered 'Task Force Able Sentry' to the rescue. I spoke to John Craddock, the US Brigade

Commander, and advised him to make haste slowly. 'You do not want to become part of the problem,' I suggested. Luckily the Macedonian riot police arrived first and dispersed the mob, which moved off to disport themselves outside the British and German embassies. It seemed to me more than likely that this civil disorder had been orchestrated from Belgrade. The Macedonian Government was rattled, and called an emergency Cabinet meeting that night. Much of my time in the next few weeks would be spent calming them, reassuring them that we had the situation under control. I saw support to the Macedonian Government as fundamental to our operation.

Yet later that same evening we received a SITREP (situation report) from the American battalion that the Serbs had crossed the border. I was sceptical. It emerged that an American U-2 spy plane had mistaken French forces for invading Serbs. I was not at all happy about the confusion, and complained vigorously to Mike Short, the three-star US Air Force commander at the Air HQ of AFSOUTH (Allied Forces Southern Europe) in Vicenza, from which the air strikes were being coordinated. This was the kind of mistake that could have easily led to a 'blue on blue' disaster.

SACEUR was under a lot of pressure. I observed Clark each morning on the video conference (VTC) held twice daily among all the NATO centres involved in the Balkan operation. He seemed tired already, not helped by having to work Washington hours. This was a concern to us all. We knew that Wes was having trouble with his superiors at the Pentagon, many of whom saw little reason for America to become involved in Kosovo. President Clinton's administration had shown itself to be extremely reluctant to commit ground troops to overseas operations. The President declared that he 'had no intent' to use ground troops against the Serbs. But this seemed to make Wes all the more determined. At first he argued that the bombing would bring the Serbs to heel. 'I know Milosevic,' he would say time after time. It was a peculiarity of the Kosovo War that all the main protagonists had met beforehand.

My old friend Rupert Smith had by now succeeded Jeremy Mackenzie as Clark's deputy. He and I spoke at least once a day on the secure phone. Rupert was a moderating influence on Wes, as Jeremy had been before him. When the bombing started, Wes had wanted to come down to inspect personally the arrangements we had made for our defence should the Serbs come across the border. The implication was that we wouldn't know what to do, which didn't go down well with the Headquarters staff. In the end, Rupert persuaded SACEUR that he should come instead. Rupert knew perfectly well that we didn't need any guidance from him or anyone else. He arrived, had a briefing, had lunch with us and then went back to Belgium again without inspecting anything.

Clark's attitude to the Serbs convinced many that he was spoiling for an all-out war. He seemed dangerously stuck in a Cold War mentality of confrontation. At the end of March, he became very excited by reports that the Russians were planning to send warships from their Black Sea Fleet into the Mediterranean. On the morning VTC that day, he declared that they had to be stopped. Jim Ellis was clearly unhappy with this approach. 'What exactly do you want me to do?' he asked.

Clark told him to lean on the Turks to keep the

Russians bottled up in the Black Sea by denying them access to their territorial waters.

'SACEUR, I can't do that,' Ellis replied. 'The Montreux Convention guarantees the right of free passage through the Bosphorus.' Clark went on to suggest that he should establish a maritime exclusion zone, rather as we had done in the Falklands. Fortunately nothing came of this.

I had more cause to question Clark's judgement a week or so later, when during a VTC he asked CINCSOUTH to confirm that he had received a detailed map reference sent the day before. That the Supreme Commander should be personally passing such minutiae to another four-star officer was worrying.

A fortnight or so later, there was another extraordinary piece of rhetoric from Wes on the morning VTC. He gave the kind of gung-ho address the commander of a small unit might give immediately prior to battle, when the soldiers need to be fired up. It was totally inappropriate for a VTC with thirty or forty senior officers in a multi-national force, watching in ten or so different locations.

'We are moving to total war,' he announced portentously. 'If there is a battle, it will be tough, very tough, hill to hill, house to house, street to street. It will be bayonets and close combat in guerrilla war. NATO soldiers must relearn the spirit of the bayonet.'

Listening to this stuff back at Skopje, we were all stunned. I glanced at my senior American staff officer, Brigadier General Mike Maples, and I could see that he was staring at the ground.

'Do you understand the spirit of the bayonet?' Clark asked. He addressed one of the German generals on the VTC. 'Klaus, do you understand the spirit of the bayonet?'

The general shifted uneasily. There was an embarrassing pause. 'Oh yes, SACEUR,' he replied eventually.

The next day Clark issued a statement. 'I wish to clarify any misunderstanding that may have arisen from what I said yesterday. All I meant was that the campaign would have administrative implications for NATO's staff vacation plans.'

Word began to get around regarding some of Wes's extraordinary behaviour. I remember a visit to Naples some time that spring, when Jim Ellis had called together a conference in his own Headquarters. At a supper party he gave that evening, I noticed a group of American three-stars in a huddle. 'Is this Americans only or can a Brit join in?' I asked jocularly.

'Of course,' one of them said. 'You'd better come in on this, because we're all having a beef about Wes.' It was alarming to encounter mutterings about Clark's judge-ment among his American subordinates – not from Ellis, but from those at three-star level and below.

All this took me back to a conversation I'd had in Sarajevo with the commander of SFOR, US Lieutenant General 'Monty' Meigs, not long before the Kosovo oper-ation started. Monty and I had become quite good friends by this point. We were talking generally about the Balkans, and the likelihood of the ARRC being deployed to Kosovo, when Monty came out with an unexpected question. 'Have you thought about how you are going to handle Wes?'

The last of the Red Cross personnel to leave Kosovo painted a grim picture of a breakdown in law and order, with rape, executions and looting taking place on the streets of the capital, Pristina. One young woman broke down as she described finding the sole survivor of a burned-out village, a baby girl trying to feed from a bottle filled with her mother's blood. As the fighting worsened, the prospect of a humanitarian disaster loomed once more. Hundreds of thousands of displaced persons or those fearing for their safety were making their way west and south to the mountainous border regions, hoping to cross into Albania or Macedonia. Others were loaded on to trains by the Serb security forces and shunted to the border, where they were compelled to cross on foot, told to walk down the track because if they strayed off the road they risked walking into a minefield. At the height of the crisis, it was estimated that three-quarters of a million people, approximately one-third of the entire population, had fled Kosovo. The refugees came in waves, sometimes five thousand or more in a day, completely overwhelming the small number of personnel from the UN High Commission for Refugees on hand to provide them with food and shelter. Refugee assistance was not, of course, part of KFOR's mission as stated. But we had to take on the problem – in the first instance, on purely humanitarian grounds; secondly, because it was operationally essential in order to deny Milosevic his political goal, namely the fall of the Macedonian Government.

I was in constant contact with NATO HQ during this period, speaking several times a day to either Rupert Smith or Wes Clark. KFOR did most of the spadework, literally and metaphorically, of establishing the refugee camps, and we ran them until UNHCR and the various NGOs got their act together. We had a handover programme, camp by camp: somebody will take over water, somebody will take over food, somebody will take over medical aid; and then, when they were able to cope with the whole thing, we felt able to leave with a clear conscience. The lion's share of the administrative support for the refugee crisis was taken by the British 101 Logistic Brigade, under the inspired leadership of Brigadier Tim Cross. Some of the NGOs and professional relief people took a certain exception to the military being involved in the humanitarian effort. But this was a case of needs must.

NATO also assembled a force of about two thousand lightly armed soldiers in Albania to provide humanitarian aid to the refugees arriving there. Known as the Albania Force (AFOR), its HQ was formed by HQ Allied Command Europe (ACE) Mobile Force (Land), commanded by yet another member of the Airborne tribe, Major General John Reith, who back in 1986 had succeeded me as commanding officer of 1 Para, itself then part of ACE Mobile Force (Land). John was given the rank of lieutenant general for the duration of the operation.

The refugees had been only reluctantly allowed across the border by the Macedonian authorities, who feared the effect of adding so many ethnic Albanians to their own significant Albanian minority. Like us, they recognized that this ethnic cleansing was a tactic of Milosevic's, intended to destabilize their Government. The huge numbers of refugees formed a substantial addition to Macedonia's Albanian population, already around 30 per cent of the total before their arrival. At the beginning of the refugee crisis over Easter, the Macedonians had denied the refugees entry, confining them to the no-man's-land between the two countries where they squatted on the ground, exhausted. Under pressure from international opinion, the Macedonian Government had relented and allowed the refugees in, but restricted them to camps only a short distance into the country. Though we could just about cope with the refugees during the warmer summer weather, it was obvious that if they were still there when the harsh Balkan winter arrived, many of them would die.

The refugee crisis was of intense interest to the world's media, attracting hundreds of journalists to Skopje. During this period we received innumerable visits from VIPs, many of whom were nothing more than a nuisance and some of whom appeared to be seeking photo-opportunities. I became irritated with the constant refrain, 'I'm here to help.' After hearing this for the umpteenth time, I handed one of the worthies a spade. 'Take this up to the camps,' I said, 'and start digging latrines.'

Clare Short, Secretary of State for International Development, arrived in Skopje on Easter Sunday. She successfully bullied the Macedonians into allowing the refugees to leave no-man's-land and to be dispersed into camps. Less helpfully, she tried to bully me too, breathing fire about the need to 'defeat Serb aggression' and accus-ing me of being 'weak-willed' in not wanting to march straight into Kosovo. I countered that we had no authority to do any such thing, and when she sniffed, I suggested that we withdraw to my office for a private chat. When we were alone I didn't mince my words. I explained to her the facts of life – that I had at that time approximately eight thousand soldiers under my command to oppose a Serb army more than twenty times that number; moreover, that we had only twenty or so tanks, a mere 380 fewer than the Serbs. 'I'm too old for a heroic but futile gesture,' I told her.

She calmed down after that. I offered her a whisky, and

we parted on good terms. My staff, who had earlier heard raised voices coming from my office, were surprised to see her come out grinning.

In fact my planning team had been looking at the options for a forced entry into Kosovo if all other options failed. This had to be done very discreetly, as it was extremely politically sensitive. For one thing, NATO rules did not permit us to start formally planning a ground offensive without the prior authorization of the NAC. For another, the Macedonian Government would not countenance their territory being used as a base for an invasion – at least, not publicly. A ground offensive was anyway a daunting prospect, given the formidable size of the Serb army and the challenging terrain. We reckoned we would need at least three corps of fifty thousand soldiers each. Even with those numbers, and complete command of the air, it would still be very difficult. Apart from anything else, there were only a few routes into Kosovo, all of which could easily be blocked. And there was little political support for a ground war. When Clark began to argue for an all-out ground offensive against the Serbs, he found himself cold-shouldered in Washington and denied access to the President. Immediately afterwards he gave a press conference in which he talked freely about the limitations of bombing and appeared to advocate a forced entry into Kosovo. His superiors in the Pentagon were livid. Clark received a call from General Hugh Shelton, Chairman of the US Joint Chiefs of Staff, who announced that the verbatim guidance he was about to give came directly from the Secretary of Defense, William Cohen. 'Get your fucking face off the TV,' he said. 'No more briefings, period.'

This was an extremely busy time for my team. We worked long hours, often late into the night. This suited my habits, though I occasionally compensated with an afternoon nap – known jocularly in the Factory as 'strategic thought'. This ability to cat-nap is something that you learn in the Army. There's always a lot of waiting around between intense periods of activity, and any soldier will have a kip if he's got nothing to do, whether he's sitting in the back of an aeroplane or waiting for orders to move off. Most nights I would telephone Sarah just before going to bed. This sometimes led to some incongruous conversations. I remember Sarah holding forth about car insurance at one particularly tense moment. But talking to her helped me to keep a sense of proportion.

There was a great deal to be done while we waited for the bombing campaign to force Milosevic to concede: not least the complex task of coordinating the disparate national forces into one effective fighting formation. We also steadily built up our strength as new units and supplies arrived by road, rail or air. I spent a lot of time in helicopters, on visits to the brigades dispersed across northern Macedonia. Then there was the need to keep our plans under constant review to take account of rapidly changing circumstances. The refugee relief effort complicated all of this, of course. Throughout I had to work hard to keep the Macedonians on side. There were also problems with the Greeks: over 90 per cent of the population there opposed the bombing campaign against another Orthodox country, and once the bombing began there was a succession of demonstrations and other difficulties. We relied on the Greek port of Thessaloniki for our line of

communication, and from time to time I had to go down
there – and once to Athens – for meetings with concerned
Greek officials who were worried that public unrest would
affect our logistics. Then there was the constant need to
put out small fires. Early on, I had to deal with a panic
about a Serb incursion when three American soldiers out
on a patrol near the border reported that they had come
under fire, and were subsequently captured by Serb forces.
Wes Clark's version of this was that Serb special forces had
kidnapped them from inside Macedonia. It turned out
that they had strayed across the border before being
detained by the Serbs. Later, a Norwegian captain driving
up the wrong side of the road from Thessaloniki was
involved in a head-on collision, killing the son of a
Macedonian minister.

All the time we were operating in the spotlight of the
world's media. I was very fortunate in having a quite
excellent media operations staff, ably led by Lieutenant
Colonel Robin Clifford. I gave press conferences only
when there was some new development, rather than providing a running commentary on the situation. I also gave
occasional one-to-one interviews, and informal off-the-
record briefings to the press, some of them to journalists
from non-English-speaking countries – particularly
Germany, Italy and Greece, to say nothing of Macedonia
itself – aware that world opinion was a weapon in the
struggle with Milosevic. My aim was always to be open
and straight whenever possible. I have found that, by and
large, journalists respond well to this. Weasel words
and spin are generally counter-productive. I bridled
when London tried to tell me what to say. 'If that's
what you want, you're going to have to find someone

else,' I told one of the more intrusive spin doctors.

In the process I came in for rather too much personal attention, including a *Sunday Telegraph* profile which caused much amusement at the Shoe Factory. 'He likes whisky and cigars . . . prone to work all night . . . keeps going in Churchillian style with an afternoon nap . . . the pace is furious but his aides seem to adore him.' Why my staff seemed to think this so funny I couldn't imagine.

Early in May the Prime Minister, Tony Blair, visited Macedonia to see the refugee situation for himself. He sent advisers ahead to arrange the details of his visit. They were obsessed with the media angle, of course. I enjoyed teasing them by saying that I intended to give him a public broadside. It was worth it just to see the look of horror on their faces. Blair arrived accompanied by a large party, including his wife Cherie, his chief press officer Alastair Campbell, and Anji Hunter, known as the gate-keeper, who ran his private office. I disliked the accompanying media circus, but the Prime Minister knew what he was about. He was relaxed and well briefed, and asked shrewd questions. Blair was leading the inter-national community on this issue, and I felt that I was speaking not just to the British Prime Minister, but also to the political leader who would make the case inter-nationally. Throughout the whole Kosovo crisis, the UK was the nation most on the front foot. Blair was arguing to the world that we couldn't let this appalling situation continue, that we must take action, however difficult or dangerous it might be. A few weeks before coming to Kosovo he had made an important speech in Chicago, outlining what he described as 'a new doctrine of inter-national community', setting out criteria for intervention in the internal affairs of a sovereign state – in particular, the imperative of coming to the assistance of the oppressed.

Also with the prime ministerial party was the CDS, General Sir Charles (now Lord) Guthrie. I'd known Charles from the late 1970s, when he had commanded the Welsh Guards in Berlin and then in South Armagh, where my company had been under his command for a while. I had appreciated his guidance down the years, and it was good to see him, not least because I knew of his strong influence on the Prime Minister.

The most important part of the visit from my point of view was undoubtedly the hour and a half I spent in private with the PM and the CDS. It was a warm afternoon, and we sat under a camouflage net on one of our training areas, just hammering through where we were and what we might have to do, analysing the timelines for a decision on a ground invasion. At this point Blair had been in power two years and this was the first time that he had committed British forces to a strategic military operation, so of course he was on a serious learning curve. I stressed to him the urgency of prompt action: humanitarian disaster loomed if the refugees remained in the camps into the winter months.

The Prime Minister asked me to estimate the likely casualties if we had to fight our way into Kosovo. He wanted to know what the butcher's bill might be. I remember telling him that it was very difficult to say, but used the Falklands War as an analogy. In the worst case we might be talking about several hundred British deaths and well over a thousand wounded – to say nothing of the casualties which might be incurred by the other NATO nations.

This visit also provided an opportunity for the Prime Minister to speak to the soldiers and to thank them for what they were doing. After that, he and his wife visited the refugee camp at Stankovic, a few miles south of the Kosovo border. Both were visibly shocked by what they saw and moved by stories they were told of rape, murder and brutality. The refugees lionized him, and it was obvious that they saw him as a key to their future. The very fact that he'd bothered to go and see them was a statement that they were not being ignored. Blair made a powerful speech. 'This is not a battle for NATO,' he declared. 'This is not a battle for territory. This is a battle for humanity.' He demanded an end to Serb atrocities, so that the refugees could return to their homes. 'NATO will prevail. The butchers of Belgrade will be defeated.' The crowds cheered and chanted, 'Tony, Tony, Tony.'

By now, NATO's objectives had been simplified to sound-bites: Serbs out, NATO in, refugees back. NATO's strategy, as championed by Clark, had been to bomb the Serbs into backing down. But this was taking a long time to work. The bombing campaign continued for more than two months with little sign that Serbs were on the brink of capitulation. Overall, NATO aircraft flew more than thirty-eight thousand combat missions with surprisingly little effect on Serb military capability on the ground, as we discovered when we eventually occupied Kosovo. A few obvious buildings had been destroyed, but there were hardly any burned-out tank hulks to be seen. In part, this was because the Serbs had dispersed their formations and found clever ways to conceal their weaponry. In part too, this was because pilots were instructed not to fly lower

Main picture and above left: *In the first half of 1999, almost one-third of the entire population fled Kosovo. A quarter of a million people were living in camps just inside Macedonia, run by the NATO Kosovo Force (KFOR) under my command. A humanitarian disaster loomed if the refugees were forced to remain in the mountain camps through a Balkan winter.* **Above right:** *The British Prime Minister Tony Blair visited us with the Chief of the Defence Staff General Sir Charles Guthrie. Blair was convinced of the need to stop Serbian President Slobodan Milosevic's ethnic cleansing, and took the lead in persuading the world community that military action was necessary.*

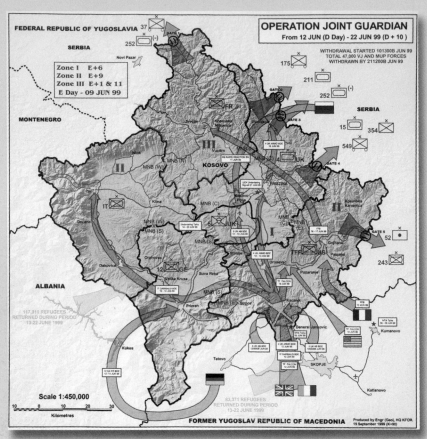

Operation 'Joint Guardian' provided for KFOR's entry into Kosovo and Serb withdrawal. Negotiation with the Serbs took over one hundred gruelling hours, with constant amendments to the draft agreement.

KLA 'Commander in Chief' Hashim Thaqi signs an undertaking renouncing the use of force and acknowledging KFOR's sole authority, 21 June 1999.

Main picture: *Northern Macedonia, 11 June 1999: paratroopers and Gurkhas preparing to move forward into Kosovo by Chinook helicopter.*

Disarming the Kosovo Liberation Army (KLA) was essential to the peace-keeping operation. British soldiers escorting KLA fighters.

A British soldier carries weapons surrendered by the KLA during the demilitarization process.

Shaking hands with KLA 'Field Commander' Agim Ceku on a visit to a weapons storage site. Ceku played a key role in the process of normalizing Kosovo and is now its Prime Minister.

As KFOR entered Kosovo, a column of Russian troops occupied Pristina Airport. Orders from my superior officer, NATO's Supreme Allied Commander, Europe, General Wesley 'Wes' Clark, could have led to a dangerous confrontation, but I was able to avert this and establish good relations with the Russian commander, General Viktor Zavarzin.

Left: *Russian armoured personnel carrier at Pristina Airport.*

Below: *with General Zavarzin at the airport, 26 June 1999.*

American President Bill Clinton, his wife Hillary and daughter Chelsea visit US troops in Skopje, Macedonia, 22 June 1999. I flew down from Pristina to meet them. Wes Clark stands at right.

US Secretary of State Madeleine Albright visits KFOR HQ, Pristina, 29 June 1999. With her is Bernard Kouchner, Special Representative of the Secretary General (SRSG) and head of UNMIK, the UN 'international civil presence'. I jokingly called Bernard 'le roi'.

With Wes Clark and Prince Charles in Kosovo.

Negotiations on the transformation of the
KLA into a peacetime organization were
very difficult and continued until after the
KFOR-imposed deadline. We held regular
meetings in the 'Bat Cave' at KFOR HQ,
a huge room in a deserted film studio.
Artist in residence Nick Bashall (top
right) painted a moment in one of our
sessions when I confronted Ceku across
the table (above).

Right: In October 1999, after seven months
in the Balkans, I handed over command of
KFOR and returned with my immediate
staff to HQ ARRC's permanent base in
Rheindahlen, Germany. It was a great party.
With Caroline Everard, wife of my Military
Assistant (MA) James; Caroline had given
birth to twins Sam and Tilly while we were
in Kosovo.

than 20,000 feet for fear of being shot down. There was also, rightly, much sensitivity about 'collateral damage'. Pilots often found that their targets had been changed after they had taken off on a mission.

Inevitably, there were mistakes. Early in May, NATO aircraft attacked and largely destroyed a Kosovar refugee convoy, mistaking it for a convoy of Serb military vehicles and killing the very people it set out to protect. Then NATO in error bombed the Chinese Embassy in Belgrade, prompting a diplomatic uproar.

But there was a sense that the end-game might be in sight. Britain, ever on the front foot, decided to make the necessary arrangements to reinforce its existing contingent, then still largely based on 4 Armoured Brigade, commanded by Brigadier Bill Rollo. In the event, HQ 3 Division under Major General Richard Dannatt and 5 Airborne Brigade under Brigadier Adrian Freer deployed as reinforcements. Richard Dannatt took on the national role of Commander British Forces (COMBRITFOR) from Bill Rollo.

On 16 May Rupert Smith summarized the progress of the air campaign on the VTC by quoting from a little-known speech by Churchill. We were 'buggering on'. For the benefit of those watchers whose first language was not English, he explained what was meant by the term: 'an unnatural act . . . committed in a dark and unpleasant place . . . that produces nothing . . . but has a certain rhythm to it'. There was a lot of laughter in the Shoe Factory, but I could see on the monitor that some of the Americans were not amused. KBO ('Keep Buggering On') became our unofficial mission statement after this.

As it became more likely that we were headed for a

showdown with the Serbs, I flew back to London for a private audience with Her Majesty The Queen at Buckingham Palace, with only the two of us present. This was unusual, but then it was an unusual situation. As ever, she was most perceptive and encouraging, and showed a very impressive grasp of the situation.

Late in May Viktor Chernomyrdin, President Yeltsin's special envoy to Serbia, issued a stark warning to the West. 'The world has never in this decade been so close to the brink of nuclear war. I appeal to NATO leaders to show the courage to suspend the air raids . . . it is impossible to talk with bombs falling.' Unless the bombing stopped soon, he warned, he would advise Russia's President to suspend Russian participation in the negotiating process, put an end to all military/technical agreements with the West, delay ratification of the SALT II arms reduction agreement and use Russia's veto to block any UN Security Council Resolution on Yugoslavia.

This was a chilling statement, but there was an element of bluster in it. The Russians felt protective towards their fellow Slavs and extremely sensitive about NATO's attack on a former Communist country – unauthorized by any UN Security Council Resolution. Nevertheless, they recognized the need to end the fighting in Kosovo. On behalf of the G8 group of industrialized nations, they put pressure on the Serbs to compromise.

On 2 June, Milosevic received Chernomyrdin and Finland's President Ahtisaari in Belgrade. Later that day we received a diplomatic telegram (DIPTEL) indicating that 'real progress towards some form of agreement may be genuinely possible'. I didn't get too excited, even when we heard a report that Milosevic had made an announcement to the effect that he would withdraw all military and para-military forces from Kosovo. We'd heard this sort of thing before. An annual conference of the ARRC's peacetime-assigned divisional commanders was scheduled to begin the next morning, and there seemed no convincing reason to postpone it. The conference had begun when the star-tling news came through that the Serb parliament had reluctantly approved the Kosovo plan presented by Ahtisaari and Chernomyrdin, which Milosevic had approved the day before. Suddenly it began to look as if there were some substance to Milosevic's concessions. Even today, it's still unclear why he backed down, but one can surmise some or all of the following: the bombing campaign, now including strategic targets in Serbia proper, rather than just tactical targets in Kosovo, was at last really hurting Milosevic and his coterie; NATO had not splintered under the political strains of going to war against his country; the threat of an eventual ground attack was known to him; Russia had made it clear that, in the last analysis, he would be on his own; on 27 May he had been indicted by the ICTY at The Hague for crimes against humanity in Kosovo. Less than three years later, Slobodan Milosevic would find himself in the dock.

Nobody knew what would happen next. Rupert Smith, chairing the VTC on the morning of 4 June, character-istically put it well: 'Give me two minutes to think about what I am going to say—' and then added sardonically, '—the first person to do so today.' The Russians were insisting on a suspension of the bombing, but NATO resisted this. The argument was that if we stopped bombing, politically we would never be able to start again, even if the Serbs didn't withdraw. The agreement provided for an international security force 'with substantial NATO participation under unified command and control'. This in turn implied a unified NATO chain of command, under the political direction of the North Atlantic Council. Talks were taking place in Moscow about the involvement of Russian forces, negotiated by the US Deputy Secretary of State, Strobe Talbott. Russia's opening position was that the Russian contingent would not be under NATO command, which would make life very difficult on the ground. Wes Clark was determined not to allow the Russians a sector of their own. If Russian troops occupied the northern part of Kosovo where most of the Serbs lived, it could result in *de facto* partition. In Bosnia, a Russian brigade had deployed as part of IFOR/SFOR within the American Sector. This was the model we were keen to adopt in Kosovo, but it was by no means certain that the Russians would go along with it.

Much debate followed about the wording of the so-called Military–Technical Agreement (MTA) that would determine the arrangements to be made between the withdrawing Serb security forces and the incoming KFOR. Such an MTA would provide for the replacement of one force by another. Within KFOR itself, we were naturally concerned that the MTA should not commit us to anything that we felt unhappy about doing. SHAPE was circulating a draft MTA but had not thought to copy it to us. At the daily NATO press conference on 4 June, the spokesman Jamie Shea announced that a meeting with the Serbs to finalize the details of the MTA would take place the following day, and that I would conduct it. This was the first any of us had heard of it. Imperturbable as ever, Andrew Ridgway made the necessary arrangements. Brigadier Jonathan Bailey, who in the last few days had joined us from Rheindahlen, was dispatched to the border to act as a liaison officer with the Serbs. He set up a meeting with Serb representatives for the following morning at the Café Europa, a small, run-down establishment similar to a British transport café 500 yards inside the Macedonian border. All day drafts of the MTA pinged backwards and forwards. At 01.20 hours on the morning of Saturday 5 June a 'final' MTA arrived – containing a number of errors. It looked as though I would be flying by the seat of my pants.

I spent an hour working through the text and finally got to bed at 02.30 hours. Half an hour later the telephone rang. It was the office of the Supreme Allied Commander. There was another draft of the MTA. It arrived at 04.00 hours. I sat up cross-checking the new version line by line with the previous version. It was mind-numbing, painstaking work, but it was vital to get it right. By 08.15 the next morning, after little enough sleep, I was waiting in our nearest base to the Café Europa, where apparently a hundred or more press were gathered. Jonathan Bailey phoned me and explained that the Serbs weren't prepared to cross the border, claiming that SACEUR had agreed to a meeting 500 yards on their side. I had had a hunch that the Serbs might be reluctant to come across, which was why I hadn't gone up to the café, not wanting to be seen waiting for them. It was an impasse, with neither wanting to give way. In the next few hours the phone rang hot. By 11.00 hours it seemed that I was faced with three choices: cancel, meet in no-man's-land, or go across the border myself. We looked at the possibility of erecting a tent right on the bridge that marked the border. Still undecided and getting impatient, at 11.45 I went up to the café; as luck would have it, very shortly afterwards the Serbs arrived. We could start.

The demeanour of the Serb delegation was resigned. They were obviously depressed. I was determined not to show any hint of triumphalism on our part, which would have been inappropriate and gratuitous. The atmosphere was workmanlike and professional. One sensed that the Serbs didn't really understand why we were there. 'You are an honourable officer, a general from Britain, a fine country, our allies in two world wars,' one of their officers said to me while we were chatting during a break. 'Of course we in the Serb army will treat you with honour. But Albania is not a proper country. The Albanians are not a proper people. There is no requirement to treat them with honour.'

Occasionally while we were negotiating I reflected that if the talks broke down, I would be going into battle against the Serb generals on the other side of the table. The same thought must have occurred to them too.

On our side of the table I had my own small team: Mike Venables, an MOD civil servant who had been with us since deployment to Macedonia as my political adviser – inevitably nicknamed 'the Commissar'; US Air Force three-star general Robert H. Fogelsong, representing US national interests; Admiral Kaskeala, a Finn who had accompanied President Ahtisaari to Belgrade; and, of course, taking notes, James Everard (by now known to all as 'Ever-Ready').

The first thing we discovered was that the Serbian delegation had spent the night driving down from

Belgrade and didn't have the latest version of the MTA. So we had to go through it again line by line, translating this time, of course. It was slow, ponderous work. The Serbs were insisting on a UN Security Council Resolution (UNSCR). It soon became clear that the delegation was not empowered to sign the MTA without consultation. At 18.00 hours the Serbs withdrew to consult with Belgrade. They announced that they needed further time and said they wouldn't be coming back that night. I was knackered and happy to agree. They also suggested that the next day's meeting should be up at Kumanovo in north-east Macedonia, where the French-led brigade was based. The advantage for them was that Kumanovo shared a border with Serbia proper rather than Kosovo, which was much more secure for them. They didn't like the idea of driving back into Kosovo each evening, with the KLA at large.

This was fine by me. Kumanovo was only a short helicopter ride away, and it was much easier for us to administer the talks within a KFOR base than a café. The next morning I woke up refreshed, to find that yet another version of the MTA had arrived. I flew up to Kumanovo and we reconvened in a tent at 09.23 hours. Then one of the Serb delegation announced that he could only discuss certain parts of the MTA and that everything else must be done through the Security Council. I insisted that the document must be considered as a whole. It was deadlock. At 09.37, after just fourteen minutes, the meeting broke up.

It was very difficult to negotiate when amended drafts of the MTA kept arriving in short order. I was aware that there was a lot of talking going on, but it seemed to me that all that should have been done before I was asked to

311

start negotiating with the Serbs. What was happening here was, to some extent, a piece of theatre designed to keep the media happy while much of the game was played out elsewhere. To make matters worse, all sorts of hangers-on appeared, including the inevitable spin doctors from the Prime Minister's office who offered their unwanted views. I became quite cross. I phoned Clark and said to him that this was now a political, not a military matter. He told me to stick with it. A little later Charles Guthrie called to smooth things over.

Negotiations restarted. The Serbs proposed that the international security force be under UN auspices. After what had happened in Bosnia we could not accept this. After three hours of change and counter-change we found that we were back to where we had started. It was ridiculous. In another interesting twist, the Russian defence attaché from Belgrade arrived at Kumanovo later that afternoon; after some conversation with the Serb delegation, he seemed content to act merely as an observer.

An indication of the high level of interest in what was going on came in phone calls asking for a personal update from both Prince Charles and Tony Blair – among many others. Both the Prince and the Prime Minister offered me their encouragement and support.

By midnight on the second day we had reached another deadlock. The Serbs wanted a text which was unacceptable to NATO and vice versa. At 01.15 hours I spoke to Wes back at SHAPE, not for the first time in the previous thirty-six hours. I told him that we had reached an impasse and that the Serbs wanted to leave. We had to get in first with the press if we didn't want to lose the initiative. Clark told me to wait while he sought clearance. The next thirty-five minutes were a farce: at one stage we had the Vice-President on one line, Strobe Talbott on another and Wes on the third. Eventually I'd had enough. I went back to tell the Serbs we couldn't make any progress for the time being. We arranged to keep our communication channels open. Afterwards I went outside to tell the press that the talks had stalled. It was about two o'clock in the morning, and all the hacks were waiting in a sort of grandstand. I made my statement and the Serbs made a short statement afterwards. Then it was back to the Shoe Factory for whisky and egg and chips at 03.10 hours.

Monday 7 June was a quiet day. I received welcome telephone calls from Wes, Rupert and others offering support for the way I had been conducting the negotiations. The media blamed the Serbs for failure to comply. Jonathan Bailey had a rendezvous with one of the Serbs at the border purely to keep the lines of communication open; the press mistook this for a resumption of the negotiations, encouraged by one of the spin doctors who wanted the impression given that progress was being made. General Fogelsong started muddying the waters by talking to the Serbs independently. It looked as though the Americans were negotiating separately, outside the NATO chain of command. I wasn't impressed. All that day and the next there was a great deal of confusion, with much talk of a new agreed text of the MTA which no one had seen. I was becoming very annoyed. At some point Anji Hunter arrived.

'I'm here to see what I can do to help,' she beamed.

In normal circumstances I would have been pleased to see her, but this time frustration got the better of me.

'We were fine until the spinners fucked it up,' I said furiously.

She backed off.

By now we knew what we were trying to achieve. The aim was to choreograph several different events which all had to be sequenced: first, the text of a Security Council Resolution had to be approved by the G8; then the MTA had to be agreed and signed; then a verifiable withdrawal had to be agreed which would bring about an end to the bombing; then the Security Council Resolution had to be ratified – and only then would KFOR go into Kosovo. The MTA provided for phased Serb withdrawal from three designated zones of Kosovo, ending in complete withdrawal eleven days from signature. The concept was that we would enter the zones in phases as the Serb forces withdrew.

I flew back up to Kumanovo on the evening of 8 June, the fourth day. The Serbs arrived ten minutes after I did. But they still had a number of concerns. I had some sympathy with them. Once they withdrew their security forces, the Serb minority population in Kosovo would be unprotected. After all that had happened in Kosovo in the past year or so, one could well imagine that the Albanians might carry out reprisals on Serbs remaining there.

The Serbs weren't ready to sit down and discuss the document until 02.47 hours. We worked through the document until 05.34 hours, by which time it was light. Then the meeting broke up, with both sides seeking approval for changes negotiated to the text.

The next meeting was scheduled for midday. We were all weary. There was another text which needed to be painstakingly checked. I was constantly dragged to the telephone to speak to Wes. He couldn't or wouldn't leave it to me.

The meeting ended at 14.23 hours, without much progress. By late afternoon the Serbs were talking about going back to Belgrade. At this stage we felt nothing but relief at the prospect of a decent meal and a proper night's kip. We were just climbing into the helicopters to go back to the Shoe Factory when Jonathan Bailey telephoned to say the Serbs wanted to reconvene immediately. At 17.25 hours they returned. They asked for some minor changes, which I approved. Then they indicated that they were content. 'I'm buying,' one of them announced. I suggested that they might like to delay signing until a minute past midnight, which would give them an extra day, but they said, no, we want to sign now. A helicopter arrived with a fresh supply of KFOR headed paper. We printed out clean copies. When everyone was happy, I penned my signature, and the Serbs added theirs. It was 21.07 on Wednesday 9 June 1999. We had been negotiating for more than a hundred hours.

12

An Airfield too Far

Our daily routine at KFOR HQ began with a morning update at 08.00 hours, when twenty-five to thirty members of the command team would gather in the conference room in the Shoe Factory. The morning update on Friday 11 June was good-humoured. We were all very tired, but there was a feeling that at last all the ducks were lined up. After much buggering about, we had a signed agreement with the Serbs for withdrawal of their forces. The bombing campaign had been suspended and we had the authority of UN Security Council Resolution 1244, passed the previous evening. We had agreed to a Serb request to postpone D-Day, provisionally agreed for Friday, to Saturday – they weren't ready, and we could use the extra twenty-four hours ourselves. H-Hour was now set for 05.00 hours the following day, Saturday 12 June. I planned to spend the day visiting each of the six brigades that would be moving into Kosovo at dawn the next morning, to answer any last-minute queries and to wish them all good luck. I didn't know then that all these plans were going to be overtaken by events.

The morning update was followed at 09.00 hours by the morning VTC, chaired by Wes Clark. On this occasion Jim Ellis, who was visiting KFOR, attended the VTC at the Shoe Factory.

Clark's anxiety about the Russians dominated that morning's VTC. Talks taking place in Moscow between the Russians and the Americans were not going well. There was still no agreement about the command and control or the deployment area of any Russian contingent to KFOR. SACEUR was particularly concerned by reports that a Russian column in Bosnia was on the move – despite vehement protestations to the contrary from SFOR in Sarajevo.

It was immediately obvious that other plans would have to be put on hold while we studied the implications of this news and acted accordingly.

At 10.34 we received confirmation from SHAPE that a Russian column of approximately thirty armoured vehicles carrying an estimated 250 soldiers had crossed the River Drina into Serbia, presumably headed for Kosovo. Moments later, images of the column on the move appeared on CNN. Interestingly, the Russian vehicles had 'KFOR' freshly painted on their sides. To some extent this was a conciliatory gesture, indicating that they were coming to take part in the peacekeeping mission as authorized by UN Security Council Resolution. We knew that the Russians were desperate to avoid the intervention in Kosovo being seen as a NATO operation in a former Communist country, one that had historically looked to Russia for protection and support.

SHAPE's assessment was that the Russians would try to secure the airfield at Pristina prior to the arrival of air-delivered troops from Russia. Pristina airfield was the only airport in Kosovo for both civilian and military aircraft. It looked as if the Russians might be trying to pre-empt us, establishing themselves on the ground prior to a possible partition of Kosovo. The Russians had initially wrong-footed the American negotiators by referring to the airfield by its local name, Slatina. The column was expected to reach Pristina by 15.00 hours. Clark phoned and gave me a warning order to secure the airfield before the Russians arrived.

I didn't like this idea one bit – and I could tell from his body language that Jim Ellis didn't either. This was only a warning order, to make a detailed plan and get preparatory moves under way, and it could not be executed without a confirmatory order. But if confirmed, it meant sending helicopter-borne troops into Serb-held territory where they could easily be isolated. We had already looked at a similar option – as part of KFOR's main force advance into Kosovo – a week or so before, at the instigation of the French, who were keen to have television pictures of French troops jumping out of helicopters. I had had a personal conversation over the telephone with the French Chief of Defence, who agreed with our own conclusion that it was too risky.

By going into Kosovo ahead of time we would be breaching our newly signed agreement with the Serbs, providing them with a pretext not to withdraw and perhaps to fight. They could say, well, bollocks to you; if you're tearing up the agreement now, then so will we, thank you very much. Though our bombing campaign had damaged the Serbs' capability, their armed forces remained formidable, with well over three hundred tanks in Kosovo alone. At the time KFOR was comparatively small, only about fifteen thousand men in six brigades – two of them British – with forty-odd tanks. The airfield was only 35 miles or so from the border, but intelligence had revealed that the bridges and tunnels on the road through the narrow Kacanic defile into Kosovo had been prepared for demolition. If any one of them were blocked or blown, we would have been in real difficulty. It would only take one bolshy Serb engineer and we'd have lost our overland route for quite a while. So even if we didn't have to fight our way in, it might be days or even weeks before we could relieve our soldiers at Pristina overland. Moreover, there would be a serious risk of a confrontation when the Russians arrived. The Russians had played a key part in persuading the Serbs to withdraw from Kosovo, and we needed their continued participation to make the agreement stick. We knew how raw Russian feelings were at the time, especially with the recent accession to NATO of three former Warsaw Pact nations. The situation might quickly escalate and become extremely dangerous.

Despite my misgivings, I instructed my staff to prepare a plan to secure the airport with at least one battalion of heliborne troops. I directed that the plan should be kept on very close hold, i.e. that only the bare minimum of people should be told about it. One person who had to be informed was COMBRITFOR Richard Dannatt, so that he could clear this with London. I then left with Jim Ellis for a pre-arranged meeting at Skopje airport with US Secretary of State Madeleine Albright, who was passing through. Perhaps she could tell us what the hell was going on.

As Commander of KFOR I was responsible for the welfare and safety of all the soldiers under my command. But at the back of my mind was another consideration. I knew that 5 (UK) Airborne Brigade would have to provide at least some of the force necessary to secure the airfield. Among those soldiers I would be ordering to Pristina airfield would be my son Mark, one of thirty or so of 5 Brigade's Pathfinder Platoon with an advance force reconnaissance role.

Madeleine Albright didn't seem to appreciate fully what was happening. In the VIP lounge at Skopje airport Jim Ellis persuaded her to call her opposite number at the Russian Foreign Ministry, Igor Ivanov, who assured her that there was nothing underhand in the Russian troop movements. But then perhaps he didn't know what the hell was going on either.

It was now 11.45. I received a call from my staff telling me that I was needed back at HQ. Their assessment was that a decision to launch the operation to secure the airfield needed to be taken by 14.00 hours at the latest, given the Russian convoy's estimated time of arrival (ETA) of 15.00 hours. Pristina airfield was not more than thirty minutes' flying time from northern Macedonia, where a battalion from 5 Airborne Brigade was based, so this left a maximum of half an hour for our soldiers to load up and take off, and then another half an hour to deploy to defensive positions when they arrived. I put the battalion – my old friends, 1 Para – on fifteen minutes' notice to move.

We had decided before I left the HQ that this had to be a multinational operation if at all possible, and while I had been away the French had offered to contribute a battalion and twenty-three Puma helicopters. That made the equivalent of two battalions – good news, but NATO's Combined Operations Air Centre in Vicenza had refused to provide close air support without a direct instruction from Jim Ellis. Their lack of enthusiasm was another reason for our waning confidence.

To say that I felt frustrated would be to understate the position. The helicopters might well attract Serb anti-aircraft fire on the way in. The Serbs had, after all, been firing at NATO aircraft until only a few days before. It was also unclear what the troops were supposed to do when they reached the airfield: were they supposed to block the runway to prevent the Russians from landing? If not – and worse still – were they to open fire on Russian soldiers as they deplaned? Or would the Russians initiate a firefight? To launch such an operation without close air support would be inviting disaster. We had not come to Kosovo to lose several hundred men on the first day. The pressure on me personally was intense – 'the stuff of heart attacks', as James Everard noted in his journal that evening.

The feeling among my staff was that Clark was shooting from the hip. I respected Clark's record and his overall aims, and of course I felt a duty to act loyally towards my superior in the chain of command, but my confidence in him was being severely tested. We had already been mucked about over the agreement with the Serbs, several times receiving fresh drafts of the agreement after the negotiation had already begun.

I arrived back at the Shoe Factory just as information was received from a Russian news agency that six aircraft had taken off from air bases near Moscow carrying a thousand airborne soldiers. It was alarming – but

I wondered who had leaked this information, and why?

At 13.15 hours I received a written order from Clark 'to move and occupy Pristina Airfield'. But it contained a constraint. No move was to take place before Clark had approved a 'back-brief' of the operational plan.

To 'use the long screwdriver' was characteristic of Clark, and indeed of the US military in general. They were always reluctant to delegate, always interfering. In general I didn't much like this. To have your boss looking over your shoulder when you were already under such pressure was asking for trouble. But in this instance it gave me another chance to make the case against the operation.

Andrew Ridgway was down at the border liaising with the Serbs. Somewhat going through the motions, I got him to make a formal request for early entry into Pristina. The response was predictably negative. You could read this one of two ways. Maybe they were colluding with the Russians; or maybe they had perfectly understandable reasons for not wanting us there before the time agreed. I thought back to that Serb request to delay D-Day from the Friday to the Saturday: at the time, the request seemed to us to be nothing more than practicality; now, in the light of the Russian manoeuvre, it could be seen in a most conspiratorial light. The Serbs had MiG aircraft housed in bunkers at Pristina airfield, and you could see that they might not want us around when the MiGs emerged for take-off. After all, we had been bombing them until two days before. The control tower at the airfield and many of the surrounding buildings were badly damaged.

In the middle of scribbling notes of my own analysis of this extraordinary situation, at 13.30 I received an intelligence re-assessment of the Russians' progress. The new estimate was that the column would not reach Pristina until 18.00 hours. There seemed, moreover, to be no hard evidence that any military planes had left Russian airspace. These two pieces of information bought us a little more time. I telephoned Rupert Smith and ran through the logic behind my very grave reservations. He agreed that this was not a sensible operation. There was another potential problem with this order: the operation fell outside the terms of the UN Security Council Resolution, and so the commander of each national force was entitled to consult his superiors back home, and if the response was negative, he could decline to participate.

Sure enough, ten minutes later the French played their 'red card'. Paris had conducted a risk assessment and decided to pull out. Earlier we had also contacted the American Brigade. They offered six of their Apache attack helicopters to support the operation, but no ground troops. The view of my staff, including those Americans attached to KFOR HQ, was that Washington wanted the operation to take place but not at the risk of American lives. 1 Para – now lined up in a cornfield close to the border on fifteen minutes' notice to go – was on its own. This was not the way to do it. When all my staff had gone, leaving me alone with James in my office, I unbuttoned my rank badge and flung it on the table. 'I cannot do it; it makes no fucking sense.' James looked at me apprehensively. I knew that Richard Dannatt had been closely in touch with London. Almost certainly he was holding the British national red card in his pocket. But as KFOR commander I felt it would be a cop-out for me to rely on this. The planning staff agreed with my own analysis, but this was my call. Since my military judgement was so strongly against this operation I should be prepared to oppose it publicly, even if it meant putting my own career on the line.

Clark had called a video conference for 15.00 hours. This was obviously to be the decision point. I asked Richard Dannatt to attend. As we assembled in the conference room before the video camera, I was ready to resign. For the first time in my almost forty years in the army I had been given an order that I felt I could not in principle accept. In a few minutes' time my career could be over. But Clark had a surprise in store. 'We are not now going to execute this option,' he announced as the conference began. 'We will now wait to see if Yeltsin has lied to the President.' Clearly, there had been some communication between the two leaders. He had just begun to say that he wanted the plan to seize the airfield kept in readiness when the power went down and we lost the connection.

It seemed that I was not going to have to resign, at least not straight away. As I looked around it was obvious that I was not the only one in the room to feel relieved that the operation had been put on hold. By the time we had re-established the connection, Wes Clark was gone and Rupert Smith was in the chair. He took us through the arguments that had led to the stand-down of the operation. Apparently the decision had been founded on 'a balance of risk versus advantage'. Indeed; but my feeling was *that* sort of *key* judgement should be made before you put all these wheels in motion, not afterwards.

It was an interesting insight into Clark's thinking. He had perceived the Russian troop movements as a 'threat', and had drawn an analogy with the race to Berlin in 1945. It was the language of the Cold War.

We were back to Plan A, entry into Kosovo at first light the next morning. I was relieved that the operation to seize the airfield had been put on hold, but irritated that events had prevented me from making my planned final visits to all the brigades. But it was too late now. We just had to trust the mission.

After so much chopping and changing I felt I ought to at least fly up to 5 Airborne Brigade to explain why they had been mucked about all day. After all, they had been on fifteen minutes' notice to go, which is just about enough time to fire up the helicopter engines, get the boys on board and strapped in, carry out all the checks and lift off. The soldiers had been sitting for several hours by the helicopters in a cornfield under a hot sun, with all their equipment lined up on the ground beside them. One moment they were told they were flying into a potentially hostile situation and had psyched themselves up accordingly, the next moment they were back to the original peace support operation. In such circumstances a soldier can begin to lose faith in his superiors.

I flew up to the cornfield, where 1 Para had just received the order to stand down. There was the unforgettable sight of a dozen or so big twin-rotor Chinook helicopters stretched out in a long line ready for take-off, with rows of soldiers behind each aircraft sitting on their kit. I apologized to Adrian Freer, the Brigade Commander, a punchy character nicknamed 'Angry of Aldershot', at least in part because of his shock of ginger hair, and explained some of the background. Then I said, 'Right, I'm going to see my son,' and walked across to find Mark. He greeted me cheerily – 'Hello, Dad' – and we had a brief chat. He'd been in Macedonia almost a week, but this was the first time we'd seen each other. It was good to have him there. 'There's no way we'll be going to the airfield today,' I told him. The mood of the Pathfinder Platoon was mixed, a combination of frustration and disappointment. I lined up for a photograph with Mark and the Platoon before flying back to Skopje for the regular evening update at 18.00 hours. This was followed by the daily conference call at 19.00 hours, when the form was that I would speak by radio to all the brigade commanders and other senior staff, including Rear Support Command at Thessaloniki. The conference call that night was a fiasco. First we could not get hold of everybody, then the power collapsed again. After a day of so much tension I was not in a good mood. The difficulties with the conference were particularly worrying with H-Hour due next morning, but eventually the hard-pressed communicators got the net up and running again. It seemed the last straw when we heard that a large number of the refugees had broken out of their camp to celebrate the impending Serb withdrawal. The bloody idiots were blocking our route into Kosovo.

At 22.15 hours that night I received a personal message from Her Majesty The Queen, asking me to convey the following message to all the British servicemen and women under my command:

> I have nothing but admiration for the way in which you have carried out your duties over recent weeks during this difficult time of preparation and improvisation in caring for the refugees. I have no doubt that much greater pressures now lie ahead as you prepare to move into Kosovo as part of KFOR with the eyes of the world on you.

I am confident in your ability to rise to these challenges and I am proud of every one of you, as are your families and friends who watch and wait. My thoughts and prayers are with you all.

I replied as follows:

Your kind and gracious message has been most gratefully received by all British servicemen and women here in Macedonia. We plan to enter Kosovo tomorrow 12 June at first light. God save Your Majesty.

I got to bed about midnight and had just fallen asleep when the telephone rang. It was the Joint Operations Centre in Naples, informing us that H-Hour, scheduled for 05.00, was to be delayed twenty-four hours: 'Reason unknown'. None of us could believe that the operation could be postponed at such short notice, considering all that we had been through in the day that had just finished. The phone rang repeatedly in the next few hours, while an oddly dressed group of us gathered in the conference room. Mike Venables, my usually dapper political adviser, was wearing just a pair of trousers. James Everard, not known for his sartorial elegance at the best of times, had just a towel wrapped round his waist. Andrew Ridgway was the most appropriately clad in his dressing gown. I was wearing boxer shorts, a glass of whisky in one hand and a cigar in the other.

I tried to call Clark but I could not reach him. I managed to get hold of Jim Ellis, who was aware of the delay but knew nothing more. He promised to chase an answer down and called back fifteen minutes later. All he

had been able to discover was that the delay was something to do with the need to integrate the Russians into
the deployment plan. I was fairly irritated at this point. I
told Jim in no uncertain terms that we would be into
'damage limitation like you have never seen before. If we
carry on like this, the whole chain of command will be
exhausted before we start.'

The logistical problems of delaying H-Hour at such
short notice were bad enough. Six brigades from five different countries were ready to move across the border in a
few hours' time from many different locations scattered
across northern Macedonia. It was a complicated plan
with plenty of opportunity for cock-ups. The plan had 5
(UK) Airborne Brigade securing the Kacanik defile, with
4 (UK) Armoured Brigade passing through and on to
Pristina; at the same time the German Brigade would head
for Prizren, in south-west Kosovo, through Albania; the
French Brigade would move into south-east Kosovo over
the mountains, before moving on to their final deployment area in the north; the Italian Brigade was to follow
on through the Kacanik defile on their way to north-west
Kosovo; and the US Brigade, with a complicated US
Marine Corps/US Army handover, was to relieve the
French in the south-east.

Perhaps even worse was the psychological effect of
delay. Soldiers are used to being mucked about, but I was
very reluctant to muck them about any further – particularly as I had a strong suspicion that the delay might be
revoked. There was also the effect of further delay on international opinion and KFOR's credibility, and on the
refugees – not to mention the Serbs. It had not been
announced that we were due to go in that morning, but

since the press conference on Thursday after the agreement was signed everyone had known that it was imminent.

After discussing the problem with my immediate staff in my office I thought: Bollocks, I'm not going to do this. I took the decision not to pass on the order to delay H-Hour – at least, not for the time being. Sky News and CNN were showing pictures of Russian troops in Pristina being welcomed by jubilant Serbs. There was much speculation from the pundits about the significance of what was happening. President Clinton was said to be 'stunned' by this development.

I called Rupert Smith at home. Rupert was a very old friend, pragmatic and highly operationally experienced, with an offbeat sense of humour, who understood the difficulties of multinational operations. His wife answered the phone rather sleepily. 'Suzie, it's Jacko,' I said. 'I'm really sorry, but I've got to talk to him.' Rupert came on the line. He hadn't even been aware of the delay. Oh, he said when I told him. I asked: 'Any bright ideas, Rupes?' He called back a few minutes later and I ran through the advantages and disadvantages of delaying H-Hour with him. We felt that the disadvantages overwhelmingly outweighed the advantages. I told Rupert, 'I'm going to have to have it out with Wes. I just cannot go on being buggered about like this – it's getting to the stage when I can't look my own people in the eye.'

At 02.29 hours Ivanov announced on television that the Russian troops should not have been deployed and would 'withdraw immediately'. But there was no evidence that they were doing so.

Jim Ellis called five minutes later. I took him through

the arguments against a delay. A land operation like this involved multiple small units carrying out different functions, all of which needed to be coordinated. 'It's not like a ship, Admiral,' I said. 'In a ship, the captain says to the bloke at the wheel, thirty degrees starboard, and everyone turns to starboard. With an army, particularly with a multinational army scattered over different assembly areas, it's a different matter altogether.'

Over the next hour or so I spoke to Jim several times. I knew that the CDS, Sir Charles Guthrie, and George Robertson, Secretary of State for Defence, were both putting pressure on the Americans to keep to the original H-Hour. It was clear that the mood was changing and that the decision to delay might be revoked. I informed Jim of our assessment that the last safe moment to put the operation back on was 04.00 hours. Of course, this was also the last safe moment to delay it, but I didn't go into that. Jim called at 03.46, fourteen minutes before our deadline. H-Hour was back on again at 05.00. We were back in business. Good call.

At 05.05 Sky TV showed the first Chinooks flying 5 Airborne Brigade forward across the border into Kosovo. We were all knackered. The whisky bottle was empty. Someone from SHAPE called to ask where we would be holding our press conference in Pristina. My ADC told him where to get off.

As the morning progressed, reports came in that the advance was going smoothly, though minefields and the very difficult terrain which they had to cross were delaying the French. We had expected to come under fire from scattered Serb units opposed to the order to pull back, but it seemed that there was very little resistance. I had to restrain 5 Airborne Brigade from confiscating weapons, which was not allowed by the terms of our agreement with the Serbs. Later in the day we received reports that Serb police and militia were coming under attack from the Kosovo Liberation Army. I tried to relay a message to the KLA leadership to get them to stop.

Not long after H-Hour we received a call from Jim Ellis's Chief of Staff, Lieutenant General Jack Nix, who commented that he was amazed we had managed to remount the operation at such short notice. He was much amused when James Everard told him that I had never passed on the order to cancel it.

I emerged from updating Clark at the morning video conference to find a Russian colonel in full dress uniform, peaked cap and all, waiting for me. I was introduced to Colonel Gromov, the local military attaché in Skopje. He handed me a letter from the Russian Ministry of Defence, informing me that 'the leading element of the Russian KFOR contingent' now controlled the airfield at Pristina. So Gromov had been told by his superiors in Moscow to come and see me. This bizarre performance was confirmation that the Russian column in Pristina wasn't just a rogue element of soldiers doing their own thing. They were part of 'the Russian KFOR contingent'. The other fact I noticed was that the letter was addressed to me by name as 'Commander, KFOR'. It seemed to me a significant acknowledgement. The Russians were saying that they were willing to be part of what we were doing. I had to fax the letter to both SHAPE and Jim Ellis's Naples HQ.

I've thought about this quite a bit since and my view is that the Russians were making a point by sending a column into Kosovo. They had been worsted in the Cold

War, and there was considerable upset, even indignation, on the Russian side about NATO's expansion and the fact that the Alliance had undertaken military action against Serbia without a UN Security Council Resolution. The intervention was a reminder that the Russians were still players on the world stage, that they still needed to be treated with respect.

If Clark was thinking in these terms, he didn't show it. He wanted me to do all that we could to prevent the Russians from 'creating facts on the ground'. Over the secure telephone line he urged me to increase the tempo. He was planning to fly down to Skopje himself early the next morning. I rejigged our plans, ordering 5 Airborne Brigade to push on towards the airport as quickly as possible. By mid-afternoon they had got there and Adrian Freer had established contact with the Russian command-ing officer, who turned out to be a two-star general, a mark of the importance of this relatively small column in Russian eyes.

By 18.30 hours we had secured the 10-mile-long defile into Kosovo, and the leading British elements were clos-ing on Pristina itself. The weather had turned filthy, with heavy clouds and a thunderstorm moving in, but the media people were very keen for me to fly in to give a short press conference at Pristina Airport that evening to mark KFOR's entry, and somewhat against my better judgement I said OK, I'll do it. It occurred to me that I could kill two birds with one stone: do the press con-ference and make contact with the Russians, to establish some kind of relationship, whatever might be happening at a higher level. We climbed into two Lynx helicopters and took off. This was the first time I had crossed the border, and it was quite a sight to look down and see columns of vehicles streaming north into Kosovo. As we came out of the defile we flew into driving rain and when we were about halfway to Pristina the pilot said that he would have to put down. He said that if we let the worst of the storm pass we would probably be all right to continue. The Lynx landed close to a filling station by the main road, where a bunch of British soldiers were having a brew. I walked over and joined them for a coffee before the weather eased and we took off again for the airfield.

The press conference was a bit of a washout, literally and metaphorically. Afterwards I introduced myself to one of the Russians and asked if I could see General Viktor Zavarzin. I was ushered into the back of his command vehicle. My first impression was of a burly man who seemed somewhat nervous. I greeted him in Russian, even though I had an interpreter with me. He was a bit frosty at first, and it was pretty hard going. Then the rain must have got into the electrics because the vehicle filled with acrid black smoke. We got out and stood in the rain, which was still bucketing down. I said to Zavarzin, 'Hey, listen, I used to get wet as a company commander, but generals don't need to get wet.' We found a dry place in what remained of the wrecked airport terminal. I had a flask of whisky in my map pocket and I dug it out and offered it to Zavarzin. Relations warmed up after that.

When I got back to the Shoe Factory I found that Clark had spoken personally to Andrew Ridgway. He seemed obsessed by the threat of Russian troops invading the Serb enclaves, particularly in the north, and establishing a *de facto* partition of Kosovo. To prevent this happening, he wanted the runway blocked by KFOR helicopters. My team failed to see the logic in this order. We already controlled the airspace, so the Russians would have to run the NATO gauntlet if they wanted to fly in fixed-wing aircraft. Putting helicopters down on the runway would simply confuse the situation, and provoke the Russians. Despite the team's reservations, Andrew had contacted the US Brigade, the only force with uncommitted helicopters available. Shortly afterwards the Americans called back: they were playing the red card! They declined to take part in the operation. Two hours later the Americans were on the phone again: they would do it after all. Obviously Clark had been talking to Washington. But by now the weather had deteriorated further. The American brigade commander felt that it was not possible to implement the order without serious risk. Andrew recommended that the operation be put on hold until Clark arrived in the morning and it was possible to 'clarify SACEUR's intent'. I agreed. I managed to get some sleep that night.

Clark arrived at 08.40 hours on Sunday and caught the end of the morning update. He still seemed obsessed by the Russians, and would not focus on anything else. Clark was convinced that they intended to reinforce their troops at the airport. We gave him our intelligence assessment, which was that the Russians had neither the capability nor the political will to confront the international community in this way. Again and again I stressed that confrontation was not the answer. Russian support had been crucial in delivering the deal with the Serbs. They were major players and must be treated as such. To alienate them would be counter-productive in both the short term and the long term. I argued for a more subtle approach, isolating the Russians as a prelude to obtaining their participation.

Either Wes wasn't listening, or he wasn't convinced. It seemed that he had discussed the situation by phone with the NATO Secretary General Javier Solana on the flight down to the Balkans, and they had agreed a common position. Clark ordered me to block the runway one way or another. I don't mind admitting that I was furious. We were all tired, frustrated with the stopping and starting, and fed up with being buggered about. After the morning update I indicated to Clark that I wanted a word with him in private, and led the way to my office, closing the door behind us.

'SACEUR, we cannot go on like this,' I said with some feeling: 'We need to move on. Let me sort it out with the Russians.'

But Clark was unmoved, and insisted that we should block the airfield.

'I won't do it! Sir, I just won't do it,' I said heatedly.

Clark seemed taken aback. 'Mike, let's talk about this,' he said.

Once again I ran through the reasons for my very grave reservations about implementing the order. We had established liaison with Russians on the ground. Blocking the runway would not help bring the Russians onside. They were dislocated anyway. Our troops were in position and had effectively isolated the Russians already. The airfield had no current operational value at this point. We controlled the airspace. Apart from anything else, the Russians could have flown reinforcements into Serbian airfields and then moved across the border into Kosovo by vehicle. As for us, we could continue to use Skopje. Pristina Airport just wasn't that important. Finally, the order fell outside the terms of the mandate.

I made it clear to Clark that I was fed up with taking orders from Washington, from people who seemed to have no appreciation of the problems on the ground.

'Mike, these aren't Washington's orders, they're coming from me.'

'By whose authority?'

'By my authority, as SACEUR.'

'You don't have that authority.'

'I do have that authority. I have the authority of the Secretary General behind me on this.'

'Sir, I'm not going to start World War Three for you.'

Again Clark stated what he wanted done.

I said to him, 'Sir, I'm a three-star general, you can't give me orders like this. I have my own judgement of the situation and I believe that this order is outside our mandate.'

'Mike, I'm a four-star general, and I can tell you these things.'

He insisted that he was giving me a direct order. I told him that I would have to talk to my superiors in London. He telephoned Charles Guthrie, and outlined the discussion that had just taken place. Guthrie asked to speak to me. I took the phone and moved away from Clark to speak to Guthrie in private. 'I cannot go on,' I told him, 'I'm going to have to resign.'

'For God's sake, Mike, don't do that,' Guthrie replied hastily. 'It would be a disaster.' He asked to speak to Clark again. 'Well, I must say, Wes,' he said, 'that I agree with Mike – and so does Hugh.'

Clark was visibly nonplussed. Hugh Shelton was his boss. He had gone out on a limb, and now he found that he had gone too far. I left the room so that he could call

Shelton in Washington. I gathered later that Shelton told him that Washington did want the runways blocked, but not at the expense of a confrontation with the Russians – which seemed to me an outright contradiction in terms. When Clark said that I was resisting his orders, Shelton suggested that he had an 'authority problem'.

Clark called me back into the room. 'Mike, do you understand that as a NATO commander I'm giving you a legal order, and if you don't accept that order you'll have to resign your position and get out of the chain of command?'

'SACEUR, I do.'

'OK. I'm giving you an order to block the runways at Pristina airfield. I want it done. Is that clear?'

SACEUR was insistent, despite the risk of a confront-ation with the Russians. I suggested that armoured vehicles would be better suited to blocking the runways than helicopters, in the almost certain knowledge that the UK would decline such a provocative move. Clark agreed that the vehicles would be preferable. I went out to pass the order for 4 Armoured Brigade to place a combat team on short notice to move to the airfield, knowing that it would be referred to Richard Dannatt for national approval. Meanwhile Clark called Shelton again. Apparently Shelton had been trying to reach Charles Guthrie, but had been told that he was in a meeting with the Prime Minister.

I returned to the room and reported to Clark that I had given the warning order. He tried to change the subject, but I wasn't prepared to leave it there. 'SACEUR, you're just testing me, aren't you? You don't really want me to do this, do you?' He denied any such motive. After a little more discussion I left again to check on what was happening. Andrew informed me that London had played the red card.

Clark seemed to feel somehow that this was my doing. On the contrary, I had deliberately not spoken to Richard Dannatt to avoid any accusation of collusion, as I felt very strongly that as a commander of a multinational force I should not act as a Brit per se, or favour any particular national contingent. And though Wes didn't seem to credit this, I also felt a soldier's loyalty to my chain of command. But I felt very strongly that it would be a mistake to confront the Russians, whichever nation's troops were on the spot.

Clark again phoned Shelton, and then tried to contact Guthrie, who was still unavailable. He didn't say anything to me, and I didn't say anything to him. There was nothing more to be said. After a short time Clark and his team left to return to SHAPE HQ in Belgium.

I telephoned Charles Guthrie, who had George Robertson with him, and my words were relayed to them both on the speakerphone. I told them what had happened. 'You may take the view I should go, Secretary of State, CDS,' I concluded. But both Guthrie and Robertson were very supportive of the line I had taken. Meanwhile the MOD had been in contact with Richard Dannatt as COMBRITFOR. He was authorized to deploy 4 Armoured Brigade to Pristina Airport and if necessary to isolate it, but not to block the runways. James Everard telephoned Wes Clark's MA to inform him of this. Clark's British MA (Lieutenant Colonel David Limb, also by chance a Parachute Regiment officer) assured James that he understood the problems, but he was less sure that SACEUR did.

Ten minutes later one of Clark's American MAs called, anxious about a CNN report of tanks with Russian markings at the airfield. It sounded unlikely, and we soon established that the report referred to VJ tanks with Federal Republic of Yugoslavia (FRY) markings moving past the airfield as they withdrew. My view was that Clark's people needed to get a grip, and stop panicking in response to every unfounded rumour or ill-informed press report. The next ridiculous, poorly thought-out order I received would be the last, as I would refuse to implement it.

In fact, the crisis was over. We had avoided an unnecessary and potentially dangerous confrontation with the Russians. But my relationship with my superior officer, General Wesley Clark, had suffered. I had come to the brink of refusing a direct order, though in the event it had not quite come to that. And Clark himself had been damaged. Two months later it was announced that he would be replaced as Supreme Allied Commander earlier than expected. When Clark announced that he would be standing as a candidate for the Democratic Party's presidential nomination, Shelton said, in a public forum, that Clark being short-toured 'had to do with integrity and character issues', adding, 'Wes won't get my vote.' Despite my differences with him, I thought that this was a less than fair judgement. Wes Clark had not spared himself to achieve a successful outcome to the Kosovo campaign.

There was one last twist in the tale. At 01.00 hours the next morning, after I'd gone to bed, I received a call from Jim Ellis. Again it was the Russians. There had been a report that six aircraft had taken off from Moscow, headed for Pristina. This was the third such alarm. We were as sure as we could be that this scare contained no more substance than the previous two (and so it would turn out). I was exhausted, and I'm afraid that I replied rather sardonically to Ellis, a man I liked and respected: 'Admiral, if Russian planes are on their way I will go to Pristina and welcome them with open arms to KFOR.' Fatigue had made me facetious. 'If SACEUR wants to shoot them down with US aircraft, that's his business. Goodnight.'

13

Nation-Building

Operation 'Joint Guardian' proceeded according to plan. Within a few days units of KFOR had penetrated all parts of Kosovo. Whenever a KFOR vehicle drove through a village, children would run out waving and cheering. It was obvious that most of the inhabitants saw us as deliverers. The atmosphere was euphoric. People would applaud when they recognized me in the street, in Pristina and elsewhere. It was all rather embarrassing.

I flew around the brigades in the first few days, meeting the commanders and dealing with their immediate problems. From the air you could see plumes of smoke curling up from burning buildings: the Albanian Kosovars were indulging in the typical Balkan behaviour of burning the houses of the enemy. The Serbs fulfilled their obligations under the MTA, withdrawing their security forces on schedule and in good order, though some tanks had plunder strapped to their sides. Before long we began to discover grisly evidence of their activity: sites of mass graves scattered across the country. Jonathan Bailey was my liaison man at the Serb Army HQ in Pristina; he witnessed scenes of frantic activity, as files were hurled out of the windows into the courtyard below to be burned in the incinerator. On their last night they drank the place dry. Despite the difficult circumstances Jonathan forged a good relationship with the Serbs, and he continued to liaise with them after they'd left Kosovo. Once a week he would go over the border into Serbia proper, and they'd discuss issues arising over a Balkan lunch.

Many Serb officials – administrators, judges, prison warders, utility workers, teachers and doctors – had chosen to quit Kosovo when the security forces left, presenting KFOR with the task of filling the vacuum they left behind. The Serbs remaining in Kosovo were fearful – justifiably so – of revenge attacks by ethnic Albanians. Plenty of scores were settled in those first few days. Armed KLA units began to emerge from the woods and come down from the hills. There was widespread looting, burning of abandoned houses, grenade attacks, beatings and shootings. In the worst such incident, we found the bodies of fourteen Serb farmers lying in fields about 12 miles south of Pristina. It was one of our core tasks to try to retain as many Serbs as possible. If too many of the Serbs left, the Western ideal of ethnic balance would appear to be hollow. Their security was at the heart of this. The attitude of the Kosovo Serbs was a curious mixture of fear and defiance. On D+13 I attended a meeting of Serb teaching staff at the university after the murder of one of their professors: their anxiety was palpable, but when they spoke they alternated between arrogance and venom. They wanted my help, but they could not resist a litany of complaint and grievances. Bloody mindedness is a defining Serb characteristic; appropriately enough, they have a word for it, *inat*. There were intelligence reports of a Serb plot to assassinate me, but I didn't take this seriously. If they had any sense, they would realize that we were there to protect them.

On 14 June, D+2, we had put our so-called Tactical Headquarters (Tac HQ) – a group of core staff from the main headquarters – forward into Pristina. Somewhere between the airport and the city they found a half-built industrial building, and settled in there. I joined them the next day. We quickly realized that we needed to be closer to town, and less than a week later we moved main HQ up from Skopje to a new location, a film studio on a ridge overlooking the city. At night you could see many fires burning in the city below and in the surrounding country-side. The building was a modern office block which we referred to as the Film Factory, with a cavernous studio below which quickly became known as the Bat Cave. There was no accommodation, so to start with everybody was in tents. We set up a field kitchen, and every meal was al fresco. It was summer, the weather was warm and settled, and a copse of Mediterranean pine provided some welcome shade – and a place to relax and to entertain visitors, whether VIPs from abroad or local worthies. I and my immediate staff tended to eat later than the others, after the evening conference call. It was good to be back on fresh rations, after living for days in Tac HQ on field rations: a daily box of 'boil in the bag' food. I made a point of thanking the resourceful and enthusiastic Army chefs, who supplied us with excellent food whatever the local difficulties.

We built a large helipad about two or three hundred yards behind the building. There were also two smaller helicopter pads right in front – known, no doubt a bit optimistically, as the 'VIP LS' (landing site). Aircraft could be summoned from the main pad to be waiting there in the front, rotors whirling, ready for immediate take-off. In those early days my time was so precious that I needed to conserve every minute. Having a helicopter waiting at the front meant that I could dash straight out of the building, board and lift off immediately.

My six-man command group occupied the first floor of the office building, and here, just as at the Shoe Factory, we slept in our offices. At the far end was an 'executive' bathroom, which would have been an improvement on the field alternative had the shower been working. A Macedonian plumber arrived to mend it, but didn't bother to check that the waste pipe was connected to the outfall, with the inevitable consequences. I was first to use the shower. Jonathan Bailey had the misfortune to occupy the room below, and after a while my shower water began to drip through the ceiling on to his desk, causing much amusement to everyone except Jonathan and me.

This was a reminder – not that we needed one – that it was crucial to get the infrastructure working as soon as possible. If you don't get the water supply working pretty quickly, you start getting problems with hygiene and disease, and since many of the Serb doctors had left with their Army compatriots we couldn't afford to allow this to happen. But without electricity the pumps couldn't operate. Many of the Serb specialists who made everything work, the technicians and the engineers, had disappeared when the security forces withdrew. And without a working telephone exchange it would be more difficult for Kosovo to get itself back on its feet. So we set our Army signallers to sort out the telephone exchange, put Army medics into the hospitals and allotted Army engineers to reconstruction projects – just to keep as much as possible functioning until the UN civil administration was ready to shoulder the burden. I sent an engineer squadron up to the old lignite-fired power stations outside Pristina to see if there was anything they could do. The squadron commander used the satellite phone to speak to his uncle in the UK, who worked for the Central Electricity Generating Board. One can imagine the uncle's surprise on receiving a call from Kosovo. 'It's me – I need a bit of help!' And the uncle talked him through the process of how to run this less than state-of-the-art power station which used the dirtiest fuel of all. After that we had intermittent power. You could look out of the window at the power station on the skyline, and if you could see smoke belching out of one of the chimneys, you knew that the power was likely to be on. We had our own generator as a back-up, but of course that didn't pump the water, which came and went. Without regular water, living conditions rapidly become rather sordid. Later on the CEGB sent out two very capable engineers who soon had the power station running as well as – probably better than – it had ever done.

The Territorial Army railway gang came into their own, getting the train line south to Skopje up and running by D+14. I remember riding on the footplate for a while to celebrate its re-opening. Once the railway was working again it took a lot of traffic off the road. The line continued all the way down to the port of Thessaloniki, so from that moment on we could bring in supplies and vehicles by rail.

To me all this was basic stuff, which was why I was surprised by the failure to address infrastructure issues promptly in Iraq in 2003. It's not as though we haven't had enough experience to learn from. That hard-won experience should have impressed upon governments that if people's lives don't quickly improve, they rapidly become disenchanted. It's difficult enough to build a civil society in a country devastated by war; without the basics of life it's near impossible. Gilbert Greenall's rule of thumb of the first hundred days being crucial remains very pertinent. I go back to my analogy of a length of rope, made up of strands: a military strand, a security strand, a reconstruction strand, a humanitarian strand, a demobilization strand, a political strand, and an economic strand. The individual strands are easily cut, but once they are woven together, the rope is strong.

I think it was Donald Rumsfeld who said, 'We don't do nation-building.' To my mind, that kind of dismissal on principle is nonsensical – and operationally detrimental as well, because the overall success of the operation will depend upon reconstruction. In Iraq, the Americans had the naïve idea that the people would be so happy to be liberated that nothing else mattered; that once they had pushed over the statue of Saddam Hussein, democracy would flourish overnight. It's a very ideological approach, and one which is intellectually bankrupt. This difference in doctrine between us and the Americans would be a recurrent difficulty in the years ahead. Military force should never be used for its own sake, but always to achieve a political objective. The generic political objective of any intervention must be to bring about those circumstances in which the country becomes at peace with itself; at peace with its neighbours; with its boundaries unchanged; stable therefore; with a representative government accepted by at least a respectable majority of its citizens – and that doesn't necessarily mean a Western liberal democracy; and the prospect of a better future for all.

Early one morning, a few days after our entry into Kosovo, I was sitting outside Tac HQ on a camp stool talking to Andrew Ridgway and enjoying the sunshine when I heard somebody exclaim, 'What on earth—?' I looked up to see the most extraordinary sight: a group of figures in long black robes, striding towards us across the fields in a sort of arrowhead formation. As they approached, we saw that they were clergy of the Serbian Orthodox Church, led by the Patriarch himself, carrying a crozier.

I greeted him with great respect. The Patriarch of the Serbian Orthodox Church is not somebody to be treated lightly, and indeed he cut a very distinguished figure. We found some chairs and offered them some coffee. With the Patriarch was the Bishop of Kosovo, and among the retinue was a very tall young priest who spoke immaculate English and acted as translator. It turned out that he'd spent some time in America, and was an absolute IT wizard; at the Film Factory he soon acquired the nickname of 'Cyber-monk'.

The Patriarch told us that he had come to Kosovo to see for himself what was happening to his people. He told us tales of burning, rape and ethnic cleansing of Serb civilians, all the dreadful things that were being done to his long-suffering Serb parishioners by these terrible Albanians. He lamented the failure of KFOR to protect the Serb population. It was apparent to me that the Church was just about the only surviving institution from the former Serb regime, and the clergy the only surviving figures of authority: everyone else had fled to Serbia proper. So it was logical for the Bishop of Kosovo to represent the interests of the remaining Serbs. Subsequently he became one of two Serb members of the Transitional Council set up by the UN.

I laid out what KFOR was doing and the security that we intended to bring to *all* the people of Kosovo. We agreed to place a static guard on the main Serb Orthodox churches and monasteries, in case some Kosovar hothead decided to burn them down. I appointed a British Army chaplain as my liaison officer to the Orthodox Church: Kingsley Joyce, an outgoing and jovial priest. The Patriarch and I ended the meeting on good terms, and he left with a KFOR escort. Later he addressed a crowd in the courtyard of the fourteenth-century monastery at Gracanica, the seat of the Bishop of Kosovo. 'I call on you to be able and persevere to the end, because everything will pass. He who perseveres to the end will be saved.' That was very Serbian: we are downtrodden, but we will endure.

Afterwards the Bishop asked me to lunch two or three times, which was always a very splendid affair. We sat down with half a dozen or so of the clergy, the Bishop at the head of the table, being waited upon by nuns, in the medieval splendour of the monastery, drinking 'the best wine in Kosovo'.

On D+3 I had held another meeting with General

Zavarzin. Any sense of threat was fast fading. The real obstacle to an agreement with the Russians was political, not military: they wanted a slice of the action. It rapidly became obvious that poor old Viktor Zavarzin had no real negotiating power. Everything had to be referred back to Moscow, because the situation was so political. I decided to play it long. I met Zavarzin regularly, without pushing for an immediate solution. Our relations became more cordial. Since the first time we met, when I had offered him that swig from my hip flask, he reciprocated with vodka on every occasion, no matter what the time of day. It was all very Russian. Soon after KFOR's entry, a chance meeting with his deputy revealed that his men were short of drinking water; so I arranged to have sent over to them all the spare bottled water we could find. They appreciated the gesture. Two or three days later I had another chat with Zavarzin.

'So, how's it going up at the airport?' I asked him.

'We are having problems with the KLA. They have snipers. We are vulnerable up here.'

I couldn't resist remarking, 'Well, Viktor, you did choose to go there.' He smiled.

'I'll tell you what we'll do,' I said. 'I will put some of my British soldiers around you in an outer security cordon. I don't think the KLA will give us any trouble. Would that help?' Indeed it would, was the reply. Then inspiration struck. 'Furthermore,' I went on, 'this force of British soldiers will be commanded by my own son.'

Zavarzin beamed, and advanced to give me a bear hug. The Russians are a very sentimental people.

The trouble with sending Mark and the Pathfinders to the airport was that it meant acting contrary to the philosophy of delegation that we in the British Army hold so dear. We have a guiding principle, whereby the senior commander tells the subordinate what he has to do, what objectives he has to achieve, what effect he is to bring about, what resources he has to do it – but not *how* he has to do it. That is always left to the subordinate commander. We call this 'mission command', and it's an essential part of the way we operate. What I had done went against everything I had been taught and believed in. Needs must, however, I thought to myself.

At the time 5 Airborne Brigade was established in a small market town about 6 miles south of the airport. I got on the radio to Adrian Freer.

'I've just had a meeting with Zavarzin,' I told him. 'He's feeling a bit insecure. Your task, Adrian, is to make the Russians feel loved and protected.'

Adrian said that he understood.

'Adrian, I'm now going to break the rules of mission command, because I am going to tell you how I want this done. I've told Zavarzin that Mark will be in command. So I want Mark and his merry men involved, whoever else you decide to use for whatever. Furthermore, find a bottle of whisky from somewhere, give it to Mark, and tell him to give it to General Zavarzin with his father's compliments.'

The bottle was a message to Zavarzin. He would appreciate that I had sent my own son to look after him. I am no psychologist, but I sensed that this would mean a lot. It seemed to work. Russian forces eventually deployed into the sectors headed by the French, German and Americans; they turned over responsibility for air traffic control and logistics at the airport to the British, while keeping the security function. The airport was soon functioning normally.

As I said, the Russians are a sentimental people.

The refugee crisis solved itself, melting away like spring snow in a thaw. When D-Day arrived, most of the people in the camps in Albania and Macedonia just got up and went home, many of them on foot. It was an amazing sight, these tens of thousands of people at any one time streaming back into Kosovo. It was extraordinary to think of hundreds of thousands of families repossessing their former homes, finding some of them burned out or occupied by squatters, picking up the threads of their former lives. There was one hell of a traffic jam on the road coming up from Macedonia, as our convoys of military and UN vehicles struggled to pass the slow-moving masses. But within a few days it was clear. The refugee problem was over.

The UNHCR had put together a complicated plan for the return of the refugees, but as things turned out their help was not required. The people returned of their own accord. I remember talking to the regional head of UNHCR, a man called Denis McNamara, a New Zealander, not long after D-Day. 'The refugee problem is over,' I observed.

'Yes,' he conceded somewhat grudgingly, 'but they didn't follow *our plan*.'

Before KFOR moved into Kosovo, a negotiating mechanism had been set up with the KLA. Most of the talks took place in Albania, because that was their base. As AFOR Commander, John Reith had conducted the negotiations on NATO's behalf. We had hoped to have concluded an agreement before we went in, but that didn't happen. So we didn't have rules telling us how to deal with the KLA on entry, as we had in our dealings with the Serb armed forces. NATO had not forced the Serbs out in order to leave Kosovo in the hands of 'warlords' – though if KFOR was going to restrain the KLA, clashes were almost unavoidable. The issue became more and more pressing as each day passed. The Serb withdrawal resulted in a dangerous vacuum. Armed KLA fighters emerged, unrestricted by any Serb security presence. Many of them seemed to imagine that they were now free to lord it over the population. Despite our best efforts, different KFOR brigades took different national lines with the KLA. The British wanted the KLA fighters disarmed, which annoyed them no end. The Germans and the Dutch, on the other hand, were somewhat cosy with them – too cosy, in my opinion. These differences in attitude mirrored contrasting views of the KLA within NATO: some regarded them as not much better than terrorists, whereas others saw them as freedom fighters.

The concluding phase of NATO's negotiations with the KLA took place in their field headquarters in the hills, some 25 miles west of Pristina. John Reith continued to represent NATO, with the help of Jamie Rubin, Clinton's State Department spokesman and the husband of CNN's star reporter Christiane Amanpour, whom I had come to know well during my tours in the Balkans. Negotiations continued until D+8, the last day of the eleven given by the MTA for the Serbs to withdraw. Eventually the KLA agreed to sign an Undertaking, renouncing the use of force and acknowledging KFOR's sole authority under UNSCR 1244.

At 22.50 hours an RAF Chinook landed at our Tac HQ, bearing Reith, Rubin and the KLA leaders. The two most important were the self-styled 'Commander in Chief' Hashim Thaqi, a tall young man with wavy swept-back hair, and Agim Ceku, the Field Commander. We convened in a muddy tent, sitting on canvas chairs around a long trestle table. I was amused to note that Thaqi was wearing a patterned tie and a shiny suit, indicating his future political ambitions. Ceku, a big, heavy-jowled man, rather older than Thaqi, said little, but stared hard at me throughout; I realized after a while that he was trying to take my measure. Ceku's combat kit contrasted with Thaqi's civilian clothes. Before he joined the KLA, he had served with the Croats in Bosnia and the Krajina, and before that in the old Yugoslav army. It was strange to think that he'd been fighting a guerrilla campaign against the army in which he'd once served.

Jamie Rubin was a tall man with dark hair and a no-nonsense manner. He did most of the talking with Thaqi while I scrutinized the paper on the table in front of me. This was the KLA's 'Undertaking' to renounce the use of force and demilitarize. They'd been hedging about this for weeks, trying to avoid committing themselves while they extracted as much as they could from our side. The KLA leaders were insistent that their 'military contribution' should be recognized, and that they should enjoy 'special consideration in the administration and police force' – otherwise known as jobs for the boys. Even more contentious was their ambition for an army of Kosovo on the lines of the US National Guard. Western governments were nervous about being seen to reward 'terrorists'. I'd been under pressure not to give anything significant away.

My instructions from NATO were that I could 'receive' the document, but not 'accept' it. Then someone pointed out that in Albanian the same word is used to mean both.

I took my specs off my nose and swung them in one hand as I explained our position. Thaqi nodded. We moved to the main tent, where others were waiting to witness the signing. Jamie handed Thaqi a pen. His hand shook as he signed.

'Right,' said Jamie. 'Now you get your reward.' He whipped out a satellite phone and called the President. After a few words of explanation he handed the phone to Thaqi, whose hand continued to shake as he spoke.

After Thaqi had finished his call, somebody poured out glasses of the local gut rot, and we drank a toast to Kosovo. This was an important moment in the transformation of the KLA into what would become a legitimate organization. The terms of the Undertaking committed the KLA to a timetable for their disbandment as a military force, commencing on its signature. Monday 21 June became 'K-Day' in our diaries, with a programme dating from then onwards. Within seven days (K+7) the KLA agreed to establish secure weapon sites, to be registered and verified by KFOR, to clear minefields and booby traps, to vacate any fighting positions, and to move to assembly areas as agreed with me as COMKFOR. Thereafter, only personnel authorized by COMKFOR would be allowed to bear arms outside these assembly areas: I restricted this concession to senior officers of the KLA with their close protection personnel (not exceeding three), carrying side arms only. By K+30 the retention of any rifles would be subject to my authorization, and all personnel not of local origin would be withdrawn. (The Americans were worried about *mujahedin*, as they had been in Bosnia.) And so on, up to K+90 (19 September), when KFOR would assume full control of the weapons storage sites. By then the KLA were to have completed their processes of demilitarization and would cease wearing either military uniforms or KLA insignia.

In the weeks that followed, I flew around the country meeting KLA regional commanders and enduring a series of yet more elaborate Balkan lunches. It seemed to me important to make contact with the lower levels of the KLA as well as the leaders, to get everyone involved in the process of demilitarization. Meanwhile, I began to develop a good working relationship with Ceku. We had a Joint Implementation Committee (JIC) which met regularly to monitor the progress of demilitarization. At these meetings I would tell Ceku what he should do: we're not satisfied with this, you must do that. Periodically he would remind me of the 'special consideration' due to the KLA for their role in liberating the country. 'I'm still considering it, General Ceku,' I would say.

KLA members of the JIC carried a card entitling them to carry side arms. At the Film Factory we referred to these as the 'Get Out of Jail Free' cards.

The day after the Undertaking was signed, the President of the United States (POTUS) and the First Lady (FLOTUS) arrived in Skopje. They didn't come to Kosovo because of fears about security. I was asked to go down to the airport to meet the President. It was one of those events that the Americans love, but the British find embarrassing. A large group of American soldiers made their presence felt by whooping and cheering. Wes made a triumphal speech, referring to Milosevic personally: 'We won, he lost, and we won with the President behind us all the way. Mr President, I would like to thank you for your wonderful leadership, the guidance you have provided and I thank you for your support.' I imagine that Wes had his fingers crossed behind his back as he said these words. The President also made a short address, paying tribute both to KFOR and to me personally as the KFOR commander. Afterwards we had an exchange of pleasantries. This was before my clash with Wes had been made public. If the President had heard about it, he made no comment on the matter. Even in this very brief encounter, I was impressed by his ability to communicate. He seemed completely at his ease. I am not the first to make the observation that Bill Clinton is a very charismatic man.

My schedule was becoming alarmingly crowded. No two days were the same, but the programme for the next day, 23 June, gives an indication of how busy we were: morning update 08.00, DSACEUR telephone call 08.30, VTC 09.00, Ambassador Petritsch (EU envoy to Kosovo) 09.30, Ambassador Eiff (NATO Secretary General's Civil Representative in Macedonia) 10.15, General Zavarzin 11.00, the Bishop of Pristina and numerous clergy 14.30, British Foreign Secretary and foreign ministers of Italy, Germany and France 16.30, visit UN Headquarters for discussions with the SRSG and foreign secretaries 17.30, evening update 18.00, Minister Vujovic, Deputy Foreign Minister of Serbia (quite brave of him to come, but he did) 18.45, my conference call with the brigade commanders 19.00. Just another day at the office. All the time the telephone was ringing and messages were coming though on the radio. That's why it was so important to have a first-rate staff, who took as much off my shoulders as possible. I can't praise them highly enough for their professional and constant support.

High-level visitors continued to arrive in quick succession. The following day it was Javier Solana and Wes Clark with their accompanying multitudes. They did a tour around Pristina, conducted with an air of triumphalism, many hurrahs and much glad-handing. The Albanian community, as if on cue, shouted 'NATO! NATO! Solana! Solana!' I found it embarrassing, frankly. It was as if they'd won an election.

At my meeting with General Zavarzin the previous day I had explained the KLA Undertaking, and after that the conversation became more light-hearted. He expressed delight at having met Mark, and complimented me on having such a fine son. He thanked me too for the whisky. Then he shared with me some of the difficulties he had been having with Moscow. 'I am hacked off with the politicians,' he told me.

I raised the inevitable glass of vodka in his direction.

'You too, eh, Viktor?'

One person for whom I had a lot of time was the Brazilian SRSG Sergio de Mello, who was later to be killed by a suicide bomb attack in Iraq. Sergio and his small UN team were in Pristina almost as soon as KFOR were there; he immediately began building up UNMIK, the UN 'international civil presence' set up under UNSCR 1244 to work alongside the 'international security presence', which was of course KFOR. He was a great man, a true internationalist, and he saw the civil administration off to a flying start. But his appointment was only a temporary one, until a more permanent candidate was in place. Just before he left, he instituted the Kosovo Transitional Council, which was an attempt to bring together leaders of the various factions in Kosovo under his chairmanship. UNMIK's role was to provide an interim administration until such time as it should be replaced by a locally elected government. At the time of writing, UNMIK is still the constitutional power in Kosovo, although the situation has been complicated by Kosovo's declaration of independence early in 2008.

Sergio was replaced by Bernard Kouchner, the founder of Médecins Sans Frontières, who'd been a government minister in France before and in 2007 was appointed French Foreign Minister. I made a point of going down to Pristina Airport to greet Bernard and to salute him, as a symbolic gesture as much as anything: it seemed to me important to show that in a civilized society the military should be subject to the civil authority. After that I always made a point of deferring to Bernard on public occasions; in private I sometimes teasingly addressed him as 'le roi'. We worked hand-in-hand, meeting daily at 17.00 for as long as it took, sometimes half an hour, sometimes more.

There were no police; but also there was no system of justice, because the judiciary, prison warders and so on had all been Serbs, and almost all of them had chosen to leave. Under UNSCR 1244 KFOR had responsibility for maintaining a 'secure environment', so in effect we were the police – at least until the UN police had built up their strength. To stem the tide of killings you needed a system of justice. But it was very difficult. You'd catch an individual about to murder somebody, arrest him, and hold him. But what were you to do then? Sergio de Mello empanelled a number of judges, both Serbian and

Kosovar Albanians. Initially the judges were given the power only to hold a prisoner on remand, but not actually to sentence him; that came later. There were no rules for this situation: Sergio and I had to make them up as we went along.

In the early days, when we were still feeling our way, a prisoner from one ethnic background was brought in front of a judge from another. The main witness was a British military police corporal. The corporal gave his evidence, and was alarmed to observe the judge frowning. 'I am not happy with this confession,' the judge announced.

The corporal assumed that he was being accused of mistreating the prisoner. 'I didn't lay a finger on him, Sir,' he hastened to assure the judge.

'No, no, corporal,' the judge said. 'You misunderstand me. This evidence is not good enough. Take him away and beat him harder.'

Tony Blair would be the first world leader to come to Kosovo after KFOR's entry. He was due to arrive at Pristina on the afternoon of 30 July. I was having lunch that day in the field kitchen behind the Film Factory when James Everard's mobile phone began to ring. It was in my pocket for some reason: I must have borrowed it and failed to give it back. James wasn't around, so I pulled it out of my pocket and answered it.

'Hello?' I said, and a female voice said 'Hello' back.

'Who is that?' I asked.

There was a pause and a deep sigh down the line, followed by, 'It's Caroline.'

'Ah,' I said, beginning to take in the situation. Another

pause and another deep sigh. 'Caroline,' I said, 'it's Mike. Are you, um . . . has it started?'

'Bloody right it has!'

I had promised James that he could be back for the birth of his twins, and I like to think that I am a man of my word. It turned out that there was an early evening Lufthansa flight from Thessaloniki direct into Düsseldorf, the nearest international airport to Rheindahlen. The timing couldn't have been better. So we put James in a helicopter and flew him down to Thessaloniki – but Sod's Law meant that the flight was an hour late. Caroline had to have the twins by Caesarean section. James didn't quite make it before she went under the anaesthetic, but he was the first person she saw when she came round. If only the flight had been on time he'd have been with her before she went under, but there we are. I have a lovely photograph of Caroline with the twins and myself at the tremendous homecoming party we held at RAF Brüggen on our return from Kosovo.

On these deployments you live alongside each other and you share these extraordinary moments. It's much closer than a working relationship – it's more like an extended family.

Torrential rain and low cloud did not bode well for the Prime Minister's visit, but the weather cleared in time for his plane to land only thirty minutes behind schedule. After a walkabout on the streets of Pristina, Tony Blair met assorted but very much arranged groups, spoke to the press and posed for a number of photographs. The locals lionized him, because they knew what a key part he'd played in persuading other NATO countries to take military action in Kosovo. Then he and I had a one-on-one meeting, before being joined by Bernard Kouchner. My conversation with him showed that he had a real grasp of the political and security realities, of the need to lock the KLA into a democratic framework while retaining as much of the Serb population of Kosovo as possible. Afterwards he made time to go and talk to the soldiers.

It was good to see the Prime Minister taking a personal interest in our progress. Even though as COMKFOR I was commanding a multinational force, I was still a Brit, and I was proud of what we were achieving. Britain had played the lead role in KFOR and Tony Blair had played the lead role in mobilizing world opinion to intervene in Kosovo.

That evening Tony Blair and Alastair Campbell were our guests in the field kitchen behind the Film Factory. The atmosphere was much more relaxed than it had been during the Prime Minister's visit to Macedonia earlier in the year, when it seemed that we might be on the brink of a major war. It had been decided that the Prime Minister should not stay overnight in Pristina because of security concerns – in my view overplayed – but would fly down to Skopje and return the next day. His party decided that they wanted to depart somewhat earlier than expected. I sent word to get the helicopters up and running. A muddle ensued as to which of the two landing sites the PM's party was going to leave from: either the main one at the back, which was nearer the field kitchen, or the VIP site at the front. We were headed towards the main heli-pad at the back when we heard the aircraft taking off, and realized that they were expecting to pick up the Prime Minister's party at the front. By now it was dark, of course, and the ground was muddy after the heavy rain that had fallen earlier. Meanwhile, the Army Air Corps captain who'd come to guide the Prime Minister to the aircraft had got lost somewhere. We had to stagger through the woods in the dark, slipping and sliding in the mud. The Prime Minister was very good about it, but I felt embarrassed by the cock-up.

There was much political activity among the Albanian Kosovar activists, both KLA and others, to the extent of attempting to establish a 'government', which contravened the terms of UNSCR 1244. With hindsight, one can see that the KLA Undertaking should have included a prohibition on political activity by its members. Early in August the self-styled 'Minister for Public Order' Rexhep Selimi, a KLA regional commander, was stopped at a military checkpoint and became very abusive when a soldier from the Royal Irish Regiment asked to see his weapon. On the return of his Smith & Wesson, Selimi ostentatiously reloaded it, retaining one bullet which he held up to show the soldier with the message 'This one is for you'. At this point he was promptly arrested and had his weapon and JIC card confiscated.

I was furious to hear that one of my soldiers had had to endure this kind of thuggish bullying. Thaqi asked to see me to discuss the matter. In the end he didn't turn up to the meeting, but sent three self-styled officials in his place, including the 'Deputy Prime Minister' and the 'Deputy Defence Minister'. They began to argue that as 'war heroes' they were not subject to the same law as other Kosovo citizens. I'd had enough of this. I gave them a little lecture about what the rule of law means in civilized countries. They started to challenge the soldier's account of what had happened – which riled me even more. When one of them stood up, I lifted the table off the ground and banged it down again. 'Sit down!' I shouted. That shut them up.

Immediately afterwards I had a private meeting with Ceku. I cut him off before he could start speaking. 'I don't like being lied to,' I snapped as I strode into the room. All this time there was a JIC meeting waiting to begin. When it finally started, more than an hour later than scheduled, I restated our position on the unacceptability of any KLA challenge to KFOR's authority. They could not remain an armed force if they wanted to be recognized by the international community.

More high-level visitors followed, including the American Secretary of State Madeleine Albright, and from Britain the Foreign Secretary Robin Cook and the Defence Secretary George Robertson. There was a routine for visitors, depending on their importance. I might meet them at the front door or arrange for somebody else to do that and bring them up; we would give them a full briefing on the situation; and then, depending on who they were, they might go and visit units on the ground. If they were politicians they'd go and see Bernard Kouchner. We strung the programme together and the boys took care of most of it.

Early in September, when the Adjutant General, the number three on the Army Board, was visiting us, I received the worrying news that my daughter Amanda had been taken into hospital for an emergency operation, after an ectopic pregnancy. Apparently she was out of danger and had been sent home. Sarah had rushed to be with her, but of course I wanted to get back to see her myself as soon as possible. My ADC put in several hours' work and no fewer than sixty-five telephone calls trying to get me home and back. The Adjutant General came up with a solution. He had come out in an HS-125, a small RAF executive jet, and was due to fly back the next day. He turned one of his party off the plane, and persuaded me that I must take the seat. We flew direct to RAF Lyneham, which handily was close to where Amanda and her family lived. She didn't know I was coming. We landed about eleven-thirty in the morning, and I reached the house at about midday. I quietly unlatched the front door and pushed it open to see Amanda's first child, young Casper, sitting in his high chair facing me, while she was shovelling goo down him. 'Hello, darling,' I said, my voice cracking a little as I spoke. Amanda looked round, amazed, and then tears filled her eyes. It was a very poignant moment.

I couldn't stay in England more than a few hours, because I was due back in Kosovo the next day for a visit by the Prince of Wales. Ed Sandry had arranged for an RAF Puma helicopter to pick me up from a field near Amanda's house in the small hours of the morning and fly me on to Mons, where the plan was to hitch a lift from Wes Clark, who was flying down to Skopje in his personal jet, before taking a helicopter ride up to Pristina. I 'appointed' Sarah as my helicopter marshaller: we brought the Puma in to land on the kale field across the lane in pitch darkness at 04.30 using a couple of torches. I was back in Kosovo before lunch, in time to greet Prince Charles.

The flight from Mons had given Wes and myself plenty of time to review the whole situation in Kosovo, particularly in the run-up to the K+90 deadline. Early in August, an account of my altercation with Wes had broken in the press, and I took the opportunity to assure him that I was not responsible for the leak. I am quite clear that nobody at my end was responsible for it.

Like Wes and me, the Prince of Wales was dressed in combat kit. The real purpose of his visit was to see some of the British soldiers serving in Kosovo. Since I had become Colonel Commandant – the tribal elder – of the Parachute Regiment in 1988 and would continue as such until 2004, I was to see a lot more of HRH Prince Charles in his capacity as Colonel in Chief. He is a very warm human being, much warmer than the press generally give him credit for. The soldiers enjoy meeting him, and are hugely appreciative of the trouble he takes to come and see them.

Wes made no secret of his belief that Milosevic had left behind in Kosovo some special police units in civilian clothes, with communications and weapons hidden, ready to foment trouble at a moment's notice. I didn't share this anxiety. I thought it very likely that the Serbs had left behind agents who would keep them informed of developments. But I was less convinced that there were still Serb fighting units in Kosovo.

As K+90 approached, our focus was increasingly on the transformation of the KLA into a legitimate organization. The pressure increased as the deadline drew nearer. The major issues of demilitarization had been agreed, but the emotional issues remained unresolved. The KLA had accepted that their weapons should be held in KFOR-controlled storage sites, but only reluctantly: for many of their members, possession of these was a virility symbol. 'They can go there and stroke them if they want,' I told Ceku. He smiled grimly.

Richard Holbrooke rightly commented that in this final negotiation we were caught on the horns of a dilemma: we had to persuade the KLA to change, but if we pushed them too hard they might go underground again. It would be a horrible irony if we found ourselves in the same position as the Serbs, fighting a counter-insurgency campaign against a national resistance movement. Inevitably there was going to have to be an element of compromise on both sides. Holbrooke told Thaqi that 'the degree of international support' for Kosovo depended on its commitment to democracy, and that democracy was the way to independence. Thaqi didn't seem to understand. It was not just the organization that had to change, but its leaders. I negotiated with Ceku, observing his difficult and often painful metamorphosis from a guerrilla commander into a national leader.

The KLA's insignia may have seemed a small point, but the symbolism was potent. The KLA had worn on their combat uniform the red and gold insignia of the double-headed Albanian eagle. Such an emblem would have been unacceptable to the international community, suggesting as it did to many an aspiration for a Greater Albania, incorporating Kosovo. Moreover, it would have been intolerable to the sizeable Serb minority remaining in Kosovo. Ceku took the point intellectually, but he would have to sell any changes that he accepted to his military commanders, and it would be hard to overcome their emotional attachment to the double-headed eagle. This was the symbol under which they had fought; to abandon it would be insulting to the memory of those who had been killed. But I told Ceku that the eagle would have to go all the same. Even if I had agreed to it, NATO would have vetoed the proposal. At this, Ceku put his head in his hands and leaned forward on the table.

Ceku accepted that it was politically impossible for Kosovo to have its own army in the immediate future, and that the transformed and demilitarized KLA would have to be called something different. The name then being bandied around was the 'Kosovo Rescue and Protection Corps'. Ceku didn't like the word 'corps', which he felt was weak. His people came up with suggestion after suggestion, all of which needed to be carefully translated from the Albanian and then the nuances explored. We couldn't allow any name with a military connotation. They kept trying it on. He gave us a copy of a proposed new 'Kosovo Corps' ID card, which when translated read 'Kosovo Army Corps'.

As the eleventh hour arrived, the negotiations became extremely tense. Up until now we had been bouncing ideas around, but now the time had come to settle. Ceku was going through hell. His brain was telling him, 'I've got to play ball, for the long-term future of Kosovo, I've got to,' but his heart was working in the other direction. I kept saying to him, 'Don't be emotional,' 'You must comply with UNSCR 1244,' 'the world is watching' – banging on, repeating the same points again and again. We reached D+89. Thaqi turned nasty. 'Nobody plays games with the KLA,' he shouted at me. 'If you think you can issue directions to us, then you are mistaken and you will regret it.'

'I am too old to play games with anyone,' I replied

wearily. 'If we don't get this right tomorrow, the KLA will cease to exist. There will be no successor organization, you will have no identity, you will be nothing. Anybody found with a weapon will be arrested. Your magic little JIC cards will be worthless.'

I was under a lot of pressure too. I received a cryptic message from Rupert Smith, saying that there was deep discomfort within NATO about some of the concessions I was making to the KLA. 'The ghost is not laid to rest,' he wrote.

The following day, Sunday 19 September, was K+90. The press were speculating that the talks had collapsed. We reached the evening. Thaqi sent a message that I should go downtown to meet him. 'Bollocks to that,' was the universal reaction up at the Film Factory. Eventually Thaqi was tracked down having supper in the Grand Hotel. He tried the same ploy, received the same answer, then agreed to come up to the KFOR HQ. He and his colleagues arrived at just after 22.00 hours, complaining about being kept waiting. Our meeting started at 22.15. It was clearly going to be a long night. Seventeen minutes before midnight we took a break.

Outside, my staff had set up a sweepstake on the time the pen would hit the paper. Jonathan Bailey had 06.00, Andrew Ridgway 05.50 hours. In the event nobody won. As the night wore on it was clear to me that we weren't near to closing the deal. At 06.10 hours I decided to stop the clock. I went outside to tell the press that we hadn't made it. In a statement, I reminded the KLA that the Undertaking had expired, and that officially they no longer existed as a legal organization. If there was no agreement by midnight on the following day, and their members continued to carry weapons or wear uniforms with the old KLA insignia, they would be deemed to be non-compliant and would face arrest.

I spoke to Wes Clark, who suggested that he should fly in to add weight to the negotiation. That seemed sensible to me. I finally got to bed at 06.30, and was up again at 10.00. Wes arrived at 14.00 hours, and the KLA delegation was with us forty-five minutes later. Wes was in his element, working the room confidently, telling stories about his experiences in Vietnam which had the KLA's zone commanders hanging on his every word. Afterwards he made a rousing, virulently anti-Serb speech that would have had our diplomats reeling if they could have heard what he was saying. It became clear that the differences between the two sides had narrowed. We resolved the issue of the insignia, agreeing on an outline of the shape of Kosovo itself. Off the top of her head, our new Canadian political adviser Wendy Gilmore came up with a wording on one of the remaining issues, access to weapons, which satisfied everybody. More names were bandied about. Would we be prepared to call the organization the Kosovo Guard? Silence.

'It sounds too military,' Ceku responded, and then everyone started laughing.

'Hey, that's meant to be my line,' joked Wes. And eventually we settled on the name Kosovo Protection Corps.

It was early evening on K+92, Tuesday 21 September, when we signed the agreement. We had got there at last.

Two days later there was a football match between a KFOR XI – including a young Russian soldier – and Pristina FC. Our team lost 4–0, but the crowd applauded both teams enthusiastically none the less. I returned to the Film Factory to find Ceku dressed as I had never seen him before, in smart civilian clothes.

Ceku became Prime Minister of Kosovo, before being replaced by Thaqi. I have met him several times since, and when he came to England recently we had lunch together. He is proud of the fact that Kosovo still has a significant Serb population, and that one of his personal staff is a Serb. I saw him grow in stature, from 'freedom fighter' to statesman, renouncing violence and embracing democracy. It was a fine thing to watch.

Wes Clark was at his best in the negotiation with the KLA. When I saw him operating like that, I reflected on his outstanding qualities. It seemed tragic that his military career should be ending in bitter disappointment.

But only a few days later Wes began obsessing about the Serbs again. He was fixated on the possibility of a Serb reinvasion of Kosovo. Of course we'd considered that possibility, but it seemed to me extremely unlikely. For one thing, it wouldn't have made military sense to withdraw, to allow your enemy to occupy the ground, and then to have to fight your way back. I have no doubt that, having withdrawn, the next thing the Serb General Staff would have done was to examine the options should they be ordered to go back in. But that was very far from saying that it was a real possibility. Planning is one thing, execution is very much another. Even Milosevic would have known that NATO could not have allowed Kosovo to be retaken by the Serbs. However formidable the Serb Army, it would have been crushed by NATO's overwhelming strength. By September KFOR was fifty thousand strong, and of course we could call on a vast pool of potential reinforcements in an emergency.

'When the Serbs come over I am going to do everything I can to finish the fight,' Wes told me on the VTC from Mons. This time, he said, 'we will go the whole way' – presumably all the way to Belgrade. Clark talked a lot about Serbs coming back in. He said that we should 'welcome' a Serb attack. Can he really have wanted an all-out battle – a battle that would have meant thousands, maybe tens of thousands, of casualties?

I was not alone in thinking that this was barking mad.

HQ ARRC was due to go back to Germany in October, and though this could have been postponed, I knew that once we had implemented the KLA Undertaking, we had done what we set out to do – and more. The tempo had been non-stop for seven months, ever since we had deployed in March. We were tired, and it was beginning to show. A sluggishness was creeping in, a reluctance to do more than the minimum. It was time to go home.

In the last week the weather changed dramatically, and for the first time since our arrival in Kosovo we needed pullovers and jackets. I went on a round of farewell engagements. Even Thaqi was all sweetness and light. I gave Ceku a framed copy of the painting I had commissioned, showing us negotiating at a JIC meeting, him at one side of the table and me at the other. He absolutely loved it, and it seemed to seal the bond between us. It had been painted by Nick Bashall, who for a month had been an artist in residence with the Headquarters. Towering over most of us, Nick had cut a splendidly bohemian figure in his grotty, paint-stained shorts and bare feet.

Wes came down for the handover ceremony, at which I relinquished command of KFOR to a German four-star, General Dr Klaus Reinhardt. I reflected that this was almost certainly my last day of operational command in the field. The ceremony, which was presided over by Wes Clark, was a bit over-the-top for my taste, with a parade and a military band, followed by flowery speeches delivered from a lectern while the rest of us sat in a panel on a dais like the competitors in *University Challenge*. Andrew Ridgway described it as 'a press conference with music'. I was embarrassed when my own brief address was greeted with disproportionate cheering. Afterwards I went down to the big football stadium which we used as a helicopter landing site and flew to the airport, where the aircraft was waiting. There was still half an hour or so to kill before we left. General Yeftokovitch, the Russian commander who'd taken over when Zavarzin had returned to Moscow, had gone to great efforts to provide us with a farewell drink, so we had a vodka or three. There were many handshakes and lots of 'Do zvidaniya' – farewell in Russian. Then, together with my immediate staff, I boarded the BAe-146 aircraft and we took off. I'd ensured that we were well stocked with fizz, which we cracked open as soon as possible. The stewards were unused to our high spirits, and disapproved when I declined an offer to close the sliding doors separating the VIP cabin from the 'steerage' passengers. The similar flight home from Bosnia three years earlier inevitably came to mind.

Many commentators had predicted genocide in Kosovo. Bad things had happened there, but we'd largely put a stop to them, and set Kosovo on a road to a better future. We reckoned that it had been a job well done.

* * *

Soon after my return from Kosovo, I attended a special dinner at No. 10 Downing Street to commemorate the Kosovo operation. Margaret Thatcher had hosted a similar occasion after the Falklands War. Wes Clark was among those attending, as was George Robertson, who had just succeeded Javier Solana as NATO Secretary General. It was a very select gathering: numbers were restricted to about sixty and very few wives were present, but I insisted that Sarah should come. I felt that she had played a vital role in keeping the home fires burning while I had been away.

On 2 December 1999 I went to Buckingham Palace to receive the Distinguished Service Order (DSO) from Her Majesty the Queen. This is the decoration which every officer, if given a choice, would probably most covet. It is a tri-Service medal, requiring a very strong element of leadership on operational service. In this respect it stands outside the hierarchy of medals awarded purely for gallantry. I received many gratifying messages congratulating me on the award, and on what we had achieved in Kosovo. Some came from soldiers, some from political and civilian leaders, and others from members of the public. I received a magnanimous letter from Wes Clark, which caused me to reflect once again on the character of that contradictory man.

More than five years later I would go to the Palace again to be invested as a Knight Grand Cross of the Order of the Bath (GCB) – jocularly known as the 'Very Deep End of the Bath'. At the same investiture, Private Johnson Beharry, a Commonwealth soldier from Grenada, was presented with the Victoria Cross for his outstanding gallantry in twice rescuing comrades from an armoured vehicle during an ambush in Iraq, even though wounded. This was the first VC to be awarded since the Falklands; 'It's a long time since I've presented one of these,' the Queen remarked.

'I was overshadowed today by Private Beharry, and quite rightly so,' I commented to the press afterwards. 'It was an honour to stand alongside him.' I'd got to know Johnson Beharry beforehand and I knew him to be both modest and self-effacing, though obviously as brave as a lion. It was entirely appropriate that on that day he should be first of the hundred or so to be presented with an award by Her Majesty. He led, and I followed: the private soldier first, and the Head of the Army second.

14
High Command

While still in Kosovo I had learned what I'd be doing next. When my three-year tenure as COMARRC elapsed at the end of 1999 I would be succeeding Mike Walker – not for the first, or indeed the last, time – as Commander in Chief, Land Command (CinC Land), headquartered at Wilton, just outside Salisbury. This was the number two position in the Army, and entailed promotion to the rank of full general, four-star command. As Commander in Chief, I would automatically become a member of the Army Board, the formal institution that runs the Army. The promotion also meant that I would be a strong candidate to become CGS in due course.

The job came with a fine house, Bulford Manor, with four even gables and mullioned windows. It had plenty of bedrooms and a lovely drawing-room. Best of all, there was a glorious garden running down to the bank of the crystal-clear River Avon. We knew the house well, because it was close to Bulford Camp and opposite the church where Sarah and I were married. I had been dining at Bulford Manor in the summer of 1995 when the then Commander in Chief, John Wilsey, had warned me that I might have to go to Bosnia very soon.

I was of course delighted by the appointment, but I have to admit that the job took a bit of adjustment after the excitement of the previous year. Then I had been commanding a force in the field; this job was more sedentary and more managerial. By contrast with the intensity of what had gone immediately before, the work could be considered routine. It was, of course, important: the Commander in Chief has between two-thirds and three-quarters of all the Army's manpower under his command, and there's a very big budget to run, about £4.5 billion – not that you have much real control over it, as the MOD's overall spending pattern is largely in the hands of civil servants.

As Commander in Chief, your principal job is to run the Army on a day-to-day basis: to ensure that it's in good shape, that it's sufficiently trained and exercised, that it's structured properly and that it's ready to be deployed on operations. Of course, the future is very important – and that's where membership of the Army Board comes in. One of the most important aspects of the job is 'force generation', i.e. putting a force together to fulfil a particular task. I make the analogy with an orchestra: its make-up will vary, depending on the piece of music you want to play; similarly, the make-up of a force will vary depending on the requirements of the task. Just as for a piece of chamber music you might need only a string quartet, for example, so for a limited operation you might only need Special Forces. There are certain constants: in an orchestra you will always need violins, and in any operation you'll almost always need infantry. But other instruments are optional – percussion, for example – and some you use only rarely, like the organ (the Army equivalent might be artillery). Just as in an orchestra you don't always need every instrument, and for some pieces you may require more of one and less of another, so for a particular Army operation you may want to vary the proportions. Of course, you also have to ensure that your musicians are competent, which is where the training cycle comes in. The analogy also holds good for the force commander and the conductor of the orchestra: both have to get the best from their teams.

During my time as Commander in Chief I restructured the command and control system. When I took up the post I had a three-star deputy and a dozen or so major generals reporting to me. I asked my Chief of Staff, Freddie Viggers, my erstwhile artillery commander in Bosnia, to look at how the command might be better organized. On his recommendation, I decided to split Land Command in two: on the one hand what we call the 'field army', i.e. the two manoeuvre divisions – the 3rd Division in Britain and the 1st Division in Germany – and the specialist brigades such as air defence, engineers, signals and logistics; and on the other the regional chain of command, including all of the TA. I was able, perhaps surprisingly, to cajole the MOD into authorizing another three-star post, so that a lieutenant general ran each of these two, both reporting to me. It was a much more efficient set-up.

In May 2000, soon after I took over Land Command, a desperate Sierra Leone Government requested British help. A group of tribal thugs calling themselves the RUF, the Revolutionary United Front, had virtually overrun the country and were getting very close to the capital, Freetown. One of the RUF's more gruesome activities was chopping off people's hands and legs.

There was a huge UN force in Sierra Leone of around 17,500 soldiers, the biggest UN deployment anywhere in the world at the time. But though there were some good units among them, the challenge once again showed the weakness of UN forces, with national governments deciding what their soldiers could and could not do. The result was a humiliating failure to deal with the rebels. Kofi Annan appealed for international action. Tony Blair's Government made the decision to deploy a national force to stop these brutes taking control of Freetown, which had to be done with great urgency as they had already reached its outskirts. A force of around six hundred soldiers, largely from 1 Para, was flown to Sierra Leone under the command of Brigadier David Richards. Most travelled aboard RAF Hercules aircraft, but a pair of Chinooks which had been conducting mountain-flying training in Scotland flew all the way, with two crews 'hot-seating'. On landing, the first task of the battlegroup was to push out and secure the airport.

Captain Mark Jackson, then second-in-command of the Pathfinder Platoon, found himself part of the operation. After a journey to the British High Commission to deliver a mysterious briefcase, he then took part in the operation to evacuate EPs ('entitled persons'). With a patrol of four soldiers Mark cadged a helicopter ride across the estuary dividing the airport from the main part of the city. The situation in Freetown was very tense; as they arrived at the High Commission there was a firefight going on down the street. But the arrival of British soldiers effected a complete transformation, and the rebels withdrew. A while later rebels advanced on the airport in the hope of capturing a British soldier to use as a hostage. They were repelled after taking heavy losses in another firefight: the first and last time the rebels took on the British Army directly.

The British intervention in Sierra Leone was a huge success, preventing the fall of Freetown and stopping the insurrection in its tracks. Once again a small force of British soldiers, inserted rapidly at the *moment critique*, had succeeded where a much larger multinational force had failed. In 2002, elections were held in Sierra Leone for the first time in thirty years. Today the country is returning to normal, though there remains a small British presence of a hundred or so soldiers, acting as trainers for the Sierra Leone Army.

Another feature of my time as Commander in Chief was being called in to assist the civil authorities at home to help with a series of national emergencies. Within the Army these came to be known as the 'four Fs', the 'Fs' standing for flooding, the fuel-tanker drivers' strike, the firefighters' strike, and the crisis over foot-and-mouth disease. The first two were straightforward enough, but the firefighters' strike was a serious drain on our resources in the build-up to the second Gulf War. We had up to thirteen thousand soldiers on firefighting duties, which would be very difficult today, given the pressure on manpower arising from the current level of overseas deployments.

In principle, it could have been politically contentious to have the Army filling the gap – strike-breaking, to some – but in the case of the firefighters' strike, with lives potentially at risk, it was a no-brainer. Obviously most of our soldiers were not trained in the more esoteric firefighting skills, though the Navy and the Air Force do have a small number of very high-tech specialists. But a lot of firefighting is straightforward, and on the whole we didn't let people down. To have the necessary manpower trained in the basic skills and available right across the country was quite a logistical exercise. Some of our soldiers were camping out – in TA centres, for example. The famous – or infamous – old Green Goddesses trundled out of their depots. Now retired from service, these iconic vehicles had been procured for civil defence in the 1950s to put out fires after a Soviet nuclear attack on Britain. But though by now very ancient, they still did a good job. The soldiers quite enjoyed the firefighting, even if some might have been irritated to have to cover for people who were already paid a damn sight more than they were. There was always a chance that the boys might rescue a pretty girl from a blazing house . . .

The epidemic of foot-and-mouth disease in 2001 was a disaster for British agriculture. The Ministry of Agriculture, Fisheries and Food (MAFF) was struggling until we were called in to help. We put a logistics Brigade Headquarters into the Ministry to provide command and control, and used the regional chain of command to administer the crisis, treating it much like any other operation, using standard battle procedure, with command groups, morning updates and so on. MAFF were shown to be so hopelessly overwhelmed that soon afterwards they restructured and changed their name to the Department of Environment, Food and Rural Affairs (DEFRA). I flew up to Great Orton airfield in Cumbria with Geoff Hoon, the Secretary of State for Defence, to see for ourselves what was entailed in the slaughter and burial of thousands of animals in mass graves. The piles of corpses made a grisly sight, and the stench was appalling.

Among the soldiers, the 'four Fs' were inevitably known as the 'eight Fs': 'fookin' floods', 'fookin' fuel', 'fookin' fires', and 'fookin' foot and mouth'.

I was in the middle of a briefing in London in the late summer of 2000 when I received the news that Mark had been severely injured in a parachuting accident.

I left the briefing immediately, and within ten minutes or so had found out the details. Mark had gone out to north-east Spain for a week's holiday with a friend, Ed Paxton, who happened to be ADC to Rupert Smith. They had been free-fall parachuting, and Mark had misjudged the turn necessary to check his lateral speed (known in the sport as a 'low hook') just before he landed. He hit the ground too fast at the wrong angle, shattering a hip and fracturing his pelvis. From what I was told, it was clear that he was lucky to be alive.

Immediately after the necessary surgery, Mark was recuperating at the Haslar military hospital near Portsmouth when half a dozen or so wounded soldiers arrived from A Company, 3 Para. They'd been taking part in a spectacular rescue mission in Sierra Leone, to recover some British Army hostages taken by another bunch of lawless hoods called the West Side Boys. On the same ward as Mark, the wounded were in fine fettle, benefiting greatly from being together; here again was proof positive of the psychological advantage which wounded soldiers gain from being in a military environment, giving each other support and encouragement.

After his recovery, Mark started a junior staff course that summer, but abandoned it when 16 Air Assault Brigade undertook another short-notice deployment, this time a stabilization operation in Macedonia. This put him behind an ops-room desk. It was around this time that Mark decided against staying in the Army – with the permanent damage to his hip, transfer to another part of the Service would have been inevitable, and this had little attraction for him. More fundamentally, perhaps, he had always had a passion to be an artist and would probably have left the Army within the next decade to follow that course; now he would just go that bit sooner. Having identified the Charles H. Cecil Studios in Florence as where he wanted to study, he decided to stay with the Army for a year or two to save up the necessary money, and booked himself another tour to Sierra Leone for a year as an acting major.

I went back to the Balkans in June 2001. After consultation with the British Ambassador, I had arranged to pay a visit to Belgrade. This was my own initiative: it seemed to me an opportunity to extend a hand to the new, democratic Serbia, and perhaps to heal a few wounds. Slobodan Milosevic's regime had fallen the previous October, and at the end of March Milosevic himself had been arrested by the Serb authorities on charges of corruption and abuse of power, following an armed stand-off at his fortified villa. Back in 1999 he had been indicted by the ICTY to answer charges of crimes against humanity at The Hague, but despite strong international pressure the new Serbian government was resisting his extradition.

I flew into Pristina beforehand, and over lunch with Ceku I bet him a bottle of whisky that by the end of July Milosevic would be in The Hague. Afterwards I flew on to Belgrade. The effect of NATO air strikes could be seen as we came into land: broken bridges and bombed-out buildings. I was conscious that only two years before I had been one of the most public faces of the enemy that had caused this destruction. Nevertheless I was received with courteous formality by both politicians and the Serb High Command. In the course of the visit I had an amicable meeting with a member of the Serb delegation with whom I had negotiated the MTA just before KFOR's entry into Kosovo.

The Serbs made a point of telling me how they were dealing with the unrest in the Presevo valley, the area east of Kosovo where ethnic Albanians are in the majority. They described how they were handling the violence and outlined their rules of engagement. This was a message: they were telling me that they'd learned a lesson, that they weren't going to make the same mistakes as had been made in Kosovo.

The situation regarding Milosevic's extradition was developing rapidly, and at one stage during our visit it looked as though our seven-seater RAF aircraft might be retasked to fly him out to The Hague. As things turned out we flew out of Belgrade on 28 June, the anniversary of the assassination of Archduke Franz Ferdinand by Serb extremists in Sarajevo in 1914, the event that triggered the

First World War. On the very same day Milosevic was transferred to UN custody in Bosnia, pending his extradition to The Hague. I have yet to claim my bottle from Ceku!

A year later I paid another visit to Belgrade, when again I was received courteously. In London I had come to know Crown Prince Alexander, heir to the throne of Yugoslavia, whose last crowned king had been deposed (with British support) in 1941. Since the fall of Milosevic the Prince had returned to Belgrade and installed himself back in one of the palaces built for the Yugoslav Royal Family, later commandeered by Tito to be his official residence, and later still occupied by Milosevic. The Crown Prince asked me to go and see him there. He showed me around the ornately decorated palace, including the room used as a personal office by Tito and then by Milosevic – the very room where the latter had conceded to Ahtisaari and Chernomyrdin two years earlier.

In the second week of September 2001 I was in Canada, on a routine visit to watch one of our brigades in action at the Army's largest training area on the prairies of Alberta. It's a hell of a place, like a huge Salisbury Plain but thirty or forty times as big, so the Army can do almost anything it likes there, including plenty of live firing. On the morning of 11 September I came down to breakfast in the visitors' accommodation on the base camp to find my MA, Mark Carleton-Smith, and my ADC, Jez Rostron, glued to the television. 'There's mayhem in New York, General,' Mark said. It was 7.00 a.m. Alberta time, 9.00 a.m. New York time. Minutes afterwards we watched, horror-struck, as the second aircraft deliberately flew into the second tower – and then came the collapse of both towers. Just conceivably, the first aircraft hitting the Twin Towers might have been an appalling mistake, but now it became obvious that this was a coordinated terrorist attack of unprecedented scale – a conclusion reinforced when the third aircraft hit the Pentagon. Our immediate assumption was that this was the work of Islamic terrorists, almost certainly Al-Qaida. 'We've just witnessed the start of a new kind of war,' I commented to Mark and Jez, 'and now we're going out to see training for the old kind of war.' We flew out by helicopter to the exercise area. Knowing that the troops out on the prairie had little or no access to the media, I gathered the senior officers together and told them as much as I knew. I do remember saying to them, 'Life is not going to be the same after this.' Rather obvious, perhaps, but worth saying none the less. Like everybody else, I couldn't immediately see where this one was going, but I did make the comment that the attack would put an edge to their training. Other thoughts were in my mind: Was London next? Would it be a similar attack? Canary Wharf? The NatWest Tower? The Houses of Parliament? Buckingham Palace? And where were Sarah and the family? Were any of them in London?

I was in utterly the wrong place and needed to get back to the UK as soon as possible. It was hard to know what was happening back at home and how people had reacted. For some hours no telephone communication across the Atlantic was possible. After considerable difficulty I managed to get hold of my Chief of Staff back at Wilton, Freddie Viggers. Typically, he had already worked out what Land Command could provide if required. There was a sense of great uncertainty. While our intelligence services had been aware of a threat from Al-Qaida, an attack on this scale was totally unanticipated. Nobody knew if the attacks on the Pentagon and New York would be followed by attacks elsewhere. On both sides of the Atlantic, politicians were faced with the possibility of having to make a terrible decision: to order fighter aircraft to shoot down hijacked airliners filled with innocent passengers.

Though aircraft across North America were grounded for the next four or five days, I was able to take advantage of an opportunity to get back to England. Several days earlier there'd been a serious training accident on the range in which four or five soldiers had been wounded, and an RAF VC10 had arrived the day before to take them home. Since this was a casualty evacuation, the Canadians made an exception to allow this one aircraft to fly on humanitarian grounds, and we were able to cadge a lift on it. We took off at about 10.30 local time on 12 September. 'We are the only aircraft in Canadian airspace,' the captain told me.

Some hours later, as we were approaching the east coast of Canada, one of the crew came to tell me that the captain wanted a word.

'You know I said we were the only aircraft flying in Canadian airspace?' the captain asked, when I arrived on the flight deck.

'Yes,' I replied.

'Well, we're not any more. Down below us is a pair of F-16s.'

'Bloody hell,' I said. 'I hope they know who we are!'

We flew non-stop from Alberta to England, arriving back at RAF Brize Norton around 02.00 hours the next morning. Freddie's typically comprehensive written brief was waiting for me on landing. He'd answered all the questions in my mind, and so I felt able to spend what was left of the night at home. I was very relieved to be in Britain again. In Canada I was isolated from my HQ; back at Wilton I was in a position to deal with whatever force generation might be called for. Nobody knew then what the requirements might be. There still seemed the possibility of further attacks, including attacks on the UK itself. We were clear about our responsibility. In the event of a national emergency the lead service is the civil police, and it's for them to ask for military assistance, whether it be engineering assistance, specialist assistance in the event of a nuclear, biological or chemical attack, or just raw manpower. Soon after the attack on 11 September, intelligence was received of a possible terrorist threat to Heathrow Airport, and the police did request a military presence, which we provided, once ministerial approval had been granted.

The attacks of '9/11', as it became known, had come as a complete shock to the American body politic, and indeed to the world. Mainland America had been attacked for the first time in two centuries. Americans felt that they were 'at war'. Now they thought: These people have declared war on us, and therefore we will take the war to them. It was not immediately clear what this would mean for Britain and the British Army. We were, of course, ready to do whatever was asked of us in the event of an attack on British territory – but, more generally, there was a sense in the Army that overseas involvement was probably inevitable. Where and when was still unknown. Pretty soon attention focused on Afghanistan, particularly the Afghan–Pakistani border area, the heartland of the Taliban which had provided a refuge for Al-Qaida. The Americans decided that they had to go into Afghanistan to deal with this threat. President Bush's immediate reaction was: 'You're either with us, or you're against us.' On 12 September George Robertson had demonstrated NATO's solidarity with the United States by invoking Article 5 of the founding treaty, for the first time in the organization's history. In essence, the Article says that an attack on one member is an attack on all, and its invocation was of enormous symbolic importance. At home, the Prime Minister pronounced his support for the United States, speaking – then, at least – for the country as a whole.

The first missile strikes on Afghanistan came less than a month after the 9/11 attacks. By 19 October the first US Special Forces had entered the country. The UK con-tributed to the air campaign and sent in a modest number of our own Special Forces, who as ever punched way above their weight. But most of the ground fighting was carried out by the Afghani Northern Alliance, an umbrella organization of *mujahedin* fighters who had been active in the resistance to the Soviet occupation in the 1980s. By 13 November Kabul was a free city. It was a neat solution to employ indigenous forces, assisted by the use of devastating air power, to get rid of the Taliban, rather than sending in a Western army. But this success had the effect of bolstering, rather than diminishing, the status of the warlords.

After the collapse of the Taliban, the UN convened a meeting in Bonn of the various factions to address the future of Afghanistan. There were three urgent priorities: the search for a new political order in the country, the desperate need for humanitarian supplies, and the hunt for Bin Laden and the remnants of Al-Qaida. The four Afghan factions signed a deal which promised a new future for the country. Shortly after Bonn, a *loya jirga*, a traditional meeting of the clans, was held in Kabul and appointed a provisional government under President Karzai, pending elections. The Americans did not seem much interested in what would happen within Afghanistan after the Taliban had gone. While they were entirely right to prosecute the counter-terrorist campaign as vigorously as possible, their aversion to 'nation-building' was evident. But Tony Blair had made it clear that 'we will not walk away from Afghanistan as the outside world has done so many times before'.

The Bonn Conference provided for an International Security Assistance Force (ISAF) to support the embryo government in Afghanistan, to provide security and to train new Afghan security forces. Tony Blair volunteered Britain to lead ISAF first time around. This was essentially a political decision, though of course we were consulted on the operational factors. As Commander in Chief, I had to generate the necessary forces very quickly: as usual, we had to find a force commander and headquarters, and inevitably the finger finished up pointing at the 3rd Division, under its commander Major General John McColl. John, whom I knew to be a very able and humane officer, was to establish a remarkable personal rapport with President Karzai – so much so, that after the end of his tour in Kabul he became Tony Blair's personal envoy to Karzai.

I made my first visit to Afghanistan in January 2002, travelling with a small personal staff. It was very cold, with snow on the ground. This was a purely military visit: my purpose was to support John McColl, to receive briefings from local commanders and to see the situation on the ground for myself. There was still fighting going on in the south-east when I arrived, and the situation in Kabul had still not returned to normal: there was no mains electricity supply and aircraft were making only night-time landings at Kabul Airport. Once again I was able to snatch some time with Mark, who had deployed to Kabul before going on to Sierra Leone.

Introducing an international force into a country with its infrastructure in ruins, in the immediate aftermath of conflict, was a real challenge for the British Army, particularly as this had to be done during the winter. But this kind of challenge had become familiar to us in recent years after our experiences in Bosnia, Kosovo, Sierra Leone and elsewhere.

Under UNSCR 1386, ISAF's area of responsibility was restricted initially to the area around Kabul, which with hindsight was probably a mistake. In August 2003, NATO assumed command of ISAF – the first time the Alliance had operated outside Europe. ISAF gradually expanded its writ, but the critical area, the Tora Bora mountains adjoining Pakistan in the south-east, remained under a US-led Coalition command, with its emphasis on counter-terrorist combat operations. Now, this may sound a technical distinction, but to have two chains of command in the same country is to invite friction. It was not until the autumn of 2006 that a unified command structure under NATO was achieved.

Why was it so difficult to unify the chain of command? The Americans have always been wary about multinational forces, and perhaps understandably they regarded the ISAF with a jaundiced eye, because it was mainly, though not exclusively, composed of European troops and, as ever, hindered by various national caveats – they can't do this, they must do the other, they can't fly at night. These caveats are there because European governments are particularly nervous of the political effects of military risk-taking, not least when casualties are concerned. Britain has always been more sanguine in this regard. As for the US post-Vietnam aversion to body bags, 9/11 changed all that in a trice. The idea that somehow military operations can be risk-free is an absolute contradiction in terms. Unless a multinational force is prepared to accept a certain degree of risk it will never be able to fulfil its mission.

The American administration that had come to power in 2000 under President George W. Bush took a very different approach to foreign policy from its predecessors. Bush surrounded himself with neoconservative thinkers, who viewed the world in more aggressively ideological terms. Among these was his powerful Vice-President, Dick Cheney. The 'neocons' took the view that victory in the Cold War had demonstrated the superiority of American-style democracy, and that with American encouragement this model could spread across the world. Unlike the Clinton Administration, they were ready to intervene in other countries when they believed that American interests were at stake. Bush's Secretary of State, General Colin Powell, was an isolated figure among these ideologues. In a conversation with the British Foreign Secretary Jack

Straw, Powell was quoted by the respected American journalist Sidney Blumenthal as having described the neocons within the Bush Administration as 'fucking crazies'. Powell was a professional soldier; his thinking had been formed by the chastening experience of Vietnam, and he was habitually cautious about risking American lives in overseas adventures. The Secretary of Defense, Donald Rumsfeld, and especially his deputy, Paul Wolfowitz, pursued radical neoconservative policies aimed at reshaping the world in the American image. While Powell was Secretary of State there was a running battle between the State Department and the Pentagon.

Rumsfeld proposed a new doctrine for the American military, seeking to increase force readiness and to decrease the amount of supply required to maintain forces by reducing the number of troops in theatre. A key component of what became known as the 'Rumsfeld Doctrine' was the use of light forces to seek out the enemy and call down air strikes. In contrast, Powell favoured the use of overwhelming force, with well-defined objectives and exit strategies. The apparent success of the Rumsfeld Doctrine in Afghanistan took little account of the major part played by the Northern Alliance. There was great tension between Rumsfeld and his senior generals, particularly the Army Chief of Staff, Eric Shinseki, who had been fighting a rearguard action against Rumsfeld's desire to slim down the army. Rumsfeld felt that the American army was too cautious, too resistant to change and too unwilling to take risks. I believe events have shown him to be wrong.

In my view, Rumsfeld is one of those most responsible for the current situation in Iraq. He rejected the advice given to him by his generals, while at the same time he discarded the detailed plans for the post-conflict period prepared by the State Department.

Her Majesty Queen Elizabeth the Queen Mother died in March 2002, and I was privileged to take part in the cortège that followed her coffin from St James's Palace to Westminster Hall, where it would lie in state before her funeral. I took the part of the CGS immediately behind the Royal Family, since Mike Walker was acting as a pall-bearer, in his capacity as Colonel of the Royal Anglian Regiment.

My driver and I believed that we had allowed plenty of time to get to the Palace, but we had reckoned without the special measures put in place by the Metropolitan Police. In the event we arrived only just in time. I emerged from the car still a little bedraggled, my full ceremonial dress not yet complete. Greeting me was the awe-inspiring figure of the Garrison Sergeant Major, a very tall Guardsman called Mason and known inevitably as 'Perry'. He looked at his watch ostentatiously and sniffed. He sniffed again as I dragged on my frock coat and buckled my ceremonial sword.

'Very good to see you, Commander in Chief,' he said in a voice radiating disapproval. 'If you will move along smartly to the room on the left, you will find the other mourners, who have been here *for some time.*'

I felt duly put in my place. Only in the British Army could a four-star general be rebuked in such a way by a warrant officer.

Immediately after 9/11, President Bush announced that the war in Afghanistan was part of a broader battle against states sheltering terrorists. This caused a certain amount of discomfort in Britain, where public opinion didn't share that same sense of being 'at war'. Indeed, the phrase 'the global war on terrorism', much used by Washington, struck me as rather odd. Any use of military force must, by definition, be in pursuit of a political objective: this linkage is at the core of strategy. If we use the simple but powerful analytical tool of ends, ways and means, the end is the political objective; the means are the tools – diplomacy, sanctions, military force, etc.; and the ways are how you apply the tools to achieve the objective. Al-Qaida's end is not terrorism – that is their way of applying the means of violence; their end is the political one of achieving the ascendancy of Islamic fundamentalism.

So 'the global war on terrorism' equates to a war on a means, which makes little or no sense. Our objective – our end – must be the physical and intellectual defeat of Islamic fundamentalism as a threat to us. The means to this end certainly include the use of armed force, but also, very importantly, engagement in the battle of ideas. It is here, for me, that the US approach is inadequate: it focuses far too much on the single military means. Nation-building and diplomacy are fundamental to demonstrate the advantages of political and economic progress, both to nations as a whole and to individuals. Furthermore, it has to be understood that this 'war' is not conventional force-on-force war-fighting, in which the use of violence is maximized: in this 'war' the degree of violence has to be very carefully judged to avoid a detrimental effect overall.

In his State of the Union Address in January 2002, Bush

identified three countries – Iraq, Iran and North Korea – as an 'Axis of Evil'. He accused these regimes of sponsoring terrorism and seeking to obtain weapons of mass destruction (WMD). As 2002 progressed, there was a sense that Washington's next priority would be Iraq. The Prime Minister's judgement was that Britain had to be alongside America – indeed, that the United Kingdom and the United States should always stand together, even if the cause is seen by some as muddled or misguided. Tony Blair believes passionately in the strategic importance of the Anglo-American alliance. There is no doubt in my mind that this belief, together with the 'doctrine of international community' he had set out in 1999, guided his decision to join the American-led Coalition against Iraq.

It has been suggested more recently that there should be an inquiry into why we went to war in Iraq. In February 2007 the Leader of the House, Jack Straw, indicated in the Commons that the Government would be open to an inquiry 'at the appropriate time', by which he seemed to mean once our troops were no longer involved on the ground. Speaking for myself, I would have no objection to such an inquiry. This seems to me a political rather than a military matter.

In Washington, a vigorous debate ensued about the number of troops required for the invasion of Iraq. Rumsfeld favoured using only a relatively small force of sixty thousand or so, on the model of Afghanistan – disregarding, or at least minimizing the contribution of the Northern Alliance in the defeat of the Taliban. The American military wanted four hundred thousand. The eventual number decided upon was a compromise between these two. From the earliest stage, British concerns focused not just on the war itself but also on what would happen afterwards – so-called 'Phase 4'. At issue was not so much the number of troops needed to topple the regime as the number needed to maintain the peace afterwards. Within meetings of the Chiefs of Staff, I voiced my concern that management of the post-conflict period was essential to the success of the operation. There was no divergence of view between the Chiefs on this issue, and the then CDS, Admiral Sir Mike Boyce, represented our concerns both to the Prime Minister and the Secretary of State – though it may not have helped that he didn't have an easy relationship with Geoff Hoon. In our discussions it became clear that the American State Department had done plenty of planning for Phase 4, and we placed our confidence in this.

By the autumn of 2002 it had become the received wisdom that Saddam Hussein's regime had and was continuing to develop WMD. This was not spin: every major intelligence agency on the planet was saying the same thing, including the Russians'. It was known that Saddam Hussein had used chemical weapons against the Kurds, and it seemed therefore entirely plausible to conclude that what Iraq sources were saying was accurate, i.e. that he was attempting to develop nuclear and biological weapons as well.

Since no evidence of WMD was found after the invasion of Iraq, some commentators have speculated that the scare about WMD was invented as a pretext for the invasion. I have no reason to give this any credence. We in the British Army were certainly not willing to discount the intelligence; to do so would have been extremely foolhardy. I know that our soldiers in northern Kuwait before the invasion were very concerned about WMD – particularly chemical weapons – being used against them. I myself visited the forces in the build-up to the invasion, and, like everyone else, I had to lug a respirator and chemical suit about with me. Our forces out there had to do a lot of training in respirators and pro-tective clothing to rehearse their response to a chemical attack. You would not do this in the heat and dust of the desert unless you judged that a chemical attack was a serious possibility.

We know now that the intelligence was fool's gold. I can't pretend to know why this was. Intelligence-collecting in Saddam Hussein's Iraq was peculiarly difficult, and intelligence gathered there required cautious handling. I suspect there was only a very small number of high-ranking sources in Iraq. It's possible that these sources didn't have first-hand knowledge of what was happening, but had themselves been told that Iraq was developing WMD and believed it to be true. Perhaps the regime allowed this belief to circulate because it was thought to act as a deterrent to intervention. The obstruc-tive Iraqi behaviour towards the UN weapons inspectors before the invasion reinforced the conclusion that they had something to hide. Of course, it's possible to draw the opposite conclusion: that the Iraqis hindered the inspectors to conceal the fact that they had no WMD – in other words, that they had been bluffing all along. That was a very high-risk game for the Iraqis to play, and as it turned out they lost.

Another possibility is that the sources knew that there was no WMD programme, but lied to their handlers to deter an attack. Much depends on what they perceived Western intentions to be. One could equally well argue that they lied to their handlers because they knew that intelligence of a WMD programme would provoke an attack and they wanted Saddam Hussein removed. Washington in particular was locked into a dialogue with some disgruntled and ambitious Iraqi expatriates, based both in America itself and in Jordan, no doubt working to an agenda which suited them. It's possible that they were telling their paymasters what their paymasters wanted to hear. These are recurring problems with intelligence.

The intelligence assessments produced by the Joint Intelligence Committee (JIC) are very measured documents indeed, and normally full of caveats. Every word is carefully considered. As Commander in Chief and later as CGS I used to receive such assessments on a regular basis, though in neither role did I sit on the committee myself. On 24 September 2002 the Government took an unprecedented decision to release a dossier, based 'in large part' on the work of the JIC, into the public domain. The wording of the dossier was less measured than was usual for JIC assessments. It concluded that Saddam Hussein's regime possessed chemical and biological weapons, some of which 'are deployable within forty-five minutes of an order to use them'. This was taken by some commentators to mean that the UK could face a threat of attack at forty-five minutes' notice.

It was understood that the dossier was intended for public consumption. Nevertheless, its release caused a stir in military circles. We all knew that it was impossible for Iraq to threaten the UK mainland, even if the dossier left that impression open. Saddam's SCUD missiles could barely have reached our bases on Cyprus, and certainly no more distant target. We took the vague warning to mean that chemical warheads could be fitted to missiles in the field within forty-five minutes – though the public may have been left with a rather different impression.

I learned that I was to be the next CGS after an Army Board meeting in the MOD in the autumn of 2002. The Army Board meetings would last all morning, and then there would be an informal lunch in the office, after which members of the Board would drift away. At the end of one of these lunches Mike Walker asked me to stay behind, and afterwards he told me that he had been chosen as the next CDS once his time as CGS was up, early in 2003. I was to take over from him. For the third time in succession, I would be stepping into his shoes.

The choice of a new CGS is ultimately made by the Prime Minister and subject to approval by the Sovereign. In practice, the existing CGS puts forward a recommendation to the CDS and the Secretary of State after off-the-record discussions with a number of senior officials, including the Military Secretary. The recommendation is forwarded to No. 10 and finally to Buckingham Palace.

Of course I was delighted. To become head of the Service is a huge honour. To me personally, it meant staying in the Army for another few years. The alternative would have been retirement, because there was nowhere else for me to go – it was up or out at that point. I would take up the post of CGS fewer than seven weeks before my fifty-ninth birthday. I was already at least a couple of years or so older than the average CGS on appointment. Being somewhat older than the optimum age probably blew any chances I might have had of becoming CDS in due course – that and my discomfort with the MOD, which I found hard to conceal.

I knew that the job of CGS would be high-profile, especially as it was looking increasingly likely that we would be going into Iraq at some point. I discussed the matter with Sarah, and we thought that I should brief the whole family. Although Amanda and Mark now had their own lives, my taking this job would affect them none the less, as well as Tom. I told them my news over supper in the kitchen at Bulford. The first thing I wanted them to know was that I would be staying in the Army for another three years or so, and that we would be living in an official residence in London – in a small but charming apartment above the old stables of Kensington Palace, as luck had it. Any CGS inevitably becomes involved in difficult and sometimes unpopular decision-making, and there was no reason to suppose I would be exempt. I knew that taking the job meant that I would come in for a lot of criticism, often without being able to answer back. I have always held very strongly to the principle that soldiers should never become embroiled in politics: I would therefore have to defend decisions which were not mine, and to refrain from speaking out openly on issues about which I felt strongly. I would have to accept compromises even if I felt these were shabby ones. It was my constitutional duty not to express dissent in public for as long as I was in post. There was sure to be some sniping; it was important that, as a family, we would be able to take the rough with the smooth. I had a sense that it was not going to be an entirely easy ride. Though aware of the downside, the family was entirely supportive.

*In Kabul, on a visit to
Afghanistan as Chief of
the General Staff.*

My elder son Mark with an unidentified colleague on active service in Sierra Leone. **Below:** *Mark later left the Army after a serious parachuting accident and has made a new career as an artist.*

Left: *Cadet Lance Corporal Jackson: my younger son Tom photographed with the Eton CCF, 2007.*

Below: *My daughter Amanda's wedding to Jason Gard, 21 October 2005. Standing in front of the picture are my grandchildren Jemima, Phoebe and Casper.*

Inspecting officer cadets at the Sandhurst Sovereign's Parade, 10 December 2004.

Right: *At the Palace after being presented with the DSO for my service in Kosovo, 2 December 1999.*

Above: *With Princes William and Harry at the Sovereign's Parade, 12 April 2006, Prince Harry's commissioning day.*

Below: *With Private Johnson Beharry VC, at Buckingham Palace, 27 April 2005.*

Above: *In the Kabul HQ of 16 Air Assault Brigade, early in 2002, during a visit in my capacity as Commander in Chief. In the middle of the picture is the Brigade Commander, Barney White-Spunner.*

Below: *In 7 Armoured Brigade HQ talking to Brigadier Graham Binns. His Brigade played a leading role in the Iraq operation.*

Above: *Overlooking the River Euphrates from the terrace of the British Embassy in Baghdad, April 2003. The Embassy had been closed for the previous thirteen years. The man not in uniform is Major General Tim Cross.*

Below: *Addressing British soldiers in southern Iraq.*

As Chief of the General Staff, presenting a wreath at the Cenotaph during the service to commemorate the sixtieth anniversary of VJ-Day on 21 August 2005.

* * *

Before the invasion of Iraq there was much speculation about the legality of going to war without the backing of a specific UN Security Council Resolution authorizing military action. There was a bit of inconsistency about this. People forgot, or chose to forget, that the intervention in Kosovo, which had broad public support, was made without a UNSCR. It seems that it had been acceptable then, but wasn't acceptable when it came to Iraq. Cynics have pointed to Iraq's oil as a motive for going to war; I saw no evidence of this myself, and in any event it doesn't alter the principle. In the case of Kosovo, the legal argument used to circumvent the absence of a UNSCR was the emerging doctrine in international law that intervention on humanitarian grounds to prevent genocide or 'ethnic cleansing' may be adequate legal justification in itself. And indeed the fact that this had happened in Kosovo served as a kind of precedent. This is quite a controversial area: some accept the argument, some don't, but of course international law is a strange beast. It often doesn't have the precise clarity of domestic law, and often it applies to a particular country only if that country has signed up to a particular treaty or convention. In the case of Iraq, we were the junior partner in a coalition led by the United States, which doesn't acknowledge the authority of certain aspects of international law to the extent that the UK does. In particular, the Americans do not accept the authority of the International Criminal Court. The relevant legislation had been introduced into UK law in Charles Guthrie's time as CDS and he was on record as having been rather unhappy about it; but he had accepted an assurance given to him by the Government that it could not envisage circumstances in which a British soldier would find himself in front of the International Criminal Court. Now, an assurance given by a politician is one thing, but in law there was at least the theoretical – and worrying – possibility that a British soldier might find himself being tried by the ICC. The same applied right up the chain of command, up to the very top.

Mike Boyce was CDS in the run-up to the Iraq War. He had been due to hand over to Mike Walker before the war started, but it was decided that it wouldn't be very sensible to change the Chief of the Defence Staff in the very early stages of the Iraq campaign, so he remained in post for a few months longer than originally intended. Tony Blair wanted a new UNSCR if possible, for internal political reasons as much as for anything else. It became clear that the Security Council were not going to back a so-called 'second' UNSCR (there had already been seventeen concerning Iraq); of the permanent members of the Security Council, the Russians would veto any Resolution authorizing military action, and the French might do the same.

The matter came to a head after I'd become CGS, in the immediate run-up to the war, but of course the debate had been running for some while before this. A lot of people had asked me in casual conversation, 'Are you sure you're OK on this one?' The Chiefs of Staff discussed the matter and collectively agreed that we needed to be sure of our ground. So Mike Boyce, on behalf of us all, sought the Attorney General's assurances on the legality of the planned military action. I remarked at the time that, having had some part to play in putting Slobodan Milosevic into a cell in The Hague, I had no wish to be his next-door neighbour. Notwithstanding the Attorney General's advice that the war was legal, I decided to do my own homework. I dug out what to me were the critical Security Council Resolutions (particularly 678, 687 and 1441) and went through them very carefully. By the end I had satisfied myself independently that military action against Iraq was legitimate under international law without a 'second' Resolution. There was much debate about whether or not UNSCR 1441 carried with it 'automaticity', i.e. whether nations were entitled to take military action if Saddam failed to comply with its provisions. But my own reading of the Resolutions is that the first Gulf War had ended in a ceasefire, and that if Saddam failed to do what he was obliged to do under UNSCR 687, the ceasefire no longer held. Indeed, it is entirely possible to regard the two Gulf Wars of 1990 and 2003 as being a single war, with the two ground actions separated by a long operational pause.

The political reasons for action against Saddam Hussein propounded at the time have proved to be flawed: Bush's position that Iraq was an Al-Qaida hotbed does not now withstand scrutiny; and Blair's reliance on WMD proved to be a chimera. It is something of a mystery to me why Blair did not extend the argument, as Bush did in mid-December, when he declared Iraq to be in material breach of various past UNSCRs. For a decade, Saddam Hussein had defied and obstructed the United Nations. Unenforced UNSCRs can only diminish and weaken the institution; he was a brutal tyrant who treated his own people with appalling cruelty, including gassing a Kurdish town; even if he did not possess WMD in 2003, it is likely that his intent was to obtain them.

I have given my own view as to the legality of the Coalition action, and certainly the Chiefs accepted the Attorney General's advice. In conversation with critics of the Iraq action, I have heard some seem to suggest that the British Armed Forces should have refused to take part. This is very dangerous ground. The Armed Forces of this country take their oath of allegiance to the Sovereign as Head of State, and they are constitutionally bound to follow the lawful directions of the duly elected Government of the day. It would be unthinkable for the Armed Forces not to do as they are directed – or, worse, to act without authorization. That is the road to anarchy.

The legal status of UK soldiers after the invasion was also an issue. I remember that the Army lawyers worked very hard on this, because military occupation was not an area of international law which had been used in the recent past (in the Balkans, international forces had intervened with the agreement – however reluctant – of the appropriate governments). During the Iraq War itself, British soldiers were operating under the international Law of Armed Conflict and, as ever, British military law. What happened once the war ended was more complicated. International law defined the Coalition as 'occupying forces' under the Geneva Convention until a sovereign Iraqi government was re-established. Once Iraq formally regained its sovereignty under the interim government in the summer of 2004, agreements were made which changed the status of the Coalition forces from that of occupiers to that of a military presence at the behest of the sovereign government, which is perfectly valid in international law. So the period of occupation lasted just over a year.

* * *

In the autumn of 2002, as options for military action against Iraq were being explored within the MOD, the initial proposal was that the British contribution should be based on naval and air contingents, without any significant ground force. I never quite got to the bottom of that. It was true that there was a groundswell of anti-war opinion at home, though opinion polls showed that public opinion was about two to one in favour of military intervention in Iraq. I argued strongly that we would never get traction with the Americans without ground troops. In a coalition, as in a formal alliance, both political and military risk must be shared.

If you are going to commit a ground force to a major military operation, whether on an independent national basis or as a partner within a coalition, you need to do it on a scale which gives you the confidence to say: Well, if it all goes wrong, we can look after ourselves and we can fight our way out. In circumstances such as prevailed in Iraq, you needed a division to do that. A brigade would not have been big enough.

There were problems about deploying a sizeable ground force. Not only were there some ten thousand soldiers still committed to firefighting in the UK because of the continuing firemen's strike; such a commitment would also be outside the MOD's 'Defence Planning Assumptions'. These assumptions define force structures and equipment stocks. In 2002 the assumptions provided for nothing more than what we call a 'small-scale' effort in desert conditions (small-scale being below a brigade, medium-scale being brigade level, and large-scale being the level of a division or more). The most charitable judgement is that this assumption lacked prescience. I am reminded of the definition of such an assumption produced by one of my fellow-officers: the genesis of a cock-up. So the MOD had based its procurement on equipping no more than a few thousand soldiers to operate in the desert. This is not something that you can change overnight. For example, you can't produce thirty thousand sets of desert combat kit in a few weeks; it just isn't possible.

There was a political element in this, too. The British Government wanted to demonstrate that the decision to invade was not a *fait accompli*, i.e. that Saddam Hussein would not be attacked if he cooperated fully with the weapons inspectors. Such political sensitivities delayed the necessary military preparations.

A further complication was that we had planned for the main British force to move south from Turkey into Kurdistan, which would have given greater autonomy to the British campaign, despite the very considerable logistic challenge of an overland line of communication six or seven hundred miles long from the nearest available port in the eastern Mediterranean. But by early January 2003 it had become clear that the Turks were highly unlikely to give the necessary permission for an invasion from Turkish soil, and the decision was made to switch to the south. So then the plan had to be rejigged at short notice, adding the complexity of having to mesh closely with the American entry plans, and increasing the pressure on time.

The switch to the south also required a re-appraisal of the ground force's size and shape. The outcome was the decision to adopt a full divisional structure comprising three brigades – a larger force than the northern option. This increase to full scale brought additional logistic pressure. The eventual British ground contribution would be approximately thirty thousand soldiers, around one-fifth of the total ground troops deployed. Time was not on our side. The logisticians went into overdrive. Personnel and materiel were moved to the Gulf much more quickly than in 1989–90. The build-up was helped by the fact that the UK had held an ambitious joint-Service exercise in Oman during the autumn of 2001, after which a lot of equipment was held in the Middle East rather than being returned to Britain.

Lack of proper equipment at the start of the war has become something of a *cause célèbre*. The main problem was that political decision-making had left too little time for the Defence Logistic Organization to equip every soldier with desert camouflage clothing and with the latest body armour. But in the judgement of the in-theatre commanders, this was not what we in the Army call a 'show-stopper'. None of them said, 'We can't go in this time frame.' And too much emphasis on logistical difficulties was not the right message to send to the enemy just before the invasion. The alternative would have been to delay the operation until the autumn of 2003. But there were overwhelming counter-arguments: it would have been a nightmare to have kept the Coalition forces in their assembly areas in the Gulf during the fierce summer heat – and Washington was simply not prepared to wait that long.

There was a mood of keen anticipation in the Army in late 2002. It's very much part of the job of the Commander in

Chief to get around, visiting units in the barracks, visiting the Brigade Headquarters, seeing what's going on in field training exercises, talking to officers, talking to soldiers. In my last few months as Commander in Chief, during the build-up to the invasion of Iraq, I was lobbied wherever I went to favour the battalion I was visiting over others. This remarkable desire to get involved in operations gives the British Army the can-do character for which it is renowned.

I took over as CGS on 1 February 2003. By this time the invasion of Iraq was imminent. Many of our troops were already in their assembly areas in northern Kuwait, a flat landscape of greyish desert. I flew out to visit them in the second week of March, just a week before hostilities began. They were training hard and doing plenty of live firing. The weather was awful, with sandstorms making it unpleasant to venture outside. As the wind howled around our camps, sand found its way everywhere, into your clothes and into your equipment. I shared a tent with Major General Robin Brims, the UK Land Component Commander. While I was there I went off to find Mark, who was what we called 'watch-keeping', i.e. working in the ops room, taking the radio messages and all of that. We had about three-quarters of an hour together before I had to move on.

During this visit I had a memorable chat with a young private soldier from the Royal Regiment of Fusiliers, a northerner.

'How are you doing?' I asked him.

'Doing fine, Sir,' he replied. I asked him if he was getting the newspapers from home, and he told me that he was.

'Well, as you probably know then, there's a bit of a fuss

going on about boots and bog rolls and whatnot,' I said. 'Are you all right for boots?' He told me that he was.

'Any worries, then?'

'Aye, Sir,' he said firmly. Wait for it, I thought. 'When are we going in, Sir? Fucking when?'

'I don't know,' I told him, stifling a grin. 'A week, ten days perhaps – you know, it's all down to the politicians.'

'Because what we need to do is get across that bloody border, kick that bugger's arse, get home and have a few bloody beers.'

As a succinct mission statement, I couldn't have matched it.

War began on 20 March. The Chiefs of Staff moved to meeting on a daily basis, as I had witnessed during the Falklands – only this time I wasn't a minion sitting in a cubby-hole manipulating the vufoils (now, of course, long out-of-date), but one of the Chiefs myself. At that point, I was the only soldier among the five Chiefs of Staff, because Admiral Mike Boyce was CDS, and his deputy, the Vice Chief, was Air Chief Marshal Tony Bagnall. These daily meetings were held in the morning in the splendidly appointed Old War Office building, which served as the MOD HQ while the main building was being refurbished. Meetings would begin with an intelligence and operations update, before moving on to discuss any special developments, logistics and 'force flow' – the coordinated movement of men and materiel. Day-to-day operational matters were overseen by the Permanent Joint Headquarters (PJHQ) in Northwood, which had permanent responsibility for all operations worldwide (except operations on the UK mainland). The Chief of Joint

Operations (CJO) at the time was my old friend John Reith, now a lieutenant general, and he would participate in the Chiefs' meetings by video conference from Northwood.

During the war a dedicated Cabinet sub-committee met most mornings, attended by the Prime Minister, the Deputy Prime Minister John Prescott, the Foreign Secretary Jack Straw, the Attorney General Peter Goldsmith, the Defence Secretary Geoff Hoon, the International Development Secretary Clare Short and others. I attended in place of Mike Boyce on several occasions when he was busy elsewhere. This was my first experience of so-called 'sofa government'. I was included in the Prime Minister's discussion group, which would meet in his unprepossessing study beforehand. The room was furnished with a small desk and a couple of sofas, where I sometimes found myself perched on one of the arms. Informal agreement on the day's issues would be reached prior to rehearsing the discussions in Cabinet. Alastair Campbell was always present in the PM's study.

I was quite confident that the conventional war – what we in the Army call the 'manoeuvre war' – would be a resounding success, because this is what the US Army does best. My concerns centred on the aftermath of the inevitable fall of Saddam Hussein. One could see it was going to be very difficult: Iraq is a very much larger country than any other in which we had recently operated, and there was the constant problem of American aversion to nation-building. The difficulties were greatly exacerbated by the President's fateful misjudgement in transferring responsibility for the post-conflict period from the State Department to the Pentagon. All the planning carried out by the State Department went to waste. Rumsfeld and his fellow neocons paid little attention to the Phase 4 period; for them, it was an ideological article of faith that the Coalition forces would be accepted as a liberating army. Once you had decapitated Saddam Hussein's regime, a model democratic society would inevitably emerge.

As always in the British Armed Services, our inclination was to leave the tactical decisions to the commanders on the ground. There were plenty of Cassandras, both in the press and within the MOD itself, warning that the fighting in the Iraqi cities would be like Stalingrad, a grim struggle to the death in rubble-strewn streets. These ignoramuses didn't know what they were talking about. Graham Binns, the brigade commander responsible for taking Basra, bided his time, using probing attacks to test how the Iraqis would react. Graham had been my Chief of Staff in 39 Brigade, on my last Northern Ireland tour; I knew that 7 Armoured Brigade could not be in better hands. In close consultation with Robin Brims, his divisional commander, Graham fought a brilliant battle. He wore down the Iraqi defences on the periphery of Basra until – with exquisite timing – he was able to take the city in one fell swoop.

The Cassandras were always looking for something to go wrong. I well remember doing a press conference on the afternoon of the first Friday of the ground war, six days after the invasion began. In the morning meeting of the Chiefs of Staff, John Reith had given us an operational update on the VTC from Northwood. At that point the American spearhead had paused just short of the town of Karbala, where the only practical route north is through a narrow gap between the River Euphrates and a very large salt pan. They had advanced 300 miles or so in less than a week. And some of the press commented that the Americans were 'bogged down'!

'They've just advanced three hundred miles in contact with the enemy in a mere six days,' I told the press conference. 'Do you understand what an enormous military achievement that is?' After such a rapid advance the American soldiers needed to catch up on sleep, and stock up on fuel and ammunition. And of course they needed to regroup and replenish, to plan what they were going to do next, how they were going to advance through the Karbala gap and on to Baghdad. 'If you think that's being bogged down,' I went on, 'words fail me.'

Civilians might find it remarkable that the Iraqi Army, which had fought for many years against the Iranians in the 1980s, collapsed so quickly. But it was all a matter of manoeuvre, of paralysing your enemy by speed and by decisiveness. The Iraqis were completely outmanoeuvred and outfought, cut off from their lines of communication and logistics. I suspected, too, that many Iraqi soldiers had no wish to die for Saddam Hussein. I remember saying shortly before the war began: 'What we need is the mobile phone number of every Iraqi divisional commander. Our commanders on the ground should give each of them a ring twenty-four hours out and say something along the lines of, "Ahmed, my friend, you don't know me but I know about you. You and I are going to meet: we can either meet with a handshake or we can meet over the dead bodies of your soldiers." ' I was pretty sure how they would have reacted to such an approach. Before the manoeuvre war began, I predicted that it would be finished in two weeks. In fact it took almost three. By the middle of April, that relatively straight-forward bit was over.

Three weeks later I flew out to Iraq myself. Robin Brims had settled his Division down into its post-conflict areas of tactical responsibility. I was taken on several tours to see where the fighting had taken place, in particular to the large bridges outside Basra where the Iraqis had put up a stubborn resistance. My overall impression was that those who had taken part rightly felt a quiet sense of satisfaction for a job well done. The main purpose of my visit was to congratulate and thank the soldiers who had done so well – but I also wanted to get a feel for the place. Basra is a big city of low-rise buildings surrounded by flat desert. At that stage the insurgency had not begun, and the atmosphere seemed relaxed and good-natured. I remember walking through the souk in Basra and stopping to buy a carpet, haggling with the moneychanger in the traditional manner.

I listened to a lot of soldiers telling me their individual experiences. One of the most memorable accounts came from Lance Corporal of Horse Mick Flynn of the Blues and Royals, a redoubtable character who afterwards would be awarded the Conspicuous Gallantry Cross for his part in the Iraq War. Remarkably, he had also fought in the Falklands War as a very young soldier. Twenty years on, as a veteran vehicle commander in a squadron of the Household Cavalry in the armoured reconnaissance role, he was very much in the thick of the fighting. While 'turret down' behind a bund north of Basra he spotted several Iraqi T-55 tanks and called in airpower to destroy these. When the aircraft failed to find the tanks, Flynn made the decision to fire tracer rounds to indicate the targets. This would be visible from the air – but it meant moving forward to a 'hull down' position to allow the 30mm cannon to fire, thereby exposing the vehicle to retaliatory fire from the tanks. On being given the order to move, the young driver, fresh out of recruit training, hesitated. Flynn reached down from the turret and put his hand on the young man's shoulder. 'Steady, lad, steady,' he said comfortingly, before issuing the order again: 'Driver, advance!'

Three years later, in Afghanistan, Mick Flynn, now a Corporal of Horse, would be awarded the Military Cross for his exceptional courage and presence of mind during an ambush by the Taliban. His actions undoubtedly saved the lives of the crew of his Scimitar armoured vehicle, and contributed to saving the lives of the crew of another vehicle in his Troop.

Afterwards I flew up to Baghdad to talk to the Brits there. I stayed in the old British Embassy, a colonial-style building right on the banks of the River Euphrates, which had been evacuated after the invasion of Kuwait more than a dozen years earlier. Very soon after the end of hostilities, a platoon of Paras had deployed to Baghdad to secure the building at the request of the Foreign Office. The ambassador-designate arrived more or less the same time that I did, and the boys decided that this was reason enough to host a party that evening. Somehow they found cold beers and supplies for a barbecue. With the Union Jack flying above the Embassy, an eclectic mixture of guests arrived, Brits of all sorts materializing out of the darkness.

I found myself talking to the old caretaker, who showed me that the Royal coat-of-arms was once more up over the entrance to the building, and that framed photos of HM The Queen and HRH The Duke of Edinburgh had been re-hung on the Embassy walls.

'I have guarded these in the cellar all these years,' he said proudly. I made the appropriate noises of appreciation.

'One small thing,' he added. I looked at him quizzically.

'Thirteen years' back pay.'

When I got back to London I did raise the matter with Sir Michael Jay, Permanent Secretary at the Foreign Office. The records showed that the caretaker had continued to receive pay throughout those years when the Embassy was closed. I asked how the money had been sent. Apparently payments had been made through the Russian Embassy. I am pleased to say the caretaker was paid in full, and received an MBE as a further recognition of his efforts.

As CGS I was twice present at RAF Brize Norton to pay my respects when the bodies of those killed in combat were repatriated. Each was a sombre occasion. The relatives of the dead were present. This was essentially a private ceremony, but not a secret one, and one set of cameras was present on the basis that the film would be shared out among the broadcasters as required.

We gathered before the aircraft landed, and were seated on the edge of the apron outside the terminal building to watch the C-17 aircraft land and taxi into position, coming to a rest with the nose of the aircraft facing diagonally away from the mourners. Then the ramp was lowered. A bearer party of six soldiers in parade dress advanced and marched up the ramp to take the first coffin. As they came into view down the ramp carrying the coffin, a band began playing and everyone stood. We all saluted as the bearers marched past in slow time, carrying the coffin to the waiting hearse. This simple, but profoundly moving, ceremony was repeated for each coffin on board the aircraft.

The war was a quick fix, but predictably the peace hasn't proved so easy. The scale of the looting at the end of the manoeuvre war came as a surprise to everyone. It was perhaps the first indication that things were not as they should be. Our people on the ground found it very difficult to control, because the indigenous security forces were in disarray and there was no judicial system worth the name to deal with the looters. Since then, the insurgency and the appalling inter-ethnic violence have both made it extremely difficult to rebuild Iraqi society.

Going back to my analogy of the strands of the rope, in a post-conflict situation you need security and you need political authority. Once Saddam Hussein's regime collapsed, there was a complete vacuum at the top. It took a long time to establish a provisional government, and even today the Iraqi politicians continue wrangling while their country is torn by sectarian and tribal strife.

Reconstruction is another essential strand of the rope. Maybe it's apocryphal, but there is some substance in the Iraqi complaint that the Americans could put a man on the moon, but they couldn't fix the Iraqi power supply. Repair work to the infrastructure has proceeded at an agonizingly slow pace. Gilbert Greenall's maxim of the first hundred days being vital comes to mind here. It seems strange that the Washington planners didn't seem to have learned from our experiences in Kosovo and Bosnia. The waste of all our accumulated knowledge of how to manage post-conflict situations is a tragedy. We had a very good man inside the Coalition Provisional Authority, the body which ran Iraq after the collapse of Saddam Hussein's regime until an elected Iraqi government was ready to take over: Major General Tim Cross, who had run our logistics in Kosovo. The reports we received from Tim were alarming: 'This is a madhouse,' he was saying, 'the situation is terrible.' Tim had been with the Pentagon planners in Washington before the war and he had been saying then that they hadn't got their act together.

The first British envoy to Iraq, Sir Jeremy Greenstock, has recently commented in a BBC *Inside Story* television documentary that the Prime Minister took his 'eye off the ball' in the crucial first days and weeks after the liberation of Iraq.

> In the days following the victory no one, it seems to me, was instructed to put the security of Iraq first, to put law and order on the streets first. There was no police force. There was no constituted army except the victorious invaders. And there was no American general that I could . . . establish who was given the accountable responsibility to make sure that the first duty of any government – and we were the government – was to keep law and order on the streets. There was a vacuum from the beginning in which looters, saboteurs, the criminals, the insurgents moved very quickly.

It is hard to argue with Sir Jeremy's conclusions, though in fairness to the Prime Minister one should acknowledge that, as the junior partner in a coalition, we were not in a position to call the shots. I have no doubt that Tony Blair has found this position frustrating at times. It should also be recognized that most of the Iraqi infrastructure was run down, and the utilities were creaking along after years of underinvestment, made worse by the sanctions imposed by the UN after the first Gulf War. The British Army may be able to get the odd power station working again, but it cannot build new ones. Such work requires highly skilled construction companies. I have to say once again that we found the DfID less than wholehearted about helping us in the reconstruction effort. Not for the first time, one had the impression that some of their people see soldiers as part of the problem rather than part of the solution. When the British Government has such a huge amount at stake, politically, economically and militarily, it does seem extraordinary that a key Government department should be dragging its heels.

It's very difficult to start rebuilding a country without proper security. I shared the view that the Washington-inspired decision to disband the Iraqi army was very short-sighted. I can remember stressing in a Chiefs of Staff meeting that we should not be doing this. We should have kept the Iraqi security services in being and put them under the command of the Coalition. I know that Mike Boyce shared this view and argued it with our political masters. To what extent the British Government communicated our concerns to the Americans I have no idea. For much too long the Coalition soldiers have had to carry out a policing function, which is very difficult indeed, especially as few of them speak the language. In the short run it is a case of needs must, but in the long run I don't think it's possible for a foreign army to provide security, or for a foreign police force to maintain law and order. At the end of the day, internal security must be a matter for the people who live there. It is a question of consent: with it, the intervention force can hold the ring while indigenous security forces are brought up to scratch; without it, the intervention forces can only be seen as repressive. And consent in Iraq has dwindled since Saddam Hussein's downfall.

I had a similar reaction to the decision – again made in Washington – to ban members of the former ruling Ba'ath Party from participating in the new government or holding other official posts. There is a precedent in the occupation of Germany after the Second World War, when it was accepted that at any time up to 1945, if you had been a schoolteacher and wanted to become a headmaster you'd probably have needed a Nazi Party membership card in your back pocket – but that didn't mean to say you were a Nazi, just that you wanted to get on. Interestingly enough, President Bush announced a reversal of this policy of 'de-Ba'athification' in October 2006. But by then much damage had been done.

Some people find it difficult to understand why, with all the resources at its disposal, the Coalition has been unable to suppress the insurgency. One answer is troop numbers. At the height of the Troubles in Northern Ireland, for example, we had twenty thousand or more soldiers in the Province to keep the peace, and even then we were unable to suppress terrorism altogether. Northern Ireland has only around 5 per cent of Iraq's population; a similar presence would thus equate to four hundred thousand soldiers, but the Coalition struggled to reach half that figure. Furthermore, in Northern Ireland the

Army was working alongside a highly competent police force, which doesn't yet exist in Iraq. On the contrary, many of the Iraqi police are corrupt and making matters worse.

Since my first visit immediately after Saddam Hussein was deposed, I have made a number of subsequent visits to Iraq, and I have seen the Iraqi Army rebuilt from scratch. When I first visited the Iraqi Divisional HQ in Basra, it was still functioning on a very makeshift basis. I have watched the new Iraqi Army become gradually more capable, undertaking joint operations with British forces. I have also visited the Iraqi equivalent of Sandhurst just outside Baghdad, which under largely British guidance has grown from nothing into an impressive institution. Throughout, I had the sense of the Iraqi Army acquiring its own ethos of service to the nation – something which sadly cannot be said of the police force.

The insurgent tactic of suicide bombing has been particularly difficult for the Coalition forces. In Northern Ireland, we at least knew that the IRA would not initiate an attack unless they were very confident of their escape route. Defence against suicide bombers, however, requires almost instantaneous reaction, and therefore split-second decision-making. This is an enormous responsibility for the British soldier – and of course, the use of suicide bombers increases the risk that innocent civilians will be caught in the crossfire. Sooner or later it will be alleged that someone has overstepped the mark. There have been a minute number of cases in which British soldiers have been charged with murder – and no convictions – following allegations that they may have used excessive force. Other than in conventional war, the legal test is whether the amount of force used was 'reasonable'. It must be difficult for people who have not served in the military themselves to judge what is, or is not, 'reasonable' in confused and dangerous conditions (and this is one reason why a separate military justice system provides for courts martial made up of military personnel). I have the greatest sympathy with soldiers in such circumstances.

But I draw a clear line between alleged excessive force in the heat of the moment, and prisoner abuse in cold blood. Very sadly, a handful of British soldiers in Iraq have been found guilty of the latter; a few others have been tried and, thankfully, acquitted. Photographs of alleged prisoner abuse irresponsibly published in the *Mirror* without proper verification turned out to be fakes, but shockingly similar events to those shown have actually taken place. I made it clear at the time that I deplored any such behaviour, not least because of its detrimental effect on operations. How can we expect to win the support of the Iraqi people if they believe that we are abusing their compatriots?

It has to be recognized that within an Army approximately a hundred thousand strong, there are bound to be a few who will take it out on prisoners if the opportunity arises to do so, particularly in a unit which has been taking casualties. We do our best to screen out such individuals, but inevitably some slip through the net. So abuses will occasionally happen – but they can never be tolerated. I am quite clear about this. During my time as CGS I came in for a certain amount of stick for not 'standing up for soldiers' accused of prisoner abuse. It beats me what people who say such things think should happen. Do they want cases of alleged prisoner abuse swept under the carpet? I am certain that any cover-up would do the Army great harm; we must adhere to the rule of law. The British public must be able to trust our soldiers at all times. In addition, once proceedings reach a certain stage, senior officers have to be mindful of the need to avoid making comments that could prejudice a fair trial.

I am appalled by the view that prosecutions of soldiers alleged to have abused prisoners in Iraq were politically driven. Such opinion is tantamount to saying that the Army Prosecuting Authority dances to some political tune. Any prosecuting authority has difficult decisions to make, but those decisions are made on the evidence presented and emphatically not on the basis of personal whim, political direction or how the media may react. We are fortunate indeed in Britain to live under the rule of law, the bedrock of a civilized society. The absence of the rule of law, as one sees in far too many other countries, can only result, by definition, in lawlessness. I am saddened by criticism of decisions by an independent authority to prosecute: such criticism which, of itself, is political in nature and fails to give proper weight to the due process of law. I think it's crucial that the head of the Army speaks unequivocally about such matters; he sets the standard. The mistreatment of prisoners tarnishes the fine reputation of the British Army, and constitutes a blatant breach of discipline; furthermore, it is an affront to the soldiers' pride in their profession. Ultimately it is detrimental to operations, because it creates suspicion and hostility in the minds of the civilian population. The Army cannot condone such behaviour.

I had operations overseas always very much in mind during my time as CGS, but these weren't my only concerns. I am always reluctant to use 'management speak', but it may help civilians to understand their different functions to think of the CGS as the Chairman and the Commander in Chief as the Managing Director of the British Army. It's the Commander in Chief's job to keep the Army machine ticking over; the CGS's job is at least as much about the future as it is about the present. His priority is to maintain the Army's ability to achieve operational success over the coming years.

For me, the biggest challenge of my time as CGS was without doubt getting the optimum future capability for the Army from the resources the Labour Government had seen fit to devote to increasingly hard-worked Armed Forces. The Government had already carried out a Strategic Defence Review soon after it came into power, the effect of which was to concentrate more resources on expeditionary forces. Fair enough; but it rapidly became clear that the programme of defence expenditure laid out for the future could not be met from the budget allocated. And so, besides dealing with Iraq, my first eighteen months as CGS were spent fighting the Army's corner in a cost-cutting exercise bizarrely entitled 'the medium-term work strands' – in effect, a mini defence review. The outcome was that the RAF had to shed about 10 per cent of its manpower and the Royal Navy lost some of its older ships. In the opinion of the MOD civil servants, the Army got away 'relatively lightly', losing some 1,500 soldiers from an establishment of about 104,000. In fact, we were in some ways ahead of the game: the Army staff in the MOD had already come to the conclusion that the balance of capabilities within the Army was out of kilter. Given finite resources, you have to make the best possible use of them, even if you have concluded that the resources allocated do not match the commitments you have been given. So what the Army staff did was to sit down and, on the basis of the Defence Planning Assumptions, try to work out what the best balance would be. The result was the 'Future Army Structure'. Some of this rebalancing was relatively uncontroversial. Field artillery, for example, was reduced because we decided we had too much of it, relative to the overall size of the Army. On the other hand, we actually increased the number of engineers, because experience told us that we would need more engineers for the kinds of operations we were likely to expect.

But the real rub was the future size and structure of the infantry. Under the Strategic Defence Review of the early 1990s, the Army had made the case for an infantry of fifty-five battalions, but that was deemed too many for the post-Cold-War budget and the figure of forty had emerged. Now the MOD was proposing an infantry of fewer than thirty battalions, based on the assumption that Northern Ireland would soon go non-operational. After a long attritional battle with the MOD Central Staff bean-counters, we got the figure up to thirty-six. At thirty-six, we ran out of specific arguments, and had to rely on the general justification of being prepared for the unexpected, of having resilience, of maintaining a reserve. Entirely sensible as this may seem, such justification cuts no ice in the MOD (or 'Head Office' as they like to call themselves) – or in the Treasury, which second-guesses the MOD in all such matters. None the less, given that so much infantry manpower had previously been allocated to Northern Ireland, these thirty-six battalions would in fact give us more general-purpose battalions available for use elsewhere. That said, the Army Board was faced with the agonizing decision of which four battalions were to be removed from the Order of Battle.

There was another, parallel, problem which was overdue for a definitive solution. The infantry was run on a system known as the 'Arms Plot', by which individual battalions were moved every few years – moved geographically and very often moved in role. The justification for this was that each battalion and every soldier needed variety, to maintain the interest of the job, to produce soldiers who were adaptable and versatile with a wide range of experience, and to even out geographical advantages and disadvantages. But the system had evolved largely in order to maintain the existing infantry regimental structure. Previous reductions in the infantry and previous decisions about its structure had produced a situation whereby approximately half the infantry were in single-battalion regiments. In such regiments there could obviously be no rotation between battalions. So the Arms Plot prevented battalions stagnating in one place for ever, while preserving regimental identity.

But the result of this system was that at any one time a significant number of battalions – up to 20 per cent of our infantry overall – were not available, because they were either changing their location, retraining, taking on new roles or generally in some form of 'baulk', as the cry had it. It was a high price to pay for the regimental system as it was then organized. To have battalions moving from one role to another was very inefficient and wasteful of expertise. For armoured infantry, for example, the perceived wisdom was that they didn't really master their job for about two years; and then after another four years they'd be moved to a different role. Given that the average length of service for a private soldier is about four and a half years, the loss of capability was impossible to justify. We were getting breadth at the expense of depth, an outcome which particularly concerned the other major combat arm, the Royal Armoured Corps. The Arms Plot also went against brigade coherence; each brigade had, on average, at least one battalion changing over each year.

Once or twice a year the Army Board would have an 'away-day', in which we would try to stand back and look at the way we did things. On 27 November 2003 the Board held an all-day session at the former Staff College at Camberley to concentrate on the infantry Arms Plot, comparing it with other models of how we might do things. We scored the options, just as a selection board scores individual candidates. The results made it quite clear that the Arms Plot could no longer be justified. It was so detrimental to operational effectiveness, and had so many inherent disadvantages built into it, that it would have to go. No one doubted the value of the regimental system to the British Army. But if all the infantry was organized in large regiments, you could move individuals between battalions when their career and personal circumstances suited, while still keeping them as members of the same tribe.

It was the obvious solution. Much of the rest of the Army had long been asking: 'Why should the infantry get this special deal?' Reform was long overdue. For many informed observers, the issue concerning this reorganization had been a question not of if but of when. But the loss of any cherished regimental names was bound to cause pain and grief, particularly to the Old and Bold. I myself felt considerable sadness at the prospect, and I knew that we would face a lot of opposition. But we had to grasp this nettle: staying as we were was not a realistic option for the future. If the British Army had never accepted the need for change, we'd still be in red coats and fighting in squares. I felt that it was the primary responsibility of the CGS to lead the Army Board in facing up to the Army's future.

I, along with my fellow Army Board members, thought that some historical research was needed. The structure of the British infantry has changed a number of times over the centuries. In the late nineteenth century, the then Secretary of State for War, Edward Cardwell, had decided to reform the system of the time by which all infantry battalions were numbered. He devised a structure whereby the infantry was put into regiments with county affiliations, each of two battalions, one battalion to be serving overseas and the other to be serving at home, with its own training depot. There was a predictable outcry from serving and retired alike, protesting that they didn't want to be part of these new-fangled regiments, they wanted to stay in their numbered battalions, the 49th, the 68th or whatever. *Plus ça change.* During the two world wars these county regiments expanded enormously, by twenty and more battalions each; but as the Army drastically reduced in size afterwards, the stage was reached where there were fewer battalions than counties, so that one started to get amalgamated regiments: the Devon and Dorsets, or the Ox and Bucks, for example.

With the end of conscription at the beginning of the 1960s, the then Army Board concluded that the only sensible way to produce a flexible infantry for the future was to put it on a 'large regiment basis', with three or four battalions in each regiment. But this, of course, implied the loss of many much-loved county names. The Army Board at the time funked the decision: it urged the infantry to adopt a large regimental system but did not make this compulsory. In broad terms, half the infantry accepted that urging and the other half didn't. The latter chose to remain as single-battalion regiments. The Army Board had promised that those who opted for this large regimental structure would be looked upon favourably if there were to be further reductions in the future – but when there was another reduction in the early 1990s as a result of the end of the Cold War, the Board of the time reneged on the undertaking given by its predecessors, removing the third battalions from the existing large regiments. A little later, the infantry of the Territorial Army was reduced in similar fashion. For reasons I have never fully understood, this reduction resulted in the invention of entirely new regiments in the TA; the TA infantry thereby lost their tribal links with their regular counterparts. I suspect this was done to avoid change in the regular infantry regimental structure. Whatever the reason, the outcome for the TA infantry was a complete mish-mash.

I remember saying on that fateful away-day, 'Are we all clear about the conclusion we've come to? The Arms Plot has run its course, but are we all clear about what the ramifications of that are? Because the current infantry structure cannot survive without the Arms Plot.' The Army Board was unanimous, even though some members were aware that they would face criticism and accusations of disloyalty from within their own regiments. Indeed, the Adjutant General, Sir Alistair Irwin, knew that one consequence of the decision would be that his own position as Colonel of the Black Watch – the tribal elder – would cease to exist. He was also Colonel Commandant of the Scottish Infantry as a whole. He deserves special credit for committing himself to a decision which would leave him particularly exposed.

As details of what we had decided emerged, people began saying to me, 'At long last somebody's got the balls to do it.' Others, of course, took a very different view. I had to face some pretty unpleasant comments, some addressed to me personally – as did Alistair. The accusation that we had destroyed the regimental system was nonsensical: the regimental system has changed again and again over time. What matters is that the regimental system adapts to changing circumstances and operational requirements.

At a subsequent Army Board meeting a couple of months later, we looked at how we would implement our decision, and came up with a set of principles and a direction to the infantry that those regiments which were not already on a large basis must now form regiments of two or more regular battalions. In fact, we thought that the optimum size for a regiment should be around four battalions, but that in some cases this might be too hard to achieve. We urged the infantry to give as much weight in their deliberations to the formation of what we called 'large-large' regiments of four or five battalions as to the formation of 'small-large' regiments of two or possibly three battalions. Some perceptively saw that large-large was the end-state that they would need to be in, and went for it straight away. To my surprise the Scots did that, forming themselves into the Royal Regiment of Scotland with five battalions. I had thought that a Highland/ Lowland divide would prevail. In Yorkshire, for example, there were three single-battalion regiments which combined into the Yorkshire Regiment of three battalions. The Light Infantry and the Green Jackets were both regiments with two battalions each, which meant that they weren't obliged to change; but both regiments had a tradition of being unafraid of change and decided of themselves to combine anyway to form the Rifles, a name going right back to the Peninsular War. As part of this process we realigned the Territorial Army structure to put the TA battalions back in the new regimental structure, which is where they always should have been.

At the same time as all this was going on, we had to decide which four battalions were to go, as part of the reduction from forty to thirty-six. This was very difficult. We used a set of objective criteria: statistical data on recruitment and population figures in the recruiting area. The results showed which regiments were finding it most difficult to maintain their strength. Of the four lowest-scoring regiments, two were Scottish, which was no surprise because the Scots were trying to maintain a disproportionate number of battalions for their population. The figures suggested that two of the Scottish battalions should go, but we decided that for the Scots to lose two out of a total of only six would be seen as unfair, so our decision was for five. Then it was clear that one of the three in the north-west had to go, and that one in southern England would have to go too. Deciding which should be the fourth to go was very difficult, but Yorkshire was in the frame. But the sense of being singled out for the chop was softened by incorporation into the large regiment structure.

By the autumn of 2004 we were ready to announce all the final decisions. I knew that there were going to be ructions, with constituents writing in to their MPs and other pressures. I had sought political approval at the outset. I briefed Geoff Hoon, the Secretary of State for Defence, and told him that we could anticipate flak. He was very supportive about the whole thing. 'If that's what the Army has to do for the future,' he said, 'let's do it.'

The plan was for the announcements to be made after quite a long period of consultation. There was an understandable concern about the proposed changes, with the inevitable protests from the retired community, MPs, mayors et al. I received some angry letters. The outcry was loudest in Scotland, where it became overtly political when the Scottish Nationalist Party jumped on board, claiming that this was yet another example of the English 'screwing the Scots'. The 'Save our Scottish Regiments' campaign was run by a chap who had never even been in the Army. Some commentators suggested that this had been a political decision which the Army had been forced to carry out, with Jackson doing the Government's dirty work. They couldn't be more wrong, of course, because this was an Army Board decision. (An article in the *Spectator* attacking the proposed reforms spuriously linked them to a minor operation conducted on my eyelids the previous summer. In a riposte I explained that the surgery had been carried out for medical rather than cosmetic reasons: it had been a matter of 'vision not vanity'.)

Tony Blair was concerned about the political fuss,

especially in Scotland. In particular, he had come under pressure from Scottish Labour MPs to save the Black Watch. There had been much speculation in the press that the Government would announce a U-turn. I was determined not to let this happen. Such a decision would make a mockery of our carefully considered plans. Shortly before the announcements, Geoff Hoon and I were summoned to see the Prime Minister at Downing Street. What he was looking for was a change to the plan which would turn down the political heat, particularly from north of the border. 'I need you to get me out of a hole,' he said.

'Prime Minister,' I replied, 'selection and maintenance of the aim is a fundamental principle of war.' The Secretary of State reiterated that we must stick to our guns. We ran through the logic with the PM. 'I know it's difficult,' I continued, 'but actually that's where we are and this is what we have to do.' Eventually the Prime Minister accepted what we were saying.

One of the ceremonial tasks of the CGS is to lay a wreath at the Cenotaph on Remembrance Day, along with the other Service Chiefs. It's the job of the CGS, who as an Army officer is deemed to know more about drill, to give the words of command to the other Chiefs. It's a tradition that many of the participants gather beforehand in one of the large rooms in the Foreign Office before going out on to Whitehall. Among those present are leaders of all the political parties. In 2004 I took the opportunity to speak to the SNP leader, Alex Salmond, about the Scottish regiments. 'I understand you're not happy with the changes,' I said, 'but they are for the overall good.'

'You're massacring our tradition,' he replied.

I told him that he was absolutely wrong, and explained the demographic problem underlying the difficulties the Scottish regiments were having with recruitment, as evidenced by the two hundred or more Commonwealth soldiers – mainly Fijians – who were serving in the Scottish infantry. 'The fact is that the Scots are over-represented in the British Army,' I told him; 'which is fine by me, provided that they can recruit enough soldiers.' Salmond seemed to be uncomfortable with this argument.

Just before the announcement of the new regimental structure, due to be made in December 2004, there was a last-minute twist to the story. The Director of Special Forces had taken stock that autumn, following three years of intense operational activity since 9/11; among other things, he had concluded that the Special Forces needed bolstering with additional manpower. To avoid Special Forces soldiers being employed on supporting tasks, and thus wasting their specialist skills and capabilities, they were having to find back-up from outside their own numbers; there were ad hoc arrangements to produce this back-up from elsewhere in the Armed Forces, but ad hoc arrangements are never very satisfactory. Here was a crystal-clear requirement for dedicated support to the Special Forces, with an equally clear recommendation that it should be based on a dedicated infantry battalion under command of the Director of Special Forces. This new role would raise the future number of battalions from thirty-six to thirty-seven.

So far, so obvious, one might conclude – as I did. But then comes MOD process: such a proposal is regarded as an 'enhancement', i.e. an improvement to capability, and the process requires all proposed 'enhancements' to be judged in competition, one against another, as part of the annual budget round. Fair enough, as a general principle. But in this case, circumstances had produced an out-of-process situation. It would have been ridiculous to have announced in December a reduction of four battalions, only to have announced in June that this 'enhancement' had been approved and only three battalions were to go. My recommendation that only three battalions be cut was accepted by Geoff Hoon, much to his credit – albeit at the eleventh hour, the night before he made his announcement in the House of Commons; his approval was given in the teeth of opposition from most senior MOD staff, some of whom seemed to think that their beloved process was more important than operational capability. Within the MOD, I made few friends and, I dare say, quite a few enemies over this – but it was the right solution.

Events throughout my time as CGS produced a sharply increased media focus on the Armed Services, and on the Army in particular. When I took over the job, the man who looked after media relations for the Army was the improbably named Director of Corporate Communications (Army), the new management-speak title for the post of Director of Public Relations (Army) – the post I might have gone to after commanding 39 Brigade in Belfast.

In this job you needed someone who was savvy, who knew the media personalities, who could explain the whys and wherefores. But this implied a degree of autonomy, which rested somewhat uneasily with the Labour Government's insistence on being 'on message'. By the summer of 2004 Geoff Hoon had become exasperated by what he perceived as a poor press. He took the view that the DPRs – and particularly the Army DPR – were briefing against the Government in general, and against him personally in particular. I do not believe there was any substance in this allegation, but it was his personal wish to abolish the DPRs. The Chiefs of Staff were unanimously opposed to this proposal, and trooped in to see the Secretary of State en masse; but in vain. It was interesting to observe that the Permanent Secretary remained sitting on the fence. It was humiliating enough that the Chiefs had to seek ministerial approval for any contact with the media, but this was an outrageous move, explicable only in terms of a lack of confidence. I thought long and hard about resigning, but eventually concluded that, important though this issue was, there were bigger fish to fry.

Had there still been a DPR (Navy) in place in the spring of 2007, when fifteen Royal Navy personnel from HMS *Cornwall* were detained by the Iranians in the disputed waters of Shatt al-Arab, it seems likely to me that the media handling of the whole affair would have been rather better managed. Leaving aside the question of whether those personnel should have been patrolling there without full tactical precautions, the subsequent handling of the story was damaging to the reputation of the Navy, and to that of the Services as a whole. We pride ourselves on our fighting qualities, and I found it very unsavoury that the captured sailors allowed themselves to be paraded by their captors in the way that they did. However, this much was beyond the control of their superiors. But I thought it was appalling that they should have been greeted after their release as if they were returning heroes. In my view they should have been flown to an overseas base for a couple of days before being returned to their ship. And to crown it all, it was inept – to say nothing of unfair – to allow two of them to sell their stories to the media and to forbid the others from doing so.

Poor media handling was again evident in the coverage of the decision whether to allow Prince Harry to deploy to Iraq in the summer of 2007 with the rest of his squadron from the Blues and Royals. We had anticipated this problem during my time as CGS, and had carefully considered the methodology of reaching a decision about whether either of the two Royal Princes should serve on any particular deployment. Each situation is different, and has to be assessed separately. I discussed the matter with the boys' father the Prince of Wales, and their grandmother the Queen, and we laid out a set of principles. It was agreed then that there should be a certain amount of consultation, but that the final decision should rest with the CGS. When it came to it, this difficult decision-making process was played out in the press, to nobody's advantage. The Prince himself was rightly keen to go. Months of speculation followed the MOD's announcement in February that the Prince would be accompanying his regiment to Iraq. In mid-May, my successor Richard Dannatt announced that the Prince would not be deployed there. I believe that none of this need have been made public, and that if necessary a D-notice should have been issued to prevent its becoming so.

The MOD is an extraordinary place. It has two discrete roles. One is as a Department of State handling the policy issues, just as, for example, the Department of Education handles policy issues to do with education and schools. But it's also the supreme headquarters of the Armed Forces. These two functions are not, however, discrete in terms of personnel or, if you like, office space. There's a lot of intermingling here: uniforms and suits, side by side. Some servicemen 'go native', absorbing the culture of the MOD, but these are the exceptions. Half a century back, each of the Services had its own department and its own minister, with a Secretary of State for Defence above them all. But since then the bureaucrats have increasingly accumulated power in their own hands. There is a story, perhaps apocryphal but nevertheless symbolically true, of a senior MOD civil servant who remarked: 'The Ministry of Health is not full of doctors, the Ministry of Education is not full of teachers, the Ministry of Ag and Fish is not full of farmers and fishermen, so why on earth do they have all these bloody people in the Armed Forces in the MOD?' The same philosophy lay behind the decision to spend a quarter of a million pounds on specially commissioned abstract paintings as part of the refurbishment of the MOD. The Government art collection has many military paintings which would have been in keeping with the purpose and ethos of the Department and which would have been available at no cost; but civil servants preferred to spend on abstract art money which might otherwise have directly benefited soldiers and their families. It may seem a small point, but to me it was so indicative of the cultural divide in the MOD.

I didn't always find the MOD wholehearted about the interests of the soldiers. I was constantly battling the civil servants, and it was often very frustrating. I'd come back from a visit and say, 'We've got to do something about the state of those barracks,' but it was like trying to fight your way through cotton wool. A soldier's approach is very straightforward: this is the problem, all right, give me the tools and let's crack on. But bureaucrats are not like that at all. I remember the Army Board being told by the then Second Permanent Undersecretary that we must reduce our recruiting – then buoyant because we had taken on more soldiers that year than the budget had forecast – to meet the funding line. Quite absurd, but absolutely true. We all knew from hard-won experience that it would take years to recover from such a sharp application of the brakes.

Not many people realize, I suspect, that the Army Board has a statutory duty under the Army Act to investigate allegations by soldiers that they have been wronged, and in effect to ensure that they have been fairly treated. This is especially important in areas where soldiers cannot take a complaint to a civilian tribunal, for example an allegation of unfair dismissal, when the Army Board is the arbiter and protector of their rights. The Board takes this responsibility very seriously, and cases are considered in enormous detail. But I noticed a tendency for civil servants to want to limit the Board's power, especially in relation to the ability to grant compensation, and I fought a long battle with the MOD to retain as much of this as possible. As I stepped down, the issue was still rattling around the MOD, with lawyers arguing over the exact scope of the Board's powers. My determination to do what I saw as my legal duty and the 'right thing' in the face of those who cannot see beyond Government accounting rules did not endear me to the mandarins, who like the Chiefs to be more 'collegiate'.

The public doesn't realize that until a welcome change in April 2008, the Service Chiefs had no direct control over the way the money was spent. But much expenditure remains centrally controlled, and the MOD keeps the Armed Services on a short rein. The Defence Planning Assumptions often seem to be given more importance than reality. That's why there wasn't enough of the right equipment in stock when the decision was made for a large-scale commitment in Iraq. It comes back to the contract with the soldier. If you will the end, you must will the means.

Decisions about arms purchases were made by the Defence Procurement Agency (now Defence Equipment and Support), whose record for acquiring the right equipment, at the right time and – crucially – at the originally contracted cost, is less than impressive. And housing, for example, is in the hands of the 'Defence Estates', as they are called, run by a chief executive. He gets a tick in his box for coming in on budget, and another one for not making waves within the MOD. Within the Ministry they use a lot of management jargon, talking about targets and indicators. One of these is the 'balanced scorecard', with a 'traffic lights system' of green, red and amber, according to whether you are doing well, badly or indifferently. Doing 'well' is not about ensuring that soldiers and their families have decent accommodation: it's about whether or not you've met your budget. You can get a 'green' even if some of the houses you're responsible for have green mould sprouting on the inside walls. This whole culture I found to be Kafka-esque.

I did not find the MOD a comfortable place to be. Its values were not mine.

* * *

In the previous few years I had gained two more grandchildren to add to my grandson Casper, born in 1997: two lovely girls, Jemima, born in 2001, and Phoebe, born a year later. Sadly, though, Amanda's marriage broke down. Sarah and I were therefore delighted when she married Jason Gard, an ex-Royal Green Jacket, at Chelsea Town Hall in October 2005. It was a wonderful family day, with all the children taking part. The following year they had a new baby brother, Charlie.

My youngest son Tom was by this time at Eton. In the same year he joined the CCF, a first indication that he would continue the family tradition of service in the Army. In the winter of the following year he would make the train journey to Westbury to undertake the admissions course before the Army Officer Selection Board. I am proud to say that he was accepted. When he finishes his university education Tom will be headed for Sandhurst, following his elder brother, his brother-in-law, his father and his grandfather into the Army. This was a few months after I stepped down as CGS, so nobody could claim that I had any hand in his being selected!

As CGS, one has the opportunity to make visits to one's opposite numbers abroad. And as it turned out, one of the earliest overseas visits I made was to Argentina. I was the first CGS to go there since the Falklands War. For the most part I was treated with great courtesy, though every briefing room I entered seemed to have a sodding great map on the wall with the unmistakable outlines of the Falkland Islands, captioned 'Las Islas Malvinas Argentinas'. The Argentinians' official position is that they do not in any sense cede their claim to sovereignty over the Falklands, though they accept that military force is not the way to achieve their objective. I had a couple of set-tos while I was there. I remember in particular an altercation when a somewhat worse-for-wear colonel came up to me after a dinner and started finger-poking. He began ranting about how they would throw us out of the Islands. 'It's very foolish what you're saying,' I told him at last, 'because if you try it again, we'll come down here again, and we'll do what we did to you last time – so best not do it, eh?'

Another early visit was to Russia, which was fascinating for me. The last time I had been there, in 1976, I had been one of the most junior members of the party; this time, I had the red-carpet treatment. It was amazing to reflect on how much had changed in the interim. In 1976 the main strategic function of the British Army had been to prepare to fight the Warsaw Pact, the alliance dominated by the Russians; now we were serving alongside them in the Balkans.

Whenever I could I tried to make use of my Russian, though it has become rusty over the years. The Russians seemed to be aware of my long-term interest in their country. They knew of me from Bosnia, where there had been a Russian deployment in the American Sector, and of course they were well aware of the Pristina Airport episode, which occasioned the odd jocular remark. I did ask after General Viktor Zavarzin, but unfortunately it turned out that he was in the Far East at the time. One of the highlights was a visit to Rostov-on-Don, the headquarters for the military district which includes Chechnya. I gather that this raised a few eyebrows among the American Embassy staff in Moscow, because their attaché had not been allowed to go there.

My visit took place in June, during the short period of 'white nights' when it never gets dark in the north of the country. On the night of the summer equinox I strolled through St Petersburg at one o'clock in the morning, among thousands of other people out on the streets because it was still light. On this occasion, I was pleased not to be in uniform as I had been almost thirty years before; it was more than enough just to be one of the crowd.

I made many other interesting visits during my time as CGS. One of the most fascinating was to Vietnam; as far as I could tell, I was the first CGS to visit the country. This time Sarah came with me, and for her it was particularly exciting because she had vivid memories of living there in the late 1960s. Sarah's father had been the British defence attaché in Saigon during the Vietnam War, and she had gone out there to stay with her parents during her school holidays. After she left school she had lived in Saigon for a while, working as a stringer for *Newsweek*. This gave her a much-valued American press pass, and access to operational areas with American Huey helicopters to get her there.

Our visit started in Hanoi, which of course Sarah had never been to before, since it had been the enemy capital during the war. We were both captivated by the city, which retains its French influence even though half a century has passed since it was a French colony. Despite the heavy bombing it received from the USAF during the war, it remains a lovely landscape of lakes, shaded boulevards, parks and French colonial-style architecture.

These visits are always programmed from morning

until night, so there are not often any surprises. But a few days after my arrival I received an unexpected invitation: General Giap wanted to see me.

Giap was a legendary figure, the victor at Dien Bien Phu, the battle which forced the French out in 1954. Until then the French had been fighting a counter-insurgency campaign against Vietnamese revolutionary forces known as the Viet Minh. Dien Bien Phu was a remote outpost up on the northern border of Vietnam, with a large garrison. The Viet Minh cut the road access and then besieged the French positions. They pounded the French with artillery which they had assembled from pieces carried through the jungle on the backs of pack animals. Eventually the French garrison surrendered, and more than eleven thousand of their soldiers were taken prisoner, of whom only three thousand or so ever saw France again. This was the first time the forces of a non-European independence movement had ever defeated a Western army in pitched battle. Later Giap had been the Commander in Chief of the North Vietnamese army, which had successfully defied American military might during the Vietnam War. After the Americans had withdrawn and the South Vietnamese had been defeated, Giap had fallen out of favour with the Communist authorities; but now in his tenth decade he was revered, a hero of the Vietnamese resistance.

The following morning I was taken to his home in Hanoi, quite a modest house with a small garden, but a shrine to his achievements with memorabilia everywhere. Giap himself was a diminutive old gentleman, physically frail but still bright as a button mentally. We had about half an hour together, talking mostly about the Indo-China war, but towards the end he asked me questions about the British Army. We were conversing in French, which he preferred to speaking through an interpreter. At the close he got up and put his arm through mine as we walked towards the door. 'It is interesting, isn't it,' he said, his eyes twinkling, 'that both of our countries have had some problems with the French, and that both of our countries appear to have resolved those problems satisfactorily?'

Sarah and I travelled south from Hanoi, calling at the old imperial capital of Hue before going on to Saigon. Once there, after a bit of jiggery-pokery with changed street names, we found the old residence of the British military attaché, now the headquarters of the All-Vietnam Engineering Union. This had been Sarah's family home almost forty years before. We hovered outside for a while, until I began a conversation in French with a young girl who invited us in. Inside it had changed somewhat. The old dining room was now a conference room adorned with a bust of Ho Chi Minh. The splendid mahogany staircase was still in place, though, and on the upper floor Sarah found the bedroom she had occupied as a teenager, and the balcony where she would go out and have a surreptitious smoke, watching the flares and red tracer bullets light up the night sky while the percussion of bombs dropped from B-52s rattled the stained-glass windows. For her it was extraordinary to be back in the same house so many years later, after all that had happened in between.

During my time as CGS I made several visits to Afghanistan. After Iraq, Afghanistan represents Britain's second largest operational commitment in recent years. It may in the long run prove to be strategically more important. The war in Iraq had to some extent taken eyes off the Afghan ball; without doubt, the initial intervention in Afghanistan had been a great success, but yet again events showed that it was not enough to remove a regime; you then had to rebuild the country. ISAF's initial deployment, to the immediate region of Kabul only, was able to give essential, although only local, support to the Karzai government. The flaw here was that this limited focus allowed the regional warlords to continue to put their own territorial interests and that of their regions ahead of the future of Afghanistan as a whole.

By the second half of 2005 it had become obvious that a much greater effort was required in Afghanistan – if for no other reason than that, though the Taliban had been defeated in 2001, they had not been completely destroyed. Despite heavy casualties, survivors had retreated to the Afghanistan/Pakistan border area, particularly to the Tribal Territories – Waziristan – just across the border in Pakistan. Eventually, it became more than clear that it was essential to bolster the Karzai government in establishing its writ throughout the country – not least, by taking on the now familiar role of helping to build up and train the indigenous Afghan security forces.

And so NATO developed a plan to take security responsibility throughout the country, region by region. In the early years of Karzai's government this was achieved by NATO establishing so-called Provincial Reconstruction Teams (PRTs) in the comparatively benign north and east of the country. The PRTs worked by influence. They were anything but manoeuvre or combat forces: rather, their mission was to support the expansion of the central government's remit, to help subordinate the regional warlords to Kabul, and to assist in local reconstruction and in the training of the Afghan security forces.

But the real challenge was NATO's further expansion to the south – into Helmand and Kandahar provinces – and eventually to the Pakistan border area in the east. In the autumn of 2005 the UK carried out an assessment of the situation in the south. It was clear that PRTs alone would not be nearly enough; given the Taliban influence in the region, combat forces would be required. The fundamental questions were: how big a force, with what capabilities? And could a sufficient force be generated, given our other commitments, notably Iraq? When we were working out the numbers there was an assumption that the commitment to Iraq would draw down more sharply than in fact it has done. In the event, the balance of judgement was for a relatively small force of around 3,500, based on a single infantry battalion, but with significant combat support – notably Harrier ground attack aircraft, artillery and, for the first time, the Apache attack helicopter.

There has been a lot of press comment about the supposed lack of equipment and support for the troops in Afghanistan. The Prime Minister was quoted as saying that the Army could have anything it needed – to which the cynical response was, 'Tell that to your next door neighbour.' For example, the RAF has found it difficult to meet the demands of current operations where transport aircraft and support helicopters are concerned. The RAF has an impressive programme for new fast-jet fighters, but their ageing VC10 and Tri-Star transport aircraft are unreliable and increasingly difficult to maintain.

My last visit to Afghanistan came in the early summer

of 2006, just as the British effort in southern Afghanistan was ramping up. Our forces, serving under NATO command, took over security responsibility for the southern provinces of Kandahar and Helmand. Hard, but successful, fighting against the Taliban followed, including set-piece battles in which attacks by Taliban forces were repulsed after they had taken heavy casualties. 'We have not yet lost one tactical engagement,' commented our commander in the field, Brigadier Ed Butler, 'but we have yet to win at the operational level.' I was exasperated by some of the initial press reaction to our relatively few casualties, which seemed to conclude that any casualty meant mission failure. Here again was the absurd and naïve assumption that military operations against a determined enemy can be risk-free. The critics made much of the statement by John Reid, who succeeded Geoff Hoon as Secretary of State for Defence, that 'if we came here for three years to accomplish our mission and had not fired a shot at the end of it, we would be very happy indeed'. This was a hope, not a prediction; it was also sending a message to the people of southern Afghanistan that we were not, ourselves, choosing to prosecute an offensive mission. But Reid went on to say that 'it would be a complex and dangerous mission, because the terrorists will want to destroy the economy . . . and the government that we are helping to build up'. He also emphasized that 'if this didn't involve the necessity to use force, we wouldn't send soldiers'.

I have no doubt that we must continue to support the now democratically elected government of Afghanistan. To allow the Taliban to overthrow that government and once again to give succour to Al-Qaida would be strategic folly.

There is a sub-set of the British approach to Afghanistan: counter-narcotics. No doubt in the knowledge that the vast majority of heroin consumed in Britain originates in the poppy-fields of Afghanistan, the Prime Minister volunteered Britain to take the international lead on counter-narcotics. Well and good; but I would emphasize that the Foreign and Commonwealth Office, as the responsible Department, must understand that eradication is contrary – right now – to strategic success. In my view, we would be far better emulating the EU's set-aside policy.

My last reflection where Afghanistan is concerned has to do with the crucial position of Pakistan, a country of great contrasts: the gulf between the sophistication of Islamabad, for example, and the feudal Tribal Territories puts President Musharraf into a most difficult position. I have a vivid memory of flying by helicopter from Peshawar over barren mountain ranges to South Waziristan to visit the Pakistani Army division responsible for that area. The highly impressive divisional commander briefed me in some detail on the high intensity of fighting his soldiers had experienced as they carried out their mission to extend central government's writ to the region in which the Taliban and Al-Qaida had found refuge. Subsequently, President Musharraf has cut some sort of deal with the tribal leaders and largely withdrawn the Army. The wisdom of this remains to be seen . . .

On the morning of 7 July 2005 I was in London for a Defence Management Board meeting at the MOD. This is a meeting chaired by the Permanent Secretary and attended by all the Chiefs of Staff, various other civil servants, the Government's Chief Scientific Adviser and others, and normally starts around 10.00 a.m. I remember Sir Kevin Tebbit, then the Permanent Secretary, telling us that news was coming through of explosions in London: he wasn't quite sure what was going on, but we might have to adjourn the meeting.

As subsequently became clear, four bombs had exploded that morning in a coordinated terrorist attack, the worst bombing in London since the Second World War. In fact the meeting went ahead as planned. As a general principle it is a bad idea for senior officers to start interfering when systems are already in place to cope with the situation. The police had primacy in handling domestic terrorism, and the Armed Forces' role was to act in their support if so requested. Accordingly, we did supply a certain amount of specialist help to the police.

On 28 August 2006, I relinquished the post of CGS to my successor Richard Dannatt, and shortly afterwards retired from the Army. In fact, my last day in the office had been a month earlier, at the end of July, the date when most of Whitehall closes down and everyone goes on summer leave. There was no formal ceremony to mark my departure from the MOD, nor would I have wanted one. In the previous few weeks I had made a round of farewells. On that last Friday morning, I invited all the colonels and the brigadiers on the MOD Army Staff to join me in my office for a glass or two of champagne; and then all of us, down to the most junior of the military clerks, made our way to one of those boats moored off the Embankment that serve as floating pubs. Sarah, Mark, Tom and the house staff led by Colour Sergeant Mawby joined us there. We continued with a drink or three, and a bite to eat as well, until mid-afternoon, when people began to wander off for the weekend. It was a warm day, and the Thames glittered in the sunshine as the dwindling party chatted on deck. The moment came when I felt that we had said our goodbyes and that we should go home. It was time to move on.

15
Reflections

When I retired from the Army in 2006, I was within one month or so of forty-five years' service. I count myself fortunate indeed to have spent so long a time doing what I loved. It has been a wonderful career, so full of reward, variety and – above all – comradeship.

I have been lucky enough to have been on operations at every level of command from company to corps, apart from the battalion level, for some seven years in total. All these tours were some form or other of 'peace support operation'. To my regret – because it is the ultimate challenge for a soldier – I have not taken part in a conventional war. There were but two opportunities, and I missed them both: the Falklands, because the cards didn't play my way; and the First Gulf War, when I was otherwise engaged, as a brigade commander in Northern Ireland. *C'est la guerre* – or rather, in my case, it wasn't.

Soon after I retired I was asked to give the annual Richard Dimbleby Lecture, delivered at a Territorial Army Centre in central London on 6 December 2006 and broadcast live on BBC TV. This offered me the opportunity to reflect on the changing role of the Army, and the challenges it is likely to face in the future. This chapter draws heavily on the text of that lecture, entitled 'The Defence of the Realm in the Twenty-First Century'.

My years in the Army have spanned three very different sets of strategic circumstances. The Cold War dominated the first half of my career, when the Army's focus was on defending north-west Europe against an invasion by the Warsaw Pact. This focus shifted abruptly after the fall of the Berlin Wall and the collapse of the Soviet empire at the end of the 1980s; and it shifted again after the dramatic events of 9/11.

While the importance of the Army's war-fighting capability remains paramount, training is now for war in general, not for *the* war against the Warsaw Pact. And it has become clear that the wars we may have to fight in the future will in all probability be at a strategic distance from the UK. We have fought two very short major wars since the end of the Cold War, both in the Middle East against Saddam Hussein. But the Army, in particular, has spent the years conducting operations other than war – in Northern Ireland, the Balkans, Africa, Iraq and Afghanistan; and so the balance between war-fighting and the capability to conduct peace support operations – both in an expeditionary mode – has to be very carefully judged. The result has been a shift in emphasis from the 'heavier' end of our capability to the 'lighter', with the intention to improve our medium-weight forces by equipping them with a new family of armoured vehicles. This rebalancing has also put yet more emphasis on the helicopter as a major means of manoeuvre. These changes have been brought together under the 'Future Army Structure', with its modest shift of emphasis towards operations other than conventional war.

History may well judge that the so-called 'peace dividend' was too sharply taken in the euphoria and relief that followed the end of the Cold War. The effect of that momentous shift has proved to be rather like that of removing the lid of a pressure cooker, a lid screwed down by bilateral superpower rivalry. Once that lid was off, the pressures erupted – pressures of disputed boundaries, ethnic rivalry and regional conflict. The West in general, and NATO in particular, moved from its Cold War posture of strategic defence and groped its way towards a new policy of intervention on humanitarian grounds. Tony Blair's Government has taken a lead in this new role. Acting in some cases unilaterally and in others together with our NATO allies, we have chosen to deploy military power to contain the resulting conflicts – particularly in the Gulf, in the Balkans and in Africa. Operational tempo has increased markedly.

These events also highlighted the importance of international law. The United Nations – perhaps the most important fount of international law – is of course a major player on the world stage. But the UN has been criticized, particularly since the end of the Cold War, for failing to meet its founding ideals. I find this somewhat unfair. I would be more inclined to look critically at the behaviour of the member nation-states than at the institution itself. On a more general legal point, I am convinced from experience that the establishment and maintenance of the rule of law is the bedrock of both national and international stability – and that this principle applies in the national context to the Armed Forces of this country.

However, legality and legitimacy in international affairs are not necessarily the same concept. In an ideal world, what is legal is legitimate, and vice versa. But it doesn't always happen that way. The Iraq intervention was in my opinion legal but has perhaps ceased to be legitimate – in the eyes of certain beholders, at any rate. The Kosovo intervention was probably illegal, but has been largely deemed to be legitimate. The general principle holds that one shouldn't intervene in another sovereign state except in the most extreme circumstances. But if the Kosovo action was legitimate, then it was because of an emerging doctrine which holds that the inviolability of the sovereign state should not legitimize genocide. There are circumstances in which rapid and determined intervention by a relatively small but well-equipped force can prevent large-scale slaughter. In such circumstances it seems that it is not only legitimate to intervene but that there is a strong moral case for doing so.

The history of intervention after the Cold War starts with the West's decision – under UN auspices, to be fair – to become involved in the Bosnian war. Thus was established a precedent of intervention. The received wisdom of the time was that of the three warring factions in Bosnia, it was the Muslim population who were at greatest risk of ethnic persecution; and of course, when it came to Kosovo in 1999, the West's intervention was almost entirely predicated on the protection of a Muslim population who were at risk. In the current difficult relations between the West and the Islamic world, it seems to me that this risking of Western blood and treasure on behalf of beleaguered Muslim populations has been somewhat, if not largely, forgotten. It is also worth noting that when NATO took military action over Kosovo without a UNSCR, that action was largely regarded as legitimate.

A second major change in strategic circumstances took place towards the close of my career, with the self-proclaimed declaration of war by Al-Qaida against the West and its values. The gauntlet was thrown down. Before 9/11, possession of terrain had much to do with the outcome of conflict, but we have now moved to a position in which terrain seems to be rather less important, and a battle of ideas has commenced.

Possession of terrain is a vital matter in war between states, in which opposing countries use military means to achieve their objectives, or in war within a state, when factions vie to rule that state. Wars between states are often described as 'symmetric' or 'force on force'. However, 9/11 – and, indeed, the Madrid bombings and the terrorist attacks on 7 July 2005 ('7/7') in this country – represent a very different sort of struggle, in which the battleground is people's attitudes, allegiances, values – their very identities. It seems to me that Clausewitz's famous dictum that 'war is nothing but a continuation of politics with the admixture of other means' holds good even in these different circumstances. This 'asymmetric' struggle is emphatically not one which can be solved by military means alone – far from it.

We are again confronted with terrorism on mainland Great Britain. The threat such terrorism poses should not be underestimated, even though we may find the ideology underlying it difficult to comprehend. At home, the Security Service and the police quite properly have the onerous responsibility of taking the lead in the counter-terrorist role, while the Armed Forces act in their support. Overseas, military intervention may be needed to counter the parallel threat of terrorist attack on British interests and personnel, say in the evacuation of non-combatant nationals, as in the case of Sierra Leone. Next, there can be rogue states which may be inclined to military adventurism in breach of international law, and we have seen examples of that in the recent past. Such adventurism, by definition, is likely to be gravely destabilizing. And in the face of instability, whether caused by ethnic conflict or by failed or failing states, the Armed Forces may well be required to respond. We should not ignore, also, the grim prospect of future conflict over access to sources of energy and water.

Defence of the Realm is difficult and complex in today's world. In particular, the terrorist threat, especially when the terrorist is willing to die in the course of his actions, is a grave challenge. This terrorism can originate in the UK itself, as we saw on 7/7, or abroad. We have to address both sources.

So how should the United Kingdom position and defend itself? Pulling up the drawbridge of a Fortress Britain is not a sensible strategy. The UK cannot isolate itself from the wider world. For us in Britain, the most fundamental strategic issue is how we position ourselves between the United States and Europe. While we are geographically much closer to the continent of Europe, politically we have often been closer to the United States. This has been a dilemma for many decades, one that requires careful strategic judgement, not merely tactical reaction. The judgement must be whether our own national strategic objectives are served by our American ally's proposed course of action, imperfect though it may be. A rational choice about any new deployment should not be decided by whether we like or dislike this or that President or, indeed, Prime Minister: such an *ad hominem* approach can serve only to distort our thinking. It is self-evident to me why we describe our relationship with America as special, by dint of common origin and therefore values and language, of history both before and after independence (and particularly the history of the last century), and of political, economic and military ties. But we are also part of the continent of Europe, and a member of the continent's polity, the European Union. I believe that we have to remain sitting on this fence; we should not come off it one way or the other, even if it is sometimes an uncomfortable place to perch. We are so closely involved strategically with both the United States and Europe that our strategy must embrace both. British and American strategic ends may be much the same, ways and means may – almost certainly will – differ. I say ends may be much the same, because strategy must be directed towards a political goal. A war on terror is not a strategy *per se*, for terrorism is no more than a means of fighting; the strategy must address the politics behind that terrorism.

At the same time, we must be careful to guard our historic values, long and hard won: our freedoms, the supremacy of the rule of law. These attributes of our mature democracy are beyond price. But equally, we must accept that Western liberal democracy may not export itself that easily. And that means we should make an even greater effort to improve cultural understanding, to appreciate how any given situation looks through the eyes of others, while still firmly supporting the principle of representative government.

At home, we should make greater efforts to ensure that a clear national identity and a multicultural approach can sit more comfortably together. But we must not delude ourselves; clarity of thought is essential. I am a great believer in live and let live, but not at the expense of my British way of life. The fundamental political question here is what degree of tolerance the body politic should afford to those whose intolerance looks to destroy that body politic, and the rule of law which underpins it.

I served three tours of duty in Northern Ireland, and have witnessed the British Army's engagement in the Province almost from the start. For many of those years, violence there threatened the territorial integrity of the United Kingdom itself. Now a settlement has been achieved, and the British Armed Forces went non-operational in Northern Ireland on 31 July 2007. This represents a remarkable achievement, notwithstanding the cost in blood and treasure: that of preventing unlawful violence from dictating political outcomes. With proper application, and perhaps a modicum of good luck, I believe that our commitment to the Balkans will also come to a successful conclusion. Note that the operation in Northern Ireland was thirty-eight years in duration, and at the time of writing Bosnia will have been sixteen, Kosovo nine. There is no quick fix.

We have then, of course, the major effort of our joint campaigns in both Iraq and Afghanistan. There is much noise about both, but the noise is as much about what is happening on a day-to-day basis as it is about the strategic issues. We must acknowledge that the success of the initial manoeuvre war in Iraq was not followed by similar success in the immediate aftermath, to the detriment both of Iraq and of the Coalition forces. In particular, the disbandment of the Iraqi Army and the de-Ba'athification programme resulted in a worse security situation than probably would otherwise have prevailed. We are where we are, however, and the difficult question before Iraq and the Coalition is to decide on how best to secure the country's future. That future could still be bright, because Iraq has much going for it: a popularly elected government at long last, natural resources, a well-educated and energetic population. But that potentially bright future is threatened by brutal, and largely unforeseen, intersectarian strife. What is to be done?

It is strategically vital to all concerned that we get the right answer to this question. There has been growing pressure in both the United States and the United Kingdom for our forces to be withdrawn in relatively short order. As I said in a press interview while I was still CGS, the sooner our troops leave Iraq, the better for everybody – but we should not leave before it's right to do so. Our withdrawal from Iraq should not be defined by a date, but rather by conditions. To leave Iraq against the wishes of the sovereign Iraqi Government, and before the Iraqi security forces are fully able to deal with the current violence, would be both morally wrong and a fundamental strategic mistake. Great efforts are being made to bring on the Iraqi security forces: largely successful where the army is concerned, less so in respect of the police. Even when Coalition forces have handed over full responsibility for security across Iraq – and that process is well under way, province by province – there well may be an Iraqi request that we continue training assistance, as we do in many other countries. That said, the long-term solution to the Sunni/Shia violence must be political, not military.

It would be an equally flawed decision to stay in Iraq when no longer invited by the Iraqi Government to do so, with consent, patchy enough today, failing to hold. So we should not become mesmerized by dates: we must make the best judgement we can as to when the conditions are right to leave.

I also think it is worth emphasizing that while it may be that two-thirds of the British people now disapprove of our involvement in Iraq, in contrast to the two-thirds who approved three and a half years ago, such disapproval must not, of itself, dictate future strategy. The future will in all probability require a British Government to decide whether to intervene elsewhere in the world; such a decision must be taken on its merits, and not through the prism of the current campaign in Iraq. By the same token, lessons must be learned from the mistakes of the past. The tragedy of the planning for post-conflict Iraq is that we knew from our experiences in the Balkans what should have been done – but the message didn't get through to those taking the decisions.

In Afghanistan I see a long haul yet – and not only a military, but also a civilian, long haul. We must help Afghanistan to progress, we must support the sovereign and popularly elected government, and we must prevent the Taliban from once more taking control and providing Al-Qaida with a safe haven. That would indeed be a return to square one. Such a commitment means a preparedness to take casualties; the proposition of a casualty-free military campaign is a contradiction in terms. NATO is now very much the driving force in Afghanistan, and I would wish all contributing nations, NATO or otherwise, to pursue the common strategic goal – essential to us all, and particularly to Afghanistan itself – with a common vigour, accepting, if need be, the price to be paid. Faint-heartedness is not conducive to campaign success.

I emphasize again that the Defence of this Realm in the twenty-first century cannot be confined to our shores alone. I think it was Machiavelli who said that 'wars begin when you will, but they do not end when you please'. In principle, therefore, we must see these campaigns through to their proper conclusions. Not to do so would be a disaster. My coda is that a political settlement between Israel and the Palestinians is essential. The difficulties are immense, but I refuse to believe that they are insurmountable.

Over the last few years, both before and after 9/11, we have seen a pattern in the way campaigns have evolved: often an initial short, intense campaign which involves more or less conventional – 'symmetrical' – fighting is followed by long, sometimes very long, periods of peace support operations, nation-building, post-conflict oper-ations, call them what you will. I cite here Bosnia, Kosovo, Macedonia (FYROM), Afghanistan and Iraq, to say nothing of Sierra Leone and East Timor – all involving British forces. We must maintain – enhance where possible – our capability in such asymmetric operations. This means preserving and improving our ability to put and to keep boots on the ground.

Experience of post-conflict situations has shown me time and again the importance of improving everyday life for the majority of the population as soon as possible. There is a sense that you must make a difference within a hundred days, or you may lose an opportunity. It gives me no pleasure to say that I fear this was not the case where Iraq was concerned.

This multifaceted approach requires the combined effort of the Government Departments involved, not just the Armed Forces. We have not yet got this as right as we should. Our ability to integrate the Departments of State in pursuit of strategic national objectives is hampered by a lack of sufficiently authoritative machinery in Whitehall.

My career in the British Army has provided plenty of reminders of that old adage, too easily forgotten: expect the unexpected. Two examples that spring to mind are the unpredicted attacks on the Falklands in 1982 and on Kuwait in 1990. The clear deduction to me is that we must retain our significant capability to fight conventional force-on-force manoeuvre wars, as well as the ultimate shield of our nuclear deterrent. We should indeed maintain our ability to create a terrible and terrifying uncertainty as to what we would or would not do *in extremis*. While terrorism is clearly today's dominant threat, it would be very imprudent to assume that we will never again be required to fight a conventional war. I strongly believe that we must retain the ability to fight and win such a war, if only as a form of national life insurance policy.

The defence budget, at some £34 billion, is just over 2 per cent of our gross national product, having been at the end of the Cold War double or more that figure. That is only 5.5 per cent of today's government spending. While 2 per cent of GNP is similar to France's spending on defence, it is higher than that of other European countries, reflecting the importance and significance of Britain's international role. Indeed, readers may question whether this is sufficient to represent the importance, the proportionate importance, of what the Armed Forces do for this country today, and what they may have to do in the future. But there we are; we have the defence budget we are allocated, and once that is defined, the question then for the Ministry of Defence is how most effectively to spend it. It is a complex and intellectually challenging exercise, leading to a set of assumptions which – at least in theory – define the military effects required, and so in turn the size and shape of the Armed Forces; for example, how much infantry, armour, logistics etc. should there be in the Army, how much anti-submarine warfare or amphibious capability in the Navy, how much fast jet or transport capability in the Air Force. Some may question whether we really need 232 Eurofighters, for example.

The difficulty, though, is that events have long since overtaken the formal MOD planning assumptions. There seems to be a considerable inertia in recognizing this and thereby adjusting those assumptions. The virtual world defined by those assumptions has been superseded by the real world. There is a mismatch between what we do and the resources we are given with which to do it.

How stretched is the Army? Although arithmetically the Army is on average more or less within its deployment guidelines, by definition the average includes those parts of the Army which are outside those guidelines. Some parts of the Army are well below the target of twenty-four months between operational tours. We could well be asking too much of our soldiers in terms of frequency of operational deployment over the long haul, to say nothing of the conditions of service under which they continue on this long haul. For example, some of our soldiers have undertaken three – or even more – tours in Iraq.

Decisions about the allocation of resources come down to a question of balance: balance between capabilities within the defence budget – how much of this, how much of that; balance between current operations and what may be required in the future – and not only current operations, but current training, which is the investment for our capability in the future; balance between people and technology – pay and accommodation, for example, against current and future equipment. This is not how it should be. We ought to be able to provide what is required for soldiers to be fully and properly equipped, thoroughly trained, decently paid and, together with their families, decently housed. They deserve nothing less. There are some difficulties here which explain, at least to some extent, why recruiting is the challenge it is.

On a different tack, have we got our procurement right? What of our ability, or is it our inability, to get the right equipment at the right time at the right cost? Large procurement cost overruns in the past have been rather meekly accepted to the detriment of spending on personnel and training. I acknowledge that the Defence Industrial Strategy, published in 2005, is designed to improve matters in this area.

The Army feels strongly that the greatest burden rests upon its shoulders, not least when it comes to numbers deployed and casualties sustained. The facts speak for themselves. It is again a question of balance; taking away from Peter to pay Paul is a difficult and dangerous exercise and one that can be avoided by better provision for both.

The Ministry of Defence, is very much part of the equation. The role of the MOD is to translate the Government's political objectives into military capabilities and military operations; it is therefore both a Department of State and the supreme headquarters of the Armed Forces. These two roles can be uneasy bedfellows, and that unease can be to the detriment of the Armed Forces. The Department of State appears to assume that commercial so-called 'best practice', with its proliferation of performance indicators and targets, can be applied to defence in general, and to the Armed Forces in particular; I don't agree. Who judges best practice? And this obsessive measurement is often against plans, not against real-world requirements. Fighting is demonstrably not a commercial activity. I am very clear about the only performance indicator which really matters to the Armed Forces, namely, the achievement of whatever objectives are set to us: that is, winning. Far too often, the MOD confuses activity with achievement.

There is far too much reverence for process. The purpose of process is to achieve an outcome, to achieve the mission; it is not the purpose of process to maintain process. As an example, I recently read of a senior MOD civil servant quoted as saying of an even more senior MOD civil servant that the latter was 'not just leading the workstream process, but driving it'. I hope he knew what he meant, because I'm not sure I do. This reverence for process matters, because process is an overhead; the more overheads can be reduced, the more capability we can obtain from a given defence budget.

I would also express my concern at the diminution, over years, decades even, of the position and authority of the single-Service Chiefs of Staff. They are seen by the public, by those serving in the Forces themselves, and by the media, as responsible for all matters pertaining to their respective Services – but this is simply not the reality. As CGS, I did not hold the budget for the Army. Neither logistics nor procurement is any longer the direct responsibility of the Chiefs. In my view we have overcentralized, and this has diminished the ability of the Chiefs of Staff to take personal charge of the running of their Services and to determine, for example, personnel matters. While this is partly budget-driven, it is also partly policy-driven. There's an assumption that central is good, single-Service rather less good. Well, I don't agree. While the successive reforms to the top of the defence structure over the last half-century or so were largely right, I believe this process has now gone too far, to the detriment of the single Services themselves. Frankly, the Chiefs of Staff find themselves in rather the opposite position to that described in the old aphorism about the ladies of the night, who are deemed to have power without responsibility. The Chiefs bear a heavy responsibility, but without the power to match. It is time that real authority was restored to the Chiefs of Staff in order to match the responsibility which indubitably and rightly they carry.

Throughout my career, I have been taught, and I have striven to instil, the message that it is the soldiers themselves who will make the endeavour succeed. As implied by the Sandhurst motto 'Serve to Lead', one's loyalty must be from bottom up. Sadly, I did not find this fundamental proposition shared by the MOD as a whole. On the contrary, in my time working in the Ministry of Defence as Head of the Army, I felt that the culture of the Department put the welfare of members of the Armed Forces and their families too low in its priorities. But without those soldiers, sailors and airmen, ministers and indeed civil servants, generals, admirals and air marshals are nothing. While I acknowledge recent modest improvements in conditions of service, it remains true that not much over a thousand pounds a month for the private soldier on operations is hardly an impressive figure. And some of the accommodation we provide is still, frankly, shaming, and hemmed around by petty regulation.

I am concerned at a failure, even an unwillingness, to understand the fundamental ethos of soldiering. It is difficult to overestimate the importance of ethos: the can-do spirit; the us–us approach, rather than me–me; the conviction that we can hack it. At the heart of this ethos are perhaps some old-fashioned words: duty, honour, self-lessness, discipline. These may not rest easily with some of today's values – but if they're not there, you will not have an Army, certainly not an Army capable of doing what it has to do. The soldiers' part of the contract with the nation which they serve and from which they very largely recruit is to take risks – if need be, to risk their lives. But this must be a two-way contract: the nation should hon-our its covenant with the soldier. Military operations exact costs in blood and treasure. It is our soldiers who pay the cost in blood; the nation must therefore pay the cost in treasure. Soldiers and their families must be properly valued – and when I talk of the soldier and his family, I am talking not only about the regular Army: I very much include the reserves, the Territorial Army, and the reserves in the other two Services. They too play their part, they too take risks, and the contract applies to them also.

The military is uniquely different from any other walk of life. Very few legislators and opinion-formers have served in the Armed Forces; they therefore find it difficult to accept this distinctness.

As CGS, I also became concerned at comment, presumably politically motivated, which seemed to imply that the Armed Services could pick and choose their tasks for themselves. This is dangerous ground. Let us be clear: the allegiance of the Armed Forces is to the Sovereign as Head of State, and it is their constitutional duty to follow the direction of the duly elected Government of the day; the alternative is anarchy. The Government takes decisions on military as on other matters, and is answerable to the electorate for these. The media sometimes produce more heat than light on these issues, and we need to be just a little careful; the British Army must remain apolitical.

It is self-evident to me that we must defend what we have, and I hope cherish, against those enemies who would remove it. We would be foolish to take our good fortune for granted. I believe that the nation knows the value of what it has in our Armed Forces, who in turn are grateful indeed for that support. The Army is one of this country's greatest national assets; but to sustain that position – and, I hope, to improve it – the Army must have the right capabilities, the right structure, the right people, the right training, the right support and the right accommodation. In return, as the Army has proven so many times, it will provide the nation with operational success, wherever that may be, whenever that may be, however that may be.

We face an uncertain and unknowable future, and a variety of threats to our way of life. Attitudes, perceptions, even theologies, are now the dominant causes of conflict. How to defend this Realm in these complex and threatening times is the stuff not only of politics, but also of professional military judgement. The Armed Forces have a vital and irreplaceable part to play, in both war-fighting and peace support operations. Our opponents are very likely to be quick-thinking, agile and unconventional – and we have to match them. All of this requires an entirely dispassionate and objective strategic approach, not one seen only through today's political prism.

The Chiefs of Staff should have restored to them the power and authority to match their responsibilities in order that, above all, they may give their best effort and effect to the fighting capability of their Services, and to the well-being of those who produce it. My various points about the higher management and organization of defence are made with a view to getting more military effectiveness from the resources we are given. The Army's motto 'Be the Best' really says it all. The Defence of the Realm requires that when you will the ends – the political objectives which require the use of force – you must will the military means. And if you will the military means, you must also will the financial means.

Though the strategic environment which we inhabit has changed beyond recognition, the operational effectiveness and well-being of the British Army remains as crucial as it has always been. We neglect it at our peril.

Epilogue

In 2001, and again in 2004, I had the honour to represent Her Majesty The Queen on the Sovereign's Parade at Sandhurst, which allowed me an opportunity to look back over my long career in the Army. I proudly made my way up the King's Walk towards Old Building Square, where spectators sat in stands around the lines of cadets dressed in their immaculate Blues, much as I had been so many years before, while a band played a stirring march. Once I was in position on the dais, the Adjutant, mounted on his horse in front of me, gave the order: 'General Salute, Present Arms.' I walked along the lines to review the cadets, stopping every now and then to have a word with one. Then the cadets marched past, first in slow time and then in quick. Afterwards they stood at ease as I gave my address.

'You will all shortly be taking up your first commands,' I told them. 'Some of you will before long be in command of soldiers on operations. Do not underestimate the responsibility placed upon you and the judgement that will be required of you – but equally, relish the authority granted to you, and rise to the challenges ever present. Always lead by example, seize the initiative when you can, and never give in. Remember the values and standards of the British Army, founded as they are in the timeless virtues of integrity, honour, duty, loyalty and selflessness.

'We are nothing without our soldiers, who deserve the best leadership we can provide. In return, they will respect you, forgive you your inevitable mistakes, and follow you wherever you lead.

'Be true to yourselves. Honesty and integrity are absolutes, but you will need more. You will need the determination and the courage to see matters through, even when fainter hearts have already taken counsel of their fears. You will need to take hardship, danger, fatigue and – perhaps above all – uncertainty in your stride; and, vitally important, you will need an unfailing sense of humour. You will need the strength of will and confidence to take the right road when it is not an easy one. You will need to be resolute and undeterred by reverses or disappointments. In the British Army, we must come first, we must win; to come second is to lose. The Army has never been found wanting; its evident success has engendered the admiration of its friends and the awe of its foes.

'As, in all of this, you Serve to Lead, you will also realize – and, I hope, revel in – the rewards of soldiering: the sense of shared and unselfish endeavour, of achievement, of doing right, of collective and personal success. These rewards are beyond price.

'I envy you as you stand on the threshold of your commissions, since I am in the evening of my service and you are at the bright dawn. Grasp your opportunities with both hands, meet the challenges, enjoy your soldiering and, above all, make sure your soldiers enjoy it. I wish you all success and all good fortune.'

Picture Acknowledgements

PICTURE ACKNOWLEDGEMENTS

Section three
1: refugee camp, Brazda, Macedonia, 6 April 1999: Associated Press; Tony Blair talking to troops, Kosovo border, 3 May 1999: Reuters
2/3: signing of military technical agreement, Kumanovo airfield, Kosovo, 9 June 1999: Associated Press
4/5: (main photo) paratroopers put on stand down, Petrovac, 11 June 1999: © Reuters/Corbis; British paratroopers escort KLA: © Reuters/Corbis; Royal Irish soldier carries KLA weapons, Pristina, 17 June 1999: Reuters/Corbis; MJ shakes hands with Agim Ceku, 20 July 1999: Associated Press
6/7: (background) a house burns in Serbian village: © Arben Celi/Reuters/Corbis; MJ and Colonel General Viktor Zavarzin, Pristina airport, 26 June 1999: Associated Press; Bernard Kouchner, Madeleine Albright and MJ, Pristina, 29 July 1999: Associated Press; MJ, Wes Clark and Prince Charles, Kosovo: Cpl David Whittaker-Smith, RAF NATO; the Clintons visit Kosovo, 22 June 1999: Boris Grdanosk/AP/PA Photos

Section four
1: MJ on a visit to Kabul to Defence Minister General Abdul Raheem Wardak, 27 June 2006: Heathcliff O'Malley/The Daily Telegraph
2/3: Mark Jackson: Julian Andrews/The Sunday Telegraph
4/5: MJ inspects Sandhurst cadets, 10 December 2004: Associated Press; MJ talks to Prince William and Prince Harry, Sandhurst, 12 April 2006: Lefteris Pitarakis/ Associated Press; MJ receives DSO 2 December 1999: © Reuters/Corbis; MJ and Private Johnson Beharry VC, 27 April 2005: © Ian Jones

PICTURE ACKNOWLEDGEMENTS

6/7: MJ with Brigadier Graham Binns at 7 Armoured Brigade planning meeting: Sergeant Wendy Summerell RLC/ MOD; MJ visits troops in southern Iraq, 16 May 2006: Corporal John Hawkes / MOD
8: MJ lays a wreath at the Cenotaph, Whitehall, 21 August 2005: Rex Features

Index